THE
ATHLETIC
Female

American Orthopaedic Society for Sports Medicine

Arthur J. Pearl, MD
University of Miami School of Medicine
Editor

Human Kinetics Publishers

Library of Congress Cataloging-in-Publication Data

The Athletic female / American Orthopaedic Society for Sports Medicine
; Arthur J. Pearl.
   p. cm.
   Papers from the AOSSM's April 1991 conference.
   Includes bibliographical references and index.
   ISBN 0-87322-410-8
   1. Woman athletes--Health and hygiene--Congresses. I. Pearl,
Arthur J., 1930-   . II. American Orthopaedic Society for Sports
Medicine.
   RC1218.W65A85   1993
   613.7'11'082--dc20   92-27038
                                    CIP

ISBN: 0-87322-410-8

Consulting Editor: Arthur J. Pearl, MD
Managing Editor: Julia Anderson
Assistant Editors: Moyra Knight, John Wentworth
Copyeditor: Dianna Matlosz
Proofreader: Laurie McGee
Indexer: Sheila Ary
Production Director: Ernie Noa
Typesetting and Text Layout: Yvonne Winsor
Text Design: Keith Blomberg
Cover Design: Jack Davis
Interior Art: Tom Janowski
Printer: Braun-Brumfield

Printed in the United States of America   10 9 8 7 6 5 4 3 2 1

Human Kinetics Publishers
Box 5076, Champaign, IL 61825-5076
1-800-747-4457

Canada Office:
Human Kinetics Publishers
P.O. Box 2503, Windsor, ON N8Y 4S2
1-800-465-7301 (in Canada only)

Europe Office:
Human Kinetics Publishers (Europe) Ltd.
P.O. Box IW14, Leeds LS16 6TR
England
0532-781708

Australia Office:
Human Kinetics Publishers
P.O. Box 80, Kingswood 5062
South Australia
374-0433

Contents

Panel of Experts   ix

Preface   xiii

Chapter 1 A 20-Year Perspective: What Has Changed?   1

Judy Mahle Lutter

Defining the Athletic Female 1

Time as an Obstacle to Athletic Activity 2

Title IX Gives Females a Chance 2

Health Concerns Related to Women's Reproductive Status 3

Media Attention to Athletic Females 3

The Decline in Females' Sport Participation 4

The Role of Melpomene Institute in Awareness of the Athletic Female 4

A Historical Perspective of Physically Active Women's Concerns 5

Older Women and Physical Activity 7

Current Perspective of the Athletic Female 8

Summary 8

References 9

Chapter 2 Problems Facing the Athletic Female   11

Mary Lloyd Ireland

Gender Differences and Inequality in Sport 11

Personal Competition 12

Problems Facing the Athletic Female 13

Personal Injury History 14

Orthopaedics as a Career 15

Viewing Obstacles as Challenges 16

Summary 17

References 17

**Chapter 3 Psychological, Sociological, and Cultural Issues   19
Concerning the Athletic Female**

Diane L. Gill

Sex and Gender Differences 20

Personality and Gender Role Orientation 21

Gender and Sport Achievement 23

Gender Belief Systems   28
Gender and Social Context   30
Future Directions   31
Body Image and Physical Activity   33
Summary   36
References   37

**Chapter 4   Osteoporosis in the Athletic Female: Amenorrhea   41
and Amenorrheic Osteoporosis**
Elizabeth A. Arendt
The Normal Menstrual Cycle   41
Delayed Menarche   44
Luteal Suppression   44
Prevalence of Athletic Amenorrhea   45
Etiological Factors of Menstrual Cycle Abnormalities   45
Mechanisms That Alter the Menstrual Cycle   46
Treatment of Menstrual Cycle Irregularities   54
Summary   55
References   56

**Chapter 5   Diet and Menstrual Status as Determinants   61
of Injury Risk for the Athletic Female**
Tom Lloyd
Menstrual Irregularity, Oral Contraceptive Use, and Injury Rates
Among Recreational and Collegiate Athletes   61
Diet, Reproductive Hormones, and Bone Density in Collegiate Athletes   63
Normative Clinical Chemistry Values of Reproductive Hormone Levels   68
Dietary Fat and Fiber as Modulators of Female Sex Steroid Levels   69
Effects of Specific Nutrients on Menstrual Status   73
Age-Dependent Changes in Bone Density and Calcium Intake:
The Peak Bone Mass Concept   76
Summary   77
Acknowledgment   78
References   78

Chapter 6   Exercise and Pregnancy   81
Judy Mahle Lutter and Valerie Lee
A Historical Perspective of Exercise and Pregnancy   81
Current Thinking on Exercise and Pregnancy: Consistent Advice?   82
Heart and Lung Considerations   83
Muscle and Bone Effects   84
Overheating   86
A Neglected Area: What About the Right Foods During Pregnancy?   87
Melpomene Research   90
Melpomene Institute Guidelines for Exercise During Pregnancy   91

Melpomene Recommendations for Evaluating Maternal Fitness Programs   94
The Effects of Exercise on Labor and Delivery   96
Considerations for Postpartum Exercise   96
Overview of Exercise and Pregnancy   99
Summary   100
Note   100
References   100

Chapter 7   Oral Contraceptives and the Athletic Female   103

Pat J. Kulpa

Noncontraceptive Benefits of Oral Contraceptive Use   105
Negative Effects of Oral Contraceptive Use   108
Oral Contraceptives and Athletic Performance   109
Summary   110
References   111

Chapter 8   Issues Specific to the Preadolescent and   113
Adolescent Athletic Female

Deborah L. Squire

Areas of Concern for the Preadolescent Female Athlete   113
Injuries to the Preadolescent Female Athlete   115
Biological Maturation   117
Nutritional Concerns for the Adolescent Female Athlete   118
Injuries to the Adolescent Female Athlete   120
Summary   121
References   121

Chapter 9   Substance Abuse by the Athletic Female   125

Herbert A. Haupt

Anabolic Steroids   125
Pathogenic Weight-Control Aids   130
Recreational Drugs and Ergogenic Aids   132
Summary   137
References   137

Chapter 10   Eating Disorders Among Athletic Females   141

Nancy Clark

Anorexia   142
Bulimia   143
Predisposing Factors to Eating Disorders   144
Dietary Treatment   144
Tips for Helping Athletes With Eating Disorders   145
Summary   146
References   147

**Chapter 11   Gender Differences in Circulorespiratory and   149
Metabolic Variables Related to
Endurance Performance**
Ben R. Londeree
Circulorespiratory and Metabolic Factors Affecting
  Endurance Performance   149
Circulorespiratory and Metabolic Factors Related to Gender Differences
  in Endurance Performance   153
Summary   159
References   160

**Chapter 12   Nutritional Problems and Training Intensity,   165
Activity Level, and Athletic Performance**
Nancy Clark
Energy Intake of Athletic Females   166
Dietary Analysis of Athletic Females   166
Summary   167
References   168

Chapter 13   Strength Training and the Athletic Female   169
Terry R. Malone and Barbara Sanders
Assessing Changes in Muscle Strength   169
Applications of Strength Training by Athletic Females   172
Recommendations for Strength-Training Programs   181
Summary   182
References   182

Chapter 14   Conditioning the Aging Female   185
Gregory A. Peters
Defining the Aging Female   185
The Aging Process in Women and Men   186
Research on Exercise and Aging Females   186
Suggested Athletic Activities   187
Benefits of Exercise for Aging Females   188
Recommendations for Future Research   189
Summary   189
References   189

Chapter 15   Off-Season Conditioning   193
John W. Uribe and Merl J. Miller
Preventing Deconditioning   194
Training Principles   196
Optimal Body Composition   197
Optimal Flexibility   198
Program Design   199

Summary   199
References   200

Chapter 16   Sport-Specific Training   203
Barbara Hoogenboom
Injury Prevention as a Rationale for Sport-Specific Training   203
Defining Sport-Specific Training   204
Developing a Sport-Specific Training Program   205
Suggestions for Further Study   206
Summary   206
References   206

Chapter 17   Muscle Imbalances in the Athletic Female   209
Shirley A. Sahrmann
Defining Muscle Imbalances   209
The Anterior-Medial Hip Impingement Syndrome   212
Recommendations   216
Summary   217
References   217

Chapter 18   Incidence and Pattern of Injury   219
in Female Cadets at West Point Military Academy
John T. McBride, William C. Meade, III, and Jack B. Ryan
Survey Population   220
Training Activities   220
Injuries in Female and Male Cadets   224
Summary   232
Note   233
Acknowledgment   233
References   233

Chapter 19   Upper Extremity Injuries   235
Letha Y. Griffin
Frequency of Upper Extremity Injuries   235
Effects of Conditioning on Upper Extremity Strength in Women   241
Occurrence of Upper Extremity Injuries in Specific Sports   242
Common Upper Extremity Injuries   243
Summary   248
References   248

Chapter 20   Dance, Gymnastics, and Skating Injuries   251
in Athletic Females
Carol C. Teitz
Incidence of Injuries   251
Types of Injury   252

Anatomical Injury Sites   255
Dance Form, Gymnastic and Skating Events, and Injury   260
The Relationship Between Technique, Ability, and Injury   261
Schedule Considerations   261
Athletic Equipment and Injuries   262
Rules of Competition That Promote Injury   262
Preventing Injuries   263
Summary   263
References   263

Chapter 21   Lower Extremity Injuries   **267**
   Jerome V. Ciullo
Injury Patterns in Female and Male Athletes   268
Proximal Segment Injuries   272
Middle Segment Injuries   275
Distal Segment Injuries   288
Overview of Lower Extremity Injuries in the Athletic Female   295
Summary   296
References   296

Provocative Issues and Recommendations for Future Research   299
Index   306

Panel of Experts

Elizabeth A. Arendt, MD
Assistant Professor of Orthopaedic Surgery
Medical Director, Men's and Women's Varsity Athletics
University of Minnesota
Minneapolis, Minnesota

Jerome V. Ciullo, MD
Medical Director
Sports Medicine Center of Metro Detroit
Detroit, Michigan
Clinical Assistant Professor
Department of Orthopaedic Surgery
Wayne State University
Detroit, Michigan

Nancy Clark, MS, RD
Nutritionist
Sports Medicine Brookline
Brookline, Massachusetts

Diane L. Gill, PhD
Professor, Department of Exercise and Sport Science
University of North Carolina at Greensboro
Greensboro, North Carolina

Letha Y. Griffin, MD, PhD
Staff Physician
Peachtree Orthopaedic Clinic
Atlanta, Georgia
Clinical Instructor
Emory University School of Medicine
Atlanta, Georgia

Ellen Hanley
Assistant Director of Sports Sciences
National Collegiate Athletic Association
Overland Park, Kansas

Sally S. Harris, MD, MPH
Clinical Instructor
UCLA Division of Family Medicine
Center for the Health Sciences
Los Angeles, California

Herbert A. Haupt, MD
Orthopaedic Surgeon
Orthopaedic Associates, Inc.
St. Louis, Missouri

Barbara Hoogenboom, PT, ATC
Sports Medicine Clinical Specialist
St. Mary's Hospital
Grand Rapids, Michigan

Mary Lloyd Ireland, MD
Assistant Clinical Professor
Divisions of Orthopaedic Surgery and Family Practice
University of Kentucky
Lexington, Kentucky

Pat J. Kulpa, MD, FACOG
Sports Gynecology
Pacific Sports Medicine Clinic
Tacoma, Washington

Valerie Lee, MA
Education Coordinator
Melpomene Institute
St. Paul, Minnesota

Tom Lloyd, PhD
Associate Professor
Department of Obstetrics and Gynecology
Milton S. Hershey Medical Center
Penn State College of Medicine
Hershey, Pennsylvania

Ben R. Londeree, EdD
Associate Professor of Physical Education
University of Missouri
Columbia, Missouri

Judy Mahle Lutter, MA
Director
Melpomene Institute
St. Paul, Minnesota

Terry R. Malone, EdD, PT, ATC
Executive Director of Sports Medicine
Associate Professor of Physical Therapy
Assistant Professor of Surgery
Duke University Medical Center
Durham, North Carolina

John T. McBride, Jr., MD
Major Medical Corp USA
Fitzsimons Army Medical Center
Aurora, Colorado

William C. Meade, III, MD
Colonel (retired) Medical Corp USA
Springvale, Maine

Merl J. Miller, ATC
Athletic Trainer
Department of Orthopaedics
Division of Sports Medicine
Doctors' Hospital
Coral Gables, Florida

Nina B. Partin, MEd, ATC
Assistant Athletic Director
United States Olympic Committee
Colorado Springs, Colorado

Arthur J. Pearl, MD
Associate Professor
Department of Orthopaedics and Rehabilitation
University of Miami School of Medicine
Miami, Florida

Gregory A. Peters, MD
Assistant Clinical Professor
Michigan State University School of Medicine
East Lansing, Michigan
President
Great Lakes Orthopaedic Associates
Grand Rapids, Michigan

Rene Revis, MS, ATC/R
Lecturer, Department of Health, Physical Education, Recreation
    and Dance
Assistant Athletic Trainer, Department of Intercollegiate Athletics
National Association for Girls and Women in Sports
Illinois State University
Normal, Illinois

Jack B. Ryan, MD
Colonel Medical Corp USA
Director
Sports Medicine Fellowship
USMA
West Point, New York

Shirley A. Sahrmann, PhD, PT
Associate Professor, Physical Therapy and Neurology
Director, Interdisciplinary Program in Movement Science
Washington University School of Medicine
St. Louis, Missouri

Barbara Sanders, PhD, PT, SCS
Associate Professor and Director
Physical Therapy Program
Southwest Texas State University
San Marcos, Texas

Deborah L. Squire, MD
Assistant Professor
Department of Pediatrics
Director, Primary Care
Sports Medicine Clinic
Duke University Medical Center
Durham, North Carolina

Carol C. Teitz, MD
Associate Professor of Orthopaedic Surgery
University of Washington
Seattle, Washington

John W. Uribe, MD
Chief of Sports Medicine
University of Miami School of Medicine
Miami, Florida
Department of Orthopaedics
Division of Sports Medicine
Doctors' Hospital
Coral Gables, Florida

Preface

Since Title IX of the Educational Amendments became law in 1972, the number of females participating in sport, with training often beginning at early ages, has increased dramatically. Title IX (which mandates that females have opportunities equal to those of males in physical education and athletics in public schools and colleges) has stimulated the public to address misconceptions about the ability, image, self-confidence, leadership, and strength of the athletic female.

The increased athletic participation of females of all ages, from the prepubescent to the aging athlete, and at every level of activity, from organized youth sports to collegiate, Olympic, professional, and recreational participation, has generated many questions. It has become apparent that we lack information about the athletic female: the epidemiology of sport injury; body and hormonal changes and physiology; training needs; and psychological, social, and cultural attitudes. While the number of females participating in athletic endeavors at every level of involvement has increased dramatically over the past 20 years, the number of physical activity educators and physical activity programs for this group of athletes has declined.

The American Orthopaedic Society for Sports Medicine (AOSSM) recognized this lack of need for information and felt that the medical community would benefit from a professional inquiry into issues related to females' participation in sport. Thus arose the impetus for the Athletic Female Workshop. The workshop was part of a series of professional inquiries into anomalous sport-related areas as part of the ongoing educational and research efforts of the AOSSM. Under the guidance of Dr. James Farmer, the educational consultant to the AOSSM, I developed the basic outline of the workshop. Drs. Letha Griffin, Herbert Haupt, Mary Lloyd Ireland, Gregory Peters, and Carol Teitz provided leadership for particular areas of the workshop, as well as presented papers. The AOSSM invited others whom it recognized as experts in the field to present papers.

The workshop, which was held in Chicago in April 1991, opened with position statements from the National Collegiate Athletic Association, the United States Olympic Committee, the American Academy of Pediatrics, the National Association for Girls and Women in Sport, the American Physical Therapy Association, and the National Athletic Trainers Association. Each speaker then presented an overview of his or her paper; issues, concerns, and problems were identified in an open forum. Sessions were devoted to discussing provocative issues (ranked by importance), and some effort was made to reach a consensus on them.

The papers presented at the workshop make up the text of *The Athletic Female*; the book represents the AOSSM's professional inquiry into females' involvement in physical activity. With *The Athletic Female* the AOSSM intends to provide sport scientists, sports medicine specialists, and other physicians with recent information on active females by focusing on the medical issues pertaining to their involvement in sport. A specific decision was made to use the term *athletic female* instead of *female athlete*, because the focus is physically active females of every age at all levels of experience and involvement.

The book follows a progression of topics related to females' involvement in athletic activity. The first three chapters provide a backdrop for an overview of the issues relevant to the athletic female. They explore the circumstances and problems of females' involvement in sport, including psychological, social, and cultural issues. Chapters 4 through 7 discuss health topics as they relate to exercise: changes in the menstrual cycle, pregnancy, oral contraceptives, bone mass density, stress fractures, and osteoporosis.

Chapter 8 provides valuable insight into the physiology of preadolescent and adolescent athletic females. This workshop presentation gave rise to much discussion about the increased incidence of anterior cruciate ligament tears among female high school and college basketball players. Concern about iron deficiency in adolescents was also expressed. (Further information on these subjects appears at the end of the book in "Provocative Issues and Recommendations for Future Research.")

Chapters 9 and 10 discuss two problems as they affect athletic females: substance abuse and eating disorders. Both behaviors may be used in an effort to give an athlete a competitive edge. Many feel that the incidence of eating disorders is connected to media promulgation of a supposedly ideal body image.

Chapters 11 through 14 examine additional areas of concern to the athletic female. Chapter 11 gives an overview of the muscle physiology, cardiorespiratory, and metabolic changes associated with athletic activity and explains how they are different between women and men. The need for nutritional education for the athletic female is explored in chapter 12; most athletic females are deficient in their intake of calories, carbohydrates, iron, calcium, and protein, while their diets are heavy in fat. Chapter 13 discusses the effects of strength training in females and chapter 14 examines the importance of exercise and conditioning for aging females.

The importance of off-season conditioning and sport-specific training and their relationship to muscle imbalance are addressed in chapters 15, 16, and 17. Off-season conditioning and sport-specific conditioning appear to enhance performance, decrease injury rates and severity, decrease burnout, and enhance strength and aerobic conditioning, but research is lacking in this area. The relationship between muscle balance, alignment of the lower extremities, and biomechanics of specific sports is also important.

Chapters 18 through 21 address specific types of athletic injuries and their rates of incidence among females. Studies indicate that upper extremities are injured much less frequently than the lower. However, these studies are biased by focusing on sports where use of the lower extremities predominates. Traumatic overuse injuries are common in traditionally female activities such as dance, gymnastics, and skating. The book closes with commentary on the provocative issues discussed at the workshop and suggestions for future research.

Arthur J. Pearl

CHAPTER 1

•

A 20-Year Perspective: What Has Changed?

Judy Mahle Lutter

I am 2 years short of having a personal 20-year perspective on the female athlete. In 1973, at the age of 33, I began running. A few years later, after completing a marathon, I surprised myself by adding "athlete" to my resume. Was that an accurate label?

Defining the Athletic Female

The athletic woman is still variously defined (16). Ten years ago when I gave talks to women, who ranged in age from 30 to 65, only a very few would raise their hands when I asked if any considered themselves to be "athletic" or "athletes." Those numbers have increased; women today are much more likely to feel that such a label describes their level of physical activity. The vast majority, however, still shy away from that designation. Upon questioning, they may tell you that they walk every day, play tennis three times a week, and do three aerobic dance classes. "But," they will quickly add, "I'm not very good at any of them." Should the term *athletic female* apply only to the young, the elite?

Some national polls, citing participation figures of 58% and higher, lead writers to decide that we have become—by some indescribable miracle—a nation of exercisers (20). In the case of statistics supplied by the National Sporting Goods Manufacturers Association, infrequent exercisers (those who exercise 6-24 days a year) are included in this figure. To most people these figures do not represent a truly physically active population. Nonetheless, women's participation has increased in the last 20 years. Women are more likely than men to be frequent

1

participants, and a greater percentage of women participate on a frequent basis than do men (20).

One reason for the increased numbers has been the creation of a new option—aerobic dance. At first written off by physical educators and health professionals as a fad, the fact that women in great numbers stuck with an exercise program for the first time finally provoked attention.

When disseminating our findings on the female athlete, we need to be as careful in our choice of words as Melpomene was in writing *The Bodywise Woman* (15). Words like *athlete* and *exercise* are intimidating to many women. Yet these same women may reap many benefits, physical and mental, through involvement in physical activity. I believe that one of our roles as health professionals is to encourage women to become more physically active, and we should consider females of all ages, abilities, and levels of physical activity. A recent study conducted in conjunction with Melpomene's walking program for older adults supports this hypothesis. We found that our typical subject had *not* received a recommendation to exercise from her doctor (even though she made annual visits), but she reported she would be more likely to exercise if her doctor encouraged it (11).

In addition to being aware of ageism, we also need to be careful not to assume that only those without disabilities or ailments can be athletic. Some of the best athletes I know are women who use wheelchairs, who are diabetic, or who are hearing impaired.

Time as an Obstacle to Athletic Activity

Both hard data and conversations with women for the past 10 years have convinced me that the bottom line is *time*. Though we are well aware of the health benefits of physical activity, we need to provide facts about the benefits of physical activity that are convincing enough for women to be willing to take time for themselves. In order to qualify as a female athlete at any age, physical activity is a priority (14, 24).

That the demands on women's time have not decreased over the past 20 years has been documented recently by Julia Schor and a 1990 Melpomene Institute membership survey (9, 14, 25). The much higher number of working mothers has placed new stresses on the majority of women. We are looking at a period of changed opportunities and changed expectations.

Title IX Gives Females a Chance

In 1972, Title IX of the Education Amendments became law. This signaled a change in the climate of athletics for women. Title IX said that sex discrimination is prohibited in ''any education program or activity receiving Federal financial assistance'' (21). Title IX further requires that educational institutions afford women equal opportunities in athletics and that they provide women reasonable opportunities for the award of athletic scholarships in proportion to their participation. The results, in terms of numbers, have been dramatic.

Most women who become college athletes have received good training at a much earlier age. Girls' sports participation stood at 294, 015 in 1971; by 1973 the total was 817,073, more than a threefold increase. The number of girls involved in sports grew enormously and peaked in 1977-78 when there were about 2,083,000 female participants. In recent years, the numbers have fluctuated between 1,750,000 and 1,850,000 (18).

Title IX effectively made the general public examine some of its misconceptions. One reason women had not been encouraged to be athletic is because some of the characteristics of athletic achievement—self-confidence, leadership, and physical strength—have been seen as contradictory to woman's image and role. A Connecticut judge, ruling in 1971 against the right of women to participate on a cross-country team, stated, ''The present generation of our younger male population has not become so decadent that boys will experience a thrill in defeating girls in running contests, whether the girls be members of their own team or an adversary team. . . . Athletic competition builds character in our boys. We do not need that kind of character in our girls, the women of tomorrow'' (21, p. 2).

Health Concerns Related to Women's Reproductive Status

Women have long been aware of sexual stereotyping that led to limitations. The feeling that sport would be detrimental to a woman's character development was buttressed by the idea that physical activity might also have negative health consequences. In the late 1880s, when women's colleges began to consider promoting physical activity and even organized sports for women, they were aware that they were challenging the stereotype of femininity. The popular medical books of the day emphasized the notion that women suffered "brain fever" during menses. According to Dr. W.C. Taylor, "We cannot too emphatically urge the importance of regarding these monthly returns as periods of ill health, as days when the ordinary occupations are to be suspended or modified . . . long walks, dancing, shopping, riding and parties should be avoided at this time of the month invariably and under all circumstances" (6, p. 100).

The menstrual cycle question remains an issue for many women. Though we clearly do not believe that women are incapable of activity during their menses, we are not nearly as clear about the implications of amenorrhea.

Media Attention to Athletic Females

The increase in the numbers of women participating in physical activity over the past 20 years has led, slowly, to increased media coverage. Though most coverage is focused on young, competitive women and sports achievement, there has also been media attention focused on health-related issues. We read headlines about bone loss in female athletes; we know when some well-known athlete, like Joan Benoit Samuelson or Martina Navratilova, has been injured or requires surgery. Stories of athletes running throughout their pregnancies are not uncommon.

Much of the media attention is desirable. It's much easier for a girl or young woman to relate to another female. Proof that role models are influential is best measured after each Olympics, when the number of girls who begin training in gymnastics or swimming significantly increases. But we also know that general sport participation, particularly among females, has declined.

The Decline in Females' Sport Participation

The Minneapolis Park and Recreation Board has identified encouraging girls to become more active in sport to be a priority after documenting that gymnastics is the only sport with high female participation. Even sports that are designed to attract girls as well as boys, including basketball and soccer, are in fact 75% male (Minneapolis Park & Recreation Board, 1990, unpublished memo).

Daily physical education from kindergarten through grade 12 is required in only one state—Illinois. New Jersey is the only other state that also requires physical education from K through 12, though it does not specify how often. Budget cuts frequently have meant a decrease in the number of specialized physical educators; often, the classroom teacher, with no training and perhaps little interest, must do the best she or he can to provide physical activity.

The fact that schools are doing less is particularly discouraging, because family-centered activities, or even the chance for girls to enjoy pick-up softball or basketball games, have actually declined over the past 20 years. One of the problems of two-job or two-career families has been a decrease in the time available for leisure (14, 25). What then are the chances that the number of female athletes will continue to grow? What is our current level of knowledge, and what are some of the issues of the future?

The Role of Melpomene Institute in Awareness of the Athletic Female

The history of the past 20 years created the appropriate climate for the founding of Melpomene Institute in 1982. Our birth was dependent on many of the changes I have described. Melpomene's mission is to link physical activity with health for girls and women of all ages through research, publication, and education. The idea began in 1977. One of the relatively few long-distance runners in Minnesota, I was getting questions about menstrual irregularity. When I looked to the literature for answers, there was very little documentation. A colleague and I decided to distribute a questionnaire to determine, in a small way, the incidence and circumstances of amenorrhea. To our amazement we received 420 responses in a very short time. Most of them included a whole page of other questions related to physical activity. A common response was, "I have not noticed menstrual cycle change, but . . ." (unpublished data, 1977 Lutter study). The respondents said they were looking for additional information on exercise and pregnancy, aging, menopause, eating disorders, body image, injuries, nutrition, and much more.

For Melpomene, the questions come at least as frequently from lay audiences as from health professionals. In general, I think our desire for knowledge about the female athlete has emerged because a larger number of women participating has increased the need to address problems that have arisen. Individual girls and women, as well as coaches and physicians who needed to find information to solve or explain a particular problem, have been the impetus for much of the change.

Although the past 20 years have seen a change in attitudes as well as an increase in medical, nutritional, and psychological information, there is still much to be done.

A Historical Perspective
of Physically Active Women's Concerns

When we look at the issues of amenorrhea, pregnancy, osteoporosis, menopause, eating disorders, and injuries, we are dealing, in many instances, with a well informed public.

The Menstrual Cycle

Twenty years ago, only professionals knew the term *amenorrhea*. Today, due to media coverage and the increased awareness of coaches and physicians, many women are aware that the condition may not be totally benign. They are likely to have read at least one headline that warns, "Too much exercise is found bad for women" (23).

At Melpomene, we take issue with those headlines because they are misleading. But we also believe that women want and need to be informed on what they can expect. What if a woman becomes amenorrheic or experiences other menstrual cycle changes? Is there reason for alarm? Are there long-term consequences? The more we know about the menstrual cycle, the more aware we become of subtle differences that may occur from month to month in the same woman. Over the past 10 years, there has been a greater emphasis on relating these changes to physical activity, but inactive women also experience fluctuations and change.

Changes in the menstrual cycle, particularly amenorrhea, usually raises two issues. One of the most frequently voiced concerns of younger women is "If my periods are irregular now, will I be unable to conceive in the future?" The answer in most cases is that lack of periods does not preclude pregnancy. The woman who has experienced anovulatory periods or cessation of periods may need to seek professional advice to achieve pregnancy, but the fear that an active woman cannot get pregnant is largely unfounded (22).

The other question of concern for a woman who is amenorrheic relates to bone loss. In the past 10 years, there have been several studies showing that athletes without menstrual periods seem to be losing mineral content in their bones, which may put them at risk for osteoporosis. Because of this evidence, some physicians and researchers suggest that women seek treatment if amenorrhea persists for 3 months (2, 3, 4). However, the question of when and how to treat athletic amenorrhea is not clear-cut. The experts generally fall into two camps. Some feel it is important to treat amenorrhea immediately to avoid the possible problem of bone demineralization. Others take a wait-and-see attitude. They believe that athletic amenorrhea is the body's way of adapting to the extra stresses of physical training, lower caloric consumption, or a change in body composition. They contend that, in most cases, amenorrhea will reverse itself without intervention (5, 17, 22).

Exercise and Pregnancy

Another area that has received increased attention in recent years has been exercise and pregnancy. Melpomene Institute began research on this subject when women who answered a questionnaire on the menstrual cycle expressed an interest in knowing more about what they could do and what they could expect when pregnant. Most studies before 1980 had been done on pregnant sheep; common sense and certain ethical questions mean that some research cannot be done on pregnant women. The result is, however, that the data are suggestive but not necessarily conclusive (26).

But women wanted answers. Those who continued to run or swim while pregnant were frequently questioned—often publicly. According to many women, it is not uncommon for total strangers to yell admonitions at visibly pregnant runners: "Are your crazy, lady? You're killing your baby!" (Melpomene Institute, unpublished data, 1983). Though the evidence is very strong that this is *not* the case, such reactions underline the fact that women need as much information as possible to be comfortable with their decision to continue to exercise. Unfortunately, questions like "How far can I ran? Can I run throughout my pregnancy? Will I experience any discomfort?" do not have single answers.

Injury

Twenty years ago, there were too few women athletes for medical circles to be concerned about injury. Of course, women who were pioneers in sports sometimes developed injuries, but they frequently were not given serious attention. Even 10 years ago, it was common for a woman to receive different treatment than a man with an identical injury. Women runners who complained of tendinitis, for example, were frequently told to stop running, whereas men were given a specific treatment program that combined rest with continued activity. Recently, there has been some suggestion that women are more susceptible to athletic injury.

Some believe that amenorrhea is related to a higher incidence of stress fractures (1). More research is needed. In some cases, careful documentation already exists but needs to be disseminated to a larger audience. A case in point is information from the University of Texas at Austin, which, if collaborated at other institutions, might change "accepted wisdom" about the amenorrhea—stress fracture link (1, 27).

Some injuries can be prevented by good coaching. Frequently, young women today are encouraged to add weights to their training programs. They may be given "programs," pretested by other athletes, specific to their sport. Off-season conditioning schedules are often provided even at the high school competitive level. Once a woman leaves an educational setting, however, it is only the dedicated or exceptional athlete who will look for and utilize coaching.

Nutrition

Twenty years ago, there was a paucity of good research on nutrition, for either men or women. Nancy Clark has been writing on that topic for the past decade, but here, too, there is much that we do not know. One area of special concern to athletic females is whether they are eating adequately for performance (5).

Athletic amenorrhea has been linked to dietary habits in some women. Some studies have shown a much higher incidence of eating disorders among collegiate athletes, though a Melpomene study conducted in 1989 did not document that trend (8, 10). It is, however, an issue that should be acknowledged by coaches, trainers, and health personnel so that help can be given when appropriate (19).

Though *young* competitive athletes are most likley to be concerned about weight issues and low body fat, many women in their 30s, 40s, and 50s are also overly concerned about slimness (7, 15, 24). Melpomene studies document that many women practice restricted eating throughout their lives. The media definition of ideal body image is exaggerated perhaps for athletic women, but today's athletic clothing does little to hide unwanted fat!

Older Women and Physical Activity

The search for an improved body shape as well as health benefits has prompted a larger number of women to *become* physically active in their 40s and 50s. The most common entry activity for this group is walking, which leads in some cases to running, tennis, biking, or a variety of other more strenuous physical activities. Though most of these women will not ever consider themselves athletic, some may be encouraged by the role models that have emerged in the last decade (13).

The Need for New Research

This new phenomenon of women defining themselves as athletes and competing at older ages also presents possibilities for new research and new understandings. Until recently, any article written about older athletes was about older men. The opportunity now exists to discover if any form of physical activity protects against osteoporosis, arthritis, or heart attacks in women (28).

One question of great interest to women is how menopause may affect their physical activity. Basically, no one knows; at best, there has been very little information published about this experience. In 1991, at the request of many women who have remained physically active into their late 40s, Melpomene initiated a study on the relationship between menopause and physical activity. Results of this study and suggestions for additional research will be available early in 1993. The many calls and letters requesting information on this topic reflect the aging of a generation of physically active women.

Current Perspective of the Athletic Female

In conclusion, I suggest that attitudes are not universally changed regarding the appropriateness of female participation in physical activity and sport. Prejudice often is not far from the surface, particularly for older women, women with disabilities, and those who are economically disadvantaged. We must be aware that current knowledge is not definitive and that the most important message we can convey to our patients and clients may be to ''stay tuned.'' It is partly our responsibility to continue to look for answers that will make a lifetime of physical activity not only a possibility but a priority for greater numbers of women. We also have a responsibility to see that the media appropriately reports our findings. We need to provide accurate information to the individual athletic woman as well as to those who provide her health and fitness services. We need to guard against information that is patronizing or does not admit that there are not definitive answers on a particular subject.

I believe this book not only will increase the knowledge but also sharpen awareness of the issues that should receive our attention over the *next* 20 years. This is not only an exciting time but a crucial time with regard to women's health issues. We need to know, based on excellent research, what impact physical activity has on a woman's mental and physical health throughout her life, and our research must have practical implications so that the questions raised by girls and women can be more completely answered in the years ahead.

Summary

1. Female participation in athletic activity has increased remarkably in the last 20 years, but there is still much room for improvement. We need to increase public awareness, knowledge, and positive attitudes.
2. Although Title IX has been instrumental in providing women opportunities for athletic activity, particularly at the college level, women still face prejudice against their participation in physical activity.
3. Time is the major obstacle preventing women from regular participation in physical activity.

4. Concerns of the athletic female include exercise's effect on the menstrual cycle and pregnancy, the potential for injury, and proper nutrition.

5. As more older women are becoming physically active, more information and research is needed on the impact of exercise on this age group.

References

1. Barrow, G.W.; Saha, S. Menstrual irregularity and stress fractures in collegiate female distance runners. Am. J. Sports Med. 16(3):209-216; 1988.
2. Drinkwater, B.L., editor. Female endurance athletes. Champaign, IL: Human Kinetics; 1986.
3. Drinkwater, B.L.; Nilson, K.; Chestnut, C.H.; Bremner, W.J. Bone mineral content of amenorrheic and eumenorrheic athletes. New Eng. J. Med. 311:227-280; 1984.
4. Drinkwater, B.L.; Nilson, K.; Oh, S.; Chestnut, C.H. Bone mineral density after resumption of menses in amenorrheic athletes. JAMA 256(3):380-382; 1986.
5. Deuster, P.; Kyle, S.B.; Moser, P.B.; Vigersky, R.A.; Singh, A.; Schoomaker, E.B. Nutritional intakes and status of highly trained amenorrheic and eumenorrheic women runners. Fertility & Sterility. 46(4): 1986.
6. Ehrenreich, B.; English, D. For her own good: 150 years of the expert's advice to women. New York: Doubleday; 1978.
7. Foster, C.; Lutter, J.; Denny, K.; Kimber, C. The Melpomene Institute body image study: a preliminary report. Melpomene Rpt. 5(1):3-8; 1986.
8. Gustafson, D. Eating behaviors of women college athletes. Melpomene J. 8(3):11-13; 1989.
9. Jaffee, L. Melpomene research reports: ten years of Melpomene membership. Melpomene J. 11(1):20-21; 1992.
10. Jaffee, J.; Webster, M.; Lutter, J. Melpomene research reports: dietary differences of amenorrheic and eumenorrheic athletes. Melpomene. J. 7(3):15-19; 1988.
11. Johnson-Hipp, S.; Deviny, A. Melpomene research reports: exercise habits of older adults. Melpomene J. 9(3):16-22; 1990.
12. Kulpa, P.; White, B.; Visschler, R. Aerobic exercise in pregnancy. Am. J. Obstet. Gynecol. 156(6):1395-1403; 1987.
13. Levin, S. Champion athletes over 50. Ms. 1992 March/April; 71-75.
14. Lutter, J.M. A question of age: similarities and differences of Melpomene members across the lifespan. Melpomene J. 11(1): 22-25; 1992.
15. Melpomene Institute Staff and Researchers. The bodywise woman. New York: Prentice Hall; 1990.
16. Miller Brewing Company. The Miller Lite report on American attitudes towards sports. Milwaukee, WI: Miller Brewing Company; 1983.
17. Monahan, T. Treating athletic amenorrhea: a matter of instinct? Physician & Sportmed. 15(7):184-189; 1987.
18. National Federation News. 1989 Oct.
19. Nelson, A. Eating disorders and female athletes: a serious and growing problem. Melpomene Rpt. 6(3):9-12; 1987.
20. NGSA News. 1990 Aug.
21. Project on the Status and Education of Women. What constitutes equality for women in sport? Washington, DC: Association for American Colleges; 1975 Sept.

22. Prior, J.C. Exercise-related adaptive changes of the menstrual cycle in exercise: benefits, limits, and adaptations. In: Macleod, D.; Maughan, R.; Nimmo, M.; Reilly, T.; Williams, C.; Spon, E. eds. Exercise: Benefits, Limits and Adaptations. London: E.F.N. Spon; 1987.
23. Reaburn, P. Too much exercise is found bad for women. St. Paul Pioneer Press Dispatch. 1988 Sept. 29.
24. Robinson, J. Body image in women over forty. Melpomene Rpt. 2(3):12-14; 1983.
25. Schor, J.B. The overworked American. New York: Basic Books; 1991.
26. Slavin, J.L.; Lee, V.; Lutter, J.M. Pregnancy and exercise. In: Puhl, J.; Brown, H.; Voy, R., eds. Sport science perspectives for women. Champaign, IL: Human Kinetics; 1987: 189-197.
27. The Performance Team Newsletter. Univ. of Texas at Austin. 2(3):1-23; 1990 May.
28. Wells, Christine L. Women report and performance. Champaign, IL: Human Kinetics; 1991.

CHAPTER 2

•

Problems Facing the Athletic Female

Mary Lloyd Ireland

"Catch a rising star . . . catch it if you can." These lines from a children's song should encourage limitless but achievable goals for youngsters. As a child I was encouraged to play as hard and run as fast as I could. If I beat the boys, that was okay.

What problems do female athletes encounter? Lack of recognition and support are the most significant problems. This means less ink, less air time, less applause, less fame and adulation. At the professional level of competition, women receive much less money. The female athlete is continually faced with certain "lacks" at many levels. This includes lack of encouragement to compete, lack of family, peer, and financial support, lack of recognition by fans and journalists, and lack of social acceptance.

Gender Differences and Inequality in Sport

Yes, women put on their uniforms the same way men do. They shoot through the same hoops, wear the same track shoes, swim the same events, ski with the same gear, and generally play by the same rules. In my career as an athlete and in my subsequent training to become an orthopaedic surgeon specializing in sports medicine, I appreciate that there are unique differences in the genders. In addition to the physical differences, there are varying physiological and psychological approaches to competition. Due to these inherent differences, the perception is often that women are inferior to men. These perceivers can be the female athletes, supporters, medical personnel, fans, and reporters.

Should these differences in male and female athletes be emphasized or even discussed? Gender distinctions, although sometimes subtle, should not be demeaning to the female sex. Comments regarding differences in the sexes should not necessarily be labeled sexist accusations, insensitive comments, or discouraging remarks. Some women use these comments in a negative way and develop a permanent inferiority complex. It is unfortunate but true that in athletics women do not have the same potential for financial prosperity, security, and public fame. This is society's statement—and society's problem.

Violence in Sport

Crowds at athletic events seem to be fascinated with violence. The fights and hostility of the crowd parallel the contact of the sport. Crowd violence is often seen at events like boxing, soccer, and rugby. Making idols of men who act in violent ways is a problem inherent in our society. Early in my swimming career, an article described me as "fiercely competitive" (31). I feel that women can be as competitive as men but are not as excited, gratified, or fulfilled by violence as men.

Hollywood has a preoccupation with portraying women as gun-toting, man-killing predators, which does not do justice to the gender. The well-known film about female athletes, *Personal Best*, depicts the female athlete in a way that causes concern—doing more drugs, building bigger muscles, and having more relationships than men. This is not a true portrayal of the female athlete.

Gender does dictate competitive situations in certain sports. Females do not compete in football, boxing, or professional ice hockey. Males do not perform on the gymnastic apparatus of balance beam or uneven parallel bars. In female sports, violence is not the goal. Unfortunately, the sporting public pays great sums and expends great amounts of energy to attend "contact sports." The crowds become more enthusiastic and supportive when there are fights or injuries on the field. Fan violence in world soccer is an example of this. These fans like blood and fights. Is attendance less at female events because of the lack of violence? Are women the losers in this scenario? Perhaps in part, but certainly not due to any lack of competitive spirit! The price of public acclaim is public mayhem in some male sports. This is really society's problem. Competing with grace and finesse should be the challenge.

Personal Competition

The importance of competition is equal to both males and females. Fans, family, and the press should encourage an individual to compete regardless of gender. The "spirit for high achievement" is dependent on the individual rather than the sex.

I competed in five sports during high school—field hockey, basketball, track and field, softball, and swimming. At age 15, I was selected to represent the United States as a member in the Canadian-American dual swimming meet. When a high school freshman, I set two records at the state's swimming championships. Swimming two events was the maximum permitted at each year's meet. I swam each of the eight events and held the state championship swimming records in all individual events. While a student at Memphis State University, I represented the United States at the World University Games in Moscow in 1973. I found great satisfaction in athletic competition, and the demands that participation placed on my time helped me develop organizational skills, which helped me achieve honors in academics and success in my chosen profession. During my swimming career, I trained hard and dedicated myself to fulfill my personal goals of improving my times, increasing my number of wins, or making national teams. I swam with the personal satisfaction that my set goals were being accomplished. The regimen I followed in athletics helped me set goals for my professional life.

Problems Facing the Athletic Female

Problems exist in three areas: support, competition, and illnesses and injury. When I graduated high school in 1970, there was little encouragement to continue competition in college. Then, in 1972, women's athletics changed with Title IX. The increase in the numbers of female teams and scholarships and other financial support caused vast changes. Both men and women were represented by a common association, the National Collegiate Athletic Association (NCAA), and equalization of the sexes in collegiate competition was possible. Title IX legislation enhanced equal support, equal representation, and equal opportunity to compete in every college athletics department in the NCAA.

Support

I was blessed with a family that was quite supportive of my athletic endeavors. I did not receive an athletic or academic scholarship. My family financed my college education and swimming events. I worked when I could to help. With more collegiate teams and scholarships available and with financial support from sport federations and the U.S. Olympic Committee, women can compete for a longer period of time. The suit doesn't have to be hung up prematurely; even comebacks are possible. As I continued swimming into college, I improved my times and was able to compete in the 1972 and 1976 U.S. Olympic swimming trials. I did not reach my goal of representing the U.S. at the Olympic level, but I tried and was fulfilled by doing my best. Family support, both emotional and financial, was vital to the success of my athletic career.

Competition

I competed in sports harder than anyone I knew. The typical attitude several decades ago labeled me a tomboy and not very feminine. That was okay with me, because I enjoyed and excelled in my athletic endeavors. Others might have changed direction. Beating boys in basketball, swimming, or running was not a popular way to get a date in my adolescent years, but that really didn't bother me either. My attitude was that I should try my best and not worry about beating, or even intimidating, my opponent—whether male or female. I kept competing to my maximum. I approach life the way my father taught me: Tee off at the men's tee. Equal rules promote mutual respect and help the athletic female to gain strong support from men as well as women.

Illnesses and Injuries

Certain injuries and illnesses are unique to the sports in which females participate (2, 3, 6, 8, 9, 12, 17, 20). Physiologic profiles on female athletes provide important information (5, 11, 13, 22, 23, 25).

Other studies comparing injury patterns of males and females (6, 8, 9, 10, 16, 32, 33) suggest that, in general, injuries appear to be sport-specific rather than gender-specific. However, some data suggest that knee disorders involving the patellofemoral joint and anterior cruciate ligament are more common in female athletes (14, 15, 17). At the level of Olympic basketball, knee injuries are more frequent in females and require surgery more often (16). The reasons for the increased rate is under investigation, though no specific causes have yet been determined.

Menstrual and nutritional disorders are unique to and in epidemic proportions in athletic females. Menstrual irregularities contribute to injury (2, 4, 26, 27). Anorexia nervosa, bulimia, and inadequate nutrition are rampant among adolescent female athletes. Nutritional disorders and hormonal imbalances are known to be associated with a higher incidence of stress fractures, general malaise, and psychological disorders (4, 12, 15, 19, 20, 24, 30).

Young female athletes require special attention in several areas—psychological (7, 28, 30), nutritional (21), gynecological (26, 27), and orthopaedic (14, 15). Studies to date have made important contributions to our knowledge, but more research is needed. Special consideration of these conditions unique to the athletic female can only improve the level of diagnostic skills and the efficiency of treatment protocols.

Personal Injury History

I do not believe that women are more prone to injury than are men. I sustained several injuries—but not because I was female. I competed all out, and I got hurt. Running in leather-soled loafers in gym class, I broke my front tooth when I crashed face-first into a brick wall; I lost the tooth, but I beat the boy in the race! My mother was upset only because I hadn't put my arm out and broken that instead. She knew an arm was easy to set and quicker to correct permanently. Did she already have a hunch that her daughter would become an orthopaedist?

At age 15, determined to compete without pain, I underwent posterior spinal fusion for spondylolisthesis. My primary care physicians discouraged me from having surgery, saying I was at the end of my competitive career. But I was *not* finished! Surgery and rehabilitation resulted in a painless back and strong legs. I continued swimming competitively at a national level for another 10 years. Who knows where the other path might have led me.

In all, I underwent three orthopaedic procedures: posterior spinal fusion, later reexploration for spondylolisthesis, and distal clavicle excision. I swam much better following my back fusion and rehabilitation. I underwent the distal clavicle resection for an injury sustained while high jumping into an unpadded pit that caused recurrent pain when swimming. Though the shoulder procedure decreased my pain, in retrospect, it may not have been the correct procedure.

These injuries and surgeries provided me with front-line experience. I can sympathize with and relate to injured athletes very well. And I learned, by personal experience, that males and female should be treated equally and with the same recovery goals by all in the medical profession, especially the orthopaedist.

Orthopaedics as a Career

My athletic experience helped me feel comfortable in orthopaedics, a male-dominated field. In my residency, I related well to my 15 peers, all male. I carried my own weight and expected no favors or concessions. The two female orthopaedic residents ahead of me, who did not share my approach, did not finish the program. I am now a member of a professional society for women orthopaedists, the Ruth Jackson Society, to support other women who desire to enter this male-dominated subspecialty.

After I completed my orthopaedic residency, I did two sports medicine fellowships, one in Boston with Dr. Lyle Micheli and another at the Hughston Clinic in Columbus, Georgia, with Dr. James Andrews. My strong relationship with Dr. Andrews and the University of Kentucky led me back to my present situation in my hometown, Lexington, Kentucky, where I was appointed team physician for the University of Kentucky.

The football coaches at Kentucky made me welcome and accepted me because of my ability to provide orthopaedic services. The team's transition to coverage by a female orthopaedist was easy, because the athletes and coaches were already being assisted by staff and student athletic trainers who were women.

But on my return to Lexington, an article appeared in the *Los Angeles Times* in the fall of 1985, with the headline, ''Woman Doctor Makes Mark on Football Team'' (18). Until then, I had been unaware that I was the only woman serving in this capacity. According to the reporter's research, there had been a woman physician on Kent State's football staff in the 1940s. Sue Hillman, one of the few female head trainers in a Division I college, said that to her knowledge I was the first female orthopaedist to take care of a football team.

Other articles and headlines appeared trumpeting the fact that I was the only female team physician for football at the Division I level. I was even pursued by Hollywood producers to star in a mini-series or a movie. My initial reaction was that this should not be newsworthy or unique. But I hoped the publicity would encourage other women to enter male-dominated fields.

I feel that my having been an athlete, although not a football player, helps me relate to athletes. This was confirmed when the *Lexington Herald-Leader* ran an article entitled "Cats Woman Doctor Wants to Mend Bodies, Not Break Any Barriers." I was quoted as saying that I didn't think of myself as a trailblazer; my job was providing orthopaedic care for the athletes. Mark Higgs, who now plays professional football with the Miami Dolphins, concurred, saying, "We don't classify her as a woman or a man, just like it doesn't matter if you're white or black. What matters is she knows what she's doing" (29).

When I became the first female head physician for the U.S. Olympic Sports Festival, held in Minneapolis in 1990, I was called one of the few people who knows what it is like to represent the United States both as a physician and as an athlete (1). I had participated in the breaststroke events in the 1972 and 1976 Olympic swimming trials, though I had not made either team. But recently, with persistence, I made the medical team for Barcelona 1992. At last, I went to the Olympics.

Acceptance as a Female Physican

Being a woman in the role of team physician is not a problem as long as it is not perceived by others as one. If a physician, either male or female, is confident and competent, he or she should be readily accepted by athletes, coaches, and other medical personnel. Athletes, male or female, need to feel comfortable when being treated in a training or medical-type room by either female or male orthopaedists. The *physician* must inspire confidence that he or she is well trained and that the illness or injury can be treated. As then-University of Kentucky football coach Jerry Claiborne stated, "Women are in everything now, industry, medicine, athletics. As long as they can do their job, it's okay" (29).

Viewing Obstacles as Challenges

In conclusion, I say "no problem" to this topic of "problems of the female athlete from the athletic perspective." Female athletes need to regard these lacks as low hurdles. As a female you may have to take a few more bounces, but the springboard effect makes you a better person, a better athlete, a better physician. In high school, my senior class motto was "In order to hit the mark, one must aim a little above it." I did not understand the full meaning then, but I did later. Robert Browning said it another way: "Ah, but a man's reach should exceed his grasp. . . ." *Everyone's* reach should exceed his *and* her grasp. Persistence and perseverance result in success and productivity.

The spirit of competition I learned in all sports enabled me to reach my adult successes as an orthopaedic surgeon and team physician. The "problems" of being a female in male-dominated pursuits became positive advancements in me as a person and now in my career. As Judy Garland sang, "When you wish upon a star, makes no difference who you are . . . your dreams come true."

Summary

1. The problems facing the female athlete are caused by lack of social acceptance and support from family, peers, fans, and the media.
2. Society should encourage all individuals to compete regardless of gender. Society presently supports male participation with money, fame, and adulation.
3. Injuries are sport-specific and not gender-specific. However, knee disorders involving the patellofemoral joint and anterior cruciate ligament are more common in females than males.
4. Illnesses relating to eating disorders are epidemic in the athletic female. Menstrual disorders are very common.
5. Male and female athletes should be treated equally and with the same recovery goals by the medical profession.

References

1. Adams, G.A. Olympic hopefuls: physicians go all out to treat world-class athletes. Minnesota Med. 73:19-24; 1990.
2. Agostini, R. The athletic woman. In; Mellion, M B , ed. Office managment of sports injuries and athletic problems. Philadelphia: Hanely & Belfus; 1988:76-78.
3. Agostini, R. Women in sports. In: Mellion, M.B.; Walsh, M.W.; Shelton, G.L., eds. The team physician's handbook. Philadelphia: Hanley & Belfus; 1990·179-188.
4. Barrow, G.W.; Saha, S. Menstrual irregularity and stress fractures in collegiate female distance runners. Am. J. Sports Med. 16:109-216; 1988.
5. Chmelar, R.D.; Schultz, B.B.; Ruhling, R.O.; Shepherd, T.A.; Zupan, M.F.; Fitt, S.S. A physiologic profile comparing levels and styles of female dancers. Physician & Sportsmed. 16:87-98; 1988.
6. Clarke, K.S.; Buckley, W.E. Women's injuries in collegiate sports. Am. J. Sports Med. 8:187 191; 1980.
7. Corbin, C.B. Self-confidence of females in sports and physical activity. Clinics in Sports Med. 3:895-908; 1984.
8. DeHaven, K.E.; Linter, D.M. Athletic injuries: comparison by age, sport, and gender. Am. J. Sports Med. 14:218-224; 1986.
9. Garrick, J.G.; Requa, R.K. Girls' sports injuries in high school athletics. JAMA 239:2245-2248; 1978.
10. Gillette, J. When and where women are injured in sports. Physician & Sportsmed. 2:61-63; 1975.
11. Good, J.E.; Klein, K.M. Women in the military academies: US Navy (part 1 of 3). Physician & Sportsmed. 17:99-106; 1989.
12. Graevskaya, I.B.; Petrov, I.B.; Belyaeva, N.I. Some medical problems related to women's sports (a review). Sports Training Med. Rehab. 1:77-83; 1989.
13. Howell, D.W. Musculoskeletal profile and incidence of musculoskeletal injuries in lightweight women rowers. Am. J. Sports Med. 12:278-282; 1984.
14. Hunter, L.Y.; Andrews, J.R.; Clancy, W.G.; Funk, J.F. Common orthopaedic problems of female athletes. In: A.A.O.S. Instructional course lectures. 31:126-151; 1982.
15. Hunter, L.Y. Women's athletics: the orthopaedic surgeon's viewpoint. Clinics in Sports Med. 3:809-827; 1984.

16. Ireland, M.L.; Wall, C. Epidemiology and comparison of knee injuries in elite male and female United States basketball athletes. Med. Sci. Sports. 14:4/90; 1982.
17. Ireland, M.L. Special concerns of the female athlete. In: Fu, F.H.; Stone, D.A., eds. Sports injuries: mechanism, prevention, and treatment, 2nd ed. Baltimore: Williams & Wilkins; In press.
18. Japenga, A. Women doctor makes mark on football team. Los Angeles Times. Oct. 8, 1985, V-1 - V-4.
19. Kowal, D.M. Nature and causes of injuries in women resulting from an endurance training program. Am. J. Sports Med. 8:265-269; 1980.
20. Lutter, J.M. Health concerns of women runners. Clinics in Sports Med. 4:671-683; 1985.
21. Morgan, B.L. Nutritional needs of the female adolescent. Binghamton, NY: Hawthorn Press, Inc.; 1984.
22. Protzman, R.R. Physiologic performance of women compared to men. Am. J. Sports Med. 7:191-194; 1979.
23. Protzman, R.R. Women athletes. Am. J. Sports Med. 8:53-55; 1980.
24. Roy, S.; Irvin, R. The female athlete. In: Roy, S.P.; Irvin, R.F., eds. Sports medicine prevention, evaluation, management, and rehabilitation. Englewood Cliffs, NJ: Prentice Hall; 1983:457-467.
25. Sady, S.P.; Freedson, P.S. Body composition and structural comparisons of female and male athletes. Clinics in Sports Med. 3:755-777; 1984.
26. Shade, A.R. Gynecologic and obstetrics problems of the female dancer. Clinics in Sports Med. 2:515-523; 1983.
27. Shangold, M.M. Gynecologic concerns in the woman athlete. Clinics in Sports Med. 3:869-879; 1984.
28. Stark, J.A.; Toulouse, A. The young female athlete: psychological considerations. Clinics in Sports Med. 3:909-921; 1984.
29. Tipton, J. Cats' woman doctor wants to mend bodies, not break any barriers. Lexington Herald-Leader, Section C, Thursday, Oct. 10, 1985, C2-C3.
30. Ullyot, J.L. Sports medicine in action: the female runner from the novice to marathoner. Muscle & Bone. 4:2-10; 1984.
31. Van Hoose, L. Fierce GLSA competition uncovers hidden spark in Mary Lloyd Ireland. Lexington Herald-Leader. March 5, 1964; 14.
32. Whiteside, P.A. Men's and women's injuries in comparable sports. Physician & Sportsmed. 8:130-136; 1980.
33. Zelisko, J.A.; Noble, H.B.; Porter, M.A. Comparison of men's and women's professional basketball injuries. Am. J. Sports Med. 10:297-299; 1982.

CHAPTER 3

•

Psychological, Sociological, and Cultural Issues Concerning the Athletic Female

Diane L. Gill

Although my topic is psychological, sociological, and cultural issues, my training and work are in sport and exercise psychology, and I'll emphasize psychological issues. I do take a *social* psychological perspective and draw upon the work of feminist scholars who take a sociocultural perspective, but I cannot do justice to the important work of those scholars.

My role here is to remind us that we cannot understand the athletic female if we ignore *who* she is and *where* she is. That is, we must consider the individual woman in her sociocultural and historical context to understand the female athlete. I must also note here that I am interpreting "female athlete" liberally. *Female athlete* conjures up images of Olympic competitors and intercollegiate teams, and likewise, the research and discussions that focus on elite competitors. I hope to extend my discussion to diverse women participants and even to nonparticipants who could be participants.

Sport and exercise psychology does not provide conclusive answers to our many questions about gender. Sport and exercise psychology research on women is limited in many ways, and psychological factors by themselves cannot fully explain women's sport and exercise behavior. Sport and exercise behavior takes place within a social and historical context, and individual differences and psychological processes operate within this context. Also, each woman brings her unique biological as well as psychological makeup to any sport or exercise setting. These factors interact in complex ways to influence sport and exercise behavior. We cannot clearly describe these complex interactions and processes, and we cannot look at everything at once, but we should keep the complexity and richness of human behavior in mind.

Sex and Gender Differences

The earliest psychological research on women and gender was dominated by studies of sex differences. *Sex differences* refers to biologically based differences between males and females, whereas *gender differences* refers to social and psychological characteristics and behaviors associated with females and males. Because the early work assumed dichotomous, biologically based psychological differences that paralleled and, indeed, stemmed from biological male–female differences, *sex differences* is the more appropriate term for this section. Current thought calls the earlier interpretation into question and suggests that psychological characteristics and behaviors associated with females and males are neither dichotomous nor biologically based. Even most biological factors relevant to sport and exercise are not dichotomously divided between males and females but are normally distributed within females and males. For example, males are taller than females, on average, but many women are taller than many men. For social psychological characteristics and behaviors, average differences are elusive; no evidence supports a biological basis, and certainly no dichotomous sex-linked connections are evident.

In terms of psychological sex differences, the most notable work is Eleanor Maccoby and Carol Jacklin's 1974 (57) compilation of the existing research. First, they suggested that few conclusions could be drawn form the vast literature on sex differences. Most discussions of Maccoby and Jacklin's work ignore that conclusion and focus on their suggested *possible* sex differences in four areas: math ability, visuospatial ability, verbal ability, and aggressive behavior. Maccoby and Jacklin's possible sex differences quickly became accepted as common knowledge, and most people assume that males are more aggressive and have greater math and visuospatial ability, whereas females have greater verbal ability.

Despite many attempts to identify sex differences and their biological correlates, the bulk of the research casts doubt even on the four possible differences cited by Maccoby and Jacklin. Several reviews, most notably the meta-analytic reviews by Eagley (29, 31) and Hyde and Linn (50), suggest that sex differences in these areas are minimal and not biologically based. Meta-analyses consistently indicate that less than 5% of the behavioral variance in these cognitive ability areas is accounted for by sex. Moreover, sex differences are inconsistent and interactions are common. For example, sex differences might show up with one visuospatial task but not another, or boys might complete a timed math test faster than girls do but do no better on math accuracy with unlimited time. In general, overlap and simlarities are much more apparent than differences.

Perhaps the most telling statement on the sex differences literature is that neither Maccoby nor Jacklin now advocate sex differences in cognitive skills and social behaviors. Jacklin (51) suggests that researchers have been preoccupied with the search for sex differences and concludes that the original conclusions cannot be supported. Maccoby (56) places even more emphasis on the social situation and suggests that behavioral differences between the sexes are minimal when children are tested or observed individually. Sex differences emerge mainly in social situations and vary with the gender composition of the group. Both Maccoby and Jacklin, along with most others who have reviewed this topic, suggest that pursuing sex differences is not a viable research line. Such an approach assumes an underlying, unidimensional cause (i.e., biological sex) and ignores the rich and complex variations in gender-related behavior.

Criticisms of the sex differences approach and its failure to shed any light on gender-related behavior led psychologists to try other approaches. Most notably, psychologists turned to personality and individual differences, topics that psychologists typically turn to for explanations of behavior.

Personality and Gender Role Orientation

Personality is one of the most prominent topics in sport and exercise psychology, as well as in psychology, so we might expect to find that much of the psychological literature on women's sport and exercise emphasizes personality. Unfortunately, sport psychology studies on personality represent much of our weakest research. Generally, personality traits are poor explanations for sport and exercise behavior. Situational factors are stronger influences, and sport has many strong situational factors including rules, coaching and teaching instructions, strategies, team norms, and societal pressures. Individual differences play a role, but global personality traits do not tap the individual differences that are most relevant to sport and exercise behavior.

Gender Role Orientation Constructs and Measures

The behaviors of most interest for our purposes are gender-related behaviors, and psychologists have focused on gender role orientation as the relevant personality construct. Specifically, Sandra Bem's (4, 5) development of the Bem Sex Role Inventory (BSRI) served as the major impetus for a large body of research and subjected the constructs of masculinity, femininity, and adrogyny to more public attention and debate. As Bem began her work, Janet Spence and Bob Helmriech (78) began parallel investigations of gender role orientation and developed their measure of masculinity and feminity, the Personality Attributes Questionnaire (PAQ). This research not only began a line of work on gender roles in psychology but also prompted sport and exercise psychologists to examine gender role issues. In fact, most of the sport and exercise psychology research on gender uses the constructs and measures developed by Bem or Spence and Helmreich. Helmreich and Spence (46) sampled intercollegiate athletes in their early studies and reported that most female athletes were either androgynous or masculine. These athletes were similar to high achieving female scientists in Helmreich and Spence's samples, but different from female college students, who were most often classified as feminine.

Several subsequent studies yielded similar findings. Harris and Jennings (45) surveyed female distance runners and reported that most were androgynous or masculine. Both Del Rey and Sheppard (25) and Colker and Widom (12) found that most intercollegiate athletes were classified as androgynous or masculine. Myers and Lips (68) reported that most female racquetball players were androgynous, whereas most males were masculine. In a second study, players were classified as competitive or noncompetitive based on their reasons for entering a tournament. All males were competitive and also androgynous or masculine. Competitive females also were androgynous or masculine, but noncompetitive females had lower masculinity scores and tended to be either feminine or undifferentiated.

Many more studies have surveyed women athletes using the BSRI or PAQ, but listing more findings would not tell us much about women's sport and exercise behavior. Moreover, both the methodology and underlying assumptions of this line of research have been widely criticized (e.g., 55, 71, 81). The androgyny construct is of little conceptual or empirical value in gender role research, and Bem and Spence and Helmreich no longer advocate its use. Most investigators accept the separate masculinity/instrumentality and femininity/expressiveness dimensions but question the meaning of the underlying constructs and the implications for other gender-related constructs and behaviors. In a recent review, Deaux (21) noted that the BSRI and PAQ do seem to measure self-assertion and nurturance and do predict specific assertive and nurturant behaviors. However, the personality measures do not go far beyond these limitations and do not relate so well to other gender-related attributes and behaviors.

Overall, the sport and exercise psychology research on gender role orientation suggests that female athletes possess more masculine/instrumental personality characteristics than do female nonathletes. This is not particularly enlightening. Sport, especially in competition, is an achievement activity that demands instrumental, assertive behaviors. Indeed, both the BSRI and PAQ include *competitive* as one of the masculine/instrumental items. The higher masculine scores of female athletes probably reflect an overlap with competitiveness with no necessary connection to any other gender-related constructs or behaviors. Competitive orientation can be measured directly (e.g., 39), and we do not need to invoke more indirect, controversial measures that are not likely to add any information.

Indeed, this is just what I found in my work on competitive orientations. In one study (40), we found that competitiveness (measured directly) clearly differentiated athletes and nonathletes and that this difference held for both females and males. We also administered the BSRI and PAQ, and athletes scored higher than nonathletes on masculinity/instrumentality. However, this difference was not very strong and a stepwise analysis indicated that competitiveness was the only important discriminating factor and that the BSRI and PAQ scores did not add anything at all. So, sport participation, and particularly participation in competition, is an instrumental behavior, and participants tend to have higher instrumentality scores than do nonparticipants. However, we can use more direct and powerful measures of competitive sport orientation without invoking gender role connotations.

Perhaps even more important, sport participation or athlete/nonathlete status is an indirect and nonspecific measure of behavior. If instrumental and expressive personality characteristics predict instrumental and expressive behaviors, we should examine some of those instrumental and expressive behaviors. Classifying sport as an instrumental or masculine activity ignores the fact that many different instrumental *and* expressive behaviors occur in sport and exercise settings. Even within highly competitive sports, expressive behaviors may be advantageous. Creative, expressive actions may be the key to success for a gymnast; supportive behaviors of teammates may be critical on a soccer team; and sensitivity to others may help an Olympic coach communicate with each athlete.

Personality traits are poor predictors of behaviors. Helmreich, Spence, and Holohan (47) recognized the limits of the PAQ, cautioned that gender role measures are only weakly related to gender role behaviors, and explicitly emphasized situational factors. For example, expressive behaviors are more appropriate in a figure-skating free program than when doing school figures. By considering the joint influence of instrumental and expressive personality characteristics along with situational constraints, incentives, and interaction processes, we move closer to understanding gender-related behaviors in sport and exercise.

Even if we recognize the limits of gender role personality measures, research on gender role orientation raises concerns. Ann Hall (44), a sociology of sport scholar and one of the first to take a feminist approach, charges that using gender role constructs and measures reifies masculine-feminine dichotomous constructs that do not really exist. Hall cautions that focusing on these particular gender role constructs leads us away from the wider range of characteristics and social psychological processes that influence sport and exercise behavior. Overall, then, the sport and exercise psychology research on gender role orientation has all the drawbacks of early sport personality research replete with limiting gender stereotypes and biases.

Most current researchers interested in gender and behavior recognize the limits of the earlier sex differences and gender role approaches and look beyond the simple male/female and masculine/feminine dichotomies.

Gender and Sport Achievement

Achievement is one research area that has progressed from early sex differences research through gender role research to more current social cognitive models. Achievement is one of the most prominent topics in psychological research on gender and in sport and exercise psychology. Most sport and exercise activities involve achievement behavior, and competitive achievement behavior is particularly relevant. Gender differences were recognized but ignored in the early achievement research (61), and researchers simply took male behavior as the norm and conducted their work on men. It was not until the 1970s that women's achievement behavior and gender influences were considered.

Gender and Achievement Orientation

Matina Horner's (49) doctoral work focused attention on the role of gender in achievement behavior. Horner proposed a motive to avoid success, popularly termed the fear of success (FOS), to explain gender differences in achievement behavior. Horner suggested that success has negative consequences for women, because success requires competitive achievement behaviors that conflict with the traditional feminine image. This conflict arouses the fear of success motive and leads to anxiety and avoidance. To test her ideas, Horner had female and male students respond to cues about Anne or John, a medical student at the top of the class. Females wrote more FOS imagery than males did, and those females scoring high in FOS did not perform as well as females scoring low in FOS in a group competitive setting. Horner's work was widely publicized and inspired much debate and subsequent research. However, subsequent work cast doubt on Horner's FOS construct and measure (e.g., 13, 83). Critics noted that FOS imagery was prevalent in men as well as women, the FOS measure confused stereotyped attitudes with motives, and the research failed to link FOS directly to achievement behaviors. McElroy and Willis (62), who specifically considered women's achievement conflicts in sport contexts, concluded that no evidence supports a FOS in female athletes and that achievement attitudes of female athletes are similar to those of male athletes.

Horner's FOS work and earlier models emphasizing global achievement motives have been replaced with multidimensional constructs and an emphasis on cognitions as mediators of achievement behavior. For example, Spence and Helmreich (78, 79) developed a multidimensional measure with separate dimensions of mastery, work, and competitiveness and found that males score higher than females do on mastery and competitiveness, whereas females score higher than males do on work. With scientists, businesspersons, and athletes, gender differences on mastery and work diminish, but males remain higher than females on competitiveness. Spence and Helmreich also report that masculinity scores on the PAQ relate positively to all three achievement dimensions, whereas femininity scores relate slightly positively to work and negatively to competitiveness. Generally, gender influence is strongest and most consistent for competitiveness.

My work on sport-specific achievement orientation (38) also suggests that gender influences vary across dimensions. Using Spence and Helmreich's (78, 79) work on multidimensional achievement orientation and Martens' (58) work on sport-specific competitive anxiety as models, we developed a sport-specific, multidimensional measure of achievement orientation known as the Sport Orientation Questionnaire (SOQ; 39) that assesses

- competitiveness—an achievement orientation to enter and strive for success in competitive sport
- win orientation—a desire to win and avoid losing, and
- goal orientation—an emphasis on achieving personal goals.

During the development of the SOQ we found that males consistently scored higher than females did on competitiveness and win orientation, whereas females typically scored slightly higher than males did on goal orientation. In a follow-up study (38), I focused on gender and examined general achievement scores along with SOQ scores in females and males who participated in competitive sport, in noncompetitive sport, and in nonsport achievement activities. Overall, males consistently scored higher than females on sport competitiveness and win orientation, and males reported more competitive sport activity and experience. However, females scored just as high as males, and sometimes higher, on sport goal orientation and on all general achievement scores, except competitiveness. Also, females were just as likely as males to participate in noncompetitive sport and nonsport achievement activities. Thus, the gender differences do not seem to reflect either general achievement orientation or interest in sport and exercise activities per se. Instead, gender may influence an individual's emphasis on social comparison and winning in sport.

Other researchers report similar gender influences on reactions to competitive sport. When McNally and Orlick (63) introduced a cooperative broomball game to children in urban Canada and in the northern territories, they found girls were more receptive to the cooperative rules than were boys. They also noted cultural differences, with northern children being more receptive, but the gender influence held in both cultures. Duda (27) similarly reported both gender and cultural influences on competitiveness with Anglo and Navajo children in the southwestern U.S. Male Anglo children were the most win-oriented and placed the most emphasis on athletic ability. Weinberg and Jackson (87) found that males were more affected by success or failure than were females, and in a related study, Weinberg and Ragan (88) reported that males were more interested in a competitive activity, whereas females preferred a noncompetitive activity.

Although several lines of research suggest gender influences on sport achievement, and particularly on competitive sport achievement, the research does not suggest any unique, gender-related personality construct. Most investigators attempting to understand gender and sport achievement are turning to socialization factors, societal influences, and a broader range of social cognitive constructs and models for explanations.

Gender and Achievement Cognitions

Cognitive approaches that emphasize the individual's interpretations and perceptions and deemphasize personality constructs currently dominate research on achievement. That is, what the person thinks is important *is* important. If you expect to do well at volleyball, you probably will. If you believe that you're an uncoordinated klutz, you'll probably perform like one in gymnastics. Most cognitive approaches focus on expectations, and research consistently indicates that expectations are good predictors of achievement behavior and performance (e.g., 2, 3, 18, 34, 36).

More relevant to this discussion, research also suggests gender influences on expectations. Typically, females report lower expectations of success and make fewer achievement-oriented attributions than do males, and this difference may explain gender differences in achievement behavior. However, gender differences in cognitive expectancy patterns are not consistent. In her review of the self-confidence literature, Lenney (53) concluded that gender differences in confidence are more likely to occur in achievement situations that (a) involve tasks perceived as masculine, (b) provide only ambiguous feedback or ability information, and (c) emphasize social comparison evaluation.

Within sport and exercise psychology, Corbin and his colleagues (14-17, 72, 80) have conducted a series of experimental studies with motor tasks that confirm Lenney's propositions. Specifically, Corbin and his colleagues demonstrated that females do not lack confidence when performing a gender-neutral, nonsocially evaluative task and that performance feedback can improve the confidence of low-confidence females. Moreover, Petruzzello and Corbin (72) found that feedback-enhanced confidence did not generalize beyond the experimental task and suggested lack of experience as an additional factor affecting female self-confidence. In our lab (41), we matched female and male competitors of similar ability on a pegboard task. Males were slightly more likely than females to predict a win, perhaps reflecting the gender influence on competitive win orientation. However, preformance expectations were similar, females performed slightly better in competition than males did, and females generally had more positive achievement cognitions (higher perceived ability, more effort attributions).

So, these studies suggest that when tasks are appropriate for females, when females and males have similar experiences and capabilities, and when clear evaluation criteria and feedback are present, females and males display similar levels of confidence. Importantly, though, these are experimental studies in controlled settings. We cannot so easily equate task appropriateness, experience, and social influence in the real world of sport and exercise. To understand the influence of gender on achievement cognitions and behaviors we must consider these socialization and social context influences.

Eccles's Model of Achievement

Several achievement orientation models have been used in sport and exercise psychology, but I particularly like Jacquelynne Eccles's (32-34) model, which incorporates sociocultural factors along with achievement cognitions. Moreover, Eccles considers gender differences and influences throughout the model and recently (35) has extended her research to sport achievement.

Eccles recognizes that expectations are key determinants of achievement choices and behaviors and also that importance or value has a direct role in determining achievement choices. Gender differences in expectations are common in most achievement domains, including sport and exercise. Also, gender influences the value or importance of sport achievement. Eccles further notes that gender differences in expectations and value do not suddenly appear but develop over time and are influenced by gender role socialization, stereotyped expectations of others, and sociocultural norms, as well as individual characteristics and experiences. To understand gender and achievement, we must take this broader look at early socialization and the social context. Recently, Eccles and Harold (35) summarized existing work and provided new evidence showing that her model holds for sport achievement, that gender influences children's sport achievement perceptions and behaviors at a very young age, and that these gender differences seem to be the product of gender role socialization.

Eccles's model does not give all the answers but does provide a framework for developing relevant and important questions concerning gender and sport achievement. First, Eccles's research indicates that gender differences in sport achievement choices and behaviors exist. Second, gender apparently influences sport achievement through self-perceptions of value and expectations. Although physical characteristics and aptitude have some influence, the sociocultural context and socialization process seem to be the primary sources of gender differences in self-perceptions. These sociocultural processes encompass many specific factors (e.g., parental influence, school influence, sociocultural stereotypes) that are interrelated in complex ways. We may not be able to pinpoint precise predictors and lines of influence, but we must consider the socialization process if we are to understand gender and achievement in sport and exercise.

Physical Activity and Self-Perceptions

Before moving away from individual differences I want to consider the influence of sport and exercise on individual differences. In particular, sport and exercise may influence self-perceptions, especially self-esteem. Potential benefits are not unique to women, but because we have missed out on such opportunities for so long, we have a lot to gain.

The important benefits are the psychological changes that accompany enhanced physical fitness and skill. Females tend to lack confidence in their sport and exercise capabilities. Thus, sport and exercise activities have a tremendous potential to enhance a woman's sense of competence and control. Many women who begin to participate in exercise and sport programs report such enhanced self-esteem and particularly a sense of physical competence that often carries over into other aspects of their lives. Although researchers have neglected the topic of exercise and sport influences on self-perceptions, a few studies do add some support to the testimonials. Holloway, Beuter, and Duda (48), Brown and Harrison (11), and Trujillo (84) all report that exercise programs, particularly weight and strength training, enhance the self-concepts of women participants.

As well as developing feelings of physical strength and confidence, sport offers the opportunity to strive for excellence, the chance to accomplish a goal through effort and training, and the psychological challenge of testing oneself in competition. Diana Nyad (69), the marathon swimmer, expressed this:

> When asked why, I say that marathon swimming is the most difficult physical, intellectual, and emotional battleground I have encountered, and each time I win, each time I reach the other shore, I feel worthy of any other challenge life has to offer. (p. 152)

The values expressed by Nyad are those we hope participants gain in our competitive and noncompetitive programs—a sense of physical capability and the satisfaction of testing oneself and meeting challenges. Such benefits should be gained in competitive sports, but too often we lose these real benefits when we focus on competitive *outcomes*. Research clearly shows that a focus on such extrinsic rewards detracts from intrinsic interest, other psychological benefits, and even detracts from performance achievements. We should focus on internal, individual standards for both performance and nonperformance goals to help women enhance their sense of physical competence and confidence and achieve the real benefits of sport and exercise activities.

Gender Belief Systems

Deaux (20) reports that psychologists have moved away from the sex differences and individual differences approaches to an emphasis on gender as a social category. Even Bem has moved away from her early focus on personality to a broader, more social gender schema theory (6). Rather than classifying individuals as masculine, feminine, or androgynous, Bem now focuses on sex-typing as an indicant of gender-schematic processing.

Gender schema theory suggests that sex-typed individuals are more likely than nonsex-typed individuals to classify sports as gender-appropriate and to restrict their participation to gender-appropriate activities. Matteo (59, 60) and Csizma, Wittig, and Schurr (19) confirmed that sports are indeed sex-typed (mostly as masculine). Matteo further reported that sex-typing influenced sport choice and that sex-typed individuals did not participate in gender-inappropriate sports.

Deaux (20-22) focuses on social categories and social context in her recent work on gender belief systems and suggests that how people *think* males and females differ is more important than how they actually *do* differ. Even though actual psychological and behavioral differences between females and males are small and inconsistent, we maintain our beliefs in gender differences.

Deaux proposes that our gender stereotypes are pervasive and exert a major influence on social interactions. Considerable evidence supports the existence of gender stereotypes. In their often cited research, Broverman, Rosenkrantz, and their colleagues (10, 75) found that people believe males and females differ on a large number of characteristics and behaviors (e.g., women are more emotional and sensitive, whereas men are more forceful and independent).

More recent work (22, 23, 30) suggests that bipolar stereotypes continue to exist and also that gender stereotypes have multiple components. We not only hold gender stereotypes about personality traits, as shown by the work of Broverman and Rosenkrantz, and with masculinity/femininity measures, but we also hold gender stereotypes about role behaviors, occupations, physical appearance, and sexuality. For example, we tend to picture construction workers as men and secretaries as women; if women are construction workers, we picture them as looking like men in physical appearance. Deaux suggests that these multiple components are interrelated and that the relationships and implications for gender-related behavior may vary with the social context. For example, Deaux and Lewis (23) found that people infer other gender-related traits and behaviors (e.g., personality, sexuality) from physical characteristics. Such multidimensional gender stereotypes certainly have counterparts in sport and exercise. We expect men with athletic body types to be athletes, and moreover, to be aggressive, competitive, independent, and heterosexual. Teachers and coaches seldom encourage a smaller young man or one with artistic talents to try out for football. We also tend to assume that women with athletic body builds or talents are aggressive, competitive, independent, and lesbian. This stereotype seems particularly prominent and has far-reaching implications for women in sport and exercise.

Such gender stereotypes are of interest themselves, but they are of even more interest because they influence a wide range of attitudes and behaviors. Considerable research suggests a gender bias in the evaluation of female and male performance and achievement, and that bias has implications for sport and exercise. In a provocative, widely cited study, Goldberg (42) reported a bias favoring male authors when women judged articles that were equivalent except for sex of author. Many similar studies followed Goldberg's initial work. Most confirmed a male bias in evaluations of females and males, but the findings are not completely consistent and suggest that the bias varies with information and situational characteristics (e.g., 73, 86).

Although sport psychologists have not examined multidimensional gender stereotypes and interrelationships, gender stereotypes and gender bias in evaluations certainly exist in sport. Gender stereotypes in sport were identified in Eleanor Metheney's (66) classic analysis of the social acceptability of various sports. For example, Metheny concluded that it is considered inappropriate for women to engage in contests in which the resistance of the opponent is overcome by bodily contact, the resistance of a heavy object is overcome by direct application of bodily force, or the body is projected into or through space over long distances or for extended periods of time. According to Metheny, acceptable sports for women (e.g., gymnastics, swimming, tennis) emphasize aesthetic qualities and often are individual activities in contrast to direct competition and team sports. Although Metheny offered her analysis over 25 years ago, our gender stereotypes have not faded away with the implementation of Title IX, and her work could serve as a model for today's stereotypes. Deaux (21) describes a shift toward more egalitarian attitudes in society, and sport attitudes seem to be moving in that direction. The Miller Lite Report (67), for example, suggests that males and females hold similar attitudes, that parents are equally positive toward sport participation of daughters and sons, and that the trend is toward increasing egalitarian attitudes. Gender stereotypes persist, though, and they seem more persistent in sport than in other social contexts. For example, Kane and Snyder (52) recently confirmed gender stereotyping of sports, as suggested by Metheny, and more explicitly identified physicality as the central feature in gender stereotyping of sport.

Several studies within sport have adopted the Goldberg approach and examined gender bias in evaluating performance. A series of studies on female and male attitudes toward hypothetical female and male coaches (70, 89, 90) revealed a bias favoring male coaches. However, Williams and Parkhouse (90) reported that female basketball players coached by a successful female exhibited not the expected male bias but a female bias, suggesting more complex influences on gender stereotypes and evaluations.

Not only do gender beliefs persist in sport and exercise, but socialization pressures toward such gender beliefs are pervasive, strong (although often subtle), and begin early (for example, see 43). For my purposes, I simply note that gendered beliefs and behaviors are apparent even in infants and that parents, schools, and other socializers convey gendered beliefs in many direct and indirect ways. An understanding of gender socialization provides the basis for understanding individual gender-related behavior within sport and exercise.

Overall, gender belief systems seem alive and well in the world of sport and exercise. Sport activities are gender stereotyped, and the sex-typing of sport activities seems linked with other gender beliefs (e.g., physicality). Gender beliefs influence social processes, and the research on gender bias in evaluation of coaches suggests that influence is at least as likely in sport as in other social interactions. Overt discrimination is unlikely, and participants may not recognize the influence of gender belief systems in themselves or others. For example, many sport administrators and participants fail to recognize gender beliefs operating when athletic programs developed by and for men, stressing male-linked values and characteristics, are opened to girls and women.

Gender and Social Context

Not only should we consider gender stereotypes and beliefs, but as Deaux and Major (24) state, we must consider the immediate social context to understand gender-related behavior in a given situation. In her book, *The Female World*, prominent sociologist Jessie Bernard (7) points out that social experiences and contexts for females and males are quite different, even when they appear to be similar. Indeed, male and female worlds are different. In the early days of organized sport from the 1920s to Title IX, we intentionally established separate sport worlds for females and males. The separate social sport worlds have not disappeared with our legal and organizational changes. The social world differs for female and male members of a volleyball class, for male and female joggers, and for the girl and boy pitching in a youth baseball game.

Carolyn Sherif (76, 77) was a persistent advocate for *social* psychology, and she emphasized social context and process when considering gender influences on behavior. Moreover, Sherif specifically pointed out strategies for incorporating social context and gender into our research on competition and sport behavior. Unfortunately sport and exercise psychologists have not adopted Sherif's suggestions or other current social psychological approaches. Indeed, our research and practice seems narrower and more oblivious to social context and process than ever before. Such isolation cannot advance our understanding of such an obviously social issue and process as gender.

Within sport and exercise science the most prominent and innovative work on gender is being done by sport sociologists. Moreover, sport sociologists are incorporating feminist theoretical frameworks and alternative approaches (e.g., critical theory, social construction) in their work. Ann Hall (44), an influential leader in feminist sport scholarship, criticized sport psychology's limited focus on masculinity and feminity and advocated a more thoughtful consideration of gender as a pervasive social influence. Other sport scholars have devoted systematic attention to gender and have developed varied feminist frameworks within sport and exercise. Helen Lenskyj's (54) coherent and provocative analysis of sexuality and gender emphasizes the historical and sociocultural pressures toward compulsory heterosexuality that influence women's sport and exercise participation and behaviors. Like other feminist scholars, Alison Dewar (26) examines the role of gender in sport and exercise, but she has moved beyond the typical focus on elite sport to a critical analysis of gender in physical education curriculum and practice. Nancy Theberge (82) writes extensively on gender issues, and her discussion of the relationship of gender to power and empowerment in sport is particularly relevant. Susan Birrell (9) traced the reserach on gender and sport from sex differences research, through gender roles, to current considerations of gender relations in a dynamic, sociocultural context.

The work of these feminist sport scholars suggests that gender pervades society, and specifically, *sport* society; that gender beliefs, relations, and processes are multifaceted; and that an understanding of the historical and cultural contexts, as well as the immediate social context is necessary to understand women's sport and exercise experiences.

Future Directions

Adopting a true social psychological perspective is critical for current and future sport and exercise research on gender. Indeed, much sport and exercise behavior is interpretable only when considering social context. As Deaux suggests, components of social context vary tremendously, and we should consider the variations in our research on gender. Moreover, as Jacklin (51) noted, social context changes in a larger sense. The social norms and beliefs about sport and exercise may be quite different today than they were 10 years ago and than they will be 10 years from now. As society changes, gender socialization, beliefs, and behaviors change. Thus, both the immediate social context and the historical-cultural context are dynamic, and we should interpret findings and draw conclusions accordingly.

Not only should we adopt more encompassing conceptual frameworks, but we should look into a wider range of issues and behaviors. Sport and exercise psychology research on gender is remarkably limited and focuses on individual characteristics related to participation in competitive athletics. Focusing our research efforts on one of the most established, limited, inflexible, and moreover, elite, male-dominated sport systems is far too restrictive an approach for the study of gender. Certainly gender influences are just as prominent in youth sports, physical education classes, and exercise settings. Indeed, we probably could find more varied gender beliefs, behaviors, and relations and more varied social contexts in such settings.

Just as we should consider gender influences across a wider range of sport and exercise activities, we should consider diversity of participants. Most notably, research on racial, ethnic, and cultural influences is virtually nonexistent in sport and exercise psychology. Duda and Allison (28), who have conducted some of the few studies that we do have, point out the striking void on race and ethnicity in the field of sport and exercise psychology. Most of the points discussed for gender could be made for race and ethnicity. That is, stereotypes and belief systems are pervasive and multifaceted; racial and ethnic socialization, self-perceptions, and social context influence sport and exercise behavior; and a grounding in sociocultural history would enhance our understanding of race and ethnicity in sport. Unfortunately, we do not even have the limited work on stereotypes and individual characteristics for race and ethnicity to parallel the gender research in sport and exercise. More important to this discussion, gender belief systems and contexts probably interact with race and ethnicity systems in many complex ways. For example, the experiences of a black, female tennis player are not simply a combination of the experiences of white female and black male players. Althea Gibson (37) described her experiences in a personal account that highlights some of the complex interactions of race and gender and illustrates some of the influences of social history and the immediate social situation in her development as a tennis player and individual. Unfortunately, few scholars have attempted to take a broader analytical perspective, perhaps incorporating personal accounts such as Gibson's, to enhance our understanding of race and gender in women's sport and exercise experiences. We can extend considerations further to incorporate other social categories such as class, age, and physical attributes. The lack of sport and exercise research on any category other than gender and the paucity of that work preclude conclusions. At this point, the most important questions have not been identified. Clearly, though, we should consider diversity within gender in our gender research.

Not only should we consider diversity within gender, but we should consider diversity across gender. That is, we should consider gender for both men and women in sport and exercise. Given that most sport and exercise psychology research (like most research) focuses on men, research aimed at understanding women's sport and exercise is essential. However, to understand gender as a social category and process, we should consider gender influences on both women and men. Certainly gender belief systems operate for men in sport and exercise. Messner and Sabo (65) recently edited an important new volume on sport, men, and gender, but otherwise gender issues in sport and exercise for men and boys are largely ignored.

Finally, sport and exercise psychologists should not dismiss biological influences. Many scholars have called for stronger feminist analyses and consideration of diversity, but most do not discuss biological factors, unless they do so to dismiss (justifiably) the biological determinism argument. Sport and exercise are physical activities; that's our unique domain, and we should not ignore biological influences. Instead we should incorporate physical characteristics and capabilities into our social psychological models so that we actually develop *biopsychosocial* models. We should not consider biological factors as unidirectional determinants of behavior, and we should not fall into the old trap of assuming biological factors necessarily dominate or underlie social and behavioral influences. Rather we should consider biological influences as part of the social dynamic of sport and exercise. As Birke and Vines (8) suggest, biological factors are not static and absolute but dynamic processes that may interact with social psychological influences in varied complex ways.

For example, by incorporating physical measures, Eccles more clearly illustrated social processes that lead to gender differences in sport achievement. Sport and exercise psychology might well consider how we take such minimal, clearly nondichotomous physical differences and turn them into dichotomous gender influences. Consideration of physical characteristics with related social beliefs, self-perceptions, and social processes may add insight to research on body image, exercise behavior, youth sport and health behavior, as well as competitive sport behavior.

Body Image and Physical Activity

At this point I will digress a bit and discuss two specific topics that merit attention in future sport and exercise psychology research—body image and psychological skills for women. Body image is a particularly relevant but neglected sport and exercise psychology topic. From a psychological perspective, our most important concerns involve the relationship of body image to the individual's perceptions and attitudes about physical activity and to participation and behavior in sport and exercise settings.

In their recent book, *The Bodywise Woman*, Melpomene Institute (64) has compiled existing research and information on women's physical activity and health, including information on body image (see also 74 for further discussion and references). First, the information clearly points to the sociocultural influence on body image. Our images of the ideal body, and particularly the ideal female body, have changed through history and vary across sociocultural contexts. The slender image of today has not always been the ideal, as evidenced, for example, by the portrayals of larger, fatter women in earlier literature and artwork. We can document changes in the more recent societal ideal by noting changes in Miss America contestants or *Playboy* centerfolds (who have lost 25 pounds over the last 20 years and are now 18% *under* the medical norm for their average age and height). Certainly the ideal of today's society is a slender, lean female body. Just as clearly, most women recognize and strive for that ideal, even though the ideal is much *less* than ideal in terms of physical and mental health. Boys and men also have concerns about body images, but the literature indicates that girls and women are much more negative about their bodies. Moreover, the concerns are gender-related. As they approach and go through puberty, girls are particularly concerned with physical beauty and maintaining the ideal thin shape, whereas boys are more concerned with size, strength, and power. We could simply encourage young women to ignore media images, but unfortunately, our obsession with body image and particularly weight loss, has justification in our society. Studies indicate that people who don't match the ideal, especially overweight, obese people (particularly women), are eveluted negatively and discriminated against.

Clearly then, society shapes body image, and this societal pressure idealizing a body image that is not particularly healthy or attainable for many women has important consequences. Specifically, most women fall short of the ideal, and this likely has a negative influence on self-esteem and psychological well-being, as well as on physical health. Research indicates that most adult women perceive an underweight body as ideal and also that women tend to see themselves as overweight even though most fall within normal weight ranges. Older women surveyed in a Melpomene study on osteoporosis were more positive about their bodies than were younger women. More important, highly active older women were more satisfied with the way they looked than were less active women, which suggested that physical activity may have a positive influence not only on body image and perceived health, but probably on physical health as well. In another Melpomene survey, mothers who were physically active were more likely to describe their children in terms of skill and personality, whereas most mothers (and most people) put more emphasis on size and shape. Perhaps physical activity not only benefits women participants, but those participants who are mothers may encourage the next generation to see themselves in relation to healthy standards rather than unrealistic, unhealthy societal images.

Biology plays an important role in body image, particularly when we consider overweight and obese women. Recent work suggests that biology is the strongest determinant of obesity, that obese people do not necessarily lack willpower, and that they cannot simply lose weight if they "really" want to. Metabolic rates and processes vary greatly among people and are largely genetically determined; some of the assumed links between obesity and health may reflect psychological and social problems rather than medical problems; and constant dieting, especially a "yo-yo" pattern of weight gains and losses, may be more detrimental to health than would be remaining consistently overweight.

Concerns about body image affect women in general, regardless of whether they participate in sport and exercise. But, we should be mindful of how such body concerns influence women's participation and behaviors in physical activities. Eating disorders are a particular concern for women, and the societal pressure for thinness is a major factor. Although the latest reports suggest that athletes are no more likely than other women to exhibit eating disorders, the general societal pressure toward unrealistic, unhealthy thinness suggests that those who are working with women in sport or exercise activities need to be aware of the possibility. Pressures toward thinness, and thus unhealthy eating behaviors, are of most concern in the "thin body" sports, such as gymnastics, dance, and running. Coaches in such sports should be especially sensitive to what they communicate about ideal and realistic body shapes to their athletes. For example, one athlete reported, "At age 14 my cycling coach told me I was 'fat' in front of my entire team . . . At 5'5", 124 pounds, I was not fat, but my self-esteem was so low that I simply believed him. After all, he was the coach" (64, p. 36). Coaches and teachers should know that pressuring an athlete already subject to tremendous societal pressure to lose weight is not a desirable approach. Most enlightened coaches and instructors follow nutritional guidelines and emphasize better nutrition and healthy eating rather than weight standards.

This emphasis on healthy eating and nutrition is advisable for overweight women, and indeed most people, as well as for athletes. In fact, the implications of body image and related perceptions and behaviors are probably more important for overweight women than for competitive athletes. Overweight and obese people, and especially overweight and obese women, typically have been excluded from sport and exercise activities by their physical characteristics and even more by social pressures and structures and by their psychological perceptions. Ironically, exercise probably is more important for obese individuals than for normal weight individuals.

Linda Bain and her colleagues (1) conducted a unique and provocative study of overweight women in an exercise program. First, they noted that these women varied in body size, background, interests, and on most characteristics, but *all* had shared the experience of social disapproval based on body size, and this experience affected their perceptions of exercise programs and decisions about participation. These women were especially critical of previous exercise programs and instructors who were not sensitive to some of their concerns including safety, comfort, skill, and especially concerns about visibility, embarrassment, and judgments by others. Exercise instructors and program organizers should avoid moralizing and particularly avoid reinforcing social stereotypes and fat prejudice, so that larger women can gain the benefits of enhanced physical competence, strength, confidence, and control that any woman can gain through physical activity.

Psychological Skills for Women in Sport and Exercise

Applied sport psychology and psychological skills training with athletes is the most rapidly expanding area within sport and exercise psychology. Unfortunately those sport psychologists doing applied work seldom incorporate information on gender to develop programs particularly suited to women or to diverse women. Typical programs are designed for highly comptitive, elite athletes, but many sport and exercise participants are not elite, not interested in competition, and are more concerned with personal health, fitness, and enjoyment than performance accomplishments. Psychological skills training designed for an Olympic skier probably is not optimal for a 10-year-old girl soccer player, a 30-year-old woman at the fitness center, or a 70-year-old woman in a walking group at the community recreation center. Yet, all of these people could use psychological skills to enhance their sport and exercise experience, probably even more than the Olympic skier could.

Some sport psychologists have discussed applied sport psychology for women, but the discussions seldom go beyond suggesting that the existing programs could be used with athletic females. Generally, applied sport psychologists have yet to actually investigate specific psychological skills interventions, program goals, structures, and procedures that might be more appropriate for women participants.

In fairness, we have done little research on any sport psychology interventions. At this time we rely on reports and suggestions of those who are developing programs that typically include such skills as anxiety management, concentration, imagery, and goal setting. As Robin Vealey (85) noted, we need evaluation research on these programs, and we need to broaden our view of the appropriateness of psychological skills training. In particular, Vealey suggested expanding such training beyond elite athletes to involve coaches and youth. She also advocated a holistic approach based on a personal development model with more attention on communication and feedback, empathy and social support, lifestyle management, and personal arousal regulation. Although she did not explicitly call for attention to women's experiences and gender issues, her suggestions fit well with feminist approaches.

Summary

1. At present our research is too limited to make the really important contributions. To contribute to the emerging body of research and discourse on women's sport and exercise, we must expand our vision.
2. We should expand our research to a broader range of activities and settings, encompassing both women and men and making a special effort to include racially and culturally diverse participants.
3. We should be familiar with the feminist scholarship from historical, sociological, and biological, as well as psychological, perspectives.
4. We could enhance sport and exercise experiences for all by incorporating such feminist values as tolerance for error, appreciation of diversity rather than elitism, relaxation rather than tension, process rather than outcome, and a sense of cooperation and sharing.
5. We might then develop a feminist, biopsychosocial perspective on women's sport and exercise that would truly enhance sport and exercise experiences for more participants.

References

1. Bain, L.L.; Wilson, T.; Chaikind, E. Participant perceptions of exercise programs for overweight women. Res. Q. Exercise Sport, 60:134-143; 1989.
2. Bandura, A. Self-efficacy: toward a unifying theory of behavior change. Psychol. Rev. 84:191-215; 1977.
3. Bandura, A. Social foundations of thought and action. Englewood Cliffs, NJ: Prentice Hall; 1986.
4. Bem, S.L. The measurement of psychological androgyny. J. Consul. Clin. Psychol. 42:155-162; 1974.
5. Bem, S.L. Beyond androgyny: some presumptous prescriptions for a liberated sexual identity. In: Sherman, J.; Denmark, F., eds. Psychology of women: future directions for research. New York: Psychological Dimensions; 1978:1-23.
6. Bem, S.L. Androgyny and gender schema theory: a conceptual and empirical integration. In: Sonderegger, T.B., ed. Nebraska symposium on motivation, 1984: psychology and gender. Lincoln, NE: University of Nebraska Press; 1985:179-226.
7. Bernard, J. The female world. New York: The Free Press; 1981.
8. Birke, L.I.A.; Vines, G. A sporting chance: the anatomy of destiny. Women Stud. Int. Forum. 10:337-347; 1987.
9. Birrell, S.J. Discourses on the gender/sport relationship: from women in sport to gender relations. In: Pandolf, K., ed. Exercise and sport science reviews. New York: Macmillan; 1988:459-502; vol. 16.
10. Broverman, I.K.; Vogel, S.R.; Broverman, D.M.; Clarkson, F.E.; Rosenkrantz, P.S. Sex role stereotypes: a current appraisal. J. Soc. Issues, 28:59-78; 1972.
11. Brown, R.D.; Harrison, J.M. The effects of a strength training program on the strength and self-concept of two female age groups. Res. Q. Exercise Sport. 57:315-320; 1986.
12. Colker, R.; Widom, C.S. Correlates of female athletic participation Sex Roles. 6:41-53; 1980.
13. Condry, J.; Dyer, S. Fear of success: attribution of cause to the victim. J. Soc. Issues. 32:63-83; 1976.
14. Corbin, C.B. Sex of subject, sex of opponent, and opponent ability as factors affecting self-confidence in a competitive situation. J. Sport Psychol. 3:265-270; 1981.
15. Corbin, C.B.; Landers, D.M.; Feltz, D.L.; Senior, K. Sex differences in performance estimates: female lack of confidence vs. male boastfulness. Res. Q. Exercise Sport. 54:407-410; 1983.
16. Corbin, C.B.; Nix, C. Sex-typing of physical activities and success predictions of children before and after cross-sex competition. J. Sport Psychol. 1:43-52; 1979.
17. Corbin, C.B.; Stewart, M.J.; Blair, W.O. Self-confidence and motor performance of preadolescent boys and girls in different feedback situations. J. Sport Psychol. 3:30-34; 1981.
18. Crandall, V.C. Sex differences in expectancy of intellectual and academic reinforcement. In: Smith, C.P., ed. Achievement-related motives in children. New York: Russell Sage; 1969:11-45.
19. Csizma, K.A.; Wittig, A.F.; Schurr, K.T. Sport stereotypes and gender. J. Sport Exercise Psychol. 10:62-74; 1988.
20. Deaux, K. From individual differences to social categories: analysis of a decade's research on gender. Am. Psychol. 39:105-116; 1984.
21. Deaux, K. Sex and gender. Ann. Rev. Psychol. 36:49-81; 1985.

22. Deaux, K.; Kite, M.E. Thinking about gender. In: Hess, B.B.; Ferree, M.M., eds. Analyzing gender. Beverly Hills, CA: Sage; 1987:92-117.

23. Deaux, K.; Lewis, L.L. The structure of gender stereotypes: interrelationships among components and gender label. J. Pers. Soc. Psychol. 46:991-1004; 1984.

24. Deaux, K.; Major, B. Putting gender into context: an interactive model of gender-related behavior. Psychol. Rev. 94:369-389; 1987.

25. Del Rey, P.; Sheppard, S. Relationship of psychological androgyny in female athletes to self-esteem. Int. J. Sport Psychol. 12:165-175; 1981.

26. Dewar, A.M. The social construction of gender in physical education. Women Stud. Int. Forum. 10:453-465; 1987.

27. Duda, J.L. A cross-cultural analysis of achievement motivation in sport and the classroom. In: VanderVelden, L.; Humphrey, J., eds. Current selected research in the psychology and sociology of sport. New York: AMS Press; 1986:115-132.

28. Duda, J.L.; Allison, M.T. Cross-cultural analysis in exercise and sport psychology: a void in the field. J. Sport Exercise Psychol. 12:114-131; 1990.

29. Eagley, A.H. Sex differences in social behavior: a social-role interpretation. Hillsdale, NJ: Erlbaum; 1987.

30. Eagley, A.H.; Kite, M.E. Are stereotypes of nationalities applied to both women and men? J. Pers. Soc. Psychol. 53:451-462; 1987.

31. Eagley, A.H.; Steffin, V.J. Gender and aggressive behavior: a meta-analytic review of the social psychological literature. Psychol. Bull. 100:309-330; 1986.

32. Eccles, J.S. Sex differences in achievement patterns. In: Sonderegger, T., ed. Nebraska symposium of motivation, 1984: psychology and gender. Lincoln, NE: University of Nebraska Press; 1985:97-132.

33. Eccles, J.S. Gender roles and women's achievement-related decisions. Psychol. Women Q. 11:135-172; 1987.

34. Eccles, J.S.; Adler, T.F.; Futterman, R.; Goff, S.B.; Kaczala, C.M.; Meece, J.L.; Midgley, C. Expectations, values, and academic behaviors. In: Spence, J., ed. Achievement and achievement motives. San Francisco: Freeman; 1983:75-146.

35. Eccles, J.S.; Harold, R.D. Gender differences in sport involvement: Applying the Eccles expectancy-value model. J. Appl. Sport Psycol. 3:7-35; 1991.

36. Feltz, D.L. Self-confidence and sports performance. In: Pandolf, K., ed. Exercise and sport sciences reviews. New York: Macmillan; 1988:423-457; vol. 16.

37. Gibson, A. I always wanted to be somebody. In: Twin, S.L., ed. Out of the bleachers. Old Westbury, NY: The Feminist Press; 1979:130-142.

38. Gill, D.L. Gender differences in competitive orientation and sport participation. Int. J. Sport Psychol. 19:145-159; 1988.

39. Gill, D.L.; Deeter, T.E. Development of the Sport Orientation Questionnaire. Res. Q. Exercise Sport. 59:191-202; 1988.

40. Gill, D.L.; Dzewaltowski, D.A. Competitive orientations among intercollegiate athletes: is winning the only thing? Sport Psychol. 2:212-221; 1988.

41. Gill, D.L.; Gross, J.B.; Huddleston, S.; Shifflett, B. Sex differences in achievement cognitions and performance in competition. Res. Q. Exercise Sport. 55:340-346; 1984.

42. Goldberg, P. Are women prejudiced against women? Trans. 5:28-30; 1968.

43. Greendorfer, S.L. Gender bias in theoretical perspectives: the case of female socialization into sport. Psychol. Women Q. 11:327-340; 1987.

44. Hall, M.A. The discourse of gender and sport: from femininity to feminism. Soc. Sport J. 5:330-340; 1988.

45. Harris, D.V.; Jennings, S.E. Self-perceptions of female distance runners. Ann. New York Academy Sci. 301:808-815; 1977.
46. Helmreich, R.L.; Spence, J.T. Sex roles and achievement. In: Christina, R.W.; Landers, D.M., eds. Psychology of motor behavior and sport—1976. Champaign, IL: Human Kinetics; 1977:33-46; vol. 2.
47. Helmreich, R.L.; Spence, J.T.; Holohan, C.K. Psychological androgyny and sex role flexibility: A test of two hypotheses. J. Pers. Soc. Psychol. 37:1631-1644; 1979.
48. Holloway, J.B.; Beuter, A.; Duda, J.L. Self-efficacy and training for strength in adolescent girls. J. Appl. Soc. Psychol. 18:699-719; 1988.
49. Horner, M.S. Toward an understanding of achievement-related conflicts in women. J. Soc. Issues. 28:157-176; 1972.
50. Hyde, J.S.; Linn, M.C., editors. The psychology of gender: advances through meta-analysis. Baltimore, MD: Johns Hopkins University Press; 1986.
51. Jacklin, C.N. Female and male: issues of gender. Am. Psychol. 44:127-133; 1989.
52. Kane, M.J.; Snyder, E. Sport typing: the social "containment" of women. Arena Rev. 13:77-96; 1989.
53. Lenney, E. Women's self-confidence in achievement settings. Psychol. Bull. 84:1-13; 1977.
54. Lenskyj, H. Out of bounds: women, sport and sexuality. Toronto: Women's Press; 1987.
55. Locksley, A.; Colten, M.E. Psychological androgyny: a case of mistaken identity? J. Pers. Soc. Psychol. 37:1017-1031; 1979.
56. Maccoby, E.E. Gender and relationships. Am. Psychol. 45:513-520; 1990.
57. Maccoby, E.; Jacklin, C. The psychology of sex differences. Stanford, CA: Stanford University Press; 1974.
58. Martens, R. Sport competition anxiety test. Champaign, IL: Human Kinetics; 1977.
59. Matteo, S. The effect of sex and gender-schematic processing on sport participation. Sex Roles. 15:417-432; 1986.
60. Matteo, S. The effect of gender-schematic processing on decisions about sex-inappropriate sport behavior. Sex Roles. 18:41-58; 1988.
61. McClelland, D.C.; Atkinson, J.W.; Clark, R.A.; Lowell, E.C. The achievement motive. New York: Appleton-Century-Crofts; 1953.
62. McElroy, M.A.; Willis, J.D. Women and the achievement conflict in sport: a preliminary study. J. Sport Psychol. 1:241-247; 1979.
63. McNally, J.; Orlick, T. Cooperative sport structures: a preliminary analysis. Mouvement. 7:267-271; 1975.
64. Melpomene Institute. The bodywise woman. New York: Prentice Hall; 1990.
65. Messner, M.A.; Sabo, D.F. Sport, men, and the gender order. Champaign, IL: Human Kinetics; 1990.
66. Metheny, E. Symbolic forms of movement: the feminine image in sports. In: Metheny, E., ed. Connotations of movement in sport and dance. Dubuque, IA: W.C. Brown; 1965:43-56.
67. Miller Brewing Company. The Miller Lite report on American attitudes toward sports. Milwaukee: Miller Brewing; 1983.
68. Myers, A.E.; Lips, H.M. Participation in competitive amateur sports as a function of psychological androgyny. Sex Roles. 4:571-578; 1978.
69. Nyad, D. Other shores. New York: Random House; 1978.
70. Parkhouse, B.L.; Williams, J.M. Differential effects of sex and status on evaluation of coaching ability. Res. Q. Exercise Sport. 57:53-59; 1986.

71. Pedhazur, E.J.; Tetenbaum, T.J. BSRI: a theoretical and methodological critique. J. Pers. Soc. Psychol. 37:996-1016; 1979.
72. Petruzzello, S.J.; Corbin, C.B. The effects of performance feedback on female self-confidence. J. Sport Exercise Psychol. 10:174-183; 1988.
73. Pheterson, G.I.; Kiesler, S.B; Goldberg, P.A. Evaluation of the performance of women as a function of their sex, achievement, and personal history. J. Pers. Soc. Psychol. 19:114-118; 1971.
74. Rodin, J.; Silberstein, L.; Streigel-Moore, R. Women and weight: a normative discontent. In: Sonderegger, T.B., ed. Psychology and gender: Nebraska Symposium on Motivation, 1984. Lincoln, NE: University of Nebraska Press; 1985:267-307; vol. 32.
75. Rosenkrantz, P.; Vogel, S.; Bee, H.; Broverman, I.; Broverman, D.M. Sex-role stereotypes and self-concepts in college students. J. Cons. Clin. Psychol. 32:286-295; 1968.
76. Sherif, C.W. The social context of competition. In: Landers, D., ed. Social problems in athletics. Champaign, IL: Human Kinetics; 1976:18-36.
77. Sherif, C.W. Needed concepts in the study of gender identity. Psychol. Women Q. 6:375-398; 1982.
78. Spence, J.T.; Helmreich, R.L. Masculinity and femininity. Austin, TX: University of Texas Press; 1978.
79. Spence, J.T.; Helmreich, R.L. Achievement-related motives and behaviors. In: Spence, J.T., ed. Achievement and achievement motives: psychological and sociological approaches. San Francisco: W.H. Freeman; 1983:7-74.
80. Stewart, M.J.; Corbin, C.B. Feedback dependence among low confidence preadolescent boys and girls. Res. Q. Exercise Sport. 59:160-164; 1988.
81. Taylor, M.C.; Hall, J.A. Psychological androgyny: theories, methods, and conclusions. Psychol. Bull. 92:347-366; 1982.
82. Theberge, N. Sport and women's empowerment. Women Stud. Int. Forum. 10:387-393; 1987.
83. Tresemer, D.W. Fear of success. New York: Plenum Press; 1977.
84. Trujillo, C. The effect of weight training and running exercise intervention on the self-esteem of college women. Int. J. Sport Psychol. 14:162-173; 1983.
85. Vealey, R.S. Future directions in psychological skills training. Sport Psychol. 2:318-336; 1988.
86. Wallston, B.S.; O'Leary, V.E. Sex and gender make a difference: the differential perceptions of women and men. Rev. Pers. Soc. Psychol. 2:9-41; 1981.
87. Weinberg, R.S.; Jackson, A. Competition and extrinsic rewards: effect on intrinsic motivation. Res. Q. 50:494-502; 1979.
88. Weinberg, R.S.; Ragan, J. Effects of competition, success/failure, and sex on intrinsic motivation. Res. Q. 50:503-510; 1979.
89. Weinberg, R.; Reveles, M.; Jackson, A. Attitudes of male and female athletes toward male and female coaches. J. Sport Psychol. 6:448-453; 1984.
90. Williams, J.M.; Parkhouse, B.L. Social learning theory as a foundation for examining sex bias in evaluation of coaches. J. Sport Exercise Psychol. 10:322-333; 1988.

CHAPTER 4

•

Osteoporosis in the Athletic Female: Amenorrhea and Amenorrheic Osteoporosis

Elizabeth A. Arendt

Women are entering sport in great numbers. Concurrent with the increase in participation is the increase in our knowledge of sport physiology and injury. Many of the earlier concerns involving exercise and its effect on a female's anatomy and physiology have been dispelled. One recent observation, however, causes concern and clearly merits further investigation, the influence of exercise on the periodicity of a female's reproductive cycle, and its role in injury of the musculoskeletal system. This chapter reviews the studies to date concerning the topic of exercise amenorrhea and, building on that foundation, offers a treatment plan upon which individual recommendations can be made.

The Normal Menstrual Cycle

The normal menstrual cycle is commonly described by its length, or the number of days in its cycle. This cycle encompasses three phases: the follicular phase, ovulation, and the luteal phase (Table 4.1). Commonly, menstrual cycles are described as eumenorrheic, oligomenorrheic, or amenorrheic, based on the occurrence of menstrual bleeding. The terms *eumenorrheic, regular,* and *cyclic* refer to cycles that occur at intervals of 25 to 38 days. The regularity of this cycle is

Table 4.1   Endometrial Cycle

Phase	Activity

1. Follicular (proliferative, estrogenic, preovulatory) proliferation of endometrial tissue, largely directed by estrogen
2. Occurence of ovulation
3. Luteal (secretory, progestational, postovulatory) edematous, secretion-filled endometrial tissue, largely directed by progesterone

   Ends in shedding of endometrial tissue, or menstruation

as important as its interval length in classifying a woman as having a regular menstrual pattern.

The terms *oligomenorrheic* and *irregular* are used interchangeably to indicate menstrual cycles that occur inconsistently. Amenorrhea is a clinical symptom that indicates a disruption of the reproductive cycle with probable anovulation. Primary amenorrhea is the delay of menarche beyond age 16. This is a more widely accepted definition than secondary amenorrhea, which is the absence of menstruation in women who previously were menstruating periodically. There is no standard definition for secondary amenorrhea, which, together with the differences between the populations surveyed in past studies, accounts for the wide range of its observed prevalence in the population (33).

The lack of standard definitions for eumenorrheic, oligomenorrheic, and amenorrheic athletes is compounded further by differences in how one describes a normal menstrual cycle. One of the most comprehensive studies of menstrual cycle length was published by Vollman in 1977 (63). His data indicate that the length of one's menstrual cycle varies depending on the age of the patient, with the greater inter and intra individuality observed in early postmenarcheal and premenopausal years. Additionally, the variability of length is mainly determined by the highly variable length of the follicular phase, whereas the luteal phase is far more constant (10 to 16 days) (Figure 4.1). Therefore, he concluded that the normal menstrual cycle has a length of approximately 28 days, with the 10th and 90th percentile of 22 and 36 days respectively, for women between the ages of 20 and 40 years.

The variability of the length of the menstrual cycle is only one factor in characterizing its normalcy. One must also consider hormonal levels that change according to follicular and luteal development. Three aberrations are identified: the short luteal phase, luteal phase insufficiency, and anovulation (29). The short luteal phase is manifested by a shortened menstrual cycle length (21 days), with hormonal pattern similar to a normal cycle. Luteal phase insufficiency is an ovulatory cycle, with deficient corpus luteum function and deficient progesterone production. Anovulation is a cycle without ovulation, though withdrawal bleeding

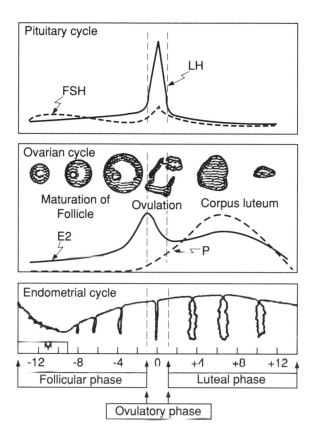

Figure 4.1   Length of the three phases of the normal menstrual cycle. *Note.* From "Menstrual Disorders in the Adolescent Age Group" by J. Kustin and R. Rebar, 1987, *Primary Care,* **14**(1), p. 145. Copyright 1987 by W.B. Saunders. Reprinted with permission.

may occur due to declining estrogen levels. These three aberrations in menses can be easily missed if only menstrual history data are available to the researcher.

A common way of looking for hormonal sufficiency is to measure basal body temperature. This has the advantage of simplicity and low cost. However, many women do not display a thermogenic response to rising estrogen levels (5, 64). Therefore, measurement of the blood levels of various hormones or their metabolites in plasma, urine, or saliva, or ultrasonographic detection of folliculogenesis is needed to establish physiologic menstrual cycles (29). However, many of the reproductive hormone levels are pulsatile and may not be accurately assessed with a single blood sample, though modern techniques for collecting elaborate endocrine data (i.e., evaluating the frequency, amplitude, and regularity of pulsatile secretory hormones) should yield more information.

True normative data representing the variability in menstrual cycle have not been adequately collected for both the sedentary and the athletic populations. Therefore, it is difficult to determine whether athletic menstrual cycle alterations represent true changes in regularity or enhancements of already established variations in menstrual cycles. The wide range of different methodologies used as well as the variance among populations studied also make comparison of studies difficult.

Delayed Menarche

That athletes have a later age of menarche has been observed repeatedly (36, 37), and a higher incidence of delayed menarche occurs in those who begin their athletic training before the age of menarche (26, 38). Frisch et al. (26) suggests that each year of high intensity training before menarche retards the onset of menstruation by 5 months. There are several explanations of the relationship between delayed menarche and athletic activity, though for decades, the sole explanation was a sociological one. Others suggest that certain physical characteristics, such as a more linear physique and less weight for the height, may effectively predispose young women to athletic success (36). Later maturation may favor athletic success, because long bones continue to grow until menarche, and later maturing growth may allow one to excel in certain sports that favor a long appendicular skeleton. However, the data base used for these retrospective studies of athletes who began training before menarche has always lacked credibility. Stager et al. (58) offered new statistical explanation for later menarche. It may be that menarche occurs at a later chronological age in athletes, but it is not clear that an earlier age of initiation of athletic training *causes* delayed menarche.

Luteal Suppression

Another reported menstrual abnormality is the suppression of luteal function in regular menstrual cycles. This was first observed in a study of regularly menstruating athletes, which compared swimmers in varying age ranges to age-matched nonathletes (7). Further studies have confirmed this change in luteal phase suppression (32, 51). A recent study by Broocks et al. (9) suggests that even recreational running may disrupt the normal menstrual pattern of reproductive hormones.

The evidence clearly points to the prevalence of more menstrual cycle alterations in athletes than in sedentary individuals, though exactly what condition this represents in the athlete is open to question. The relationship between luteal phase suppression and amenorrhea also remains unclear. One speculation is that luteal phase suppression is a mild case of athletic amenorrhea, which implies that a woman could progress to more severe amenorrhea if a more rigorous training regimen is followed or other etiological factors are changed. Or luteal phase suppression may represent successful acclimation to athletic training (32).

Prevalence of Athletic Amenorrhea

Concomitant with any discussion on prevalence of athlete amenorrhea is acceptance of the difficulties in comparing studies secondary to methodology used, and the lack of universal definitions of menstrual cycle abnormalities. Loucks and Horvath (33) discuss the wide range in the prevalence of amenorrhea found in observational studies of athletes (1 to 44%). Toriola (60) reported the prevalence of oligomenorrhea to be 25% in Nigerian athletes, compared to 10% among their sedentary counterparts. Surveys estimate the prevalence of oligo- and amenorrhea (variably defined as the absence of menses for the previous 3 to 12 months) in female runners to be 2% in recreational joggers, 24% in marathon participants, and 43% in elite distance athletes (35, 50, 53). Barrow and Saha (4) found very irregular menses (0 to 5 per year) in 29% of college-age competitive, long distance runners with irregular menses (6 to 9 menses per year) in 21%. Among female college varsity athletes, the overall prevalence of menstrual irregularities was 28%, the lowest being 13% in basketball players and the highest being 57% in cross-country runners (1).

Etiological Factors of Menstrual Cycle Abnormalities

A preliminary study by Shangold et al. in 1979 (51) was the first to investigate the idea that changes in the menstrual cycle are related to physical exercise. This early investigation looked at one woman training over 18 months. This study was followed by numerous longitudinal and cross-sectional studies, which looked at the relationship of training to menstrual cycle abnormalities (8, 11, 44). There are few longitudinal studies available in which the phases of the menstrual cycle were determined both before and after training, largely due to subject discomfort and the financial cost of such a study. Most studies rely on few subjects, a few hormonal determinations, or relatively short periods of time. Additionally, these studies may be biased by relatively short training periods, moderate training intensities, and low training frequencies. A much higher incidence of menstrual cycle abnormalities is noted when hormonal measurements are made. A carefully conducted study by Bullen et al. (12) demonstrates the inferiority of clinical assessments of menstrual cycle normalcy, compared with characteristic hormonal measurements.

The exact effects of exercise activity and training on the menstrual cycle remain unclear, and there are many confounding factors that influence interpretation. For example, few studies account for the intensity of exercise, yet factors such as volume intensity and duration of the exercise program must be considered to construct meaningful conclusions on the relationship of training programs to menstrual cycle irregularities. Also, individual women may be predisposed to reproductive disorders, or other factors, such as diet, psychological parameters, and environmental conditions, may account for these "training" irregularities (46).

In conclusion, the cross-sectional and longitudinal studies to date do support that a *sudden increase* in training volume or intensity of aerobic training may disrupt the menstrual cycle. However, this only occurs in *some* women, and it is likely that the profile that characterizes the amenorrheic woman is multifactorial. Current recommendations to decrease athletic activity as the sole treatment for athletic amenorrhea must be tempered with knowledge to date, though further research must enlighten this area before meaningful and healthy exercise prescriptions can be constructed.

Another etiological factor implicated in menstrual cycle abnormalities is diet—not only the volume of caloric intake, but the profile of nutrients consumed (6, 30, 43).

Lower percentages of body fat, greater weight loss since the onset of training, and lower initial body weight are commonly associated with amenorrheic runners when compared to their eumenorrheic counterparts. The mechanism by which body fat affects menstrual function is not completely understood, though the Frisch (critical fat) hypothesis—that is, that a critical percentage of body fat must be obtained for normal menstrual functioning to occur (27)—is a commonly held belief. However, the idea that athletic amenorrhea is caused by excessive leanness has received wide criticism because of its underlying theory and methodology as well as the many contrary observations (48, 55, 61). For example, Loucks and Horvath (33) show that the method that Frisch used to calculate the percent body fat overestimates body fat. Taken collectively, these studies confirm that there is no specific percent body fat below which regular menses cease and no percent body fat that allows a normal reproductive cycle to occur. When reviewing studies involving body fat ratios, one must consider the method used to assess body fat, as well as other factors in the nutrient profile of the athlete. Also, to offset statistical bias, training intensity and the peculiarity of the various sports must be taken into account. Despite these confounding factors, body fat continues to receive wide publicity as an etiological factor in menstrual irregularities.

Parity of women has been cited as relating to menstrual irregularities (3) with an increased incidence of amenorrhea in nulliparous compared to parous runners. Other studies suggest a link between athletic amenorrhea in runners and mood and eating disorders (28, 51).

Mechanisms That Alter the Menstrual Cycle

The exact mechanism for the alteration of the menstrual cycle in the athletic population has not been clearly defined. The majority of mechanisms cited involve the brain-hypothalamic-pituitary-gonadal axis (Figure 4.2). However obscure this mechanism is, some answers have been found. Amenorrhea is *not* caused by hyperandrogenism (33, 34, 62), hyperprolactinemia (16), psychological factors (33, 34), premature menopause (49), or excessive leanness (33, 55, 61).

Numerous theories have been developed to explain the relationship between exercise and amenorrhea (see Table 4.2), but each theory lacks a unique association to exercise. Subsets of women with *normal* menstrual function can be found who

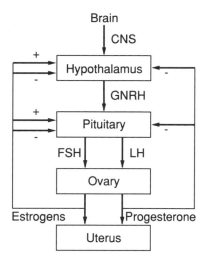

Figure 4.2   Mechanisms that alter the menstrual cycle.

have characteristics similar to those of amenorrheic athletes, such as diet, body composition, levels of stress, and reproductive maturity. The uniqueness of amenorrheic athletes appears to be exercise or physical activity. Thus a scientifically sound explanation for exercise-induced amenorrhea has not been clearly established.

One mechanism by which exercise training affects the reproductive system involves the hypothalamic-pituitary-gonadal axis. Two recent review articles (29, 32) detail the complex hormonal milieu that directs the menstrual cycle and how exercise may alter this. One mechanism cited involves endogenous opioids, which play a role in the regulation of the menstrual cycle (45, 47). Endogenous opioids act by influencing the pulsatile characteristics of luteinizing hormone and other gonadotrophin secretions. Further studies are needed to demonstrate the relationship between endogenous opioids and the hormonal regulation of the menstrual cycle.

Whatever the pathophysiology of exercise-induced menstrual irregularities, there certainly is increasing evidence that the hypothalamic-pituitary-gonadal axis plays a key role. How this axis is altered by training programs, diet, and other etiological factors is not well established. Cross-sectional studies, which make up the majority of studies to date, are hopelessly confounded by factors that cannot be controlled. Further studies are needed involving both the intensity of exercise training and energy parameters, such as caloric expenditures, intake, and deficit. There are various means to measure hormonal concentrations; however, the profile of pulsatile hormonal patterns in women is not yet fully documented.

Clinical Significance

Essential to the importance of understanding the relationship between exercise and menstrual function is its clinical significance. The most disconcerting observation is that of skeletal demineralization in nonmenstruating athletes, though its

Table 4.2   Suggested Causes of Exercise-Induced Amenorrhea

Psychological stress
  Training
  Competition
  Personal
  Society

Body composition
  Changes in lean/fat ratio
  Weight loss

Nutrition
  Poor dietary intake

Acute or chronic effects of repeated exertion

Energy drain
  Sport-specific
  Physical stress

Reproductive immaturity

Endocrinologic causes
  Hypothalamic origin
  Endogenous opioids
  Acute changes caused by repetitive exercise
  Chronic changes caused by exercise
  Pregnancy
  Hyperprolactinaemia
  Ovarian failure

Note. Adapted from Ruffin, Hunter, and Arendt (1990).

exact significance regarding the short- and long-term bone health of the individual remains unclear. Other issues can be raised, most revolving around the skeletal and reproductive health of the exercising female.

Skeletal Demineralization

Skeletal demineralization in nonmenstruating athletes was first observed by Cann et al. in 1984 (15). This was later confirmed by other studies (2, 30, 31, 39), which reported significantly lower lumbar bone mineral density (BMD) in amenorrheic athletes. Unlike their eumenorrheic teammates, these women had lower lumbar BMD than sedentary women of the same age. Although amenorrheic women who resume normal menses do regain some bone stock (24), there appears to be a net loss that is not reversible (14, 23). Cann et al. (14) also showed that decreased BMD from long-term amenorrhea (exceeding 3 years) was not reversible with calcium or estrogen supplements. Quite disconcerting are the preliminary reported results by Drinkwater (22) that suggest that young women respond to hormonal replacement therapy the same way postmenopausal women do, namely, there is no further decrease in bone density, but neither is there significant gain.

The primary clinical concern of decreased lumbar BMD is the development or advancement of osteoporosis of the skeletal spine in mature females. (The spine is the primary skeletal site where this difference is apparent.) The bulk of these studies are cross-sectional in nature, and the impact of this observation on the long-term health of the bone is not known. However, the speculation that women who experience menstrual irregularity secondary to the lack of estrogen stimulus *may never* achieve peak bone mass has a critical influence on their development of osteoporotic complications later in life. Available data indicate that peak bone mass may be reached as early as age 20 (10, 41). Suboptimal bone mass at this age may predict an increased fracture risk after menopause. The role that exercise plays in preventing osteoporosis (by maximizing peak bone mass in young women) has to be weighed against these observations of the effect of exercise on the hormonal profile of women. A summary of cross-sectional studies on exercise and bone mineral density suggest that (1) exercise may have a systemic effect on bone mass, and (2) adequate calcium intake may be necessary for a positive bone adaptation to exercise (18). However, these studies largely involve the perimenopausal woman. The role that exercise plays in preventing osteoporosis by maximizing peak bone mass in young women is still unknown. Therefore, whether a decrease in bone mass in the amenorrheic athlete will increase the postmenopausal risk factor for osteoporosis remains uncertain. Yet clearly this is an area of concern.

Knowing the timetable of bone mineral density development in young women is central to the understanding of this topic. Data on bone mineral densities in developing females are sparse, especially for ages 16 to 20. Is the number of years of estrogen exposure to developing bone a primary factor in the magnitude of peak bone mass? If yes, then perhaps the female with early menarcheal age would have greater peak BMD (see Figure 4.3). With later onset of menarche, is there a shift in the timetable for increasing BMD with peak bone mass reached at a later age (Figure 4.4)? Or does later menarche predict a lowered peak bone mass (Figure 4.3)? The role of exercise, diet, and hormonal irregularities on bone mass development is not known. Exercise could theoretically influence this timetable positively by increasing BMD at the time of exercise activity or by lengthening the time during which BMD can increase. Because the timetable is influenced by a woman's hormonal status, what is the role of the aestrogenic state, which could influence both the amplitude and duration of BMD increases in the developing female?

To date, most studies have looked at skeletal demineralization in the amenorrheic athlete, whereas few studies have evaluated BMD in a larger group, the oligomenorrheic athlete. However, preliminary studies indicate that BMD in the axial skeleton of oligomenorrheic athletes is lower than that of their eumenorrheic counterparts (42). Questions remain concerning the interrelationship of diet, menstrual status, stress level, genetic predisposition, exercise intensity, and skeletal integrity. Though studies demonstrating decreased BMD in female athletes

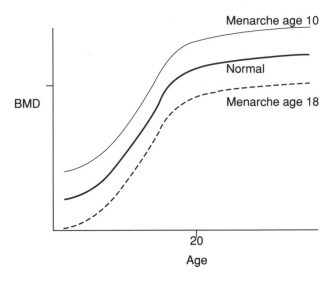

Figure 4.3   Relationship of menarcheal age to BMD.

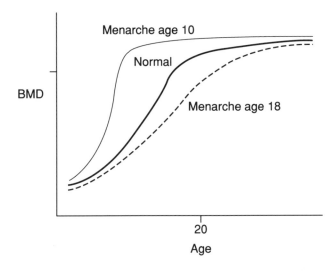

Figure 4.4   Relationship of later onset of menarche to increasing BMD.

with irregular menses are preliminary, concern and research interest should be focused on this athletic group.

Stress Fractures

In addition to the potential problems of osteoporosis in later years, there is an increase in stress fractures of the lower extremities in amenorrheic women (4,

42). These stress fractures are largely in the long bones, despite the fact that only a few studies have shown a decrease in BMD in long, or appendicular, bone (42). The primary site shown to have decreased BMD is the spine, which is largely composed of trabecular bone. Most bone surface is quiescent with less than 20% of trabecular bone and 5% of cortical bone surface being actively remodeled at any one time. Cortical, or compact, bone makes up 80% of the skeletal system and is located primarily in the long bones. It has a slower turnover rate than does trabecular, or cancellous, bone. Trabecular bone makes up the remaining 20% of the skeletal system. Because of its higher rate of remodeling, trabecular bone is more sensitive and responsive to changes in the hormonal milieu. This may explain why bone loss during early estrogen deficiency is detectable in the lumbar spine *before* it is evident in predominantly cortical bone, such as the tibia and radius (appendicular bone). This may also explain why there are few studies demonstrating a decrease in BMD of long bones in amenorrheic women.

Another reason has to do with the imaging technique used. Most studies have used the radius, which is not a weight-bearing bone, as representative of an appendicular bone (42, 56). Three standard techniques exist—single-photon absorptiometry (SPA), dual-photon absorptiometry (DPA), and quantitative computed tomography (QCT). The newest and perhaps the most useful technological development is dual-energy radiographic absorptiometry for bone densitometry (DPA-x).

• SPA is the device largely used in early studies. Its measurement of BMD is influenced by soft tissue, therefore only bones with a scant soft tissue envelope can be scanned. The radius is most popularly used and, in a few studies, the tibia. SPA measures integral bone, or cancellous plus cortical bone.

• DPA eliminates the effect of soft tissue on the absorption measurements. Its main application has been to measure BMD in the lumbar spine and the hip. DPA also measures integral bone.

• QCT's greatest advantage is its ability to measure trabecular bone independent of cortical bone. Its primary use has been in the spine.

• DPA-x is the latest development, its advantages being higher resolution, greater speed, and better precision while using less radiation than DPA. Like DPA, it measures integral bone. It can measure specific anatomic sites. Spine, hip, and total body measurements are used most frequently.

Comparisons in test time, radiation exposure, and cost can also be done (Table 4.3). As one reviews previous studies, one must bear in mind the limitations of earlier imaging techniques and the inappropriateness of comparing studies that have used different imaging techniques.

Studies of the effect of exercise on BMD have shown a difference in the *increase* of bone mass between axial versus appendicular bone mass. Three of seven longitudinal studies demonstrated an increase in appendicular bone mass (40, 54, 56), whereas only one training study showed an increase in axial bone

Table 4.3   Comparison of Bone Densitometry Techniques

Technique	Site	Time (min)	Radiation absorbed (in rem)	Cost ($)
SPA	Radius (integral bone)	15	10	75
DPA	Spine/hip (integral bone)	40	100	150
QCT	Spine/hip (trabecular and integral bone)	20	1,000	250
DPA-x	Spine/hip/total BMD (integral bone)	5	3	75

(20). This may seem contradictory. Stress fractures occur in long bones, yet long bone is the site where exercise has been shown to increase bone mass. The understanding of this relationship may relate back to the concepts reviewed so elegantly by Dalsky (19): (1) Mechanical loading through physical exercise has a positive influence on BMD; (2) lack of physical activity is a negative influence on BMD; (3) bone mass is maintained at levels appropriate to structural competence for functional loading; and (4) the positive influence of exercise on bone can be attenuated by environmental conditions, such as hormonal and nutritional status, and may not make up for the negative influence of hormonal changes in an individual.

Bone mass increases in relationship to stress and at a level appropriate to structural competence for functional loading. However, we do not have a clear understanding of how much the bone needs to increase to accommodate certain activities. For example, despite the fact that BMD in a female marathon runner may be greater than that in her sedentary counterpart, is this increase enough to withstand the impact loading that occurs during daily, long distance runs? Alternatively, at what point is impact loading of the bone dysfunctional, indicating that bone mass *cannot* be maintained at levels that will withstand the degree of loading? To answer these questions, more must be learned concerning the relationship between BMD and sport-specific stress loading of bone.

A limitation of previous studies is the lack of exercises that specifically stress lumbar muscles and lumbar bone. A recent cross-sectional study (66) compared amenorrheic to eumenorrheic athletes and rowers to nonrowers. (Rowers were looked at secondarily to the effect of intensive exercise on the lumbar spine.) Findings showed that mean trabecular BMD of the lumbar spine was significantly lower in the amenorrheic athlete compared to that in her eumenorrheic counterpart. However, mean trabecular BMD was significantly lower in nonrowers than in rowers, and there was no interaction between these two effects. The study concluded that the effect of intensive exercise on the lumbar spine partially compensates for the adverse effect of amenorrhea on spinal trabecular bone density.

There are several important considerations in the review of exercise studies to date:

1. Exercise has a positive effect on appendicular bone in the perimenopausal female.
2. Exercise *may* have a positive effect on the axial bone in the perimenopausal female.
3. The effect of exercise on developing and young bone is not known.
4. The effect of intensive exercise on the lumbar spine may partially compensate for the adverse effect of amenorrhea on spinal trabecular bone density.
5. An increased incidence of stress fractures have been reported in the long bones of athletic females.

The exact relationship between menstrual irregularity, low BMD, and stress fractures is not clearly defined. Other variables, including diet, decreased lower extremity muscle mass in females, training errors, and biomechanical, lower extremity alignment, may play parallel or confounding roles. Therefore, the exact benefit of exercise on maintaining or increasing bone mass in the active female awaits further definition, though the benefits of regular exercise on cardiovascular fitness, muscle strength and endurance, and flexibility are well established.

Other Clinical Observations

In addition to the skeletal demineralization concurrent with menstrual irregularities, other observations have been noted. In a recent study of speed skaters, training with maximal work loads was associated with a decline in T-lymphocyte function (59). This was not associated with a change in menstrual pattern, and the data are somewhat contradictory; but they suggest a relationship between the menstrual functions of athletes, the psychological stress they experience in training and competition, and a possible depression of immune response. If this observation is correct, it could have a bearing on the athlete's overall health status.

Also of clinical significance is a study of the long-term reproductive health of 2,622 former collegiate athletes compared to that of 2,766 nonathletes (25). This research from the Harvard Center for Population Studies observed a significantly lower lifetime occurrence of breast cancer and cancers of the reproductive system and a lower lifetime occurrence of benign tumors of these tissues in athletes. This may be related to the increase in estradiol by oxidation of 2-hydroxylase that has been observed during training (57). (Elevated 2-hydroxylase may be protective against breast cancer.) This increase may contribute to the lower lifetime occurrence of sex hormone-sensitive cancers observed among former college athletes.

Additionally, this increase in estradiol by oxidation of 2-hydroxylase only occurs in some females and seems to be associated with the occurrence of menstrual disturbances. This suggests a genetic basis for the development of menstrual irregularities associated with exercise.

Further research on the effect of exercise and diet on chronic estradiol function could have an impact on a variety of conditions, including not only reproductive and skeletal integrity but predisposed metabolic risk factors for coronary artery disease and diabetes (13).

The effect of menstrual cycle changes on exercise performance is also appropriate to the discussion of the clinical significance of athletic amenorrhea. A recent study by De Souza et al. (21) examined selected physiological and metabolic responses to maximal and submaximal exercise during two phases of the menstrual cycle (the follicular and luteal phases) in eumenorrheic and amenorrheic runners. They concluded that neither menstrual phase (follicular or luteal) nor menstrual status (eumenorrheic or amenorrheic) alters or limits exercise performance in female athletes.

Treatment of Menstrual Cycle Irregularities

There are two reasons to discuss the treatment of menstrual cycle irregularities in women. One involves fertility issues, which relate to gynecological concerns. It appears that there are no lasting or irreversible effects on reproduction in women with athletic menstrual dysfunction (52). However, the risk of osteopenia in hypoestrogenic, amenorrheic athletes is real and warrants therapeutic intervention.

Two recent articles review the evaluation and management of menstrual dysfunction in athletes (52, 65). The American Academy of Pediatrics Committee on Sports Medicine (17) has made these recommendations for the treatment of amenorrhea in adolescent athletes:

1. For all athletes
   - Preparticipation evaluation to include an assessment of menstrual function and dietary habits
   - Nutritional counseling for athletes, parents, and coaches
   - Routine monitoring of menstrual function, diet, growth, weight, skinfold thickness
   - Calcium supplementation of 1,200 and 1,500 mg daily
2. For all amenorrheic athletes
   - Physical examination
   - Endocrine evaluation
   - Diagnosis by exclusion of pregnancy and anorexia nervosa
3. For amenorrhea beginning less than 3 years after menarche
   - Reduced exercise intensity
   - Improved nutrition

4. For amenorrhea beginning more than 3 years after menarche or after age 16

   • Low dose oral contraceptive

These recommendations provide a foundation upon which individual treatment can be based, but for the amenorrheic athlete only. Treatment of the oligomenorrheic athlete is less well defined, and there is a question as to whether any treatment is needed. Research on this group of athletes has been sparse, and not only the clinical problems of the oligomenorrheic athlete but also the efficacy of treatment regimens have yet to be determined.

   However, a reasonable treatment outline for oligomenorrheic athletes might include these practices:

1. Full medical workup, including endocrine workup
2. Nutritional counseling with special emphasis on

   • total caloric count vs. energy expenditure
   • calcium intake of 1,200-1,500 mg/day (At least 2/3 of this should be ingested as daily dietary intake and not solely in the form of a supplement.)

3. Review of training program and exercise habits and decrease in exercise intensity if overtraining is a concern
4. Routine monitoring of diet, menstrual function, weight, training schedule, and exercise habits
5. Counseling with emphasis on possible stress factors in the athlete's environment

If following this scheme does not result in a more regular menstrual cycle, low dosages of estrogen should be considered, with appropriate counseling regarding estrogen replacement and a review of family history. Estrogen replacement therapy is thought to be important for the amenorrheic woman and for the oligomenorrheic woman whose endocrine workup reveals an estrogen deficiency in her menstrual pattern.

Summary

1. The monthly menstrual cycle from its inception at menarche to its cessation at menopause is an influential factor in women's physiology and may be influenced by exercise.
2. The influence of hormonal cycling on exercise performance seems to be fairly well defined; that is, neither menstrual phase nor menstrual status alters or limits exercise performance.
3. The influence of exercise on the periodicity of the menstrual cycle and on the normal vacillation of hormonal levels throughout the month is less well defined.

4. There is a correlation between oligomenorrheic and amenorrheic women and diminished bone mineral density.

5. There appears to be a relationship between menstrual irregularity, stress fractures, soft tissue injury rates, eating disorders, and exercise intensity, though an exact causal relationship has not been established.

6. There are a significant number of women, particularly in certain sports (dance, running, gymnastics), who have oligomenorrhea.

7. In oligomenorrheic and amenorrheic women, the amount of bone loss determined by current imaging techniques is greater in cancellous bone than cortical bone.

8. The prevalence of menstrual irregularities is greater in sport participants than in the nonsporting population.

9. Though many unanswered questions concerning this topic persist, a reasonable treatment plan can be established on current knowledge. Menstrual irregularities should be recognized and evaluated and various treatment options discussed.

References

1. Arendt, E. Unpublished study on menstrual irregularities in female college varsity athletes.

2. Baker, E.; Demers, L. Menstrual status in female athletes: correlation with reproductive hormones and bone density. Obstet. Gynecol. 72:683-687; 1988.

3. Baker, E.R.; Mathur, R.S.; Kirk, R.F.; Williamson, H.O. Female runners and secondary amenorrhea: correlation with age, parity, mileage, and plasma hormonal and sex hormone binding globulin concentrations. Fertility & Sterility 36:183-187; 1981.

4. Barrow, G.W.; Saha, S. Menstrual irregularity and stress fractures in collegiate female distance runners. Am. J. Sports Med. 16(3):209-216; 1988.

5. Bauman, J.E. Basal body temperature: unreliable method of ovulation detection. Fertility & Sterility 36:729-733; 1981.

6. Berning, J.; Sanborn, C.F.; Brooks, S.M.; Wagner, W.W. Caloric deficit in distance runners. Med. Sci. Sports Exerc. 17(2):242; 1985.

7. Bonen, A.; Belcastro, A.; Ling, A.N.; Simpson, A.A. Profiles of selected hormones during menstrual cycles of teenage athletes. J. Appl. Physiol. 50:545-551; 1981.

8. Boyden, T.W.; Pamenter, R.W.; Stanforth, P.; Rotkis, T.; Wilmore, J.H. Sex steroids and endurance running in women. Fertility & Sterility 39:629-632; 1983.

9. Broocks, A.; Pinke, K.M.; Schweiger, U.; Tuschi, R.J.; Laessle, R.G.; Strowitzki, T.; Horl, E.; Horl, T.; Haas, W.; Jeschke, D. Cyclic ovarian function in recreational athletes. J. Appl. Physiol. 68:2023-2086; 1990.

10. Buchanan, J.R.; Myers, C.; Lloyd, T.; Gerre, R.B. Early vertebral trabecular bone loss in normal premenopausal women. J. Bone Min. Res. 3:583-587; 1988.

11. Bullen, B.A.; Skrinar, G.S.; Beitins, I.Z.; Carr, D.B.; Reppert, S.M.; Dotson, C.O.; Fencl, M.D.; Gervino, E.V.; McArthur, J.W. Endurance training effects on plasma hormonal responsiveness and sex hormone excretion. J. Appl. Physiol. 56:1453-1463; 1984.

12. Bullen, B.A.; Skrinar, G.S., Beitins, I.Z.; Von Mering, G.; Turnbull, B.A.; McArthur, J.W. Induction of menstrual cycle disorders by strenuous exercise in untrained women. New Eng. J. Med. 312:1349-1353; 1985.

13. Bunt, J.C. Metabolic actions of estradiol: significance for acute and chronic exercise responses. Med. Sci. Sports Exerc. 22(3):286-290; 1990.

14. Cann, C.E.; Cavanaugh, D.J.; Schnurpfiel, K.; Martin, M.C. Menstrual history is the primary determinant of trabecular bone density in women. Med. Sci. Sports Exerc. 20(Suppl. 2):S59; 1988.

15. Cann, C.E.; Martin, M.C.; Jaffe, H.K.; Jaffe, R.B. Decreased spinal mineral content in amenorrheic women. JAMA 251:626-629; 1984.

16. Chang, F.E.; Richards, S.R.; Kim, M.H.; Malarkey, W.B. Twenty four-hour prolactin profiles and prolactin responses to dopamine in long distance women. J. Clin. Endocrinol. Metab. 59:631-635; 1984.

17. Committee on Sports Medicine. Amenorrhea in adolescent athletes. Pediatrics 84:394-395; 1989.

18. Dalsky, G. Exercise: its effect on bone mineral content. Clin. Obstet. Gynecol. 30(4):820-831; 1987.

19. Dalsky, G.P. Effect of exercise on bone: permissive influence of estrogen and calcium. Med. Sci. Sports Exer. 22(3):281-285; 1990.

20. Dalsky, G.P.; Birge, S.J.; Kleinheider, K.S.; Ehsani, A.A. The effect of endurance exercise training on lumbar bone mass in postmenopausal women. Med. Sci. Sports Exerc. 18(Suppl):96(abstract); 1986.

21. De Souza, M.J.; Maguire, M.S.; Rubin, K.R.; Maresh, C.M. Effects of menstrual phase and amenorrhea on exercise performance in runners. Med. Sci. Sports Exerc. 22(5):575-580; 1990.

22. Drinkwater, B.L. Physical exercise and bone health. J. Am. Med. Wom. Assoc. 45(3):91-97; 1990.

23. Drinkwater, B.L.; Bruemner, B.; Chestnut, C.H., III. Menstrual history as a determinant of current bone density in young athletes. JAMA 263(4):545-548; 1990.

24. Drinkwater, B.L.; Nilson, K.; Ott, S.; Chestnut, C.H. Bone mineral density after resumption of menses in amenorrheic women. JAMA 256:380-382; 1986.

25. Frisch, R.E. Body fat, menarche, fitness, and fertility. Hum. Reprod. 2(6):521-533; 1987.

26. Frisch, R.E.; Gotz Wellbergen, A.V.; McArthur, J.W.; Albright, T.; Witschi, J.; Bullen, B.; Birnholz, J.; Reed, R.B.; Hermann, H. Delayed menarche and amenorrhea of college athletes in relation to age of onset of training. JAMA 246:1559-1563; 1981.

27. Frisch, R.E.; McArthur, J.W. Menstrual cycles: fatness as a determinant of minimum weight for height necessary for their maintenance or onset. Sciences 185:949-951; 1974.

28. Gadpaille, W.J.; Sanborn, C.F.; Wagner, W.W., Jr. Athletic amenorrhea, major affective disorders, and eating disorders. Am. J. Psychia. 144(7):939-942.

29. Keizer, H.A.; Rogol, A.D. Physical exercise and menstrual cycle alterations. Sports Med. 10(4):218-235; 1990.

30. Kelsay, J.L.; Behall, K.M.; Prather, T.S. Effects of fiber from fruits and vegetables on metabolic responses of human subjects: II. Calcium, magnesium, iron, and silicon balances. Am. J. Clin. Nutr. 32:1876-1880; 1979.

31. Lindberg, J.S.; Powell, M.R.; Hunt, M.M.; Ducey, D.E.; Wade, C.E. Increased vertebral bone mass in response to reduced exercise in amenorrheic runners. West. J. Med. 146:39-42; 1987.

32. Loucks, A.B. Effects of exercise training on the menstrual cycle: existence and mechanisms. Med. Sci. Sports Exerc. 22(3):275-280; 1990.

33. Loucks, A.B.; Horvath, S.M. Athletic amenorrhea: a review. Med. Sci. Sports Exerc. 17:56-72; 1985.
34. Loucks, A.B.; Mortola, J.F.; Girton, K.; Yen, S.S.C. Alterations in hypothalamic-pituitary-ovarian and the hypothalamic-pituitary-adrenal axes in athletic women. J. Clin. Endocrinol. Metab. 68:402-411; 1989.
35. Lutter, J.M.; Cushman, S. Menstrual patterns in female runners. Phys. Sports Med. 10:60-72; 1982.
36. Malina, R.M. Menarche in athletes: a synthesis and hypothesis. Ann. Hum. Biol. 10:1-24; 1983.
37. Malina, R.M. Competitive youth sports and biological maturation. In: Brown, E.W.; Branta, C.F.; eds. Competitive sports for children and youth. Champaign, IL: Human Kinetics; 1988:227-245.
38. Malina, R.M.; Spirduso, W.W.; Tate, C.; Baylor, A.M. Age at menarche and selected menstrual characteristics in athletes at different competitive levels and in different sports. Med. Sci. Sports Exerc. 10:218-222; 1978.
39. Marcus, R.; Cann, C.; Madvig, P.; Minkoff, J.; Goddard, M.; Bayer, M.; Martin, M.; Gaudiani, L.; Haskell, W.; Genant, H. Menstrual function and bone mass in elite women distance runners. Ann. Intern. Med. 102:158-163; 1985.
40. Margulies, J.Y.; Simkin, A.; Leichter, I.; Bivas, A.; Steinberg, R.; Giladi, M.; Stein, M.; Kashtan, H.; Milgrom, C. Effect of intense physical activity on the bone-mineral content in the lower limbs of young adults. JBJS 68A(7):1090-1093; 1986.
41. Mazess, R.B.; Barden, H.S. Bone mineral density in premenopausal women: effects of age, dietary intake, physical activity, smoking, and birth control pills. Am. J. Clin. Nutr. 53:132-142; 1991.
42. Myburgh, K.H.; Hutchins, J.; Fataar, A.B.; Hough, S.F.; Noakes, T.D. Low bone density is an etiologic factor for stress fractures in athletes. Ann. Intern. Med. 113(10):754-759; 1990.
43. Nelson, M.E.; Fisher, E.C.; Catsos, P.D.; Meredith, C.N.; Turksoy, R.N.; Evans, W.J. Diet and bone status in amenorrheic runners. Am. J. Clin. Nutr. 43:910-916; 1986.
44. Prior, J.C.; Cameron, K.; Ho, Y.B.; Thomas, J. Menstrual cycle changes with marathon training: anovulation and short luteal phase. Can. J. Appl. Sports Sci. 7:173-177; 1982.
45. Quigley, M.E.; Yen, S.S.N. The role of endogenous opiates on LH secretion during the menstrual cycle. J. Clin. Endocrin. Metab. 51:179-181; 1980.
46. Ronkainen, H.; Pakarinen, A.; Kirkinen, P.; Kauppila, A. Physical exercise induced changes and season-associated differences in the pituitary-ovarian function of runners and joggers. J. Clin. Endocrinol. Metab. 60:416-422; 1985.
47. Ruffin, M.T.; Hunter, R.E.; Arendt, E.A. Exercise and secondary amenorrhoea linked through endogenous opioids. Sports Med. 10(2):65-71; 1990.
48. Sanborn, C.E.; Albrecht, B.H.; Wagner, W.W., Jr. Athletic amenorrhea: lack of association with body fat. Med. Sci. Sports Exerc. 19(3):207-212; 1987.
49. Sanborn, C.F.; Albrecht, B.H.; Wagner, W.W., Jr. Medically induced reversal of infertility in athletic amenorrhea. Med. Sci. Sports Exerc. 19(Suppl.):85; 1987.
50. Sanborn, C.F.; Martin, B.J.; Wagner, W.W. Is athletic amenorrhea specific to runners? Am. J. Obstet. Gynecol. 141:662-670; 1981.
51. Shangold, M.; Freeman, R.; Thyssen, B.; Gatz M. The relationship between long-distance running, plasma progesterone, and luteal phase length. Fertility & Sterility 31(2):130-133; 1979.

52. Shangold, M.; Rebar, R.W.; Wentz, A.C.; Schiff, I. Evaluation and management of menstrual dysfunction in athletes. JAMA 263(12):1665-1669; 1990.

53. Shangold, M.M.; Levine, H.S. The effect of marathon training on menstrual function. Am. J. Obstet. Gynecol. 143:862-869; 1982.

54. Simkin, A.; Ayalon, J.; Leichter, I. Increased trabecular density due to bone-loading exercises in postmenopausal osteoporotic women. Calcif. Tissue Int. 40(2):59-63; 1987.

55. Sinning, W.E.; Little, K.D. Body composition and menstrual function in athletes. Sports Med. 4:34-45; 1987.

56. Smith, E.L., Reddan, W. Physical activity—a modality for bone accretion in the aged. Am. J. Roentgen 126:1297; 1976.

57. Snow, R.C.; Barbieri, R.L.; Frisch, R.E. Estrogen 2-hydroxylase oxidation and menstrual function among elite oarswomen. J. Clin. Endocrinol. Metab. 69:369-376; 1989.

58. Stager, J.M.; Wigglesworth, J.K.; Hatler, L.K. Interpreting the relationship between age of menarche and prepubertal training. Med. Sci. Sports Exerc. 22(1):54-58; 1990.

59. Surkina, I.D.; Gotovtseva, E.P. The immune state of female athletes and its correlation with menstrual function and conditions of sports activities. Sports Training Med. Rehab. 1:85-88; 1989.

60. Toriola, A.L. Survey of menstrual function in young Nigerian athletes. Int. J. Sports Med. 9(1):29-34; 1988.

61. Trussell, J. Statistical flaws in evidence for the Frisch hypothesis that fatness triggers menarche. Hum. Biol. 52:711-720; 1980.

62. Veldhuis, J.D.; Evans, W.S.; Demers, L.M.; Thorn, M.O.; Wakat, D.; Rogol, A.D. Altered neuroendocrine regulation of gonadotropin secretion in women distance runners. J. Clin. Endocrinol. Metab. 61:557-563; 1985.

63. Vollman, R.F. The menstrual cycle. Philadelphia: Saunders; 1977.

64. Wetzels, L.C.G.; Hoogland, H.J.; De Haan, J. Basal body temperature as a method of ovulation detection: comparison with ultrasonographic findings. Gyn. & Obs. Invest. 13:235-240; 1982.

65. White, C.M.; Hergenroeder, A.D. Amenorrhea, osteopenia, and the female athlete. Ped. Clin. NA 37(5):1125-1141; 1990.

66. Wolman, R.L.; Clark, P.; McNally, E.; Harries, M.; Reeve, J. Menstrual state and exercise as determinants of spinal trabecular bone density in female athletes. BMJ 301(6751):516-518; 1990.

CHAPTER 5

•

Diet and Menstrual Status as Determinants of Injury Risk for the Athletic Female

Tom Lloyd

The major factors known to be associated with increased risk of injury to the female athlete are presented in Figure 5.1. The actions of these factors are often inseparable and therefore are shown intertwined. Careful studies with multivariate analysis will be required to quantitate the contribution of each factor, and these contributions are likely to differ depending upon circumstance. However, with our present experience, genetics seem to play the key role in this mosaic, followed by hormonal status and conditioning. Diet and stress appear to be more distant modulators of injury risk. However, because diet and stress influence hormonal status and conditioning efforts, they play important, though still inadequately understood, roles in injury risk.

The overall working hypothesis that our laboratory has been using for several years to design studies to evaluate these relationships is shown in Figure 5.2.

All participants in the Pennsylvania State studies provided informed consent to the protocols, which had been reviewed and approved by the Institutional Review Board for clinical studies at this institution. Details of the methods used have been previously published (6, 26, 27, 28).

Menstrual Irregularity, Oral Contraceptive Use, and Injury Rates Among Recreational and Collegiate Athletes

The results of our study of 260 women runners participating in a 10 K national championship footrace (the New York City Diet Pepsi 10 K) are presented in Table 5.1. We separated the 260 women runner respondents into two categories:

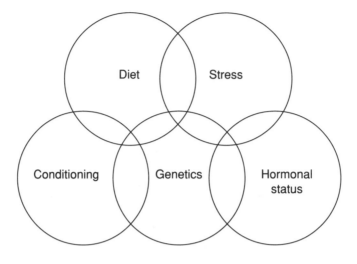

Figure 5.1   Determinants of injury risk for female athletes.

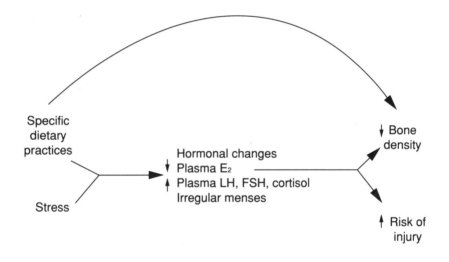

Figure 5.2   Pathways by which diet and stress may lead to bone-related injuries.

those who sustained a musculoskeletal injury that caused them to interrupt a running program or to seek medical help, and those who reported never having sustained an injury. The two groups were indistinguishable with respect to age, height, weight, menarche, parity, age started running, number of days a week, and speed of running. Where they differed was in years of running, number of miles per run, oral contraceptive use, and menstrual history. The injured women runners had been running longer, ran more miles per run, and were more likely

Table 5.1   Characteristics of Uninjured and Injured Women Runners

Characteristics	Uninjured (N = 180)	Injured (N = 80)	P value (t-test of chi-square)
Age (yr)	31.58 ± 0.62	33.65 ± 0.85	NS*
Height (in.)	64.66 ± 0.24	64.45 ± 0.34	NS
Weight (lbs)	124.44 ± 1.10	123.30 ± 1.63	NS
Menarche (yr)	12.90 ± 0.12	12.86 ± 0.17	NS
No. of children	0.49 ± 0.08	0.40 ± 0.10	NS
Age started running	27.61 ± 0.63	27.82 ± 0.90	NS
Number of days/wk running	4.80 ± 0.11	5.05 ± 0.13	NS
Number of min/mi	9.11 ± 0.11	8.82 ± 0.12	NS
Oral contraceptive use			
Yes	64	2	
No	116	78	<0.001
Menstrual history			
Regular	103	33	
Irregular	66	41	<0.025

All values are expressed as mean ± SE.
*NS – not statistically significant.
Note. Adapted from Lloyd et al. (1986).

to have irregular or absent menses and not to have been using oral contraceptives. Subsequent logistic regression analysis of these data showed that oral contraceptive use and menstrual history are independent risk factors for injury.

To examine the hypothesis that premenopausal women with exercise-associated menstrual irregularities are at increased risk for bone fractures, we reviewed the medical histories of Pennsylvania State University collegiate women athletes. The results are summarized in Table 5.2. The two groups of injured women athletes did not differ from one another or from the population of uninjured women athletes with respect to height, weight, age, or number of years in competitive sports. But the frequency of stress fractures in women with irregular menses was nearly four times the frequency of stress fractures in the group with regular menses: 15% versus 4%, $p = <.025$. When all fractures were compared, the fracture rate for the oligomenorrheic group was nearly three times the rate for the eumenorrheic group, 24% versus 9%, $p = <.025$.

Diet, Reproductive Hormones, and Bone Density in Collegiate Athletes

To evaluate the relationships among diet, hormones, and bone density, we studied three groups of collegiate women: sedentary controls, eumenorrheic athletes, and

Table 5.2   Comparison of All 1983-1984 Pennsylvania State University Female Athletes Who Sustained Bone Fractures*

	Menstrual history		
	Regular	Irregular or absent	P value
Characteristics of study Subjects+			
Height (cm)	165.5 ± 1.8	164.8 ± 1.8	NS+
Weight (kg)	60.0 ± 1.4	58.0 ± 1.7	NS
Age (yr)	20.1 ± 0.2	19.4 ± 0.3	NS
Menarche (yr)	13.0 ± 0.2	13.7 ± 0.5	NS
Fracture frequency			
Stress fractures	4% (7/158)	15% (6/41)	<0.025
All fractures	9% (15/158)	24% (10/41)	<0.025

*There were 22 reported bone injuries among 165 regularly menstruating women, of which 15 were confirmed by X ray. Of the 11 reported bone injuries in the irregular or absent menses group, 10 were confirmed by X ray. There were 148 noninjured women in the first group and 31 in the second. The denominators shown in the fracture frequencies above (158 and 41) are the sums of confirmed fractures and uninjured individuals, which are required for chi-square analysis. The number of unconfirmed bone injuries does not enter into these calculations.

+The physical data presented are for the injured athletes. However, their profiles are statistically indistinguishable from those of the uninjured group. NS+ = Not statistically significant.

Note. Adapted from Lloyd et al. (1986).

oligomenorrheic athletes. Because menstrual disturbance consequent to entering an exercise program is more likely to result in oligomenorrhea than amenorrhea, we chose to study only oligomenorrheic athletes and excluded individuals with two or fewer menses each year. The major results of this study are presented in Table 5.3. The three groups were closely matched in age, height, and weight; both groups of athletes had higher mean body mass and lower body fat than did controls. The oligomenorrheic athletes exercised more days each week than the eumenorrheic athletes, but the total time spent exercising each week was similar. The spinal bone densities of the three groups shown in Figure 5.3 indicate that the bone densities of the oligomenorrheic athletes were lower than those of either the eumenorrheic athletes or the normal control subjects at $p = 0.10$ level. Although the absolute difference in bone density was modest, this decrease gains importance when one adds the fracture threshold of about 70 mg/ml to the figure.

The nutritional patterns of the three study groups are summarized in Table 5.3. The athletes consumed significantly more kilocalories, carbohydrates, calcium, and phosphorus than the sedentary control subjects, as expected. The

Table 5.3   Physical, Menstrual, and Athletic Profiles of the Three Study Groups in Lloyd et al. (1987)

	Control	Eumenorrheic	Oligomenorr-heic
	(n = 12)	(n = 10)	(n = 6)
Age (years)	19.6 ± 0.2	18.9 ± 0.3	18.8 ± 0.5
Height (cm)	163.7 ± 0.5	168.9 ± 2.0	167.4 ± 2.1
Weight (kg)	59.9 ± 1.5	61.1 ± 2.0	58.4 ± 2.7
Lean body mass (kg)	45.7 ± 1.0	49.9 ± 1.4	49.4 ± 2.2*
Body fat (%)	23.6 ± 1.2	18.2 ± 0.8*	15.6 ± 1.2*
Menarche (years)	12.2 ± 0.3	13.1 ± 0.2	15.2 ± 0.7*
Total menses	88.8 ± 5.1	68.9 ± 4.9+	18.4 ± 4.7++
Exercise (hr/day)	0	2.9 ± 0.5*	2.5 ± 0.3*
Exercise (days/week)	0	4.9 ± 0.2+	6.5 ± 0.2++
Bone density (mg/mL)	173 ± 5	184 + 12	156 + 16
Kcal	1677 ± 126	2105 ± 119*	2218 ± 84*
Protein (g)	62 ± 3	83 ± 8*	86 ± 4*
Carbohydrate (g)	205 ± 18	261 ± 17*	289 ± 16*
Fat (g)	71 ± 6	85 ± 5	85 ± 6
Calcium (mg)	612 ± 72	933 ± 106*	1012 + 47*
Phosphorus (mg)	974 ± 56	1290 ± 86*	1355 ± 72*
Fiber (g)	12.6 ± 0.8	13.8 ± 1.3	18 ± 1.5++

*Significantly different (p < 0.05) from control subjects.

+Significantly different (p < 0.05) from controls and oligomenorrheic subjects.

++Significantly different (p < 0.05) from control and eumenorrheic subjects.

Note. Adapted from Lloyd et al. (1987).

oligomenorrheic and eumenorrheic athletes differed only in their intake of fiber. The oligomenorrheic athletes consumed nearly twice as much dietary fiber as did the eumenorrheic athletes or the sedentary control subjects. This dietary difference between the two groups was unexpected, though previous studies that have compared high- and low-fiber-intake populations—namely, vegetarians and nonvegetarians—provide some insight on this.

Vegetarian women consume approximately twice as much fiber as do nonvegetarian women and appear to have lowered circulating estrone and estradiol levels and reduced rates of breast cancer (1, 21). In contrast, fecal excretion of estrogens by vegetarians has been found to be three to four times as great as that by

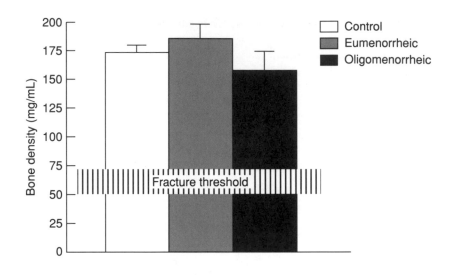

Figure 5.3 Spinal trabecular bone densities of the three study groups: controls were eumenorrheic, sedentary collegiate women; the other two groups were collegiate athletes.

nonvegetarians. The mechanisms responsible for depressed circulating estrogens and increased fecal excretion of estrogens among vegetarians are not known. A variety of mechanisms including direct absorption of estrogens by fiber subspecies and alteration of gut flora, which in turn alters enterohepatic circulation of estrogens, have been proposed (15, 18). It has also been suggested that dietary fiber binds calcium and thereby affects calcium absorption (4, 48). Calcium balance studies that have examined this issue have yielded controversial results (41, 45).

Nonetheless, the association between increased dietary fiber intake by oligomenorrheic athletes, their hypoestrogenic state, and their decreased bone density is intriguing. The decrease in bone density could have been the result of either decreased calcium availability through binding with fiber or decreased estrogen levels through the action of the fiber, both of which would have a negative effect on bone remodeling.

When we reviewed the spinal bone density data of our collegiate athletes as a function of their lifetime menstrual history, we observed a significant association between menstrual regularity of collegiate athletes and bone density (Table 5.4 and Figure 5.4; we did not use the data from the sedentary controls). We collected detailed menstrual histories and separated our athletic subjects into three groups based on those histories.

1. Eumenorrheic—six eumenorrheic women who had 11 to 13 menses a year and had not missed any menses since menarche: All subjects in this group had midcycle progesterone peaks consistent with ovulation.

2. Moderately oligomenorrheic—ten women who had missed fewer than 50% (1-39 missed menses) of their expected menses.
3. Severely oligomenorrheic—four women who missed more than 50% (> than 40) of their expected menses but had at least three menses a year.

The three study groups did not differ with respect to physical characteristics or total weekly exercise. The eumenorrheic study group had a mean of 78 previous menses a woman. We used the mean menstrual frequency for the eumenorrheic group (12.8 menses a year) to calculate the total number of expected menstrual periods for each of the oligomenorrheic subjects (age in months at time of study − age in months at menarche/12) × 12.8 = total expected menses. The two groups of oligomenorrheic athletes reported between three and seven menses a year. No participants in this study were frankly amenorrheic.

The mean bone density for the moderately oligomenorrheic group was 88% that of the eumenorrheic group; the mean bone density of the severely oligomenorrheic group was 69% that of the eumenorrheic group. To our knowledge, this was the first demonstration of decreased bone density in oligomenorrheic athletes. The mean bone density of 197 mg/ml obtained in this study for individuals who had not missed any menstrual periods is in good agreement with bone density values

Table 5.4   Physical, Hormonal, Bone Density, and Exercise Profiles of Collegiate Athletes

	Eumenorrheic (0 menses missed)	Moderately oligomenorrheic (1-39 menses missed)	Severely oligomenorrheic (> 40 menses missed)	
Number of subjects in group 6, 9, 4				
Age (yrs)	19.0 ± 0.5	18.7 ± 0.3	19.3 ± 0.6	NS
Height (cm)	169.2 ± 3.1	167.1 ± 1.7	167.6 ± 2.9	NS
Weight (kg)	61.8 ± 2.9	60.2 ± 2.4	58.0 ± 4.2	NS
Menarche (yrs)	13.2 ± 0.2	13.8 ± 0.5	13.7 ± 1.8	NS
Menses missed since menarche	0	12.9 ± 3.6	46.5 ± 1.0	a
Starting sports age (yrs)	9.4 ± 0.8	9.7 ± 0.9	10.0 ± 6.0	NS
Bone density (mg/mL)	197.2 ± 16.2	173.0 ± 8.3	135.7 ± 13.9	b

a = Moderately and severely oligomenorrheic groups significantly different ($p < 0.05$) from controls.

b = Severely oligomenorrheic group significantly different ($p < 0.05$) from controls.

NS = Not statistically different

Note. Adapted from Lloyd, Buchanan, and Meyers (1988).

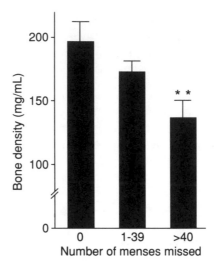

Figure 5.4   Relationship between bone density and the number of missed menses in collegiate women athletes. **Different from the control groups at *p* <0.05. *Note*. From "Collegiate Women Athletes with Irregular Menses During Adolescence Have Decreased Bone Densities" by T. Lloyd, J.R. Buchanan, and C. Myers, 1988, *Obstetrics and Gynecology*, **72**, pp. 639-642. Copyright 1988 by The American College of Obstetricians and Gynecologists.. Adapted by permission.

obtained by other investigators studying eumenorrheic women athletes (31). Recent studies by Drinkwater et al. have confirmed our observations (11). It appears that premenopausal women lose trabecular bone density at an annual rate of 1% to 2% and that this rate is accelerated after menopause to 5% to 20% (8). This information, together with data that indicate that peak bone density is reached by age 20 (32), and that atraumatic spinal fractures are likely when trabecular bone density falls below 70 mg/ml (7), suggests that young women athletes who have missed more than a third of their expected menstrual periods are likely to reach the age of 20 with a suboptimal peak bone density and therefore will be at greater risk of osteoporosis in later life.

Normative Clinical Chemistry Values of Reproductive Hormone Levels

Normal adult female sex steroid values for some of the commonly measured sex-steroids and gonadotropins are presented in Figure 5.5 next to normal adult values for plasma sodium and potassium and for resting heart rate. It is obvious that normative ranges for the steroids and gonadotropins are several times larger than those for sodium/potassium and heart rate.

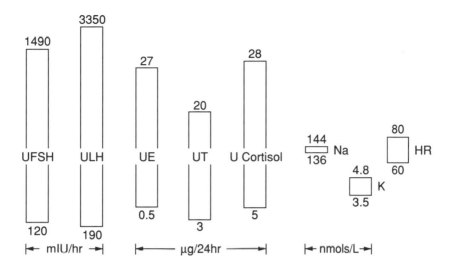

Figure 5.5 Normative adult female clinical chemistry value ranges. HR = heart rate; mIU/hr = milli International Units/hr.

There are at least three reasons for the large variances. First, carrier proteins, notably sex-hormone binding globulin (SHBG) and cortisol binding globulin (CBG), bind over 90% of the circulating steroids, allowing relatively small amounts of "free" steroid in circulation. The binding process is dynamic, and "free" steroid is constantly allowable to tissue steroid receptors. A variety of dietary factors affect the dynamics of steroid-carrier protein binding. Second, in the normally cycling, reproductive-aged adult woman, significant changes in total circulating levels of steroids and gonadotropins occur during the course of each menstrual cycle. Third, the overall concentration of sex steroids and gonadotropins is two to three orders of magnitude lower than the concentration of other circulating biochemicals. As a result of these normal variances in hormonal circulating levels, it is often difficult to accurately assess the steroid status of a given individual. Furthermore, even in large-sample studies, the ability to assess the impact of dietary or lifestyle factors on steroid status is limited.

Dietary Fat and Fiber as Modulators of Female Sex Steroid Levels

The notion that dietary practice can modify sex steroid status in humans has been supported by a large number of descriptive epidemiologic studies and a smaller number of case-control studies. Two the most widely discussed ideas concerning nutrient modification of sex steroid levels are (a) that increases in dietary fat consumption are associated with increased levels of circulating estrogens and (b) that increased dietary fiber intakes are associated with a lowering of circulating steroid levels. In a comparison of urinary estrogen profiles of vegetarian and nonvegetarian women, Adlercreutz et al. found that dietary fiber intake affected estrogen metabolism by reducing estrogen excretion (2). The recent study by Snow et al., which showed that oligomenorrheic undergraduates had a higher intake of dietary fiber and lower intake of saturated fat than their eumenorrheic classmates, is consistent with the general fat-fiber hypothesis (47). The effects of low-fat diets on steroid levels in premenopausal women have also been tested in dietary intervention protocols utilizing crossover techniques. By modification of a standard diet, which provided 40% of energy from fat, to a low-fat diet providing 20% of energy from fat, Ingram et al. observed a decrease in both nonprotein-bound estradiol and nonprotein-bound testosterone; cholesterol levels were also lowered by the low-fat regimen (22).

When short-term dietary interventions have been used, the effects on circulating steroid levels have been minimized. For example, Hagerty et al. observed no differences in plasma estrogens (E1, E2, E3), progesterone, luteinizing hormone, or prolactin among premenopausal women after an 8-week period of dietary fat reduction to 25% of calories (19). Similarly, Woods et al. saw no reduction in plasma estradiol or testosterone after an 8-week low-fat, high-fiber diet (50). However, they did observe a significant reduction in plasma estrone sulfate. Estrone sulfate, which was present in higher concentrations and has a longer half-life in plasma than estradiol, may be an important index of nutrient modification and steroid status in premenopausal women.

In addition to the complex effects of specific dietary change on circulating estrogen levels, dietary manipulations and genetic predisposition may also alter the metabolism of estradiol without affecting steady state plasma levels. Longcope et al. (29) observed that a low-fat diet resulted in a decrease in urinary excretion of the 16-hydroxylated estradiol metabolites and an increase in the excretion of the 2-hydroxy and 2-methoxy metabolites (the catechol estrogens). Subsequently, Snow et al., while studying the relationship between menstrual function and athletic activity among elite collegiate oarswomen, observed that those women athletes who consistently became menstrually irregular during peak training had significantly greater 2-hydroxylase oxidation of estradiol than did their menstrually regular teammates (46). The differences in estrogen metabolism observed in these studies may be significant, because the catechol estrogens appear to have little, if any, peripheral estrogenic activity, whereas the 16 α-hydroxylated metabolites maintain estrogenic activity.

A summary of the effects of specific dietary manipulations on female sex steroids is presented in Table 5.5. There is modest support for the idea that variation in the proportion of dietary fat and dietary fiber is a significant determinant of sex steroid status in premenopausal women. However, several caveats accompany this generalization. First, the change in fat intake must be rather large to be accompanied by a change in circulating steroid levels. The magnitude of this change has not been quantified, but it appears to be at least 15%. Second, assuming that any dietary manipulation remains isocaloric, changes in fat intake will be accompanied by significant changes in either carbohydrate or protein intakes, or by changes in both. Changes in complex carbohydrate intake will result in changed fiber intake. These dietary modalities have been associated with changes in circulating steroid levels and changes in spinal trabecular bone density (Figure 5.6). Third, although dietary fiber intake is now recognized as physiologically important, our understanding of the metabolic impact of dietary fiber intake is limited for two reasons. First, unambiguous measurement of total dietary fiber is not possible, because there is disagreement on the appropriate analytic methodologies (5, 24, 44). Accordingly, there is no complete fiber data base for computer-assisted nutrient analyses. Second, the term *dietary fiber* embraces a variety of complex chemical structures, including celluloses, hemicellulose, pectins, gums, and lignins. Just as specific fiber subspecies can modify plasma lipoprotein profiles and alter gut mobility, it is highly likely that specific subspecies modulate circulating steroids in humans. It is possible, therefore, for fiber intake to lead to decreased bone density directly by the binding of steroids to fiber or indirectly by decreasing enterohepatic circulation of estrogens, either of which would have a negative effect on bone remodeling.

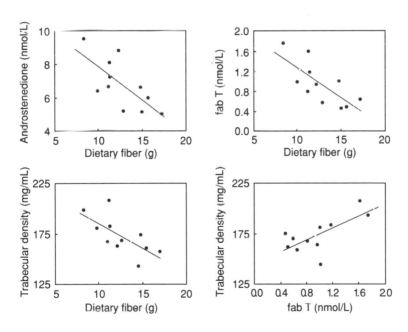

Figure 5.6 Relationships among dietary fiber intake, circulating androgen levels, and spinal trabecular bone densities in sedentary collegiate women. *Note.* From ''Determination of Peak Trabecular Bone Density: Interplay of Dietary Fiber, Carbohydrates, and Endogens'' by P.K. Leuenberger, J.R. Buchanan, C.A. Myers, T. Lloyd, and L.M. Demers, 1989, *American Journal of Clinical Nutrition,* **50**; 5:955-961. Copyright 1989 by The American Society of Clinical Nutrition. Adapted by permission.

Table 5.5   Effect of Specific Dietary Manipulation on Sex Steroid Levels in Premenopausal Women

Dietary manipulation	Hormone or metabolic effect affected	Proposed mechanism of action
1. ↑ Dietary fiber 1/3 and ↓ Dietary fat	Plasma estrogens unaffected ↑ fecal E$_1$ and E$_2$ ↑ plasma SHBG	Changes enterohepatic circulation
2. Dietary fat 40% → 25%	Plasma estrogens unaffected α ↑ 16 α estrogens ↑ catecholestrogens in urine	16-α-hydroxylase sensitive to dietary fat
3. Dietary fat 35% → 21% ↓ Cholesterol	↓ Plasma estrogens	↑ steroid binding to SHBG
4. ↑ Protein	↑ % free T and % free E$_2$ in plasma + SHBG	Effect mediated via SHBG levels
5. ↑ Dietary fiber ↑ Lignans ↑ Phytoestrogens	↑ Plasma SHBG ↓ % free T and % free E$_2$ in plasma ↑ Sex steroid excretion	SHBG levels changed

Note. ↑, increase; ↓, decrease.

Effects of Specific Nutrients on Menstrual Status

In two recent studies of premenopausal women, who differed significantly only in their dietary practices, we attempted to determine which, if any, nutrients affect reproductive capability, as measured by differences in their menstrual profiles. Sixty-one vegetarian and 78 nonvegetarian Caucasian women between the ages of 26 and 46 years who were within 90% to 115% of ideal body weight and without remarkable reproductive histories participated. As shown in Table 5.6, the incidence of menstrual irregularity was 2.6% among nonvegetarians and 21.3% among vegetarians ($p = 0.01$). The nutrient profiles of the vegetarian and nonvegetarian women presented in Table 5.7 show that the nonvegetarians reported greater intakes of saturated fatty acids, protein, cholesterol, and caffeine, and the vegetarians reported significantly greater intakes of polyunsaturated fatty acids, carbohydrates, vitamin B_6, and dietary fiber. These nutrient data were anlayzed by logistic regression analysis, which showed that the probability of menstrual regularity among all subjects was *positively* associated with increasing protein/kiloJoule (kJ) and increasing cholesterol/kJ intakes, whereas, the probability of being menstrually regular was *negatively* associated with increasing dietary fiber/kJ and increasing magnesium/kJ intakes (36). The measurement of menstrual regularity is at best an approximation of female reproductive status, because regular cycles may be anovulatory or may mask luteal phase defects. The frequency of menstrual irregularity of 2.6% among these nonvegetarians falls within the range of 2% to 5% found in large studies of normal women (9, 37).

The positive association between cholesterol/kJ and menstrual regularity may be secondary to cholesterol's role as a biological precursor for estrogen synthesis. High-protein diets are known to produce increased oxidation of 2-^{3}H estradiol at the C-2 position. Fishman et al. (12) suggested that the dominance of 2-hydroxylation may contribute to reproductive disturbances seen in these individuals. Previous studies compared the dietary practices of vegetarian and nonvegetarian women and the possible impact of these practices on health, but few of these studies used matched, premenopausal Caucasian women. Those that did reported

Table 5.6   Incidence of Menstrual Irregularity Among Vegetarian and Nonvegetarian Women*

Menstrual status	Vegetarian	Nonvegetarian
Regular	78.7 (48)	97.4 (76)
Irregular+	21.3 (13)	2.6 (2)

*Comparison by chi-square test: p = < 0.01; n in parentheses.

+Twelve women with menses 3-10 times/yr and 2 women with menses < 2 times/yr.

Note. Adapted from Pedersen, Bartholomew, Dolence, and Lloyd (1991).

Table 5.7 Nutrient Profiles of Premenopausal Vegetarian and Nonvegetarian Women

Nutrient	Vegetarian (n = 34)	Nonvegetarian (n = 41)	Nutrients having + or − effect on menstrual regularity
Energy (kJ)	7641.00 ± 364.00	7139.00 ± 406.00	
Protein (g)	63.00 ± 3.50	75.00 ± 4.00+	+
Carbohydrate (g)	264.00 ± 13.60	218.00 ± 14.00+	
Fat (g)	67.00 ± 5.00	61.00 ± 4.00	
Polyunsaturated fatty acid	13.00 ± 1.50	9.00 ± 0.97+	
Monosaturated fatty acid	15.00 ± 1.70	15.00 ± 1.00	
Saturated fatty acid	16.00 ± 1.50	19.00 ± 1.40	
Cholesterol (mg)	133.00 ± 15.00	198.00 ± 20.00+	+
Calcium (mg)	931.00 ± 69.00	873.00 ± 78.00	
Phosphorous (mg)	1159.00 ± 84.00	1138.00 ± 77.00	

Iron (mg)	20.00 ± 3.00	22.00 ± 3.00	
Magnesium (mg)	323.00 ± 25.00	250.00 ± 18.00+	—
Zinc (mg)	13.00 ± 2.40	10.00 ± 1.30	
Sodium (mg)	2304.00 ± 154.00	2649.00 ± 180.00	
Potassium (mg)	2803.00 ± 149.00	2664.00 ± 208.00	
Vitamin B_6 (mg)	20.00 ± 9.00	2.00 ± 0.38+	
Vitamin A (mg)	3.76 ± 0.49	2.98 ± 0.60	
Vitamin C (mg)	316.00 ± 92.00	184.00 ± 28.00	
Folacin (µg)	374.00 ± 44.00	385.00 ± 54.00	
Vitamin D (µg)	5.32 ± 1.0	5.62 ± 0.90	
Dietary fiber (g)	26.00 ± 1.90	15.00 ± 0.95+	—
Caffeine (mg)	16.60 ± 7.70	148.00 ± 24.00+	

*Comparison by student's t-test.

++Significantly different from vegetarians: +p < 0.05; ‡p < 0.0001.

Note. Adapted from Pedersen, Bartholomew, Dolence, and Lloyd (1991).

increased fiber intake and decreased cholesterol intake in the vegetarian groups (42, 43). Further, an inverse relationship between dietary-fiber intake and circulating estrogen concentrations was observed (15, 18, 19, 50). Differences in concentrations of circulating sex-steroids between vegetarian and nonvegetarian women may also be due in part to the effect of lignans and phytoestrogens from dietary sources. Urinary values of lignans and phytoestrogens were positively correlated with plasma SHBG and negatively correlated with plasma estrone and estradiol concentrations (3).

It is also possible that lignans inhibit the tissue aromatase enzyme responsible for peripheral estrogen formation, thereby lowering circulating estrogen concentrations. Thus, vegetarians or persons adopting high-fiber diets may be at less risk for breast cancer but at greater risk for menstrual-cycle dysfunction due to lowered plasma estrogen concentrations, which in turn may be due to direct binding of steroid hormones to fiber species in the gut (20, 49) or to alteration of steroid reabsorption caused by changes in gut flora (16, 17).

Age-Dependent Changes in Bone Density and Calcium Intake: The Peak Bone Mass Concept

Progress in measurement of the timing of peak bone mass has, until recently, been limited by reluctance to expose normal subjects to ethically unacceptable levels of radiation. However, because of the extremely low radiation used and its capability to measure total body calcium as well as bone densities at multiple anatomic sites, dual photon x-ray absorptiometry (DEXA), a recent advance in bone measurement technology, is particularly well suited for studies of normal children and of women of reproductive age (23, 33).

A host of recent studies indicate that peak bone density in women is reached by age 20 (8, 32, 35). Whether significant bone loss occurs in the normal woman between ages 20 and 40 remains under investigation. Studies aimed at identifying the major determinants of peak bone mass are underway at several institutions. To date, the major determinants of peak bone mass appear to be race, body mass index (BMI), and integrated estrogen exposure (10, 13, 14, 25, 38). The effects of calcium intake and activity patterns, although believed to be significant, are thought to be less important.

Though our understanding of the genetic contribution to peak bone mass attainment is incomplete, we know that, at all ages on a weight or BMI adjusted basis, Caucasians have lower values at all anatomic sites than do blacks (30, 34). Comparative data for peak bone attainment in the four major racial groups in the United States have not yet been collected. In contrast, body weight and BMI during adolescence are closely correlated to bone development (39). Bone accretion is accelerated during puberty, and this accelerated activity is related to integrated estrogen exposure (10, 13, 14).

However, there is a strong relationship between spinal bone loss and ovulatory disturbances between ages 21 to 42 (40), and because many young female athletes remain anovulatory even if menstruating regularly, this area of concern warrants further investigation. A more comprehensive picture of the relationships among the factors that influence peak bone development in women will emerge as more longitudinal studies of young women are conducted and reported. One such project, the Penn State Young Women's Health Study, is currently following the pubertal progression, bone development, and nutritional and exercise patterns of over 100 girls, from ages 11 through 16, to characterize and evaluate the major determinants of reproductive development and bone accretion.

Summary

1. Hormonal status in premenopausal women can be modified by diet or exercise, and the resultant hormonal changes may play an important role in bone maintenance and risk of athletic injury.
2. High circulating cortisol levels can have catabolic effects on skeletal muscle, resulting in negative calcium and nitrogen balance.
3. Birth control supplementation in oligomenorrheic women does *not* restore their hormonal levels to normal but to a level slightly greater than postmenopausal levels.
4. Many exercising females have high-fiber, low-cholesterol diets. High-fiber, low-cholesterol diets in the general population are associated with decreased bone mineral density, as noted in bone mineral studies. Nutritional data suggest that the probability of menstrual irregularity is high in individuals whose diet contains either increased fiber or increased magnesium, or low cholesterol or low protein.

   The question is, Is the exercise link to bone density related to exercise directly influencing hormonal cycling and promoting low-estrogen secondary amenorrhea, or is the loss of bone density in exercising women secondary to their dietary habits?
5. An example of a common cause-effect relationship to a third element already exists in the relationship of exercise, anemia, and diet. Many women who exercise are anemic. Anemia can result from a high-fiber diet, because fiber appears to decrease the absorption of iron. Hence, anemia in exercising women may be directly related to diet rather than to exercise. Similarly, with low bone density in amenorrhea and exercise, the diet commonly selected by exercising women may be what is predisposing them to a loss of bone density, as well as being indirectly or directly related to their oligomenorrhea.
6. Much needs to be done to see how the following are interrelated: stress, diet, sport specificity, conditioning techniques, genetics, menstrual irregularities, and bone density. Until we are able to interrelate these factors better, one should avoid the tendency to assume that one factor is directly responsible for another (e.g., exercise results in oligomenorrhea, which results in decreased bone density). The issue of decreased bone density

must be resolved in a timely fashion, because there are now in our population young, oligomenorrheic, low bone density women who need etiologic and therapeutic answers.

7. The relationship of stress fractures to the multifactorial issues of bone density and oligomenorrhea has not been well established. Although stress fractures are reported to be more common in women than men, and especially in those women with oligomenorrhea, they occur in the cortical bone of the appendicular skeletal rather than the spine or other cancellous bone areas where bone density studies have confirmed decreased density in oligomenorrheic females.

Acknowledgment

This study was supported, in part, by PHS R01-HD25973.

References

1. Adlercreutz, H. Diet and sex hormone metabolism in nutrition, toxicity, and cancer. In: Rowland, I., ed. Nutrition, toxicity, and cancer. Caldwell, NJ: The Telford Press; 1990:2-78.
2. Adlercreutz, H.; Fotsis, T.; Bannwart, C.; Hamalainen, E.; Bloigu, S.; Ollus, A. Urinary estrogen profile determination in young Finnish vegetarian and omnivorous women. J. Steroid Biochem. 24(1):289-296; 1986.
3. Adlercreutz, H.; Hockerstedt, K.; Bannwart, C.; Bloigu, S.; Hamalainen, E.; Fotsis, T.; Ollus, A. Effect of dietary components, including lignans and phytoestrogens, on enterohepatic circulation and liver metabolism of estrogens and on sex hormone binding globulin (SHBG). J. Steroid Biochem. 27(4-6):1135-1144; 1987.
4. Behall, K.M.; Scholfield, D.J.; Lee, K.; Powell, A.S.; Moser, P.B. Mineral balance in adult men: effect of four refined fibers. Am. J. Clin. Nutr. 46:307-314; 1987.
5. Bingaham, S. Definitions and intakes of dietary fiber. Am. J. Clin. Nutr. 45:1226-1231; 1987.
6. Buchanan, J.R.; Lloyd, T.; Myers, C.; Leuenberger, P.; Demers, L.M. Determinants of peak trabecular bone mass in women: the roles of androgen, estrogen, and exercise. J. Bone Min. Res. 3:673-680; 1988.
7. Buchanan, J.R.; Myers, C.; Greer, R.B.; Lloyd, T.; Varano, L. Assessment of vertebral fracture risk in menopausal women. J. Bone Joint Surg. 69A:212-218; 1987.
8. Buchanan, J.R.; Myers, C.; Lloyd, T.; Greer, R.B. Early vertebral trabecular bone loss in normal premenopausal women. J. Bone Min. Res. 3:583-587; 1988.
9. Carlberg, K.A.; Muckman, M.T.; Peake, G.T.; Riedesel, M.L. A survey of menstrual function in athletes. Eur. J. Appl. Physiol. 51:211-222; 1983.
10. Dhuper, S.; Warren, M.P.; Brooks-Gunn, J.; Fox, R. Effects of hormonal status on bone density in adolescent girls. J. Clin. Endocrinol. Metab. 71:1083-1088; 1990.
11. Drinkwater, B.L.; Bruemner, B.; Chestnut, C.H., III. Menstrual history as a determinant of current bone density in young athletes. JAMA 263:545-548; 1990.
12. Fishman, J.; Boyar, R.M.; Hellman, L. Influence of body weight on estradiol metabolism in young women. J. Clin. Endocrinol. Metab. 41:989-991; 1975.

13. Gilsanz, V.; Gibbens, D.T.; Carolson, M.; Boechat, M.I.; Cann, C.E.; Schulz, E.E. Peak trabecular vertebral density: a comparison of adolescent and adult females. Calcif. Tissue Int. 43:260-262; 1988.
14. Gilsanz, V.; Gibbens, D.T.; Roe, T.F.; Carlson, M.; Senac, M.O.; Boechat, M.I.; Huana, H.K.; Schulz, E.E.; Libanati, C.R.; Cann, C.C. Vertebral bone density in children: effect of puberty. Radiology 166:847-850; 1988.
15. Goldin, B.R.; Adlercreutz, H.; Gorbach, S.L.; Warram, J.H.; Dwyer, J.T.; Swenson, L.; Woods, M.N. Estrogen excretion patterns and plasma levels in vegetarian and omnivorous women. New Eng. J. Med 307(25):1542-1547; 1982 Dec. 16.
16. Goldin, B.R.; Gorbach, S.C. The relationship between diet and rat fecal bacterial enzymes implicated in colon cancer. JNCI 57:357-375; 1976.
17. Goldin, B.R.; Swenson, L.; Dwyer, J.; Sexton, M.; Gorbach, S.L. Effect of diet and lactobacillus supplements on human fecal bacterial enzymes. JNCI 64:255-262; 1980.
18. Gorbach, S.L.; Goldin, B.R. Diet and the excretion and enterohepatic cycling of estrogens. Prev. Med. 16:525-531; 1987.
19. Hagerty, M.A.; Howie, B.J.; Tan, S.; Schultz, T.D. Effect of low- and high-fat intakes on the hormonal milieu of premenopausal women. Am. J. Clin. Nutr. 47:653-659; 1988.
20. Hamalainen, E.K.; Adlercreutz, H.; Puska, P.; Pietinen, P. Decrease of serum total and free testosterone during a low-fat high-fiber diet. J. Steroid Biochem. 18:369-370; 1983.
21. Hayward, J.L.; Greenwood, F.C.; Glober, C.; Stemmerman, G.; Bulbrook, R.D.; Wang, D.Y.; Kumaokas, S. Endocrine status in normal British, Japanese, and Hawaiian-Japanese women. Europ. J. Cancer 14:1221-1228; 1978.
22. Ingram, D.M.; Bennett, F.C.; Willcox, D.; de Klerk, N. Effect of low-fat diet on female sex hormone. JNCI 79:1225-1229; 1987.
23. Kelly, T.L.; Slovik, D.M.; Schoenfeld, D.A.; Neer, R.M. Quantitative digital radiography versus dual photon absorptiometry of the lumbar spine. J. Clin. Endocrinol. Metab. 67:839-844; 1988.
24. Lanza, E.; Butrum, R.R. A critical review of food fiber analysis and data. J. Am. Dietet. Asso. 86:732-743; 1986.
25. Liel, Y.; Edwards, J.; Shary, J.; Spicer, K.M.; Gordon, L.; Bell, N.H. The effects of race and body habitus on bone mineral density of the radius, radium, hip, and spine in premenopausal women. J. Clin. Endocrinol. Metab. 66:1247; 1988.
26. Lloyd, T.; Bitzer, S.; Waldman, C.J.; Myers, C.; Ford, B.G.; Buchanan, J.R. The relationship of diet, athletic activity, menstrual status, and bone density among collegiate women. Am. J. Clin. Nutr. 46:681-684; 1987.
27. Lloyd, T.; Buchanan, J.R.; Myers, C. Collegiate women athletes with irregular menses during adolescence have decreased bone densities. Obstet. Gynecol. 72:639-642; 1988.
28. Lloyd, T.; Triantafyllou, S.J.; Baker, E.R.; Houts, P.S.; Whiteside, J.A.; Kalenak, A.; Stumpf, P.G. Menstrual irregularity and injury in women athletes. Med. Sci. Sports Exerc. 18:374-379; 1986.
29. Longcope, C.; Gorbach, S.; Goldin, B.; Woods, M.; Dwyer, J.; Morril, A.; Warram, J. The effect of a low-fat diet on estrogen metabolism. J. Clin. Endocrinol. Metab. 64:1246-1250; 1987.
30. Luckey, M.M.; Meier, D.E.; Mandeli, J.P.; DaCosta, M.C.; Hubbard, M.L.; Goldsmith, S.J. Radial and vertebral bone density in white and black women: evidence for racial differences in premenopausal bone homeostatis. J. Clin. Endocrinol. Metab. 69:762-770; 1989.

31. Marcus, R.; Cann, C.; Madvig, P.; Minkoff, J.; Goddard, M.; Bayer, M.; Martin, M.; Gaudiani, L.; Hashell, W.; Genant, H. Menstrual function and bone mass in elite women distance runners. Ann. Intern. Med. 102:158-163; 1985.

32. Mazess, R.B.; Barden, H.S. Bone density in premenopausal women: effects of age, dietary intake, physical activity, smoking, and birth control pills. Am. J. Clin. Nutr. 53:132-142; 1991.

33. Mazess, R.B.; Barden, H.; Vetter, J.; Ettinger, M. Advances in noninvasive bone measurement. Ann. Biomed. Eng. 17:177-181; 1989.

34. Nelson, D.A.; Kleerekoper, M.; Parfitt, A.M. Bone mass, skin color, and body size among black and white women. Bone Min. 4:257-264; 1988.

35. Ott, S.M. Attainment of peak bone mass. J. Clin. Endocrinol. Metab. 71:1082A-1082C; 1990.

36. Pedersen, A.B.; Bartholomew, M.J.; Dolence, L.A.; Lloyd, T. Menstrual differences due to vegetarian and nonvegetarian diets. Am. J. Clin. Nutr. 53:879-885; 1991.

37. Pettersson, F.; Fries, H.; Nillius, S.J. Epidemiology of secondary amenorrhea: I. Incidence and prevalence rates. Am. J. Obstet. Gynecol. 117:80-86; 1973.

38. Pocock, N.A.; Eisman, J.A.; Hopper, J.L.; Yeates, M.G.; Sambrook, P.N.; Ebert, S. Genetic determinants of bone mass in adults. J. Clin. Invest. 80:706-710; 1987.

39. Ponder, S.W.; McCormick, D.P.; Fawcett, H.D.; Palmer, J.L.; McKernan, M.G.; Brouhard, B.H. Spinal bone mineral density in children aged 5 through 11.99 years. Am. J. Dis. Child. 144:1346-1348; 1990.

40. Prior, J.C.; Vigna, Y.M.; Schechter, M.T.; Burgess, A.E. Spinal bone loss and ovulatory disturbances. New Eng. J. Med. 323:1221-1227; 1990.

41. Sandberg, A.; Hasselblad, C.; Hasselblad, K. The effect of wheat bran on the absorption of minerals in the small intestine. Br. J. Nutr. 48:185-191; 1982.

42. Schultz, T.D.; Leklem, J.E. Dietary status of Seventh-Day Adventists and nonvegetarians. J. Am. Dietet. Asso. 83:27-33; 1983 July.

43. Schultz, T.D.; Leklem, J.E. Nutrient intake and hormonal status of premenopausal vegetarian Seventh-Day Adventists and premenopausal nonvegetarians. Nutr. Cancer 4(4):247-259; 1983.

44. Slavin, J.L. Dietary fiber: classification, chemical analyses, and food sources. J. Am. Dietet. Asso. 87:1164-1171; 1987.

45. Slavin, J.L.; Marlett, J.A. Influence of refined cellulose on human bowel function and calcium and magnesium balance. Am. J. Clin. Nutr. 33:1932-1939; 1980.

46. Snow, R.C.; Barbieri, R.L.; Frisch, R.E. Estrogen 2-hydroxylase oxidation and menstrual function among elite oarswomen. J. Clin. Endocrinol. Metab. 69:369-376; 1989.

47. Snow, R.C.; Schneider, J.L.; Barbieri, R.L. High density fiber and low saturated fat intake among oligomenorrheic undergraduates. Fertility & Sterility 54:632-637; 1990.

48. Walker, A.R.P. Dietary fibre and mineral metabolism. Molec. Aspects Med. 9:69-87; 1987.

49. Whitten, C.G.; Shultz, T.D. Binding of steroid hormones in vitro by water-insoluble dietary fiber. Nutr. Res. 8:1223-1235; 1988.

CHAPTER 6

•

Exercise and Pregnancy

Judy Mahle Lutter
Valerie Lee

Can a woman be physically active during pregnancy? In the past 10 years the media have focused on star athletes like Joan Benoit Samuelson and Mary Slaney to discover what happens to an elite pregnant athlete. The information provided by their stories is anecdotal and applies primarily to high level athletes. However, this elite group is not the only one with questions about exercise and pregnancy. Women with a history of physical activity, which may or may not include competition, are still frequently told to put their feet up for 9 months and *be careful*.

At Melpomene we frequently hear from women who have been told to cut back or quit exercising completely. An ultramarathoner called to say, "I'm 2 months pregnant, and my doctor has told me that running pounds the baby, so I stopped running. But I'm bored! Can't I just run a little?" Three questions are most common: Is it safe? How will it affect me? How will it affect my baby?

A Historical Perspective of Exercise and Pregnancy

It may be helpful to put the question of exercise and pregnancy into a historical context. Ours is not, of course, the first generation of women who have been concerned about the effects of physical labor and activity on pregnancy outcome. Women throughout the world have been active during their pregnancies, often missing only several hours of field labor to deliver their babies. The main difference is that historically women had little choice about physical activity during pregnancy; most women asking questions today do have a choice.

The advice given to pregnant women in the past century is full of admonitions and warnings about exercising during pregnancy. An 1888 treatise entitled *Wife and Mother, or Information for Every Woman,* coauthored by a male and a female physician, notes, "Exercise, fresh air and occupation are then essentially necessary in pregnancy. If they be neglected, hard and tedious labors are likely to ensue" (2, p. 77). On the other hand, the same authors warn, "Stooping, lifting of heavy weights, and over-reaching ought to be carefully avoided. Running, horse-back riding, and dancing are likewise dangerous—they frequently induce a miscarriage" (2, pp. 77-78).

Current Thinking on Exercise and Pregnancy: Consistent Advice?

Have we any better advice today than we had in 1888? Today, pregnant women are still asking if they can exercise without harming their babies, and the answers they get are far from consistent. In a Melpomene study of pregnant runners and swimmers, over 90% of these women said that their health care provider was supportive of their desire to exercise while pregnant. In a comparable group of nonexercising pregnant women, however, only 60% said their health care provider made positive comments about exercise and pregnancy. Neither group of professionals were able to fully answer questions about exercise and pregnancy, nor could they supply specific information. Only 75% of the exercising pregnant women believed their providers were knowledgeable about the issue.

Why isn't research information more readily available? One reason is that we are limited in the kind of laboratory research that we can conduct on human beings. A pregnant woman obviously cannot remain in a lab for 9 months while we study her under controlled conditions. Naturally, the outcome of pregnancy will be based on many factors, of which exercise is only one. There are also ethical questions to consider when studying human beings. We cannot cause a mother to overexert herself so that we can see what effect it has on her baby. Therefore, many early studies were done using laboratory animals, which provided important background information but did not answer the practical questions of women who wished to continue to exercise.

Given all the conflicting opinions, how can pregnant women make decisions about exercise during pregnancy? Melpomene Institute has found that women want as much information as possible about the pregnancy experience. This chapter, therefore, reviews what is known about some of the specific issues, including cardiovascular and respiratory system responses of both mother and fetus, maternal musculoskeletal effects, thermoregulatory concerns, nutritional needs, labor and delivery experiences, and postpartum considerations. Remember that there are always limits to what we know. We have already mentioned the technical and ethical limits on what research can be done. In addition, what happens during a pregnancy is influenced by many personal variables, such as lifestyle and genetics, that cannot be forced into "averages." Pregnancy is different for each woman, and each woman needs to make practical, informed decisions that fit her lifestyle.

Heart and Lung Considerations

Of the many anatomic and functional changes that occur during pregnancy, those related to cardiovascular and respiratory systems show up most strikingly with exercise. The heart and lungs must work overtime to meet the increased energy needs of pregnancy. As the baby grows, the mother's heart rate increases, because more blood is being pumped through her body. Blood volume, the total amount of blood in the body, also increases.

Contrary to what many think, fitness level is not lost during pregnancy. In fact, oxygen consumption, aerobic capacity, increases throughout pregnancy until it is 30% greater than its nonpregnant level. Studies indicate that aerobic capacity can actually be increased further by exercising during pregnancy (17, 25, 28). Pregnant women may feel different when they exercise, however, because they will be carrying more weight and it will take more energy to do the same activities than before pregnancy. Exercise physiologists describe this by saying that activities have a higher energy cost during pregnancy.

Hyperventilation can occur during exercise and causes some women to question exercise patterns. One runner told us, "For me, the first month was the hardest, because my breathing was much more strained. Once I got used to it, the running was easier" (unpublished personal communication). The reason hyperventilation occurs is related to a greater sensitivity to carbon dioxide, an effect stimulated by increased progesterone. A woman's growing uterus also pushes up against her diaphragm. In response, the lower ribs flare and the chest expands in an attempt to preserve lung capacity.

In this and many other ways, the female body is adapted to handle the extra energy load associated with being pregnant. What happens, then, when the demands of exercise are added to this load? Can heart and lungs meet this increased demand? In exercise, the body deals with stress by diverting some blood flow away from the internal tissues and toward the muscles that are doing the work. Because blood is the vehicle that carries oxygen to the fetus, researchers have questioned whether strenuous exercise might divert some oxygen-filled blood away from the fetus, resulting in fetal hypoxia, or lack of oxygen (28).

One study, conducted more than 30 years ago, noted a decrease in the amount of blood flowing into the uterus while women were exercising (22). The women in this study, however, were resting on their backs, a position that in late pregnancy is uncomfortable for good reason: When a woman is on her back, the uterus can compress the vena cava, the primary vein through which blood flows from the body back to the heart. This compression naturally interferes with the amount of blood available for the heart to pump back into the uterus. Therefore, in this study, we don't know how much of the decreased blood flow was actually caused by exercise and how much was blocked by the pinched vein.

Unfortunately, we do not have a safe way to observe directly the blood flow to the uterus and the fetus. Some researchers have studied how the fetus's heart rate changes as a result of the mother's exercise (4, 6, 14, 23). They suspect that this may reveal indirectly how much blood and, therefore, how much oxygen is reaching the fetus.

Ethical considerations keep us from studying the effects of long-term, high-intensity exercise in the lab, but the body's own defenses may keep women from engaging in this kind of activity anyway. After a while, very strenuous activity becomes quite uncomfortable for pregnant women, especially later in their term. Perhaps these discomforts are a natural safety valve—the body's way of forcing a woman to cut back on activity. Pregnant women themselves have commented about their voluntary changes in exercise habits. One runner told us, "I don't feel bad cutting back my mileage. Now I run only for pleasure—it's a different type of running" (21, p. 120).

Muscle and Bone Effects

No research on exercise and pregnancy has yet been done by orthopedists or physical therapists, who work directly with the musculoskeletal system. The two major concerns for physically active women in this area are back pain and a loosening of the joints that is associated with pregnancy.

Posture and Back Pain

During pregnancy, the center of gravity moves forward and upward as the baby grows and breasts enlarge. To compensate for these changes, many women slump their shoulders and arch their backs. The resulting back curvature, lumbar lordosis, can cause fatigue and lower back pain. About 50% of pregnant women experience this kind of back pain. Whether someone's back hurts seems to have nothing to do with how much weight the woman gains or how much the baby weighs. There does seem to be an association, however, between back pain and maternal age and number of previous pregnancies.

We are not sure what role exercise plays in back problems during pregnancy. We do know that abdominal muscles help support the back as well as the uterus. Therefore, developing good abdominal muscle tone going into pregnancy may be one way to lessen backache problems (9). In any case, the shift in the center of gravity, as well as increasing weight, will mean a change in balance. Pregnant women must be alert to these changes and to the fact that they may need to change their exercise patterns as their pregnancies progress (12, 18). One runner, who decided to switch to swimming in her 7th month (because she said she felt like she was carrying a bowling ball when running), also had to make adaptations in the water. "But," she said, "I was really becoming clumsy and was afraid I might fall. That isn't much of a problem when you're in the water" (personal communication).

Women participating in sports requiring great balance and agility need to be extra alert. A physician working with downhill skiers noticed that the first sign of pregnancy in one of her clients was a rapid deterioration in skiing ability that put the skier at risk of injury.

Echoing trends in the general population, half of the runners, swimmers, and nonexercising women in a Melpomene study experienced back pain during pregnancy. As with other pregnancy-related aches, pains, and physical problems, the women tried to adjust their habits to decrease these discomforts. A triathlete who participated in our research developed back pain in the second trimester, reportedly due to an uncomfortable chair at work. Because her back was particularly sore in the evenings (the only time she could exercise), she often cut back on the duration and intensity of her workout.

Another woman who ran in the Olympic marathon trials during her second trimester experienced lower back pain. She was accustomed to running 10 miles a day but said, "I had lower back problems after running from about 5 months on. I had to decrease my mileage to 3 miles or less at a time. I learned that leaning forward while I ran helped ease the pressure" (21, p. 121).

Obstetrician and gynecologist Mona Shangold believes that all women, including pregnant women, should be encouraged to participate in some sort of strength training program to strengthen their upper body and help avoid back problems. The originators of one maternal fitness program have tried to combine strength training with aerobic conditioning to decrease discomfort and also to prepare women for labor and delivery. In their research, they found that women who were pregnant for the first time were less likely to undergo a cesarean section if they participated regularly in this program (11). Average time in labor was not affected. And *all* the women in the exercise program reported that they enjoyed it, no matter what their level of participation.

Softening Ligaments and Cartilage

The hormone relaxin, which is secreted by the corpus luteum, is detectable only in pregnant women. Relaxin causes the body's connective tissues, the ligaments and cartilage, to soften and stretch so that the pelvic outlet will be able to accommodate the baby at birth. Though this softening proves to be a great help during delivery, it may subject joints to undue strain during pregnancy. It becomes easier to turn an ankle or twist a hip, for instance, because joints are able to stretch farther than they normally would and the stabilizing ligaments are more pliable. This has particular implications for weight-bearing activities, such as walking and running.

The round ligaments that support the uterus become stretched as the fetus grows. Some women who engage in activities such as running, in which there can be movement that tugs these ligaments, experience pain. Support from a lightweight, maternity girdle or panty girdle can offer some relief.

Unlike muscle fiber, which is elastic, connective tissue does not regain its shape once it is stretched. Abdominal muscles are joined in the middle by a band of connective tissue called the linea alba. Normally, this band is 1/2 inch in width. Because of the action of relaxin, about 30% of all pregnant women experience an excessive loosening of this seam, a condition known as diastasis recti. Women who do exercises that stress the abdomen should perform a simple self-measurement for separation at the navel. If this separation is 2 or 3 finger-widths or wider, women are advised against abdominal exercises, including leg lifts and sit-ups, which can increase the gap.

By being aware of the muscular and skeletal changes that occur during pregnancy, physicians can suggest ways for women to modify their exercise patterns to accommodate these changes safely. Strengthening the upper body and the abdominal muscles and practicing good posture *before* pregnancy can help prevent or alleviate discomfort during pregnancy.

Overheating

Thermoregulation is another issue worth mention. Most recommendations and guidelines about exercise during pregnancy warn against overheating. At Melpomene, we advise pregnant women to avoid exercising in hot environments and to be sure to consume enough fluids. These recommendations are understandable when we consider the mechanisms of thermoregulation.

The body has ingenious ways of getting rid of the heat naturally generated. The heat is conducted outward to the skin and is dissipated as blood runs through the capillaries close to the surface. Sweat glands provide a water-based cooling system; as sweat evaporates, it gives up heat, thus making the body feel cooler. During pregnancy, as heat is generated by both mother and fetus, more blood is pumped to the skin, and more sweat is produced by the sweat glands. Sometimes, when the air outside the body is hot and humid, this cooling system cannot work as efficiently, and both mother and fetus can become overheated (13).

Researchers working with animals know that maternal overheating early in gestation can cause defects in the fetus. We can't necessarily apply these studies to humans however, because some of the animals have cooling mechanisms such as panting that are quite different than the mechanisms we use. Nevertheless, experts are convinced that the *possible* dangers of overheating are something to take into consideration, especially during exercise.

Of course, a woman's temperature is bound to rise somewhat during exercise. Keeping it within safe limits is the key. Researchers in Pennsylvania measured the core temperatures of four pregnant women before, during, and after they ran on a treadmill. All four women had been runners before becoming pregnant and were still running regularly. Their temperatures increased during exercise and remained elevated for at least 15 minutes afterward (13). Temperature reduction to preexercise levels was especially slow during the third trimester. The researchers felt, however, that the temperature increases they saw were not dangerous. All the women went on to deliver healthy babies. Though this is a reassuring study, it is important to note that it involved *only* four women and that these women were already accustomed to exercising. Also, the length of time that they exercised while their temperatures were measured was only 20 minutes.

Recently other scientists compared core temperatures of pregnant women who exercised for 20 minutes on a stationary bike when the bike was on dry land and when it was in water. Although temperature was affected in both mediums, it did not rise quite as high in the women who biked in the water.

Sometimes women wonder about the safety of hot tubs and saunas during pregnancy. Researchers who studied the medical histories of women with children who had birth defects did find a connection between raised temperatures and birth defects. In these cases, the mothers either had had prolonged fevers during early pregnancy or had spent long periods of time in hot tubs or saunas. These kinds of congenital problems are rare in Finland, however, where everyone takes saunas. A survey of the sauna habits of 100 pregnant Finnish women found that women who took saunas before pregnancy continued to do so when pregnant. There was a trend over the course of the 9 months of pregnancy to shorten the length of time in the sauna and to lower the temperature of the sauna. Once again, common sense leads women to protect themselves (27). Studies show that most women, even when they are not pregnant, simply don't stay in uncomfortably hot saunas or hot tubs for dangerously long lengths of time.

Practical suggestions for pregnant women to avoid overheating include these:

1. Don't exercise in hot, humid environments. Sometimes an air-conditioned health club or a pool may be the best way to beat the heat in southern climes.
2. Drink more fluid. The more fluids a woman consumes the more freely she will perspire, and the cooler she will be. Drinking enough fluids during pregnancy is also important to avoid dehydration, which has been associated with premature labor.
3. Stop exercising if you get too warm. As with many other things during pregnancy, comfort is the key. There is no reason to subject yourself to any risk, no matter how minimal, of overheating. A shorter, less intense workout may be a wise choice on warm days. Everyone who exercises tries to minimize heat stress, and the pregnant woman should be no exception.
4. Keep the sauna (or steam) at a comfortable temperature. This may be far below your normal level of comfort, especially as your pregnancy progresses.

A Neglected Area: What About the Right Foods During Pregnancy?

No research has been done on the nutritional requirements of physically active pregnant or breastfeeding women. According to Janet King, PhD, specialist in nutrition, we can only draw inferences from what we know about pregnant sedentary women and nonpregnant active women. We do know, for instance, that a woman's nutritional habits before and during pregnancy (and afterward, if she is breastfeeding) are critical for the health of both mother and child (15). The mother's weight gain will affect the weight of the baby at birth (i.e., heavier moms have heavier babies). Low-weight babies are often at risk of health and developmental problems.

Despite the evidence that pregnant and breast-feeding women need proper nutrition, many women are still tempted to "control their eating" during this time. Because women have been imbued with a cultural ideal of female slenderness, many still feel anxious about gaining weight, even if it is a normal and healthy amount. So, many women put themselves on a strict diet throughout their pregnancies.

Conventional wisdom has long encouraged this behavior by telling pregnant women they should only gain a certain amount of weight during pregnancy. In Western countries, this dates back to the 18th and 19th centuries when physicians thought they could make labor and delivery easier if babies were smaller at birth. Not only did they impose dietary controls on women to try to produce smaller babies, they even induced early labor (20).

After cesarean section became available as a delivery option, there was less concern about the size of the baby and, therefore, fewer attempts to restrict diet and weight gain. But, as nutritionists Kathryn Dohrman and Sally Ledermann note, weight gain was once again blamed at the beginning of the 20th century—this time for toxemia (5). Toxemia, a general term used to describe disorders of late pregnancy, is characterized by hypertension, proteinuria, and edema. Convulsions and coma may be associated with toxemia. Experts mistakenly believed that weight gain caused toxemia, when in reality, toxemia caused the weight gain through fluid retention. At the same time, scientists developed the mistaken theory that the fetus is a perfect parasite whose nutritional needs would always be met from the mother's stores or intake. Thus, women began to restrict their diets to prevent toxemia, thinking that the fetus would adjust to the lower food intake.

Today, although we know better, women are still restricting their diets—this time for a different reason. The myth that says women have to be thin to be attractive is alive and well, and larger women, pregnant or not, are seen as lacking in self-control. Despite the fact that it can be detrimental to both mother and baby, food restriction during pregnancy is culturally endorsed.

This leaves many women still searching for a guideline as to how much they are "allowed" to eat; unfortunately, most adult women in the United States are not in the habit simply of eating when they are hungry. There is no such thing as a "best" weight gain during pregnancy—that depends entirely on each individual. Factors to be considered include pre-pregnancy weight and level of physical activity. A thin woman may need to gain more than a heavier woman. Physically active women may need to be reminded to eat enough to cover the costs of fetal growth, added maternal tissue, and the energy needs of their greater physical activity.

When women in the Melpomene study of exercise during pregnancy were asked if they had made any changes in their health habits during their pregnancies, the majority indicated they were trying to improve their dietary and eating patterns. Some were eating more protein. Many had increased the amounts of calcium-rich dairy products they ate. Others had cut out junk foods.

They also noted that pregnancy often changed their eating habits, especially when physical changes begin to affect appetite. For example, morning sickness early in pregnancy, which may be due to high levels of chorionic gonadotropic hormone, made crackers seem more appetizing than eggs.

Some of the unpleasant side effects of pregnancy, such as nausea, heartburn, indigestion, and constipation are caused by an increase in the steroid progesterone. Progesterone causes the smooth muscles of the gastrointestinal tract to relax so that food moves through the stomach and bowels more slowly, often creating a feeling of fullness, heartburn, or nausea. Slower movement in the gut also means more water is absorbed by the intestines, a probable cause of constipation. Exercise is often recommended as a way to promote regularity, and the pregnant women in our study vouched for its effectiveness.

Progesterone is also responsible for the increase in appetite felt by pregnant women. But as pregnancy progresses and the uterus begins to displace other internal organs, some women prefer to eat several small meals rather than a few large meals. Women also need to be informed that the increased fatty deposits on hips, thighs, and abdomen, especially during the second trimester, are another natural result of increased progesterone.

Good nutrition means that we need to be concerned not only with the quantity of food but also with the quality of the diet. Research shows that some pregnant women can maintain their weight even at very low intake levels. Though the mechanism for this is unknown, it may be that a pregnant woman's metabolism becomes more efficient, allowing her to maintain her weight. Or pregnant women may instinctively decrease their levels of activity, therefore saving energy. We know from Melpomene research that recreational athletes tend to voluntarily reduce their exercise activities throughout their pregnancies.

The body seems to make the most of what it is fed during pregnancy. But again, the question arises, What if you add exercise to the equation? Will that change a woman's nutritional needs? Melpomene has the only data available on the nutritional habits of physically active pregnant and breast-feeding women (19). Based on diet histories and activity logs, we found that pregnant women runners consumed fewer calories than what would normally be required by their level of physical activity and had diets that were low in iron and calcium (below RDA standards). Yet these women were maintaining their weight, perhaps through the mechanisms already mentioned. The deficiency in iron in their diets might have been a problem, but the most of the women were taking iron supplements to compensate. Anemia is common in pregnancy, because there is an increase in blood volume without an equivalent rise in the number of red blood cells. In terms of calcium, it appears that metabolic and physiologic changes help the body conserve calcium during pregnancy (1). In general, for women who were getting enough calcium before pregnancy, supplements during pregnancy do not make much difference. However, diet logs show that most women do not meet

RDA requirements for calcium in their normal diets, so we usually suggest that they increase their intake (19).

We do not yet have enough information to know whether there are specific nutrient needs for pregnant women who exercise. To be on the safe side, women are advised to be sure their diets are high in vitamins and minerals. Nutrition from food sources is preferable to that from supplements.

Melpomene Research

Though there have been several new studies in the past 4 years, notably by Pat Kulpa, James Clapp, and their associates, women still need practical information (3, 4, 16, 17). To begin to fill that need, Melpomene Institute gathered information from a descriptive study of pregnant, exercising women in a natural, rather than a laboratory, setting. Begun in 1983, we asked 77 runners and 27 swimmers to complete a series of questionnaires during their terms. They recorded their medical histories, patterns of exercise, nutrition, discomfort, and finally, their labor and delivery experiences. We also followed a group of 27 nonexercising women so we could compare their experiences during pregnancy, labor, and delivery with those of the exercising women. At 2 months and 6 months after their babies were born, we checked up on each woman's health and exercise patterns as well as her child's health and development:

1. The women who exercised did not experience any more miscarriages or infant deaths than the general population.
2. Of the women who exercised, 22% delivered by cesarean section, which is comparable to the general population.
3. The women who exercised gained less weight than the women who did not exercise. On the average, runners gained 25 pounds, swimmers gained 27 pounds, and nonexercising women gained 31 pounds.
4. Labors were similar for all three groups.
5. The birth weights of all the infants were in the normal range. On the average, babies born to swimmers weighed 7 pounds 2 ounces, those of runners weighed 7 pounds 9 ounces, and those of nonexercising women weighed 7 pounds 14 ounces.
6. APGAR scores, a measure of newborn well-being, were similar for all groups.
7. The main benefits of exercising during pregnancy were psychological. As one woman wrote, "Exercise gives me an alive feeling—pregnancy is a natural state; you are limited, but by no means incapable. My spirits soared as I walked and dreamed and talked to our baby. You get more oxygen and so does the baby. Inactivity causes a vicious cycle of fatigue" (21, p. 115).
8. Runners decreased both their mileage and pace as their pregnancies progressed. Their average mileage per week in the first trimester was 21.2

miles at a pace of 8.87 minutes per mile. In the third trimester their average mileage was 7.5 miles per week at a pace of 10.68 minutes per mile.

9. Of the 77 runners, 41 continued to run into the third trimester. Only two swimmers stopped before the third trimester, one because of a sinus infection and the other because she was bothered by dry skin.

10. The majority of the women in the study felt exercise to be beneficial during pregnancy, even if they were not exercising on a regular basis.

What we learned from these women, and from a previous study conducted in 1981 of 195 women who ran during their pregnancies, is that neither the women nor their babies suffered negative consequences. In fact, from a psychological standpoint, it seems that the exercising women were actually better off than their nonexercising counterparts.

Melpomene research prompted us to develop some guidelines. They are among several sets of guidelines that have been developed for women wishing to exercise during pregnancy (24). Physicians frequently use the set issued by the American College of Obstetrics and Gynecology. The ACOG recommendations are conservative in nature, however, and were not created with an exercise-conditioned woman in mind.

Melpomene's recommendations, based specifically on the research we have done, are useful for the athletic woman who wants practical guidelines. They refer only to pregnant runners and swimmers and to women in maternal fitness programs. Few other physical activities have been studied, so specific guidelines for those activities await additional research.

Melpomene Institute Guidelines for Exercise During Pregnancy

These guidelines are appropriate for women without special medical histories but should be discussed with the appropriate health care professionals and modified as the pregnancy progresses.

GENERAL GUIDELINES FOR PREGNANT WOMEN

1. Discuss your exercise plans with your health care provider, especially if medical conditions might present problems (e.g., if you have a history of miscarriage).

2. Find out about special guidelines that may pertain to your own medical condition, for example, gestational diabetes; a booklet put out by the International Diabetes Center recommends exercise as a way to keep blood glucose levels at normal levels (10). Ask your health care provider about agencies or nonprofit groups that may distribute information on your condition.

3. Get psychological support for your decisions, whether you decide to exercise or not.

4. Wear comfortable clothing. Well-cushioned, stable shoes and a good support bra are important.

5. Listen to your body. ''No pain, no gain'' does *not* apply, especially when exercising during pregnancy.

6. Expect some discomfort. Learn all you can about exercising during pregnancy in order to have examples of how much discomfort is ''normal'' and what may be reason for concern.

7. Be flexible. Do not have preset goals for exercising during pregnancy. Be prepared to stop or switch to another form of exercise if you experience discomfort or fatigue.

8. Stop exercising and check with your instructor or health care provider if you have any questions about your health or a change in your condition. Seek immediate advice if you have pain, dizziness, lightheadedness, sudden confusion, lack of coordination, nausea or vomiting, vaginal bleeding, breathlessness lasting more than 10 minutes, rapid heart rate 10 minutes after aerobic exercise, or prolonged fatigue.

9. Be alert to changing conditions in your pregnancy that may call for you to change or stop your exercise, such as early thinning (effacement) or opening (dilation) of the cervix, or finding out you are pregnant with twins.

10. Avoid an anaerobic (breathless) pace. While competition may remain an option, you should expect a decrease in your times. You must control your own pace. Many women told Melpomene that they gave up competition because they were tempted to overdo. Your ability to compete will vary depending on pre-pregnancy patterns.

11. Avoid overheating and dehydration. Drink plenty of fluids before, during, and after your exercise routine.

12. Avoid injury to joints and ligaments. Take the time to adequately warm up and cool down. Avoid stretching to the point of maximum resistance. Pay attention to your balance and posture.

13. Be sure to get adequate rest. Exercising to the point of exhaustion or chronic fatigue is detrimental to both mother and fetus.

14. Be sure to meet your nutritional needs. Your diet should provide the extra energy you need for exercise, as well as the nutritional foundation for pregnancy itself. A healthy weight gain is a good indicator that you are eating enough. Iron and calcium supplements, which are normally recommended to pregnant women, are also important.

15. Once you start, stay in the habit of exercising. Exercise 20 to 30 minutes at least three times a week, preferably on alternate days. Irregular or infrequent exercise can lead to injury and fatigue.

GUIDELINES FOR RUNNERS

1. Overheating or not drinking enough can cause serious problems. Run in the coolest part of the day and wear appropriate clothing. Be sure to drink plenty of fluids before a run—even if you have to stop for bathroom breaks more often.

2. Take the time for adequate warm-up and cool-down before and after running.

3. Wear comfortable clothing. Well-cushioned, stable running shoes and a good support bra are important.

4. Some women find a lightweight maternity girdle offers support for back and ligaments. Maternity support stockings also help some women feel more comfortable.

5. Be willing to modify your runs in terms of intensity, frequency, and speed. Increasing weight and fatigue may dictate shorter, slower runs and eliminating hills and speed work.

6. Stop and walk, if necessary. You may feel a need to slow down because of heat, ligament or joint pains, Braxton-Hicks contractions (incidental contractions, not related to labor), or other indicators.

7. Run with others, if possible. Always let people know when and where you are running. Carry some money, in case you need to phone someone to take you home.

8. Be kind to your back. Pay attention to your posture and balance. You may want to experiment with posture changes that make you more stable while running.

9. Modify or stop your exercise program if medical conditions dictate (e.g., early dilation, bag of waters leaking, etc.).

GUIDELINES FOR SWIMMERS

1. Be sure the water and air temperatures are comfortable. Leave the water if you feel uncomfortably chilly or overheated.

2. Take time to warm up. Try doing some stretching on land or in the water. Start off swimming slowly until you loosen up.

3. Wear a comfortable suit. Some maternity suits may be too heavy when wet for easy swimming. Experiment with different fabrics, styles, and sizes until you find something that gives you support where you need it and in which you can swim well.

4. Swim according to your abilities. Use moderation, and be sure to breathe properly.

5. Avoid diving, jumping into the water feet first, and water-skiing while you are pregnant.

6. If you experience contractions, leg cramps, or joint pain, be ready to stop swimming, or change your swimming style (e.g., use different strokes, kicks, or turns).

7. Do not swim alone, but do try to avoid crowds.

8. Modify or stop your exercise program if medical conditions dictate (e.g., early dilation, bag of waters leaking, etc.).

Recently in an excellent paper, Clapp and Dickstein (4) suggested another way to deal with the practical aspects of exercise and pregnancy. They recommend that an individualized, flexible approach be established for each pregnant woman and discuss four management principles for health care providers:

1. Initiate frank, state-of-the-art discussions on what is known about exercise and pregnancy.
2. Set goals and plan monitoring techniques.
3. Establish general, practical considerations including the amount of activity, nutrition, and so on.
4. Indicate what precautions and limitations should be followed until further information is available.

These guidelines and management principles are most appropriate for women who have been athletic before pregnancy. What about the woman who decides to become physically active when she learns she is pregnant? An increasing number of women have decided that pregnancy is the time to modify their lifestyles for the best possible outcome. Also, some hospitals and health clubs target pregnant women as a good market for fitness classes. As a result, exercise classes, including some available on videocassette, became quite common in the mid- to late-80s. No thorough, independent evaluation of *any* of these programs has yet been done. Though some of these classes are excellent, some are not. The many questions we received from women and health professionals prompted Melpomene to suggest some evaluation guidelines to pregnant women.

Melpomene Recommendations
for Evaluating Maternal Fitness Programs

Before you begin a maternal fitness program, consult your doctor or midwife. Discuss your exercise needs in light of your medical history and your current physical condition. Get medical approval before you begin. Then select a sound exercise program with a qualified instructor. *Be choosy.*

At the heart of a good exercise program is a well-qualified instructor. Look for an instructor

- who is sensitive to the health education needs of pregnant women,
- who has an extensive background as an exercise instructor,
- who has training that includes information specific to pregnancy and childbirth,

- who will assess and monitor your health and fitness level and modify the exercise program to reflect your needs, and
- who will teach you to identify signs and symptoms of potential problems, ways to reduce the risk of injury, how to monitor your heart rate, and the importance of fluid replacement.

In addition to a well-qualified instructor, a good prenatal exercise program will include these basic components:

1. *Warm-up period* to protect joints and muscles from injury and to slowly increase breathing and heart rates
2. *Muscle strengthening exercises* to build and maintain tone and strength
3. *Cardiovascular conditioning exercises* to build and maintain heart and lung strength and endurance (*Note*: The American College of Obstetricians and Gynecologists recommends that your heart rate not exceed 140 beats per minute.)
4. *Cool-down period* to safely ease breathing and heart rates to a lower level of activity
5. *Relaxation techniques* to identify and release muscle tension and help metabolism return to normal
6. *Health education and discussion period* to foster a supportive atmosphere for the discussion of concerns related to pregnancy

MELPOMENE CHECKLIST FOR EVALUATING AN EXERCISE PROGRAM

Call several programs to determine which ones could meet your needs. We recommend asking these questions:

_____ What are the goals of the exercise program? How do you evaluate whether these goals are being met?

_____ How is a typical class session structured from beginning to end?

_____ Are participants required to check their heart rates and drink fluids?

_____ What are the qualifications of the instructor?

_____ Is a medical permit or medical history required of participants?

_____ What is the maximum class size?

_____ Is there any opportunity to evlauate the program and the instructor?

_____ What is the cost of the program? Are scholarships available?

_____ What is the registration procedure?

_____ Are potential participants permitted to observe the class?

_____ Is a postnatal program offered?

_____ Is child care available? What is the cost?

_____ What is the availability of medical help if there is an emergency?

Select one or two programs and ask permission to observe a class. Meet with the instructor and talk with class members. Then choose the program that best meets your needs. And remember: Once you begin, keep exercising. Regular exercise can increase your flexibility while strengthening your heart and lungs, bones, and muscles.

The Effects of Exercise on Labor and Delivery

Various historical sources infer that an active pregnancy is apt to make for an easier labor and delivery. Research data to support these suggestions are not as clear. Some researchers have suggested that female athletes might have more difficulty with labor and delivery because of their "overly" developed musculature. Others believe just the opposite.

Early researchers reported that elite, Olympic-caliber women athletes had easy deliveries with short second stages and a few cesarean sections (7). More recent studies of women with first-time pregnancies showed that those who took part in strength training and aerobic maternal fitness programs also had a lower-than-average number of c-sections, but their labors were of average length. A third set of results comes from Pat Kulpa, an obstetrician and gynecologist who studied women who engaged in regular aerobic exercise and some who did not. Dr. Kulpa and her colleagues found that for first-time mothers, there was no difference in c-section rates between exercising and nonexercising women; however, second stage labor was shorter for women who exercised (16).

Another conflict in results occurred when researchers examined whether exercise puts women at risk for premature births. James Clapp found that women who exercised aerobically into the third trimester not only gained less weight and had lighter babies but also delivered their babies earlier than women who had stopped exercising before the third trimester (3). This association of gestational length, maternal weight gain, and birth weight with exercise has not been duplicated by other researchers (30).

The conflicts in findings about exercise, labor, and delivery reflect some of the problems in coming to uniform conclusions about possible benefits as well as problems of exercising while pregnant. It is hard to predict the course of labor, because each women's experience is as individual as she is, and exercise, being only one variable, may not play the deciding role.

Considerations for Postpartum Exercise

While researchers struggle with the question of whether it is safe to exercise during pregnancy, women continue to get pregnant and some continue to exercise. After their babies are born, they wonder about resuming exercise and about regaining their pre-pregnancy levels of activity and fitness.

Recently the media has played up the postpregnancy athletic performances of a few elite women. Suddenly there is talk of "the training effect of pregnancy."

In an absurd leap, we have moved from wondering whether women should exercise during pregnancy to recommending pregnancy as a way to improve athletic ability. Aside from the anecdotal accounts of people like Ingrid Kristiansen and Mary Decker Slaney, however, there is not much data to back up this kind of recommendation.

Most women are advised to wait 4 to 6 weeks after an uncomplicated vaginal delivery before they start exercising again. In Melpomene's research, and from our conversations with physically active women, we know that many women do not wait this long.

In general, it is helpful to remind women that their bodies took 9 months to change and that those changes are not going to reverse themselves overnight. Relaxin-softened connective tissues in the pelvic floor and the fascia that connected these muscles stretched during pregnancy. Because its former shape cannot be regained, women should be encouraged to strengthen these muscles by doing Kegel exercises. These exercises may also help lessen the problem of urinary incontinence that many women experience after delivery, especially during weight-bearing activities such as running.

Finding time to exercise is a lesson in creative time-management for the new mother. If she chooses to breast-feed (as did more than 90% of the women in Melpomene's studies of exercise and pregnancy), there will be additional constraints in scheduling. We advise women to feed first, then exercise, to avoid the discomfort of overly full breasts. For the first few months, however, arranging child care to meet a baby's changing schedule may be as stressful an exercise as women can manage!

Besides practical problems like child care, breast-feeding women are also concerned about nutrition. Though they want to eat and drink enough to maintain a good milk supply, many are eager to return to their former weights. In our research, we found that women tend to greatly increase their exercise levels in postpartum, while eating fewer calories than they did during pregnancy. Many asked us, ''Is it all right to be losing weight while I'm breast-feeding? Is the baby getting all the nutrients needed for growth?'' (21, p. 138). Overall, we feel that infant weight gain, not maternal weight loss, should be used as the measure of appropriate maternal diet by breast-feeding women. It is also true that while a woman is breast-feeding her body will not let her lose weight too quickly. Breast-feeding slows the rate of weight loss, perhaps to conserve resources for the baby. Eventually, the breast-feeding women in our study did lose all the weight they had gained, but it took between 3 to 9 months after the birth. Women who were not breast-feeding lost it faster, but they also tended to be more active and to eat less (19).

Some researchers have expressed concern about the relation between breast-feeding and osteoporosis, a thinning of the bones that is a major health concern for women. The average woman in this country does not get enough calcium in her diet, and according to our research, this is also true for most women who exercise during pregnancy and while breast-feeding.

A recent study by Gary Chan at the University of Utah Medical Center found that sedentary women who breast-fed for more than 6 months showed bone loss even though they had calcium intakes above the RDA (1). How might these women have fared if they had been exercising? Recent evidence suggests that exercise may actually increase bone mass (29). It is important that researchers continue to explore the relationships between exercise, calcium intake, bone mass, and breast-feeding.

Another postpartum reality for many new mothers is depression, fatigue, and a feeling of being overwhelmed by their new role. At 2 months postpartum, about half of the women in Melpomene's study said they had experienced the "postpartum blues." This depression hit both exercising and nonexercising women. One woman recalled, "During the first week, I was very tired, and I couldn't stop crying" (21, p. 139). At this point, we do not know enough about the possible influence of exercise on postpartum depression.

When asked if they felt fully recovered (back to "being themselves") after 2 months, only 53% of the runners, 60% of the swimmers, and 50% of the sedentary women answered yes. Whether this refers to mental or physical recovery we do not know. All but one woman in the study reported themselves to be in good or excellent health, though many may still have been trying to recapture pre-pregnancy activity levels or weights.

Exercising After the Baby Is Born

After the births of their babies, most women are eager to resume pre-pregnancy activities, including exercise. Many come to Melpomene for guidelines or precautions. Unfortunately, we have little hard data, because very little research has been done on women who resume exercise after delivery. What we do pass along is information we have gleaned from the participants in our exercise and pregnancy research.

We encourage women to discuss their exercise plans with their health care providers and urge special precautions for those who have undergone cesarean sections. For those who had uncomplicated vaginal deliveries, we suggest several preexercise considerations.

GUIDELINES FOR POST-DELIVERY EXERCISE

1. If you had an episiotomy, you will probably want to wait until all soreness is gone before you begin exercising vigorously.

2. Because you cannot use tampons for about 4 weeks, you may find it more convenient to wait until bleeding has stopped.

3. If you exercise and begin to bleed heavily or with bright red blood, you should give yourself more time to recover.

4. Because your hormonal balance does not stabilize for several weeks, be aware of continuing joint laxity (looseness).

5. Fatigue is a common problem for new mothers. If you are tired, it might be better to take a nap than to exercise. This is especially true if you are nursing.

6. Nursing mothers should remember to drink lots of fluids.

7. For women who are breast-feeding, good breast support during exercise is important.

8. Many women are surprised to find they are incontinent after delivery. This can last for several months and can be best corrected by doing Kegel exercises.

9. Sometimes the cumulative effects of pregnancy, labor, and carrying a baby lead to back pain. Watch your posture. Abdominal strengthening exercises may help.

10. Take time to warm up and stretch before exercise, and give yourself an ample cool-down and relaxation period after exercise.

11. Be sure to practice good nutritional habits. Though it may be inconvenient to eat properly when you have a small baby and a busy schedule, it's worth the effort. There is also no reason to rush into weight loss, especially if you are nursing. Breast-feeding women lose weight more slowly, because of the body's protective mechanisms.

12. Scheduling will take some juggling. Many women find it difficult to make child-care arrangements or to find time to exercise in the early months.

13. Relax and enjoy yourself! A brisk walk with your baby may be all you can do at first. As you develop a routine and can fit in regular exercise, you will find it provides important time for yourself.

Overview of Exercise and Pregnancy

Attitudes toward women and their bodies are changing. Pregnancy is no longer viewed as a diseased state or a time when women are expected to be incapacitated. Few women "take to their beds" when they become pregnant; instead, many are simply buying a larger pair of workout clothes and continuing to exercise.

Kulpa's research indicates that cardiovascular fitness can actually be improved by exercising while pregnant. Even so, many of the specific questions relating to physiology and the effects of exercise during pregnancy are still unanswered. Yet women who are pregnant today, particularly athletic women, are not content to wait until science has "all the answers."

It is also important to offer information that will help each woman make a personal decision on exercise during pregnancy. Because of our society's emphasis on fitness, athletic women may feel as much pressure to exercise during pregnancy as not to exercise. Pregnant women also feel responsible for their decisions and need professional and personal support. Women should be encouraged to take an active role in managing their pregnancies but also be reminded that not everything can be controlled. No one can guarantee a perfect pregnancy or a wished-for pregnancy outcome. No matter how carefully women and their health care professionals try to make healthy choices, the unexpected can happen. Exercise is only one of many variables, known and unknown, that can influence the course of a pregnancy, and evidence does not show that it should be held responsible for negative outcomes.

Over and over again, women have told us that exercise helped make their pregnancies enjoyable. Many women have also told us that the questions and adjustments they made in their physical activities during pregnancy helped them remember how to enjoy exercise. Pregnancy is a time to think about priorities. As long as a woman is prepared to adapt her exercise patterns as her pregnancy progresses, she will benefit from physical activity during pregnancy.

Summary

1. Most women who exercised before becoming pregnant should be able to continue to do so. Changes in intensity, frequency, and type of exercise are to be expected, especially during later stages of pregnancy.
2. The health of both the fetus and the mother are concerns that need to be addressed in making decisions about physical activity during pregnancy.
3. Women who have not exercised before pregnancy may find that they can succesfully begin an exercise program *if* they do so cautiously without overexertion.
4. Health care providers need more information to properly advise pregnant women regarding their levels of exercise.
5. One's fitness level is not lost during pregnancy, but neither is there any evidence that pregnancy enhances fitness.
6. Women should avoid becoming overheated when pregnant by exercising during the cooler hours of the day in warmer months and drinking plenty of fluids.
7. Women reported that their primary reason for exercising during pregnancy was the feeling of psychological well-being.
8. Although women are typically cautioned against exercising during the postpartum period (the first 4-6 weeks post delivery), there have been no adverse anatomic, physiologic, or psychologic effects noted to date and more data need to be obtained.

Note

Parts of this chapter are adapted from *The Bodywise Woman*, a publication by the Melpomene Institute staff and researchers, and are used here by permission.

References

1. Chan, G.M. Human milk calcium and phosphate levels of mothers delivering term and preterm infants. J. Pediat. Gastroent. Nutr. 1:201-205; 1982.

2. Chavasse, P.H.; Stevenson, S.H. Wife and mother, or information for every woman. Philadelphia: H.J. Smith & Company; 1888.
3. Clapp, J. Exercise in pregnancy: a brief clinical review. Fetal Med. Rev. 2:89-101; 1990.
4. Clapp, J.; Dickstein, S. Endurance exercise and pregnancy outcome. Med. Sci. Sports Exerc. 16(6):556-562; 1984.
5. Dohrmann, J.; Lederman, S.A. Weight gain in pregnancy. J. Obstet. Gynecol. Neonat. Nurs. Nov/Dec:446-453; 1986.
6. Dressendorfer, R.H.; Goodlin, R.C. Fetal heart rate response to maternal exercise testing. Physician & Sportsmed. 8(11):91-94; 1980.
7. Erdelyi, G. Gynecological survey of female athletes. J. Sports Med. Phys. Fit. 12(3):174; 1962.
8. Exercise during pregnancy and postnatal period. American College of Obstetrics and Gynecology. (Press Release) 1985 May.
9. Fast, V.; Shapiro, D.; Ducommun, E.; Friedmann, L.; Bouklas, T.; Floman, Y. Low back pain in pregnancy. Spine. 12(4):368-371; 1987.
10. Franz, M.; Cooper, N.; Mullen, L.; Birk, R.S.; Hollander, P. Gestational diabetes: guidelines for a safe pregnancy and a healthy baby. Wayzata, MN: International Diabetes Center; 1988.
11. Hall, D.; Kaufmann, D. Effects of aerobic and strength conditioning on pregnancy outcome. Am. J. Obstet. Gynecol. 157(s):1199-1203, 1987.
12. Heckman, J. Managing musculoskeletal problems in pregnant patients. J. Musculoskel. Med. 7(8):29-37; 1990 August.
13. Jones, R.; Botti, J.; Anderson, W.; Bennett, N. Thermoregulation during aerobic exercise in pregnancy. Obstet. Gynecol. 65(3):340-345, 1985.
14. Jovanovik, L.; Kessler, A.; Peterson, C. Human maternal and fetal responses to graded exercise. J. Appl. Physiol. 58(5):1719-1722; 1985.
15. Kris-Etherton, P.M. Nutrition and the exercising. Nutr. Today, 21(2):6-18; 1986.
16. Kulpa, P. Exercise during pregnancy. Fam. Prac. Recert. 11(1):35-56; 1989 January.
17. Kulpa, P.; White, B.; Visschler, R. Aerobic exercise in pregnancy. Am. J. Obstet. Gynecol. 156(6):1395-1403; 1987.
18. Lee, V.; Lutter, J. Exercise and pregnancy: choices, concerns, and recommendations. In: Wilder, E. ed. Obstetric and gynecological physical therapy. NY: Churchill Livingstone, 1988; 175-198.
19. Lee, V., Koltes, L.; Schultz, B.; Trammell, J.; Slaven, J.; Lutter, J. New look at nutrition for the active pregnant woman and breastfeeding mother. Melpomene Rep. 4(2):19-24; 1985.
20. Luke, B. Maternal nutrition. Boston: Little Brown & Company; 1979.
21. Melpomene Institute Staff and Researchers. The bodywise woman. New York: Prentice Hall; 1990.
22. Morris, N.; Osborn, S.B.; Wright, H.P.; Hart, A. Effective uterine bloodflow during exercise in normal and pre-eclamptic pregnancies. Lancet 2:481-484; 1956.
23. Paolone, A.; Shangold, M.; Paul, D.; Minnitti, J.; Weiner, S. Fetal heart rate measurement during maternal exercise—avoidance of artifact. Med. Sci. Sports Exerc. 19(6):605-609; 1987.
24. Richards, D. Guidelines for exercise during pregnancy. Occup. Health Nurs. 33(10):508-509; 1985.
25. Sady, S.P.; Carpenter, M.W.; Thompson, P.S.; Sady, M.A.; Haydon, B.; Coustan, D.R. Cardiovascular response to cycle exercise during and after pregnancy. J. Appl. Physiol. 66(1):336-341; 1989.

26. Slavin, J.; Lutter, J.M.; Cushman, S.; Lee, V. Pregnancy and exercise. Sport Science Perspective for Women. Proceedings from USOC conference, Colorado Springs, Nov. 1985.

27. Uhari, M.; Mustonen, A. Sauna habits of Finnish women during pregnancy. BMJ. 1:1216; 1979.

28. Wallace, A.M.; Engstrom, J.L. Effects of aerobic exercise on the pregnant woman, fetus, and pregnancy outcome. J. Nurse Midwif. 32(5):277-290; 1987.

29. Wardlaw, G.; Pike, A. Effect of lactation on peak adult shaft and ultradistal forearm bone mass in women. Am. J. Clin. Nutr. 44:283-286; 1986.

30. Wong, S.C.; McKenzie, D.C. Cardiorespiratory fitness during pregnancy and its effect on outcome. Int. J. Sports Med. 8:79-83; 1987.

CHAPTER 7

•

Oral Contraceptives and the Athletic Female

Pat J. Kulpa

Following the presentation of the previous three papers, consensual validation process, and the evening provocative issue session, it became apparent that the role of oral contraceptives in the athletic female was an extremely controversial issue. It was agreed that there was a need for an additional paper about oral contraceptives and the athletic female. Dr. Pat Kulpa was kind enough to fill this need for our readers.

Oral contraceptives are the most popular nonsurgical method of family planning of United States women aged 15 to 44 (23% of these women, 1). Other popular contraceptive options, in order of decreasing usage, are condoms (12%), spermicides (4%), withdrawal (4%), diaphragms (3%), periodic abstinence (3%), intrauterine devices (IUDs) (2%), and douches (1%). Another recent, reversible option is Norplant, a subdermal progestin implant (levonorgestrel). Contraceptive practices of athletic women differ from those of sedentary women in their lower use of oral contraceptives and intrauterine devices and higher use of barrier methods (26). For example, female runners prefer to use the diaphragm (6).

An ideal method of birth control does not exist. Some female athletes are concerned about the potential side effects and complications associated with oral contraceptives, though only 2% to 3% of all sexually active women of reproductive age have absolute contraindications to use of the pill (Table 7.1), and exercise is not a relative contraindication. Their concern originates from the earlier use of higher dosage birth control pills containing 100 micrograms or more of estrogen. The newer birth control pills also contain less progestin, which minimizes side effects. About 1 of every 750 women on low dose oral contraceptives avoids

Table 7.1   Absolute Oral Contraceptive Contraindications

Condition	Dialogues	Precis
Undiagnosed abnormal uterine bleeding	x	x
Breast cancer	x	
Pregnancy (known or suspected)	x	
Woman smoker over age 35		x
Venous vascular disease		x
Deep vein thrombophlebitis	x	x
Thromboembolic disease	x	x
Lupus erythematous with vascular signs		x
Sickle cell disease		x
Arterial vascular disease		x
Coronary heart disease	x	x
Cerebral vascular disease	x	x
Estrogen-dependent cancers	x	
Active liver disease (benign or malignant tumor)		x
Intestinal malabsorption disease		x
Diabetes with vascular complication	x	
Uncontrolled hypertension	x	
Concomitant use of the drug rifampin for tuberculosis	x	

Note. Modified from American College of Obstetrics and Gynecology Precis IV (1990) and Dialogues in Contraception 6 (University of Southern California, 1987).

a serious disease that she would have had if she were not on the pill (1). Indeed, it may prevent an estimated 50,000 unnecessary hospitalizations in the United Sattes each year (1).

Oligomenorrheic and amenorrheic problems need to be evaluated before one starts oral contraceptives. According to some, women with hypothalamic-pituitary dysfunction or failure are better off avoiding the use of hormonal steroids for contraception (17). After their amenorrhea or other menstrual irregularities have been worked up, some women find that oral contraceptives regulate their menstrual cycles. There is no evidence that the suppression of the hypothalamic-pituitary-ovarian axis by the pill will cause future menstrual problems in an amenorrheic athlete. Whatever menstrual pattern the athlete had before using the birth control pill may resume when she stops taking it. The majority of women with exercise-induced amenorrhea resume menses and may ovulate before their first menstrual bleeding. The female athlete's fear of getting pregnant during a critical time in her training and competition is a legitimate concern. Contraceptive counseling is essential to eliminate any misunderstandings about the menstrual cycle and the use of oral contraceptives. Of course, the choice of contraceptive method for the female athlete depends on her coital frequency, medical history, and fertility plans.

Noncontraceptive Benefits of Oral Contraceptive Use

There are many beneficial effects of the low dose birth control pill that should interest the female athlete (Table 7.2). First, the pill may regulate her menstrual cycle. (Again it is vital that an adequate workup is done for any menstrual irregularity found in the female athlete before putting her on the pill.) Second, after being on the pill through several cycles, it will prevent unpredictable, heavy menstrual bleeding. The reduced menstrual flow and shorter menstrual cycle will help to minimize further iron loss and prevent iron deficiency anemia.

In particular, young female adolescent athletes may benefit from the pill. Due to the immaturity of their hypothamalic-pituitary-ovarian axis, dysfunctional uterine bleeding is common. The convenience of scheduled short menses with reduced menstrual flow and reduced dysmenorrhea, along with the contraceptive benefit of the pill make it an appropriate choice for the teenage athlete. There is no evidence that birth control pills interfere with growth after menarche. Using

Table 7.2   Noncontraceptive Health Benefits of Oral Contraceptives

Regulation of menstrual cycles

Prevention of dysfunctional uterine bleeding

Prevention of iron deficiency anemia

Decreased endometrial cancer (50%)

Decreased endometrial hyperplasia

Decreased fibroids (30%)

Prevention of osteoporosis from estrogen deficiency

Fewer functional ovarian cysts

Decreased ovarian cancer (40-80%)

Fewer ectopic pregnancies

Decreased pelvic inflammatory disease (PID)

Less dysmenorrhea

Less premenstrual tension

Decreased benign breast disease

Less gynecologic surgery

Decreased rheumatoid arthritis

Note. Modified from American College of Obstetrics and Gynecology Precis IV (1990) and Dialogues in Contraception 6 (University of Southern California, 1987).

low dose oral contraceptives only to manipulate menses around scheduled athletic events is inadvisable, except for elite world class athletes (21).

By eliminating chronic anovulatory cycles, oral contraceptives also reduce the risk of endometrial hyperplasia and endometrial cancer. The 50% risk reduction of endometrial cancer appears to be related to the duration of use (>2 years use; 25). As a result of the antiestrogenic action of the progestin in the pill, the endometrium becomes less thick, and pill users are less likely to develop menorrhagia, irregular menses, and intermenstrual spotting. This may prevent multiple visits to the doctor's office because of abnormal uterine bleeding or for endometrial samplings. Pills also prevent further growth of uterine fibroids and may help women avoid unnecessary hysterectomies (23). These factors play an important role in the health status of nonsmoking women over age 40.

The hypoestrogenic amenorrheic athlete is protected against osteopenia while on oral contraceptives. In the new oral contraceptive formulations, containing one of the two synthetic estrogens (ethinylestradiol or ethinylestradiol-3 methyl ether, i.e., mestranol), 30 or 35 mirograms of ethinylestradiol is nearly equivalent to 2.5 milligrams of conjugated equine estrogen found in some estrogen replacement regimens (12). The usual dosage of .625 milligrams of conjugated equine estrogen in some hormone replacement therapies is only one-fifth as potent as the estrogen in the oral contraeptive. This dosage is the minimum amount needed to protect women against osteoporosis (8). Of course, if the female athlete is not sexually active, hormonal replacement therapy would be preferable to use of an oral contraceptive.

Few studies have looked at the prophylactic effect on bone density associated with low dose oral contraceptive use. One study found no significant measurable effect on bone mineral density (2). Larger studies involving direct bone mineral density measurements and monitoring of calcium intake will be needed to confirm this theory.

Whether the pill increases bone density is controversial. One study measured spine bone mineral density using dual photon absorptiometry and reported a 1% increase in bone mineral for each year of exposure to oral contraceptives (in 30- to 50-microgram dosages) in a group of former users of oral contraceptives (9). This study suggests that oral contraceptives may play a role in prevention of osteoporosis, perhaps by allowing a woman to maximize her genetic bone density potential while on the pill and thus have denser bones at menopause. This study also found that long-term use of oral contraceptives (an average of 10.2 years) showed a beneficial effect on bone mass only during early menopause (i.e., the first 2 years).

The perimenopausal woman experiences anovulatory cycles and luteal phase insufficiency, results of inadequate progesterone. Progesterone receptors have also been found on bone (16). This suggests that the loss of progesterone during the perimenopausal years may also contribute to a woman's bone loss before the accelerated bone loss during menopause. Thus, the use of low dose oral contraceptives may serve theoretically to protect a woman from osteopenia during the perimenopausal period. As long as there is no medical contraindication, she may continue using the pill until she switches over to hormone replacement and therapy at menopause.

Ovulatory suppression by the oral contraceptive reduces the incidence of functional ovarian cysts. This may reduce the risk of adnexal accident or torsion of the cyst during an athletic event as well as the need for surgical intervention. This same mechanism explains the 50% reduction in the rate of ovarian cancer often seen in pill users (11).

Oral contraceptives decrease the occurrence of pelvic inflammatory disease (PID) or clinical salpingitis, as well as ectopic pregnancy. The pill must be taken for more than 1 year to confer protection against PID. It does this by reducing the menstrual flow, which decreases the availability of a culture medium for pathogens. Also, the thicker cervical mucus caused by the pill makes it difficult for pathogens to penetrate the cervical canal. Because the pill decreases cervical dilation at midcycle and at menstruation, it also reduces the likelihood of penetration by the pathogens. However, it does increase the incidence of chlamydial cervicitis.

Dysmenorrhea is caused by myometrial ischemia during myometrial contractions induced by prostraglandins (PGE and PGF_{2a}). Dysmenorrhea is independent of the physical activity level. A review on menstrual discomfort and exercise found no substantial evidence that athletic women had less dysmenorrhea than inactive women (10). Nor did exercise alleviate painful menstruation. In some cases where antiprostaglandin synthetase inhibitors (NSAIDS) fail to relieve primary dysmenorrhea, use of the birth control pill may help. The pill's effect on a woman's dysmenorrhea may improve her coordination and reduce the risk of traumatic injury during competition (13). The pill relieves dysmenorrhea by decreasing the amount of menstrual flow, thus requiring less prostaglandin. The pill may not help secondary dysmenorrhea caused by an underlying pelvic pathology. (Diagnosis of primary dysmenorrhea should be based on a woman's menstrual history and a physical exam.)

The presence of premenstrual symptoms (abdominal bloating, breast tenderness and swelling, weight gain, fatigue, joint pain, constipation, headache, and mood swings) could potentially interfere with athletic performance. Nonmedical therapies such as conditioning exercise have been shown to decrease premenstrual symptoms (18). A change in a woman's dietary patterns and lifestyle habits may ease her premenstrual symptoms. When nonmedical therapies fail, oral contraceptives may be used, because premenstrual symptoms may indicate ovulatory cycles. Thus, ovulation suppression caused by the pill may alleviate premenstrual symptoms and dysmenorrhea. However, there is no single treatment that works for all women with premenstrual symptoms.

The glandular tissue in the breast also responds to the cyclic change of the menstrual cycle. The volume of the breast can increase as much as 40% during the premenstrual phase (19). Premenstrual breast tenderness and enlargement can be avoided by use of the appropriate pill. Other regimens, like salt restriction and use of diuretics, are not acceptable options for the female athlete. Avoiding excessive intake of caffeine and nicotine also may provide symptomatic relief.

Pill use (2 years or more) and the progestin component in the pill also decreases the incidence of fibrocystic and fibroadenomatous breast disease (14). Enlarged breast cysts and breast masses resulting from these diseases, along with unnecessary breast biopsies, may be prevented. A recent study showed no evidence of an overall increased risk of breast cancer with oral contraceptive usage (22). This study included women with family histories of breast cancer, benign breast disease, early menarche, or late menopause. There may be a breast cancer-oral contraceptive relationship that varies according to age at cancer diagnosis (27). This epidemiological study shows a slightly increased risk of breast cancer (odds ratio 1.4) among women aged 20 to 34 years when compared with women of the same ages who never used birth control pills. A slightly decreased risk (odds ratio 0.9) of breast cancer was found in women aged 45 to 54 years. This new data gave no reason to change prescribing practices regarding the pill, especially as it relates to risks of breast cancer.

Depending on the progestin dose, potency, and type, the beneficial effects of the estrogen in low dose oral contraceptives on the lipid profile is clear (4). Estrogen increases high-density lipoprotein cholesterol, the cardioprotective fraction, and lowers low-density lipoprotein cholesterol, the atherogenic fraction. Whether these changes in metabolic risk markers for coronary heart disease point to a decrease in atherosclerosis is yet to be seen.

Negative Effects of Oral Contraceptive Use

The pill does not cause cervical cancer per se. Nor does it protect a woman from sexually transmitted diseases, such as human papillomavirus (HPV) and human immune deficiency virus (HIV). Of recent concern is the interrelationship of cervical dysplasia and cancer to the human papillomavirus and the role oral contraceptives may play in the oncogenic expression of those viruses (15). This is why it is essential that women who are using the pill have yearly Pap tests.

Conditioning exercise has a positive effect on the cardiovascular system that offsets any potential negative effects of oral contraceptives on lipid metabolism (5). Reducing the major coronary heart disease risk factors (i.e., elevated cholesterol, hypertension, severe obesity, cigarette smoking, diabetes mellitus, history of stroke or thromboembolic disease) and thoroughly documenting any family history of premature coronary heart disease should be top priority. Oral contraceptive users over the age of 35 who smoke and users of any age who have any preexisting vascular disease have a significantly increased risk of arterial cardiovascular disease. Thus, to reduce a woman's risks, changes in diet, exercise, and smoking habits should be made before oral contraceptives are prescribed. A woman with a relative contraindication for the pill or who has concurrent medical conditions should be closely monitored (Table 7.3). A woman may continue taking oral contraceptives until she reaches menopause as long as she does not smoke or develop any vascular disease.

Table 7.3   Relative Oral Contraceptive Contraindications

Hypertension (if diastolic pressure is > 90)

Hyperlipidemia

Gallbladder disease

Migraine headaches

Depression

Hepatitis, impaired liver function, hepatomegaly

Oligomenorrhea or amenorrhea

Renal disease

Abnormal glucose tolerance

Recent major elective surgery (less than 4 weeks postoperation)

Note. Modified from American College of Obstetrics and Gynecology Precis IV (1990) and Dialogues in Contraception 6 (University of Southern California, 1987).

Oral Contraceptives and Athletic Performance

Little is known about how the various phases of the menstrual cycle and oral contraceptives can affect exercise performance in trained women. In 1987 the International Olympic Committee banned use of birth controls pills during competition because of their potential ergogenic effect. It was thought that the progestin used in the pill had metabolic by-products that could mask other anabolic steroids or could give an anabolic steroid effect. The progestins in oral contraceptives belong to a class of synthetic sex steroids that are related to 19-nortestosterone. The majority of birth control pills contain the less androgenic 19-norprogestogen (norethindrone derivatives). Norgestrel and levonorgesterol are the other progestogens found in the same pills, and they are 5 to 20 times more potent than norethidrone and its derivatives. The androgenic potency is dose-related. The anabolic action of birth control pills has not been studied. Many of the testosterone derivatives of the anabolic steroids have been developed in attempts to dissociate the androgenic effects from the anabolic actions of the steroids. This may not be possible, because the steroids appear to be mediated through the same receptor complex; that is, the target tissue, rather than the drug itself, appears to be the important behavioral determinant (20). Compared to the megadoses of the anabolic steroids commonly used and their potency, the birth control pill has negligible amounts of sex steroids. With the advent of more sensitive urine drug testing that can distinguish between the steroids found in birth control pills and the anabolic steroids abused by athletes, the IOC has lifted its ban on the use of birth control pills during competition. Now a positive urine test for anabolic steroids means having a ratio of urinary testosterone to epitestosterone above six (24).

A few well-controlled studies have been conducted on the influence of different phases of the menstrual cycle on athletic performance of elite athletes. Earlier, most studies of the effect of menstrual phase on performance were subjective and based on the athlete's self-perception. Thus conflicting results were seen when studies tried to look at the effect of the menstrual cycle on athletic performance. Early studies were largely retrospective and anecdotal. Yet, female athletes, in every phase of the menstrual cycle, have won events in world class and Olympic competitions.

Many female athletes hesitate to use the birth control pill in the fear that it may hinder their performance, which may itself negatively influence performance. They fail to take into consideration all the other benefits of the pill that may play a positive if indirect role in performance. Similarly researchers often fail to reach any firm conclusions when looking at the effect of oral contraceptives on performance, because of the problems that arise when studying this topic:

1. Lack of large prospective studies
2. Inadequate documentation and standardization of menstrual cycle phase in the controls (i.e., nonpill users)
3. Difficulty of accurate hormonal measurements in the controls
4. Lack of trained female athletes in the study groups
5. Failure to use oral contraceptives that have the same formulations
6. The use of a wide variety of physiological testing for performance

However, one recent study examined the effects of a low dose triphasic oral contraceptive on selected measures of athletic performance in a group of elite female athletes (7). The oral contraceptive caused a slight decrease in both absolute and relative VO_2max (maximum oxygen consumption) compared to that of ovulatory nonpill users. This may exert a slight deleterious effect on aerobic capacity for the elite athlete.

Some athletes ask their physicians to manipulate their menstrual cycles around important athletic, competitive events. However, this should be done only for elite athletes. One proposed way to allow the athlete to minimize the hormonal effects of her cycle during competition involves the use of the pill. Low dose birth control pills are taken for several months before the competitive event, then stopped 10 days before the event. The athlete can expect her withdrawal bleeding 3 days before the competitive event. She may then resume taking the pills after the athletic event. Still, the female athlete should consider using the oral contraceptive pill for its other benefits—(regular menses, less dysmenorrhea, less anemia, less PMS, and endometrial and skeletal protection), which are also important determinants of performance. Collectively, these benefits may give a distinct advantage to *any* woman who engages in an exercise or sport at *any* level.

Summary

1. Oral contraceptives are the most popular nonsurgical method of family planning in use among United States women aged 15 to 44, though the sport-minded woman may still have some reservation.

2. There is no single, ideal method of birth control for any woman.
3. Oral contraceptives are not for all females. There are absolute and relative contraindications, though exercise is not one of them.
4. There are many noncontraceptive health benefits of low dose oral contraceptives.
5. Female athletes with menstrual irregularities, dysmenorrhea, or bothersome premenstrual symptoms may benefit from use of low dose contraceptives. With adequate calcium intake, oral contraceptives may provide bone protection in the amenorrheic athlete.
6. The effects of low dose oral contraceptives on aerobic and anaerobic athletic performance must be further studied. The effects of menstrual cycle phase on athletic performance, as well as on the more sport-specific measures of performance in the elite athlete, must be studied also.

References

1. ACOG Precis IV: An update in obstetrics and gynecology. The American College of Obstetrics and Gynecology; 1990.
2. Collins, C.L.; Thomas, K.A.; Harding, A.F.; et al. The effect of oral contraceptives on lumbar bone density in premenopausal women. J. Louisiana State Med. Soc. 140(9):31-39; 1988.
3. Dialogues in contraception 6. Newsletter. Los Angeles: University of Southern California; 1987.
4. Godsland, I.F.; Crook, D.; Wynn, V. Coronary heart disease risk markers in users of low dose oral contraceptives. J. Reprod. Med. 36 (3, Supplement):226-237; 1991, March.
5. Gray, D.P.; Harding, E.; Dale, E. Effects of oral contraceptives on serum lipid profiles of women runners. Fertil. Steril. 4:510-514, 1983.
6. Jarrett, J.C.; Spellacy, W.N. Contraceptive practices of female runners. Fertil. Steril. 39.374; 1983.
7. Lebrun, C.M. Effects of the menstrual cycle and oral contraceptives on athletic performance. University of British Columbia; Vancouver. 1991 December. Unpublished thesis.
8. Lindsay, R.; Hart, D.M.; Forrest, C.; et al. Prevention of spinal osteoporosis in oophorectomized women. Lancet 2:1151; 1980.
9. Lindsay, R.; Tohme, J.; Kanders, B. The effect of oral contraceptive use on vertebral bone mass in pre- and postmenopausal women. Contraception 34:333-340; 1986.
10. Linse, J.; Lutter, J.M. Physical activity and menstrual cycle discomfort: new evidence. Melpomene Rep. 6(3):15-18; 1987.
11. Merrill, J.A.; Zaloudek, K.C.; Tavassoli, F.A.; et al. Lesions of the ovary. In: Danforth, D.N.; Scott, J.R.; eds. Obstetrics and gynecology. Philadelphia: J.B. Lippincott Co.; 1986:1133.
12. Mishell, Jr. D.R.; Brenner, P.R. Menopause. In: Mishell, J.R.; Davajan V., eds. Infertility, contraception, and reproductive endocrinology. Oradell, NJ: Medical Economics Company Inc.; 1986:179-202.
13. Moller-Nielson, J.; Hammer, M. Women's soccer injuries in relation to the menstrual cycle and oral contraceptive use. Med. Sci. Sports Exerc. 21(2):126-129; 1989.

14. Ory, H.; Cole, P.; MacMahon, B.; et al. Oral contraceptives and reduced risk of benign breast diseases. New Engl. J. Med. 294:419-422; 1976.
15. Pater, A.; Bayatpour, M.; Pater, M.M. Oncogenic transformation by human papillomavirus type 16 deoxyribonucleic acid in the presence of progesterone or progestins from oral contraceptives. Am. J. Obstet. Gynecol. 162:1099; 1990.
16. Prior, J.C. Progesterone therapy increases trabecular bone in women with endocrine diseases which prevent treatment. Int. Proc. J. 1(1):204-207; 1989.
17. Prior, J.C.; Vigna, Y.M. Gonadal steroids in athletic women: contraception, complications, and performance. Sports Med. 2:287-295; 1985.
18. Prior, J.C.; Vigna, Y.; Alojado, N. Conditioning exercise decreases premenstrual symptoms—a prospective controlled 3-month trial. Eur. J. Appl. Physiol. 55:349; 1986.
19. Rankin, M.E. Changes in volume of the breast during the menstrual cycle. Br. J. Surg. 62:660; 1975.
20. Saartok, T.; Dahlbey, E.; Gustafsson, J. Relative binding affinity of anabolic-androgenic steroids: comparison of the binding to the androgen receptors in skeletal muscle and in prostate as well as to sex hormone-binding globulin. Endocrinology 114:2100; 1984.
21. Shangold, M.M.; Mirkin, G., editors. Women and exercise: physiology and sports medicine. Philadelphia: F.A. Davis Co.; 1988.
22. Stadel, B.V.; Webster, L.A.; Rubin, G.L.; et al. Oral contraceptives and breast cancer in young women. Lancet 2:970; 1985.
23. Vessey, M.P.; McPherson, K.; Johnson, B. Mortality among women participating in the Oxford/Family Planning Association contraceptive study. Lancet 2:731; 1977.
24. Wadler, G.I., Hainline, B.; editors. Drugs and the athlete. Ryan A.J., ed-in-chief: Contemporary exercise and sports medicine series. Philadelphia: F.A. Davis Company; 1989.
25. Weiss, N.S.; Sayvetz, T.A. Incidence of endometrial cancer and oral contraceptive agents. New Engl. J. Med. 1980.
26. Wells, C.; editor. Women, sport, and performance—a physiologic perspective. Champaign, IL: Human Kinetics Publishers; 1991.
27. Wingo, G.I.; Lee, N.C.; Ory, H.W.; et al. Age-specific differences in the relationship between oral contraceptive use and breast cancer. Obstet. Gynecol. 78:161; 1991.

CHAPTER 8

•

Issues Specific to the Preadolescent and Adolescent Athletic Female

Deborah L. Squire

Federal legislation created increased opportunities for girls to participate in scholastic and community sport programs, mass media exposure of female athletes as positive role models has encouraged young girls to take advantage of these opportunities. During the 1970s, girls' participation in high school sports increased by more than 600%, whereas boys' participation increased only a modest 20% (19). In 1970 to 1971, 294,000 female adolescents were on high school athletic teams; by the 1983-1984 school year, that number had rocketed to 1.8 million. Intercollegiate sports showed a similar growth; in 1971 to 1972, 30,000 women were on varsity squads, compared with 150,000 college and university athletes during 1983 to 1984 (54). Physicians caring for female athletes have raised questions regarding appropriate conditioning programs, as well as the risks for growth retardation, delayed pubertal maturation, nutritional deficiencies, and a variety of previously uncommon injuries.

Areas of Concern for the Preadolescent Female Athlete

General recommendations regarding organized athletics for preadolescent children have been published recently (1). In certain sports, such as gymnastics and swimming, girls are more likely than boys to begin intensive training regimens at an early age. The effects of such regimens on these athletes have yet to be determined.

Gender Differences

The differences in body composition, physiologic values, and actual performance between males and females are small until adolescence. Differences in $\dot{V}O_2$max disappear when indexed by weight in kilograms or by lean body mass (50). Though boys have greater stroke volumes and higher cardiac output responses, for a given work load girls have higher maximum heart rate values. Until the onset of puberty, boys and girls may participate together on athletic teams; separate competitions for racing events (e.g., running and swimming) may be indicated based on physiological differences.

Branta et al. (9) recently published a review of early studies focusing on the structural, physiological, cognitive, and socialization factors that contribute to gender differences in informal play patterns and organized sports participation. Coakley (13) proposed that a child's initial involvement in both informal and organized sports activities is influenced by (a) the availability of opportunities, (b) support from family, peers, role models, and the general community, and (c) the child's self-perception as a potential participant—the effect of identity, body image, self-esteem, and experiences in physical activities. He noted that, for boys, sport participation is seen as being directly linked to their development as men, whereas for girls, sports participation is seldom linked to becoming a woman.

In western culture, although girls may not be actively discouraged from playing sports, they are socialized differently than their brothers in at least two respects. First, they are less likely to learn that physical activities and achievements in sports can or should be uniquely important sources of rewards in their lives. Second, their play time is more likely to be regulated and controlled by their parents. This form of conditional permission not only influences the skill development of little girls, it also constrains the nature of the games and informal sports they play with their friends as they get older (13).

Discussion on sport patterns and play participation of North American youth usually cite data from a 1978 study (9, 20). Given the marked changes in attitude toward females and athletics, new studies are needed to document the current trend in female participation.

Body Composition

The body fat content of a child has been estimated typically from an adult model. Changes in the body density of both males and females during childhood growth and development are not due solely to variation in fat; significant changes also occur in the fat-free body (31). Prepubescent and pubescent children are not chemically mature, and, due to a higher water content and lower bone density, may have a fat-free body density lower than an adult. What changes in the composition of the fat-free body occur as functions of age and maturation have yet to be documented.

Thermoregulation in Children

Certain characteristics of children make them less efficient thermoregulators than adults, particularly when exposed to extreme weather conditions (5, 6). Children sweat less due to a lower rate of output from each sweat gland; in addition, the set point (i.e., the change in rectal temperature at which sweating starts) is higher in children. At a given speed of walking or running, children produce more metabolic heat per kilogram of body weight than do adolescents or adults, thus placing greater strain on thermoregulatory mechanisms (4, 52). A child's lower cardiac output at a given metabolic level places her at risk when exercising in the heat; insufficient blood supply to the skin may interfere with convection of heat from the body core to the periphery. Generally, the child's larger body surface area per kilogram promotes greater heat exchange between the skin and the environment. However, if the ambient temperature exceeds skin temperature, the net result is heat *gain*; in a cold environment, the net result may be inappropriate heat loss.

Furthermore, children acclimatize to heat more slowly than adults; with transition to a warm climate, their activities must be reduced in intensity and duration, then gradually increased over a 10- to 14-day period.

Cardiovascular Conditioning

Considerable doubt has been cast on the ability of children to improve maximal aerobic power with physical training before puberty (28, 34). This has been explained as due to the inherently greater habitual activity levels of children, which place them closer to their maximum $\dot{V}O_2$ potential. Recent studies utilizing adult criteria indicate that children do not sustain high-intensity exercise for periods of time sufficient to improve fitness. Extrapolation of adult standards suggests that sustained exercise to a heart rate of 160 to 170 beats per minute for 15 to 60 minutes at least three times a week would be necessary to increase $\dot{V}O_2$max in prepubertal subjects. Studies incorporating these standards indicate that children may achieve a level of cardiovascular conditioning similar to that observed in adults.

With the onset of puberty, it appears that, unless actively maintained, individual physical fitness (measured by $\dot{V}O_2$max levels) begins to decline (34). This observation has far-reaching implications for adolescent fitness.

Injuries to the Preadolescent Female Athlete

Physical stress is a necessary stimulant to normal bone growth. Acute traumatic injury to the extremity of the preadolescent and early adolescent is more likely to result in fracture through the epiphyseal plate than to cause ligament disruption. The vast majority of such injuries require no major medical or surgical intervention and have no long-term impact on normal growth (29).

Overuse injuries in growing athletes include stress fractures as well as the osteochondroses of the tibial tubercle, calcaneal apophysis, and distal pole of the patella. Although by anecdotal evidence the incidence of overuse injuries in young athletes has markedly increased, the actual incidence of these injuries remains unclear. Specific risk factors that predispose children to such injuries have been described (35). These include training errors, particularly sudden increases in training intensity; anatomical malalignment of the legs, such as leg-length discrepancy and abnormal hip rotation; improper footwear; hard playing surfaces; and associated disease states of the lower extremity. The role that anticipatory intervention may play in reducing the incidence of these injuries has yet to be defined.

Physicians caring for growing athletes have long been concerned about the effect that repetitive microtrauma may exert on the open epiphyseal plate. Roy et al. (48) described stress changes in the distal radial epiphysis in young gymnasts. These injuries healed with no residual growth-related problems. No conclusive data exist regarding the risk of injury to the lower extremity in growing distance runners.

Distance Running

In recent years there has been a marked increase in the participation of children in distance running. A review of the risks attendant to such participation has been recently published (2). The Academy of Pediatrics currently recommends that, if children enjoy the activity and are asymptomatic, there is no reason to preclude them from training for and participating in such events (2).

Strength Training

A detailed review of the role of strength training in the conditioning of the female athlete is the subject of another chapter, but the role of strength training in the conditioning of the prepubescent athlete deserves special consideration. Current debate has focused on three main issues:

1. Is the prepubescent child capable of strength gains from resistive weight training?
2. Does the presence of growth cartilage make resistive weight training dangerous for children?
3. If strength gains are attainable, do they improve performance or reduce the risk of injury?

Sewall and Micheli, in a small study of preadolescents, demonstrated an increase in muscle strength following participation in progressive resistance training sessions three times a week for 9 weeks (49). There was no loss of flexibility (a careful stretching program was part of the weight training regimen) and no associated injury. Studies by Pfeiffer and Francis (40) and Weltman et al. (60) also documented gains in strength by prepubertal subjects engaged in supervised resistance strength training programs. Weltman et al. suggested that the improvement in strength despite lack of hypertrophy might be due to an increased recruitment of motor units and their synchronization (60). This hypothesis is supported by other authors who found that initial increase in strength as a result of strength training can be accounted for by neural factors rather than muscle hypertrophy (25).

Rians et al. (41) examined the safety aspects of the strength training performed during the Weltman et al. (60) study using injury surveillance, biphasic musculoskeletal scintigraphy, and serum creatine phosphokinase measurements. They concluded that a closely supervised strength training program results in a low rate of musculoskeletal injury. There is complete consensus among investigators and pediatricians that any strength program for children must incorporate submaximal resistance and be well supervised by a knowledgeable adult (3).

To date, studies have primarily enrolled prepubertal males as subjects; though response to strength training should be similar in prepubescent females, future efforts must document the effectiveness and safety of strength training for girls. Furthermore, the role that such strength gains may play in improving performance or reducing the risk of injury has yet to be defined.

Biological Maturation

Early-maturing boys and girls show advanced physical growth at all ages, along with a greater lean body mass, fat mass, and heart volume. During prepubescence, static strength is positively related to biological maturity in both boys and girls. The associations with other gross motor performance components are only moderate and are partially explained by the size differences of early- and late-maturing children (8).

In adolescent girls, only static strength is positively related to biologic age. Indeed, young female athletes tend to be characterized by delayed biological maturity, especially in gymnastics, figure skating, and ballet (32). Frisch (22) postulated that the initiation of the pubertal growth spurt and the attainment of menarche is dependent on a critical body weight and percent body fat. Warren (58) noted a delayed progression of puberty in ballet dancers, which she believed to be caused by the energy drain of intensive training and not by decreased fat mass. Frisch (21) further proposed that the age at menarche of athletes is negatively related to the age at onset of training.

Stager and Hatler attempted to define the role of genetics and prepubertal training on menarche in athletes (55). Their study was confounded, however, by the tendency of the sisters of the study athletes to have also participated in sports during childhood. Using a hypothetical study population generated by a computer program, Stager et al. concluded that sampling procedures in studies investigating the effect of age of initiation of training on age at menarche result in biased estimates of the statistical parameters (56). They further stated that this bias accounts for the reported relationship between these two parameters, and that therefore, it would be more appropriate to state that menarche in some athletes occurs *later* rather than its being *delayed*.

Peltenburg et al. conducted a cross-sectional study comparing onset and progression of puberty, body composition, and growth between young female swimmers, gymnasts, and controls (39). Onset of puberty and menarche was delayed in the gymnastics group by 1 to 2 years compared to the controls and swimmers. Gymnasts were leaner than girls in the other groups. There was no relationship between training activities and pubertal events in the gymnasts; the observed relationship between duration of training each week and an increased body height, lean body weight, and pubic hair growth in the swimmers may have been secondary to the increased basal level of testosterone generally observed in women who undergo endurance training. Peltenburg et al. concluded that self-selection played an important role in the observed differences in body composition and biological maturation between females participating in various sports.

Thientz et al. (57) reported on the initial data collected at the onset of a longitudinal study of the growth and development of elite young female gymnasts, swimmers, and controls. They correlated the athletes' growth parameters with parental growth data. Despite 5 years of intensive training, the relative shortness of the gymnasts was still appropriate for parental heights. Although other studies could not correlate athletes' height with parental height (39), this study implies the importance of considering parental parameters when investigating the effects of intensive training on the growth potential of young female athletes. The results of this longitudinal study will be an important first step determining the effects of intensive training on girls.

Nutritional Concerns for the Adolescent Female Athlete

The general area of nutrition will be reviewed in a number of other chapters; three specific topics that are of special concern to the adolescent female athlete will be considered here. They are iron deficiency without anemia, calcium deficiency, and pathogenic weight-control behaviors.

Iron Deficiency

The subject of iron deficiency in the young athlete has been extensively reviewed (43, 44). As many as 40% to 50% of adolescent female athletes demonstrate some degree of iron depletion, or decreased body iron stores without overt anemia (10, 36, 37, 45, 47). Studies have tended to focus on athletes in running sports, although a similar prevalence of iron deficiency was noted in female high school swimmers (47). Runners appear to be at risk for developing iron deficiency during the training season; for other athletes, the reported prevalence may reflect a tendency for adolescents in general. Black adolescent female runners have been shown to have a twofold greater incidence of iron deficiency than their white teammates (36).

Depletion of body iron stores reduces myoglobin and cytochrome levels as well as enzymes of the electron transport system and tricarboxylic acid cycle; this may impair aerobic metabolism and limit exercise capacity, independently of the effects of iron deficiency anemia (43). A strong case for the detrimental effects of nonanemic iron deficiency can be made based on animal studies (15, 18). There is further animal evidence that age may influence the effects of iron deficiency on intracellular metabolism, with a reported 20% to 50% decrease in myoglobin concentration in iron-deficient, growing rats (23).

Human studies, utilizing treadmill times in the human performance laboratory, have failed to document a relationship between iron depletion and exercise performance in adult athletes. Rowland et al. (46), in a small, double-blind, placebo-controlled study of female cross-country runners, found a significant improvement in treadmill endurance times after correction of iron depletion. However, the implications of nonanemic iron deficiency on exercise performance remain unclear.

Iron depletion may have a greater impact on young sportswomen than that of simply diminishing athletic performance. Gastrointestinal function, mood and cognitive operations (such as intellectual performance and attention span), as well as immunologic functions may all be negatively affected by low iron stores (16, 26, 38).

Serum ferritin levels serve as an accurate marker of body iron stores (14, 27). Although higher levels may still reflect depressed iron stores, a serum ferritin value less than 12 ng/ml is generally accepted as indicative of significant iron depletion. Free erythrocyte protoporphyrins are elevated in the presence of iron deficiency. (This test is inexpensive and can be run as a screening test on a fingerstick sample.) If elevated, a follow-up serum ferritin level and hemoglobin is needed. The American Academy of Pediatrics has recommended laboratory assessment of iron status in females with "a serious commitment to exercise performance" (53).

The treatment of iron deficiency without anemia is the subject of debate. Although the implications for exercise performance have yet to be well defined, nonanemic iron deficiency may have a broad negative impact on health. Rowland (43) has proposed that iron-depleted athletes receive a 4- to 6-week course of therapeutic oral iron (180 mg elemental iron a day). Given the prevalence of iron deficiency in adolescent female athletes, routine, prophylactic iron supplementation (105 mg elemental iron a day) should be considered (37).

Calcium Deficiency

Calcium plays an important role in nerve transmission, contraction of muscle tissue, blood coagulation, and numerous enzymatic reactions. New studies suggest that an adequate calcium intake may help prevent hypertension. Most important, however, for the adolescent female athlete, is adequate calcium intake to promote mineralization of the growing skeleton. Early data presented by Gilsantz et al. suggest that spinal density reaches its peak around the time of cessation of longitudinal growth and epiphyseal closure (24).

Most adolescent females consume well below the 1,200 mg recommended daily allowance of calcium (7); for many teenage girls, their intake is even less than 800 mg calcium. A decreased consumption of milk and dairy products (sometimes in an effort to avoid high-fat foods, sometimes secondary to lactose intolerance) is often associated with an increased consumption of carbonated beverages. The high phosphorus content of these drinks may result in increased calcium excretion. A diet rich in protein (7) also causes increased urinary and fecal calcium excretion. On the other hand, the athlete who trains outdoors may benefit from both an increase in active vitamin D and the enhancement of bone mineralization from weight-bearing exercise.

McCulloch et al. (33) studied trabecular bone density in young adult women but did not find any correlation with recalled childhood milk consumption or current dietary calcium intake and bone density. Large prospective studies on the relationship between dietary calcium intake during adolescence and bone mineral density have yet to be conducted. The potentially serious, and perhaps irreversible, consequences of calcium deficiency when combined with menstrual abnormalities (11, 17, 30) are discussed in other chapters. However, future research in this area must include the longitudinal study of adolescent athletes and control for dietary deficiencies.

Providing teenage athletes with nutritional information regarding the variety of foods rich in calcium will allow them to select those foods that they prefer, and, hopefully, encourage them to assume responsibility for making wise food choices. Those athletes who are unwilling to incorporate dairy foods into their diet should be encouraged to take an over-the-counter calcium carbonate supplement.

Pathogenic Weight-Control Behaviors

A detailed review of the prevalence and management of true eating disorders among female athletes is the topic of chapter 10. However, the issue of pathogenic-weight control behaviors among athletes deserves special consideration here. Rosen et al. surveyed 182 varsity female athletes from two universities regarding their use of self-induced vomiting, laxatives, diet pills, diuretics, and more-than-twice-weekly binges to control their weight (42). Athletes were said to exhibit pathogenic behavior if they admitted to using the technique daily for at least a month. Gymnasts and distance runners showed the greatest prevalence of these behaviors (74% and 47%, respectively). This is not surprising, considering that these athletes traditionally place the highest priority on maintaining the lowest percent body fat so as to increase relative strength, speed, and endurance. However, 25% of the athletes participating in softball, volleyball, track, and tennis also used at least one of these techniques for weight control. The reported impetus was enhancement of athletic performance; few reported a concern about personal appearance.

Whether the results of this study reflect the prevalence of these behaviors nationwide is unknown. Practitioners of these techniques often were reassured by older players or coaches as to the safety of these behaviors (42). Athletes and coaches must be educated as to the risks of dangerous electrolyte abnormalities and the impaired athletic performance and cardiac arrhythmia that can result.

Injuries to the Adolescent Female Athlete

Those chronic injuries more common in the female athlete will be discussed in several other chapters. A topic of acute concern that deserves specific mention here is the increased incidence of anterior cruciate ligament (ACL) injuries in the female high school and college basketball player.

Early studies on injuries to high school athletes indicated no difference in overall rate of injury to boys and girls (51), though girls did have more serious injuries and significantly more knee injuries. A more recent study found that there was no difference in the rate or seriousness of injury between male and female high school athletes except between basketball players (12). Those girls had a significantly higher rate of injury; moreover, the injuries were more often major injuries and were more often injuries to the knee. Girls suffered more than twice as many knee sprains (the specific ligament injured was not reported), and three times as many girls as boys required knee surgery.

Although well-controlled studies on the incidence of ACL injuries in college athletes is not available, early data from team physicians and trainers throughout the country have revealed an alarming prevalence of ACL tears among female athletes. Anatomical, biomechanical, and conditioning risk factors have all been proposed. Future research should be directed at better defining those risk factors that most contribute to injury and that are most amenable to modification.

Summary

1. Females of all ages can and should participate in well-rounded fitness programs that include flexibility, cardiovascular, and strength training components.
2. The prepubertal athlete (male and female) is a less efficient thermoregulator and is more susceptible to heat stress than the mature athlete.
3. A well-supervised strength training program can increase muscle strength in prepubertal athletes without increasing their risk of injury or decreasing their flexibility. Such a program should incorporate weights that offer submaximal resistance and emphasize increased repetitions. Future study must determine if increased strength actually enhances performance or reduces the risk of injury.
4. Females who have trained intensively while premenarcheal often attain menarche later than those who have not. Ongoing studies may help define whether this represents a true delay in sexual maturation.
5. Adolescent female athletes are at greater risk of developing iron deficiency, calcium deficiency, and pathogenic weight-control behaviors. A nutritional history is an important component of the preparticipation physical for every female athlete.

References

1. American Academy of Pediatrics. Organized athletics for preadolescent children. Pediatrics 84(3):583-584; 1989.
2. American Academy of Pediatrics. Risks in distance running for children. Pediatrics 86(5):799-800; 1990.

3. American Academy of Pediatrics. Strength training, weight and power lifting, and body building by children and adolescents. Pediatrics 86(5):801-803; 1990.

4. Astrand, P.O. Experimental studies of physical working capacity in relation to sex and age. Copenhagen, Munksgaard; 1952.

5. Bar-Or, O. Children and physical performance in warm and cold environments. In: Boileau, R.A., ed. Advances in pediatric sport sciences. Volume 1: Biological issues. Champaign, IL: Human Kinetics; 1984:117-129.

6. Bar-Or, O. Climate and the exercising child—a review. Int. J. Sports Med. 1(May):53-65; 1980.

7. Benardot, D.; Schwarz, M.; Heller, D.W. Nutrient intake in young, highly competitive gymnasts. J. Am. Dietet. Asso. 89:401-403; 1989.

8. Beunen, G. Biological age in pediatric exercise research. In: Bar-Or, O., ed. Advances in pediatric sport sciences. Volume 3: Biological issues. Champaign, IL: Human Kinetics; 1989:1-39.

9. Branta, C.F.; Painter, M.; Kiger, J.E. Gender differences in play patterns and sport participation of North American youth. In: Gould, D.; Weiss, M.R., eds. Advances in pediatric sports sciences. Volume 2: Behavioral issues. Champaign, IL: Human Kinetics; 1987:25-42.

10. Brown, R.T.; McIntosh, S.M.: Seabolt, V.R. Iron status of adolescent female athletes. J. Adol. Health Care 6:349-352; 1985.

11. Cann, C.E.; Cavanagh, D.J.; Schnurpfiel, K.; Martin, M.C. Menstrual history is the primary determinant of trabecular bone density in women. Med. Sci. Sports Exerc. 20(suppl 2):S59; 1988; abstract.

12. Chandy, T.A.; Grana, W.A. Secondary school athletic injury in boys and girls: a 3-year study. Physician Sportsmed. 13(3):106-111; 1985.

13. Coakley, J.J. Children and the sport socialization process. In: Gould, D.; Weiss, M.R.; eds. Advances in pediatric sport sciences. Volume 2: Behavioral issues. Champaign, IL: Human Kinetics; 1987:225-242.

14. Cook, J.D.; Finch, C.A.; Smith, N.J. Evaluation of the iron status of a population. Blood 48:449-455; 1976.

15. Davies, K.J.A.; Maguire, J.J.; Brooks, G.A.; Dalman, P.R.; Packer, L. Muscle mitochondrial bioenergietics, oxygen supply, and work capacity during dietary iron deficiency and repletion. Am. J. Physiol. 242:E418-E427; 1982.

16. Deinard, A.S.; List, A.; Lindgren, B.; Hunt, J.V.; Chang, P. Cognitive deficits in iron-deficient and iron-deficient anemic children. J. Pediatr. 108:681-689; 1986.

17. Drinkwater, B.L.; Bruemner, B.; Chestnut, C.H., III. Menstrual history as a determinant of current bone density in young ahtletes. JAMA 263:454-548; 1990.

18. Finch, C.A.; Miller, L.R.; Inamdar, A.R.; Person, R.; Seiler, K.; Mackler, B. Iron deficiency in the rat: physiological and biochemical studies of muscle dysfunction. J. Clin. Invest. 58:447-453; 1976.

19. Five-on-one: should men coach women's sports? JOPERD 57:62; 1986.

20. Fountain, C.D. Sex and age differences in the recreational sport participation of children. East Lansing, MI: Michigan State University; 1978. Thesis.

21. Frisch, R.E.; Gotz-Welbergen, A.V.; McArthur, J.W.; Albright, T.; Witschi, J.; Bullen, B.; Birnholz, J.; Reed, R.B.; Hermann, H. Delayed menarche and amenorrhea of college athletes in relation to age of onset of training. JAMA 246:1559-1563; 1981.

22. Frisch, R.E.; Revelle, R.; Cook, S. Components of weight at menarche and the initiation of the adolescent growth spurt in girls: estimated total water, lean body weight, and fat. Hum. Biol. 45:469-485; 1973.

23. Galan, P.; Hercberg, S.; Touitou, Y. The activity of tissue enzymes in iron-deficient rat and man: an overview. Comp. Biochem. Physiol. 77B:647-653; 1984.

24. Gilsantz, V.; Gibbens, D.T.; Carlson, M.; Boechat, M.I.; Cann, C.; Schulz, E.E. Peak trabecular vertebral density: a comparison of adolescent and adult females. Calcif. Tissue Int. 43:260-262; 1988.

25. Hakkinen, K.; Komi, P.V. Electromyographic changes during strength training and detraining. Med. Sci. Sports Exerc. 15:455-460; 1983.

26. Happiness is: iron (editorial). BMJ 292:969-970; 1986.

27. Jacobs, A.; Worwood, M. Ferritin in serum: clinical and biochemical implications. New Engl. J. Med. 292:951-956; 1975.

28. Katch, V.L. Physical conditioning of children. J. Adol. Health Care 3:241-246; 1983.

29. Larson, R.L.; McMahon, R.O. The epiphyses and the childhood athlete. JAMA 196:607-612; 1966.

30. Lloyd, T.; Myers, C.; Buchanan, J.R.; Demers, L.M. Collegiate women athletes with irregular menses during adolescence have decreased bone density. Obstet. Gynecol. 72:639-642; 1988.

31. Lohman, T.G.; Boileau, R.A.; Slaughter, M.H. Body composition in children and youth. In: Boileau, R.A., ed. Advances in pediatric sport sciences. Volume 1: Biological issues. Champaign, IL: Human Kinetics; 1984:29-57.

32. Malina, R.M.; Spirduso, W.W.; Tate, C.; Baylor, A.M. Age at menarche and selected menstrual characteristics in athletes at different competitive levels and in different sports. Med. Sci. Sports Exerc. 3:218-222; 1978.

33. McCulloch, R.G.; Bailey, D.A.; Houston, C.S.; Dodd, B.L. Effects of physical activity, dietary calcium intake, and selected lifestyle factors on bone density in young women. Can. Med. Assoc. J. 142(3):221-227; 1990.

34. McKeag, D.B. Adolescents and exercise. J. Adol. Health Care 7(6S):121S-129S; 1986.

35. Micheli, L.J. Overuse injuries in children's sports: the growth factor. Orthop. Clin. North Am. 14:337-360; 1983.

36. Nickerson, H.J.; Holubets, M.; Tripp, A.D.; Pierce, W.E. Decreased iron stores in high school female runners. Am. J. Dis. Child 136:1115-1119; 1985.

37. Nickerson, H.J.; Holubets, M.C.; Weiler, B.R.; Haas, R.G.; Schwartz, S.; Ellefson, M.E. Causes of iron deficiency in adolescent athletes. J. Pediatr. 114:657-663; 1989.

38. Oski, F.A. The nonhematologic manifestations of iron deficiency. Am. J. Dis. Child 133:315-322; 1979.

39. Peltenburg, A.L.; Erich, W.B.M.; Bernick, M.J.E.; Zonderland, M.L.; Huisveld, I.A. Biological maturation, body composition, and growth of female gymnasts and control groups of schoolgirls and girl swimmers, aged 8 to 14 years: a cross-sectional survey of 1,064 girls. Int. J. Sports Med. 5(1):36-42; 1984.

40. Pfeiffer, R.D.; Francis, R.S. Effects of strength training on muscle development in prepubescent, pubescent, and postpubescent males. Phys. Sportsmed. 14(9):134-143; 1986.

41. Rians, C.B.; Weltman, A.; Cahill, B.R.; Janey, C.A.; Tippett, S.R.; Katch, F.I. Strength training for prepubescent males: is it safe? Am. J. Sports Med. 15:483-489; 1987.

42. Rosen, L.W.; McKeag, D.B.; Hough, D.; Curley, V. Pathogenic weight control behavior in female athletes. Phys. Sportsmed. 14(1):79-86; 1986.

43. Rowland, T.W. Iron deficiency in the young athlete. Ped. Clin. NA 37(5):1153-1163; 1990.

44. Rowland, T.W. Iron deficiency and supplementation in the young endurance athlete. In: Bar-Or, O., ed. Advances in pediatric sport sciences. Volume 3: Biological issues. Champaign, IL: Human Kinetics; 1989:169-190.
45. Rowland, T.W.; Black, S.A.; Kelleher, J.F. Iron deficiency in adolescent endurance athletes. J. Adol. Health Care 8:322-326; 1987.
46. Rowland, T.W.; Deisroth, M.A.; Green, G.M.; Kelleher, J.F. The effect of iron therapy on the exercise capacity of nonanemic iron deficient adolescent runners. Am. J. Dis. Child 142:165-169; 1988.
47. Rowland, T.W.; Kelleher, J. Iron deficiency in athletes: insights from high school swimmers. Am. J. Dis. Child 143:197-200; 1989.
48. Roy, S.; Caine, D.; Singer, K.M. Stress changes of the distal radial epiphysis in young gymnasts. Am. J. Sports Med. 13(5):301-308; 1985.
49. Sewall, L.; Micheli, L.J. Strength training for children. J. Pediatr. Orthop. 6(2):143-146; 1986.
50. Shepherd, R.J. Growth of physical fitness. Phys. Activity Growth 5:86-106; 1982.
51. Shively, R.A; Grana, W.A.; Ellis, D. High school sports injuries. Phys. Sportsmed. 9(8):46-50; 1981.
52. Skinner, J.S.; Bar-Or, O.; Bergsteinova, V.; Bell, C.W.; Royer, D.; Buskirk, E.R. Comparison of continuous and intermittent tests for determining maximal oxygen uptake in children. Acta Paediatr. Scand. 217 (Suppl.):24-28; 1971.
53. Smith, N.J. Sports medicine: health care for young athletes. Evanston, IL: American Academy of Pediatrics; 1983:1.
54. Squire, D.L. Female athletes. Ped. Rev. 9(6):183-190; 1987.
55. Stager, J.M.; Hatler, L.K. Menarche in athletes: the influence of genetics and prepubertal training. Med. Sci. Sports Exerc. 20(4):369-373; 1988.
56. Stager, J.M.; Wigglesworth, J.K.; Hatler, L.K. Interpreting the relationship between age of menarche and prepubertal training. Med. Sci. Sports Exerc. 22(1):54-58; 1990.
57. Theintz, G.E.; Howald, H.; Allemann, Y.; Sizonenko, P.C. Growth and pubertal development of young female gymnasts and swimmers: a correlation with parental data. Int. J. Sports Med. 10(2):87-91; 1989.
58. Warren, M.P. The effects of pubertal progression and reproductive function in girls. J. Clin. Endocrinol. Metab. 51:1150-1157; 1980.
59. Weltman, A. Weight training in prepubertal children: physiologic benefit and potential damage. In: Bar-Or, O., ed. Advances in pediatric sport sciences. Volume 3: Biological issues. Champaign, IL: Human Kinetics; 1989; 101-129.
60. Weltman, A.; Janney, C.; Rians, C.B.; Strand, K.; Berg, B.; Tippitt, S.; Wise, J.; Cahill, B.R.; Katch, F.I. The effects of hydraulic resistance strength training in prepubertal males. Med. Sci. Sports Exerc. 18:629-638; 1986.

CHAPTER 9

•

Substance Abuse by the Athletic Female

Herbert A. Haupt

Substance abuse by athletes for both performance enhancement and recreation has become pervasive in today's athletic world. It is a source of great concern for sports medicine specialists that abuse of recreational drugs, such as alcohol, marijuana, amphetamines, and cocaine, is as prevalent in the athletic population as it is in the nonathletic population (19). Females are less likely than males to use illicit drugs in the nonathletic population (38), and it is reasonable to assume that this is the case in the athletic population as well. The exception is in the use of stimulants and other medications for weight loss, which are more frequently used by the athletic female (38). Athletes, both female and male, are more likely to use substances considered ergogenic aids, such as amphetamines and anabolic steroids.

In general, the effects of the various substances subject to abuse by the athlete are similar in both the female and male, except for the unique effects of anabolic steroids and nonalcoholic carbonated beverages in the athletic female. Females are more likely to abuse substances related to weight loss (such as laxatives, diuretics, and amphetamines or their derivatives), less likely to indulge in recreational drugs (such as alcohol, marijuana, and cocaine), and less likely to abuse anabolic steroids than their male counterparts. In this chapter I will briefly review the effects of the various substances subject to abuse by the athlete and emphasize the unique effects that they have in the female athlete.

Anabolic Steroids

Anabolic steroid abuse is far more prevalent in the athletic than the nonathletic population. One study demonstrated that 20% of all athletes have used anabolic steroids compared to only 1% of nonathletes (19). Recently a study in the *Journal of the American Medical Association* demonstrated that 6.6% of all high school male seniors have tried anabolic steroids by age 18. This represents between 250,000 and 500,000 male adolescents (14). Though males are far more likely to consider the use of anabolic steroids than females (44), athletic females do use anabolic steroids (16, 54, 65).

Anabolic steroids are derivatives of testosterone and bear a close resemblance to it. There are both orally and parenterally active substances. They have virilizing effects in the female and some feminizing effects in the male and have similar effects in the liver, on lipoprotein fractions, in libido and personality changes, and on muscle and tendons.

Anabolic steroids can increase the size and strength of both athletic females and males through the same mechanisms of action and when used under proper conditions (30). Anabolic steroids are effective only when given to athletes who are previously trained in intense resistance exercise and who continue to train while using them (30). When given to subjects who are not so conditioned, steroids have little effect, even if the athletes train while using them. These effects relate to a previously noted association between the overtrained state and the ratio of testosterone to cortisol. Several studies have demonstrated that the serum testosterone:cortisol ratio increases as an athlete gains strength, a training-induced phenomenon (1, 29, 41, 42). If the level of training intensity is maintained, stress causes higher levels of cortisol (18). Cortisol has catabolic effects on skeletal muscle, which causes the negative calcium-nitrogen balance that characterizes the overtrained state. The result is a serum testosterone:cortisol ratio that is decreased by more than 30% (1). Exogenous anabolic steroid supplementation increases the testosterone:cortisol ratio, thus reversing the catabolic effects of the glucocorticosteroids (3). This anticatabolic effect appears to be mediated by testosterone's ability to displace cortisol from the glucocorticosteroid receptors on muscles and other organ systems (28, 41, 55). Therefore, anabolic steroids appear to reverse the negative nitrogen balance, loss of body weight, and muscle wasting associated with excess cortisol production during periods of stress, such as overtraining. For this reason, anabolic steroids may be classified best as anticatabolic.

Anabolic steroids have other effects that further serve to increase the size and strength of the athlete. Through receptors on muscle cells, anabolic steroids stimulate protein synthesis (30, 40, 49, 50). They can increase the release of endogenous growth hormone, which has anabolic effects (2). Finally, anabolic steroids have significant motivational and placebo effects. Athletes who take anabolic steroids become more aggressive in all activities, including their training, which results in more intense training sessions and a feeling of decreased fatigue. Yet, athletes given a placebo and told that they were taking anabolic steroids also demonstrated significant strength increases (6). However, steroid use has no effect in improving aerobic performance (30).

Though anabolic steroids can increase both size and strength, this effect is maintained only as long as their use continues. When discontinued, a significant percentage of the increased size and strength disappears. This seems to be related to the seriously depressed levels of endogenous testosterone in the male and loss of the exogenous compound in the female. Without exogenous steroid supplementation, the athlete's depressed testosterone level cannot maintain the increased muscularity. Also, the motivational effects of the steroid are eliminated and the intensity of training sessions cannot be maintained. The result is a rapid decrease in size and strength. Athletes who wish to maintain their competitive edges, or their muscular appearances, must continue to use anabolic steroids indefinitely.

Anabolic steroids have a virilizing effect on females. The younger the female, the more pronounced the virilizing effects (69, 71). These include increased muscular size and strength, hoarseness and deepening of the voice, increased facial and body hair, male pattern baldness, changes in libido, clitoral enlargement, and menstrual irregularities. In some cases, there is complete menstrual cessation (34, 69, 71).

The athletic female also suffers idiopathic hirsutism with effects best described as primary cutaneous virilism. These effects are primarily on the skin and include increased sebum production (causing oily skin and acne), increased skin thickness, increased collagen content, and increased sweat response to cholinergic stimulation (34). Idiopathic hirsutism, male pattern baldness, and voice changes may not be reversible even after prompt discontinuance of the anabolic steroid. Even estrogen therapy will not reverse these effects (45).

Athletes, both female and male, who take anabolic steroids before skeletal maturity may accelerate epiphyseal closure, thus causing shortened stature (30, 46).

The orally active anabolic steroids, the 17-alpha-alkyl derivatives of testosterone, can have a profound effect on the liver, whereas the 19-nor derivatives, the parenterally active compounds, appear to have little effect. The orally active anabolic steroids can cause transient elevations in liver function tests. Intense weight lifting alone may also cause changes in liver function tests, including SGOT, SGPT, and LDH. It is therefore recommended that more specific liver function tests, including those for the alkaline phosphatase liver isoenzyme and the LDH liver isoenzyme, be used to monitor the liver function of weight-training athletes. Altered liver functions usually return to normal after steroid use is discontinued (30, 46).

Peliosis hepatis, a rare entity historically associated with tuberculosis, is characterized by hemorrhagic cystic degeneration of the liver. Of the 23 cases of peliosis hepatis reported in the literature, all but one involved orally active anabolic steroid use for 6 to 24 months, and all were in patients being treated with anabolic steroids for medical illnesses (30). Of the 36 reported cases of liver tumors associated with the use of anabolic steroids, all but one were in patients taking anabolic steroids for medical treatment. The majority of these tumors were malignant and associated with the orally active anabolic steroids, and the patients had been treated continuously for more than 24 months with the anabolic steroids (30). However, there has been at least one report of a liver tumor in an athlete who had been using anabolic steroids for body building (22, 53).

Epidemiologic studies have demonstrated that the risk for heart disease is directly related to plasma levels of low density lipoprotein cholesterol concentrations (LDL) and inversely related to high density lipoprotein cholesterol concentrations (HDL). Though intense exercise, including body building and weight lifting, can serve to lower the LDL:HDL ratio in both females and males (35), even short-term use of anabolic steroids can cause a significant increase in the LDL:HDL ratio despite exercise. In one study, the ratio increased by 280% (35).

At least two studies have investigated the effects of anabolic steroids on the cholesterol fractions in the athletic female (16, 54) and found changes similar to those reported in males. Specifically, HDL decreased and LDL increased. In both studies, HDL_2-C was decreased more in females than males at a statistically significant level (16, 54). (HDL_2-C is considered the most important HDL fraction regarding cardiac risk.) These altered ratios returned to normal both in females and males following discontinuance of steroid use (16). The question of how detrimental short-term elevations in the LDL:HDL ratio are to coronary health is still unanswered. However, there have been two reports of strokes in athletes who were taking anabolic steroids for body building (22, 53). As athletes take anabolic steroids for longer periods, we will probably see more, severe cardiovascular disturbances.

There are anecdotal reports among athletes of increased injury to musculotendinous structures during anabolic steroid use. Three reports in the literature, two of tricep tendon tears and one of spontaneous rupture of the extensor pollices tendon after anabolic steroid use, suggest a weakening of tendinous structures (7, 31, 43). In these cases, the athletes had been taking anabolic steroids for several months before their injuries occurred. Pathological examination of the ruptured extensor pollices tendon revealed that the fibers had degenerated and there were areas of calcification, which suggested rupture secondary to inflammation (43).

It has been demonstrated that when combined with an endurance running program in mice, anabolic steroids activate cellular metabolism in the tendon accompanied by the appearance of extracellular lysosomes that induced degenerative changes in the fine structure of the muscle tendon junction (51, 52). Calcification then occurred in the area of degeneration. The collagen fibers were dissociated into subfibrils and ruptured. The fibers also showed marked variations in diameter, irregularity in contour, and highly disorganized packing. The number of dysplastic collagen fibers increased directly with the duration of anabolic steroid treatment. Thin collagen fibrils predominated so that, although the overall number of fibrils increased, the density and cross-sectional area of the tendon fibril decreased, which suggested decreased strength of the tendon. The dysplasia noted in the collagen fibrils was most marked in those animals treated with anabolic steroids and exercise, compared to untreated controls and to those animals treated with steroids but without exercise (52). Further studies on exercised rats treated with anabolic steroids demonstrated that the tendons in these animals were less efficient, had theoretically lower breaking strains, and were weaker than those in the control animals (70).

All of these studies suggest that use of anabolic steroids, especially when coupled with exercise, predispose tendons to rupture. Empirically, athletes have noted these effects. The question of reversibility with discontinuance of steroid use and the effect on the healing rate of these tendons after rupture have not been adequately studied.

The most disturbing adverse effects of anabolic steroids are their psychological effects. Both female and male athletes who take anabolic steroids suffer some degree of personality change, ranging from increased irritability to a toxic psychosis, which requires hospitalization (58, 59). Athletes on anabolic steroids often become extremely intense and aggressive, and sometimes violent. Though these characteristics allow the athlete to train in a much more strenuous and focused manner, they carry over into everyday life as well. The athletes assume a Jekyll-and-Hyde personality; even a slight provocation can cause them to react in a violent and sometimes uncontrolled manner. In extreme cases, they can become virtual sociopaths who can no longer maintain effective relationships with friends, family, or loved ones. Their only release is in the weight room or on the playing field where violent behavior may be more acceptable. These individuals not uncommonly suffer divorces, move away from family, and get into trouble with the law. Recently, there have been reports of psychotic episodes in a small number of steroid users, some of whom required hospitalization. Just as the psychoses reversed following discontinued use of steroids (59), ultimately, the personality alterations also return to normal. Unfortunately, scars on relationships with friends, family, and loved ones, as well as any arrest records, remain with the athletes for the rest of their lives.

An equally disturbing and even more devastating effect of anabolic steroid use is habituation. There is both a psychologic and physiologic component to this addiction (66). Athletes who take anabolic steroids usually do so out of insecurity. It may be the insecurity of a young athlete feeling he or she has a poorer physique than peers at a local health club. It may even be the insecurity of a world class sprinter and the current world record holder as the most important race of her life approaches. In these cases, the athlete uses the steroid to supplement *perceived* deficiencies, though under the proper conditions, anabolic steroids will, in fact, increase size and strength, even in the female. An athlete whose competitive success is contingent on this increased size and strength may find it quite difficult to discontinue use of steroids for fear of losing this competitive edge.

Even more disturbing, however, is the use of anabolic steroids for cosmetic purposes. More and more young, teenaged weightlifters take anabolic steroids simply to look bigger and stronger as quickly as possible. These young women and men are impatient with the normal, slow muscular growth patterns that occur with weight lifting alone. They constantly review their appearance in the mirror and critically perceive themselves to be smaller than their peers. They become obsessed with body image and often turn to anabolic steroids for rapid size and strength increases. While taking the steroids, they enjoy more intense training sessions, the euphoria well documented with any steroid use, and a markedly increased sexual appetite. Finally, they thrive on the attention and admiration of their peer group, which they conclude to be a result of their increased size and strength. However, when the young athlete stops taking steroids, the seriously depressed levels of testosterone in the male and the loss of exogenous testosterone in the female cannot support the intense training sessions, and the size and strength improvements quickly disappear; so does the sexual drive, the steroid euphoria, and the peer admiration. The athlete becomes obsessed with his or her decreasing size and changed appearance, and this already insecure athlete falls victim to a very real and serious depression. Most cannot tolerate this withdrawal complex and quickly return to using the steroids to maintain their distorted body image. Back on the steroids, they once again regain size and strength, sexual drive, and self-esteem. They have become psychologically addicted to the anabolic steroid. Thoughts of long-term medical consequences rarely enter their minds, though recent evidence suggests a physiologic component that resembles that of opioid dependence (66).

Compulsive behavior to maintain a distorted body image has been well known to specialists who deal with eating disorders such as anorexia nervosa. The same psychological disorder that affects the anorexic may be operating in the young body builders who become so obsessed with body image that they must continue anabolic steroid use indefinitely in an attempt to maintain their distorted body image. A disturbing consequence of this syndrome are suicidal tendencies (13, 21, 58, 63).

The degree to which these disturbing psychological effects occur in athletic females who use anabolic steroids is not clearly defined. Female athletes who take anabolic steroids do become more aggressive, which causes some social problems for them (65). Females who take anabolic steroids to attain a more muscular appearance or to improve sports performance probably suffer the same psychological disturbances and habituation tendencies that affect their male counterparts.

Pathogenic Weight-Control Aids

A recent survey of 182 athletic female collegiates showed that 32% practiced at least one of the weight-control behaviors defined as pathogenic—self-induced vomiting, binges more than twice weekly, and use of laxatives, diet pills, or diuretics (60). Sixteen percent admitted to the use of laxatives, 25% to the use of diet pills, and 5% to the use of diuretics. The problem appeared to be more prevalent among whites than blacks, and the majority indicated that their concern about weight was primarily related to enhancing their athletic performance rather than their appearance. In this study, the abuse of weight-control substances was most prevalent in young women participating in gymnastics and long-distance running. Surprisingly, a large number of those who abused these substances were involved in sports where weight control seems less important—field hockey and softball.

For the population as a whole, substance abuse occurs more frequently in males than in females, except in the case of stimulants. Substantially more females than males use stimulants for purposes of weight loss (38). Amphetamines and PPA, the active ingredient in many diet pills, are frequently abused by the athletic female pursuing weight control.

Amphetamines

Amphetamines are potent stimulants that have been used as ergogenic aids for many years. They are also potent appetite suppressants. They may be abused by not only females to maintain weight, but by males who participate in gymnastics, wrestling, or ballet (27, 47). Amphetamines are indirect-acting, sympathomimetic amines. They indirectly stimulate the adrenergic nervous system through the release of endogenous catecholamines. Of all the sympathomimetic amines, amphetamines are the most potent stimulators of the central nervous system (27), one becomes more alert and has a decreased sense of fatigue while using amphetamines. They have their most profound effect when performance has been dulled by fatigue or lack of sleep. In these conditions the amphetamines improve concentration and overall alertness despite the fatigued condition (27, 36). Athletic performance in activities involving strength, speed, and endurance improves during the use of amphetamines (36, 62).

Tolerance of and addiction to amphetamines can occur, and abrupt withdrawal may produce chronic fatigue and depression. Other adverse central nervous system effects include anxiety, insomnia, nervousness, agitation, and even the possibility of a toxic psychosis with vivid hallucinations and paranoia. Also, hyperthermia may occur as a result of peripheral vasoconstriction, a potentially serious problem in athletes exercising in the heat (36, 47). Deaths from amphetamine use have been the result of cerebrovascular hemorrhage, acute cardiac failure, and hyperthermia. Consequently, amphetamines are banned by both the NCAA and the USOC (56, 64).

Phenylpropanolamine

Phenylpropanolamine (PPA) is a sympathomimetic amine that is the active ingredient in many over-the-counter appetite suppressants, nasal decongestants, and cold remedies. Because of its stimulant characteristics, athletes are turning to phenylpropanolamine as an ergogenic aid. PPA is an amphetamine look-alike that differs from amphetamine by the presence of a single hydroxyl group that decreases its central stimulatory effect compared to that of amphetamine (25). PPA primarily affects the alpha adrenergic receptors and, thus, is a potent nasal decongestant. The stimulatory effect of PPA occurs within 30 minutes of use and can last up to 3 hours (5).

PPA use can cause significant increases in blood pressure, even at therapeutic dosages, especially when combined with the caffeine found in many over-the-counter preparations (5, 57). Life-threatening hypertension can result from overdosage and can occur in anyone attempting to lose weight or seeking PPA's stimulatory effect. Seizures have also been reported, especially when PPA is combined with caffeine (57). In addition, psychotic episodes, paranoia, homicidal behavior, hallucinations, and attempted suicide caused by use of PPA have all been reported. Acute renal failure secondary to rhabdomyolysis, cardiac arrhythmias, and myocardial infarction have also occurred (57).

Phenylpropanolamine is becoming more popular among athletes who are seeking performance aids, because of its availability and low cost. It is banned by both the NCAA and USOC (56, 64).

As we investigate substance abuse by athletic females, we must also seriously investigate pathogenic weight-control behaviors and develop effective programs in education and counseling.

Nonalcoholic Carbonated Beverages

An interesting study from the *Journal of Orthopaedic Research* studied the rate of bone fractures among former female college athletes compared to nonathletes (72). Previous studies had reported that among postmenopausal women more than 60 years old, former college athletes were at no greater risk of bone fractures than were nonathletes (73). This most recent study, however, suggests that former female college athletes who drink nonalcoholic carbonated beverages in each age decade were at excess risk for one or more bone fractures during their lifetime when compared to nonathletes. Researchers also noted a significant dose-response relationship between the number of bone fractures at all sites and the amount of carbonated beverages consumed daily. There was no association between whether the carbonated beverages were sweetened with sugar or with sugar substitutes (diet drinks). In all age groups, more former college athletes than nonathletes were drinkers of carbonated beverages.

The agent at work here seems to be the phosphoric acid in the carbonated beverages. High phosphorus intake alters calcium metabolism and the associated bone resorption (72). Former athletes also have lower levels of endogenous estrogen than do nonathletes. This lowers the athletic female's risk of sex hormone-sensitive cancers and benign tumors (72), but the lower estrogen levels also predispose her to osteoporosis. Therefore, athletic females should be made aware of the potential adverse affects of excessive consumption of nonalcoholic carbonated beverages.

Recreational Drugs and Ergogenic Aids

Female and male athletes share abuse of other recreational drugs and ergogenic aids. Cocaine, crack, marijuana, alcohol, caffeine, and beta blockers may all be abused by females who then suffer the same adverse effects as males.

Cocaine

Cocaine has a therapeutic use as a local anesthetic. However, in the past it was used more generally as a stimulant. Sigmund Freud used cocaine for a variety of maladies, and until 1903, it was an ingredient in the formula of Coca Cola (48). An estimated 28% of adults between the ages of 20 and 40, and 16% of high school seniors have tried cocaine at least once (48, 67). Abuse of cocaine by athletes received heavy media attention with the sudden deaths of basketball star Len Bias and pro football star Don Rogers. Their deaths demonstrated the potential danger in the use of this drug.

Cocaine hydrochloride is the active drug produced from the plant, *Erythroxylon coca*. It decomposes with heating, and for that reason its major mode of absorption is by snorting or sniffing the crystals. Cocaine limits its own absorption by this route by causing vasoconstriction of the nasal mucosal membranes (18).

Cocaine is a potent stimulant that may be abused by the athlete who feels that this effect improves her performance. Its stimulatory effects are the result of both the induced release of norepinephrine from neurons and the blocking of its reuptake, making more of the neurotransmitter available to the receptor sites (67). This potentiation of the effects of norepinephrine causes feelings of euphoria, decreased fatigue, and grandiosity of thought. An athlete who uses cocaine may feel that she performs at a higher level, both stronger and faster. However, this is the result of a distorted perception of performance. In fact, she is not stronger, and though her peripheral reflexes are increased, her actions are often uncoordinated and ineffective (67).

Whether an athlete takes cocaine to improve performance or simply for recreation, tolerance and addiction are likely results. Because of increasing tolerance to the drug, an athlete can be addicted and still participate in sports before this abuse significantly interferes with her activities (67).

Other side effects of chronic cocaine abuse include potential ulceration and perforations of the nasal septum, rhinitis, sinusitis, and bronchitis. Peripheral vasoconstriction caused by cocaine can cause the core temperature to elevate, which causes hyperthermia during extreme activities (48, 67). Cocaine use causes agitation, restlessness, insomnia, anxiety, and, in some cases, a toxic psychosis with hallucinations, paranoia, and delusions. Time distortion may cause the user to miss team buses and other game or practice appointments (48). Behavioral changes are the hallmarks of beginning cocaine abuse. Missed appointments, antisocial activity, restlessness, and disciplinary problems in a previously well-adjusted athlete may be the first signs.

Cocaine-induced cardiovascular disturbances can cause death. Cocaine stimulates release of norepinephrine, which can trigger serious ventricular arrhythmias or coronary artery vasospasms. As a result of the spasms, coronary thrombus formation may occur, even though the arteries are normal, causing acute myocardial infarction or sudden death (15). Cerebrovascular accidents can occur within minutes if a cerebral aneurysm or other predisposing conditions are present (15). Seizure activity has also been reported, and some experts feel that cocaine-related deaths are the result of anoxia caused by seizures (18).

Crack

Crack is essentially pure cocaine produced by removing the hydrochloride from cocaine hydrochloride. This produces a precipitate of pure cocaine that appears as a white rock. Crack, unlike cocaine hydrochloride, is not decomposed by heating. Because it vaporizes at a higher temperature, it is suitable for smoking and delivers large quantities of cocaine to the vascular bed of the lung where it is quickly absorbed. Cocaine absorption by this route is not limited as it is by nasal absorption (snorting). The result is an intense, short-lived, but accelerated cocaine effect. The rush of euphoria disappears in a "crash" that forces the user to rapidly repeat doses in order to maintain the effect. This quickly leads to addiction.

Also more intense are the potentially disastrous side effects including cardiac arrhythmias, myocardial infarction, and seizure activity (18). Overdosing with crack is a frequent occurrence. Crack is relatively inexpensive compared to cocaine and has become widely available resulting in near epidemic use, especially among adolescents (18).

An athlete may feel that cocaine and crack have positive effects on her performance through enhanced reflexes and feelings of euphoria and decreased fatigue. However, their use has potentially life-threatening cardiovascular effects, and the user risks addiction and significant behavioral alterations. Cocaine use is banned by both the NCAA and USOC (56, 64).

Marijuana

Marijuana is derived from the herbaceous plant, *Cannabis sativa*. The active ingredient in marijuana is delta-9-tetrahydrocanabinol (delta-9-THC), commonly referred to as THC (23). THC appears to act primarily on the central nervous system, but its action is not well understood. It is rapidly absorbed across the blood-brain barrier so that its central nervous system effects are rapid in onset. Because it is lipid soluble, THC and its metabolites are so slowly released from fat depots into the circulation that they may be detected in the urine for up to 30 days following use (23).

Therapeutic uses of marijuana include the treatment of asthma (it is a potent bronchodilator), glaucoma (it decreases intraocular pressure), contractures caused by chronic muscle spasticity following head injury, and the relief of nausea and vomiting caused by chemotherapy (32). Marijuana's adverse effects on the cardiovascular system include orthostatic hypotension, tachycardia, and potential hyperthermia, a result of inhibition of the sweat glands (10, 23). It may seriously hinder psychomotor functions; hand-eye coordination, tracking performance, and perceptual tasks all deteriorate for up to 24 hours after use (10, 12). Short-term memory loss and time distortion are frequent side effects (10, 23, 74). Chronic marijuana use may also cause an amotivational syndrome characterized by apathy, loss of ambition, impaired memory, and decreased concentration (10, 23, 32).

Chronic marijuana use is associated with increased incidence of respiratory disorders including bronchitis, asthma, and moderate airway obstructive disease (10, 11). The herbicide paraquat is a frequent contaminant of marijuana and can cause severe pulmonary fibrosis and even acute toxicity (32).

Marijuana has no performance-enhancing characteristics for the athlete; indeed, it may adversely affect her performance for up to 24 hours after use. Marijuana is banned by the NCAA, but not by the USOC (56, 64).

Alcohol

Alcohol is the substance most abused by teenagers today. There are an estimated 3 million problem drinkers under age 16 (9). At least half of all fatal automobile accidents in the United States can be attributed to alcohol abuse (4). Under the influence of alcohol, actions become more uncoordinated, reaction time is slowed, hand-eye coordination deteriorates, and balance is often impaired. Thus it may adversely affect athletic performance. Alcohol also may decrease muscular strength and endurance. It can impair the body's thermoregulatory mechanism, especially in cold climates, often causing hypothermia (4).

Alcohol abuse is the result of overindulgence, and athletes must be counseled regarding moderation in its use. Although alcohol is a socially acceptable drug, it *is* a drug and must be handled in a mature fashion despite peer pressure. Alcohol is not banned by the NCAA or the USOC (56, 64).

Caffeine

Caffeine, theophylline, and theobromine are all members of the group of methylated xanthines and are naturally occurring in coffee, tea, and cocoa, respectively (23). Caffeine has stimulatory effects in dosages of 250 mg to 350 mg and enhances performance in endurance athletic activities (56, 64). Improved performance occurs through a combination of central nervous system stimulation, enhanced fatty acid utilization sparing muscle glycogen, and increased skeletal muscle contractility (17, 24, 37, 47).

The stimulatory effect of caffeine is the result of its ability to block the adenosine receptors in the central nervous system. This blocks the adenosine inhibition of neurotransmitter release, decreasing its overall depressive effect (20). Other methyl xanthines have similar CNS effects, but caffeine is the most active (24). Peak blood levels of caffeine are reached within 30 minutes of ingestion (61).

Caffeine is lipolytic, thereby increasing plasma levels of free fatty acids. During exercise, this elevation of plasma free fatty acids causes increased lipid metabolism and decreased dependence on muscle glycogen. When muscle glycogen is spared, the rate of exhaustion is decreased (17), thus the noticeable effect on athletic endurance.

Caffeine strengthens the contraction of skeletal muscle and renders it less susceptible to fatigue (24, 47). So it can improve performance, even in short-term, high intensity activities such as weight lifting. Of all the methyl xanthines, caffeine has the most pronounced effect in this regard (47).

Adverse effects of caffeine include premature ventricular contractions and tachycardia that cease when the caffeine is discontinued. It is also a diuretic and may thus interfere with an athlete's performance if used over the long term (47).

Caffeine's sleep-altering effects may contribute to fatigue. Though a level of tolerance to the diuretic and sleep disturbance effects may develop, none seems to develop to its stimulatory effect (47). There is a mild withdrawal syndrome associated with its use that includes headache, drowsiness, lethargy, and, in some cases, irritability and nervousness (32). The NCAA bans caffeine only if its concentration in the urine exceeds 15 µg/mL (56). The USOC bans caffeine in amounts greater than 12 µg/mL. But these levels represent drinking in excess of 6 to 10 cups of coffee in one sitting and being tested within 2 to 3 hours (64).

Beta Blockers

Beta blockers may be used by athletes to control tremor during periods of stress and exercise in such sports as the biathlon, riflery, and archery. Beta blockers antagonize epinephrine-induced tremor in humans and laboratory animals. The antitremor effect appears to be peripheral and is most profound when the tremor is accentuated by emotional or physical stress causing epinephrine release (68). Propranolol, trade name Inderal, is the beta blocker most well known and frequently used by athletes. It is a nonselective beta blocker, blocking both the Beta 1 and Beta 2 receptors. (Specific beta blockers are Beta 1-selective, such as metoprolol.) Both selective and nonselective beta blockers are used clinically to treat certain cardiac arrhythmias, angina pectoris, and hypertension (26).

Though beta blockers are effective in decreasing tremor, especially during exercise, they can have an adverse effect on athletic performance.

Both Beta 1-specific and nonspecific beta blockers lower heart rate during exercise. At efforts above 90% of $\dot{V}O_2$max, nonspecific beta blockers lower heart rate more than Beta 1-specific blockers. This means that stroke volume is increased in proportion to the decrease in heart rate in order to allow cardiac output to remain unaltered or only slightly reduced while working at the same rate. However, the stroke volume of highly trained athletes has maximized over their years of training and can be expanded only to a limited degree. Thus, a highly trained athlete is not able to fully compensate for beta blockade, and her $\dot{V}O_2$max can be reduced by 15% or more. Because Beta 1-selective drugs have less effect on heart rate at higher rates of work, the highly trained endurance athlete does seem to perform better then using these drugs rather than the nonspecific beta blockers (68).

Propranolol and other beta blockers can adversely affect the respiratory system by increasing airway resistance, which may cause potentially life-threatening reactions in asthmatics. In addition, nausea, vomiting, mild diarrhea, and even constipation have been reported with propranolol abuse. Hallucinations, nightmares, insomnia, and depression have also been reported (26). Beta blockers have been banned by both the NCAA and USOC (56, 64).

Modifying the athletic female's abuse potential requires an integrated program of education and drug testing. Counseling on an individual basis must be available. Drug testing must be equitable, reliable, and associated with sanctions strict enough to deter abuse by athletes. Because of the pervasive availability of drugs and their rapidly growing abuse by young people, drug education and drug testing programs undoubtedly will have to be integrated into high school athletic programs in the near future.

Summary

1. Substance abuse by athletic females includes recreational drugs and pathogenic and ergogenic aids. Abused substances include anabolic steroids, amphetamines, cocaine, marijuana, alcohol, caffeine, and beta blockers.
2. With the exception of the stimulants used to promote weight loss, males are more prone to substance abuse than are females.
3. At present, statistics on substance abuse by athletic females are lacking, because there are no regular screening programs and those studies conducted are sparsely reported.
4. Females most commonly abuse substances because of body image and weight-loss concerns. Substance abuse for weight control is seen in 32% of athletic females. Concerns about body image have led to an increase in consumption of carbonated soft drinks, which increases phosphate intake and causes osteoporotic changes in bone.
5. The unique effects of anabolic steroids and nonalcoholic carbonated beverages on athletic females should be well understood by the sports medicine specialists caring for them.

References

1. Adlercreutz, H.; Karkonen, M.; Kuoppasaimi, K.; Naveri, H.; Huhtaniemi, L.; Tikkanen, H.; Remes, K.; Dessypris, A.; Karvonen, J. Effect of training on plasma anabolic and catabolic steroid hormones and their response during physical exercise. Int. J. Sports Med. 7(Suppl.):27-28; 1986.
2. Alen, M.; Rahkila, P.; Reinila, M.; Vihko, R. Androgenic-anabolic steroid effects on serum thyroid, pituitary, and steroid hormones in athletes. Am. J. Sports Med. 15:357-361; 1987.
3. Alen, M.; Hakkinen, K. Androgenic steroid effects on serum hormones and on maximal force development in strength athletes. J. Sports Med. 27:38-47; 1987.
4. American College of Sports Medicine. Position statement on the use of alcohol in sports. Med. Sci. Sports Exerc. 14:ix-xi; 1982.
5. Ando, K.; Johanson, C. Sensitivity changes dopaminergic agents in fine motor control of rhesus monkeys after repeated methamphetamine administration. Pharm. Biochem. Behav. 22:737-743; 1985.
6. Ariel, G.; Saville, W. Anabolic steroids: the physiological effects of placebos. Med. Sci. Sports Exerc. 4:124-126; 1972.
7. Bach, B.; Warren, R.; Wickiewicz, T. Triceps rupture: a case report and literature review. Am. J. Sports Med. 15(3):285-289; 1987.
8. Barron, J.; Noakes, T.; Levy, W.; Smith, C.; Millar, R.P. Hypothalamic dysfunction in overtrained athletes. J. Clin. Endocrinol. Metab. 60(4):803-806; 1985.

9. Bergman, R.T. Substance abuse in the very young athlete. Sports Med. Dig. 7(3):1-3; 1985.

10. Biron, S.; Wells, J. Marijuana and athletics. Sports Med. Dig. 6(7):3-4; 1984.

11. Biron, S.; Wells, J. Marijuana and its effect on the athlete. Athletic Training, Winter:295-303; 1983.

12. Borg, J. The effects of smoked marijuana on human cognitive and motor functions. Psychopharm. 29:159-170; 1973.

13. Brower, M.; Azizian, C. Trouble: steroids built Mike Keys up; then they tore him down. People Magazine. 1989, March 20; 107-108.

14. Buckley, W.; Yesalis, C.; Friedl, K.; Anderson, W.A.; Streit, A.L.; Wright, J.E. Estimated prevalence of anabolic steroid use among male high school seniors. JAMA 260:3441-3445; 1988.

15. Cantwell, J.D.; Rose, F.D. Cocaine and cardiovascular events. Physician Sportsmed. 11:77-82; 1986.

16. Cohen, J.C.; Faber, W.M.; Spinnler, A.J.; Noakes, T.D. Altered serum lipoprotein profiles in male and female power lifters ingesting anabolic steroids. Physician Sportsmed. 14(6):131-136; 1986.

17. Costill, D.L.; Dalsky, G.P.; Fink, W.J. Effects of caffeine ingestion on metabolism and exercise performance. Med. Sci. Sports Exerc. 10(3):155-158; 1978.

18. Crack. Med. Lett. Drugs Ther. 28:69-72; 1986.

19. Dezelsky, T.L.; Toohey, J.V.; Shaw, R.S. Nonmedical drug use behavior at five United States universities: a 15-year study. Bull. on Narcotics 37(2&3):49-53; 1985.

20. Eichner, E.R. The caffeine controversy: effects on endurance and cholesterol. Physician Sportsmed. 12:124-130; 1986.

21. Elofson, G.; Elofson, S. Steroids claimed our son's life. Physician Sports Med. 18(8):15-16; 1990 August.

22. Frankle, M.A.; Eichberg, R.; Zachariah, S.B. Anabolic androgenic steroids and a stroke in an athlete: case report. Arch. Phys. Med. Rehabil. 69:632-633; 1988.

23. Goodman, L.S.; Gilman, A. The pharmacologic basis of therapeutics, 5th ed. New York: Macmillan; 1975:306-309.

24. Goodman, L.S.; Gilman, A. The pharmacologic basis of therapeutics, 5th ed. New York: Macmillan; 1975:367-378.

25. Goodman, L.S.; Gilman, A. The pharmacologic basis of therapeutics, 5th ed. New York: Macmillan; 1975:481 & 505.

26. Goodman, L.S.; Gilman, A. The pharmacologic basis of therapeutics, 5th ed. New York: Macmillan; 1975:547-552.

27. Goodman, L.S.; Gilman, A. The pharmacologic basis of therapeutics, 5th ed. New York: Macmillan; 1975:496-500.

28. Gribbin, H.; Flavell-Matts, S. Mode of action anduse of anabolic steroids. Br. J. Clin. Pract. 30(1):3-9; 1976.

29. Hakkinen, K.; Pakarinen, A.; Alen, M.; Komi, P.V. Serous hormones during prolonged training of neuromuscular performance. Eur. J. Appl. Physiol. 53:287-293; 1985.

30. Haupt, H.A.; Rovere, G.D. Anabolic steroids: a review of the literature. Am. J. Sports Med. 12:469-484; 1984

31. Herrick, R.; Herrick, S. Ruptured triceps in a powerlifter presenting as cubital tunnel syndrome. Am. J. Sports Med. 15(5):514-516; 1987.

32. Hollister, L.E. Health aspects of cannabis. Pharmacol. Rev. 38:1-20; 1986.

33. Holma, P.K. Effects of an anabolic steroid (metandienone) in spermatogenesis. Contraception 15:151-162; 1977.

34. Houssay, A.B. Effects of anabolic-androgenic steroids on the skin, including hair and sebaceous glands. In Kochakian, C.D., ed. Anabolic-androgenic steroids. New York: Springer-Verlag; 1976:155-190.
35. Hurley, B.F.; Seals, D.R.; Hagberg, J.M.; Goldberg, A.C.; Ostrove, S.M.; Holloszy, J.O.; Wiest, W.G.; Goldberg, A.R. High density lipoprotein cholesterol in bodybuilders vs. powerlifters: negative effects of androgen use. JAMA 252:507-513; 1982.
36. Ivy, J.L. Amphetamines in sports: are they worth the risk? Sports Med. Dig. 6(3):1-3; 1984.
37. Ivy, J.L.; Cotill, D.L.; Fink, W.J.; Lower, R.W. Influence of caffeine and carbohydrate feedings on endurance performance. Med. Sci. Sports Exerc. 11:6-11; 1979.
38. Johnston, L.D.; O'Malley, P.M.; Bachman, J.G. Drug use among American high school students, college students, and other young adults: national trends through 1985. Washington, DC: US Dept. of Health & Human Services; 1986. Publication ADM 86-1450.
39. Kearns, W.M. Oral therapy of testicular deficiency. J. Clin. Endocrinol. 1:126; 1941.
40. Kopera, H. The history of anabolic steroids and a review of clinical experience with anabolic steroids. Acta Endocrinol. 271(Suppl.):11-19; 1985.
41. Kraemer, W. Endocrine responses to resistance exercise. Med. Sci. Sports Exerc. (5, suppl.):S132-S157; 1988.
42. Kraemer, W.; Deschenes, M.; Fleck, S. Physiological adaptations to resistance exercise: implications for athletic conditioning. Sports Med. 6:246-256; 1988.
43. Kramhoft, M.; Solgaard, S. Spontaneous rupture of the extensor pollices longus tendon after anabolic steroids. J. Hand Surg. 11:87; 1986.
44. Krowchuk, D.P.; Anglin, T.M.; Goodfellow, D.B.; Stancin, T.; Williams, P.; Zimet, G.D. High school athletes and the use of ergogenic aids. AJDC 143:486-489; 1989 April.
45. Kruskemper, H.L. Anabolic steroids. New York: Academic Press; 1968.
46. Lamb, D.R. Anabolic steroids in athletics: how well do they work and how dangerous are they? Am. J. Sports Med. 12:31-38; 1984.
47. Lombardo, J.A. Stimulants and athletic performance. Part 1:Amphetamines and caffeine. Physician Sportsmed. 11:128-142; 1986.
48. Lombardo, J.A. Stimulants and athletic performance. Part 2:Cocaine and nicotine. Physician Sportsmed. 1285-1289; 1986.
49. Martinez, J.; Buttery, P.; Pearson, J. The mode of action of anabolic agents: the effect of testosterone on muscle protein metabolism in the female rat. Br. J. Nutr. 52:515-521; 1984.
50. Michelson, C.; Askanazi, J.; Kinney, J.; Gump, F.E.; Elwyn, D.H. Effect of an anabolic steroid on nitrogen balance and amino acid patterns after total hip replacement. J. Trauma 22:410-413; 1982.
51. Michna, H. Organization of collagen fibrils in tendon: changes induced by anabolic steroid. Virchows Archiv B. 52:87-98; 1986.
52. Michna, H.; Stang-Voss, C. The predisposition to tendon rupture after doping with anabolic steroids. Int. J. Sports Med. 4:59; 1983.
53. Mochizuki, R.M.; Richter, K.J. Cardiomyopathy and cerebrovascular accident associated with anabolic-androgenic steroid use. Physician Sportsmed. 16:108-114; 1988.
54. Moffatt, R.J.; Wallace, M.B.; Sady, S.P. Effects of anabolic steroids on lipoprotein profiles of female weight lifters. Physician Sportsmed. 18(9):106-115; 1990.
55. Morris, D.; Garcia, M. Effects of phenylbutazone and anabolic steroids on adrenal and thyroid gland function tests in healthy horses. Am. J. Vet. Res. 46(2):359-365; 1985.

56. National Collegiate Athletic Association. The 1988-89 NCAA drug testing program. 1988 September.
57. Phenylpropanolamine for weight reduction. Med. Lett. Drugs Ther. 26:55-58; 1984.
58. Pope, H.G.; Katz, D.L. Bodybuilder's psychosis. Lancet 1:863; 1987.
59. Pope, H.G., Jr.; Katz, D.L. Affective and psychotic symptoms associated with anabolic steroid use. Am. J. Psychia. 145:487-490; 1988.
60. Rosen, L.W.; McKeag, D.B.; Hough, D.O.; Curley, V. Pathogenic weight-control behavior in female athletes. Physician Sportsmed. 14(1):79-86; 1986.
61. Slavin, J.L.; Joensen, D.J. Caffeine and sports performance. Physician Sportsmed. 13:191-193; 1985.
62. Smith, G.M.; Beecher, H.K. Amphetamine sulfate and athletic performance: I.Objective effects. JAMA 170:542-557; 1959.
63. Smith, S. Aaron Henry's dangerous journey. Reader's Dig. 1989 Dec., 116-120.
64. Sportsmediscope. Guide to banned medications. 7:1-5; 1988.
65. Strauss, R.H.; Liggett, M.T.; Lanese, R.R. Anabolic steroid use and perceived effects in 10 weight-trained women athletes. JAMA 253:2871-2873; 1985.
66. Tennant, F.S., Jr.; Black, D.L.; Voy, R.O. Anabolic steroid dependence with opioid type features. New Eng. J. Med. 319(a):578; 1988 Sept.
67. Tennant, F.S., Jr. Dealing with cocaine use by athletes. Sports Med. Dig. 6(11):1-3; 1984.
68. Wilmore, J. Exercise testing, training, and beta-adrenergic blockade. Physician Sportsmed. 12:45-52; 1988.
69. Wilson, J.D.; Griffin, J.R. The use and misuse of androgens. Metabolism 29(12):1278-1295; 1980.
70. Wood, T.; Cooke, P.; Goodship, A. The effect of exercise and anabolic steroids on the mechanical properties and crimp orphology of the rat tendon. Am. J. Sports Med. 16:153-158; 1988.
71. Wright, J.E. Anabolic steroids and athletics. Exerc. Sport Sci. Rev. 8:149-202; 1980.
72. Wyshak, G.; Frisch, R.E.; Albright, T.E.; Albright, N.L.; Schiff, I.; Witschi, J. Nonalcoholic carbonated beverage consumption and bone fractures among women former college athletes. J. Orthop. Res. 7(1):91-99; 1989.
73. Wyshak, G.; Frisch, R.E.; Albright, T.E.; Albright, N.L.; Schiff, I. No greater risk of bone fractures in former college athletes compared with nonathletes in the postmenopausal years. Obstet. Gynecol. 69:121-126; 1987.
74. Yesavage, J.; Leirer, V.; Ditman, J.; Denari, M.; Hollister, L.E. "Hangover" effects of marijuana intoxication on aircraft pilot performance. Am. J. Psychia. 142:1325-1329; 1985.

CHAPTER 10

•

Eating Disorders Among Athletic Females

Nancy Clark

In 1986, The American College of Physicians estimated that anorexia and bulimia affect 10% to 15% of adolescent girls and young women (2). Among athletes, eating problems and pathogenic disorders affect as many as one-third of females but only very few males (1, 5, 8). One might guess that athletic girls and women who participate in sports emphasizing leanness (i.e., running, gymnastics, wrestling, and light-weight crew) would be at particular risk for developing an eating disorder. However, research suggests that eating disorders are prevalent not only among athletes in weight-related sports but also among tennis and field hockey players and other nonweight-oriented activities (12).

A brief review of the literature indicates the following:

- Three percent of almost 700 athletes in midwestern colleges met the diagnostic criteria for anorexia; 21.5% met the criteria for bulimia (6).
- Thirty-two percent of 182 collegiate female athletes from a variety of sports reported some type of weight-control behavior defined as pathogenic, be it anorexia, bulimia, laxative abuse, excessive exercise, crash dieting, or other unhealthy weight-loss practices (12). Gymnasts, field hockey players, and distance runners reported the highest incidence of eating concerns.
- Responses to the Eating Disorders Inventory suggested food problems or preoccupation with weight among 20% of female athletes in sports that emphasized leanness (ballet, body building, cheerleading, gymnastics), 10% of all athletes, and 6% of nonathletes (5).
- Among adolescent female athletes in Switzerland, 11% of the swimmers, 1% of the gymnasts, and 6% of the controls were extremely preoccupied

with weight (as measured by the Eating Disorders Inventory). Thirty-eight percent of the swimmers, 1% of the gymnasts, and 9% of the controls scored high on the body dissatisfaction scale of the EDI. The authors concluded that disturbances in eating behaviors are not limited to sports that emphasize leanness (4).

- Thirty-four percent of the nation's top female runners reported a history of eating disorders, with 25% having had a BMI of less than 17, suggestive of an anorexic physique (8).
- In a survey of 494 girls (ages 9-18), 58% perceived themselves as being overweight, although only 15% actually were overweight according to medical standards. Among the 9-year-olds, 30% expressed a fear of getting fat. This fear became increasingly prevalent with age; among the 18-year-olds, 87% reported fear of fat. Thirty-one percent of the 9-year-olds reported binge eating, as did 100% of the 18-year-olds (10).
- Among ballet dancers, 80% of those with recent stress fractures had weights less than 75% of ideal and showed a greater incidence of eating disorders (9).

Obviously, dieting, binge eating, and food obsessions are not confined to the overweight population; they are also prevalent practices among normal-weight and thin females, athletes included. Among athletes, many strive to be thinner than their natural weight in the belief that a lower weight will enhance athletic performance (12). They exercise excessively and eat spartanly to attain this often unrealistic goal. Diet restrictions commonly lead to binges. The cycle deepens, and food becomes the fattening enemy. Some suffer from anorexia, others bulimia; many yo-yo between the two. The athletes lose sight of the fact that food contributes to good health, top performance, and athletic longevity.

Anorexia

Anorexia is characterized by a pursuit of thinness. The person is obviously emaciated and often disguised as a very thin athlete. The American Psychiatric Association's (3) definition of anorexia includes

- intense fear of becoming obese, which does not diminish as weight loss progresses;
- disturbances of body images, e.g., claiming to "feel fat" even when emaciated;
- weight loss at least 25% of original body weight or, if under 18 years of age, weight loss of 25% of original body weight plus projected weight gain expected from growth charts;
- refusal to maintain body weight above a minimal, normal weight for age and height; and
- no known physical illness that would account for weight loss.

Among their peers, anorexics are often considered "perfect athletes." They train harder and more than their teammates and can be seen working out at all hours of the day or night. They often push themselves to outstanding goals that bring fame and glory to their team, school, or club. Coaches often overlook the emaciated physique, denying that an athlete who performs so well could be sick.

Some anorexics look "perfectly thin," but more likely they are unattractively scrawny and wasted. (Family and friends may have trouble making that distinction.) They often have a layer of fine body hair, easily noticeable on their faces and arms. They tend to wear bulky clothes to hide their thinness and complain about the cold (even when the temperature is comfortable for others). They consume an abnormally spartan amount of food in comparison to the energy they expend. (You may never see them eating in public; if you do, you'll notice that they push the food around on a plate to fool you into thinking they are eating.) They often have other compulsive behaviors, such as studying very hard or working long hours.

Bulimia

Bulimia is characterized by a fear of food. The person may have a normal weight but abnormal eating behaviors. The definition used by the American Psychiatric Association (3) includes these characteristics:

1. Recurrent episodes of binge eating (rapid consumption of a large amount of food in a discrete time period, usually less than 2 hours)
2. At least three of the following:
   - Consumption of highly caloric, easily ingested food during a binge
   - Inconspicuous eating during a binge
   - Termination of such eating episodes by abdominal pain, sleep, social interruption, or self-induced vomiting
   - Repeated attempts to lose weight by severely restrictive diets, self-induced vomiting, or use of cathartics or diuretics
   - Weight fluctuations greater than 10 pounds due to alternate binges and fasts
3. Awareness that the eating pattern is abnormal and fear of not being able to stop eating voluntarily
4. Depressed mood and self-deprecating thoughts after eating binges

Bulimic behavior can be more subtle than that of anorexics. Common symptoms include blood-shot eyes, swollen glands, and bruised fingers (from inducing vomiting). The athlete may eat a hearty meal, then rush to the bathroom and use running water to cover the sound of her vomiting. She may hide laxatives and display other secretive behaviors. Bulimics may even resort to petty stealing of money from teammates to support their addiction.

Predisposing Factors to Eating Disorders

Eating disorders are common among people who grew up in dysfunctional families—in particular, families with alcohol problems (7). People with eating disorders often have a compulsive desire for control and perfection, two characteristics common to adult children of alcoholics (13). If as children they couldn't control their (alcoholic) parent, they now may strive to control their weight (get rid of all body fat), their food (eat minimal calories), and their training (take no rest days). They may exercise compulsively or eat compulsively (if bulimic) and may be better described as compulsive exercisers rather than dedicated athletes. An athlete, after all, incorporates good nutrition and rest days into an optimal training program.

Dietary Treatment

A medical team that includes a physician, sport nutritionist, and psychological therapist (all skilled in working with people with eating disorders) is optimal for the long-term treatment of eating disorders. The team goals are to establish a normal eating pattern appropriate for the athlete's energy expenditures; modify abnormal attitudes toward food, weight, and eating; develop alternative coping strategies; increase self-esteem; and improve family communication.

During the initial interview, the athlete will undoubtedly feel embarrassed about her abnormal eating behaviors. Hence, the professionals should try to make her feel at ease in an accepting, nonjudgmental atmosphere, letting her know that she is only one of many who struggle with food issues and that they have helped others like her. The athlete must clearly understand that *she* is responsible for changing her abnormal eating behaviors; the team's only job is to provide helpful information, guidance, and support.

Although the athlete undoubtedly wants to lose weight, the first step is to relearn how to eat normally. Often, the athlete has a warped body image and is unaware that she has no weight to lose. In such cases, body fat measurements can help identify a realistic weight goal. Even if an athlete is overweight, dietary restriction is inappropriate at this time and incompatible with breaking the binge-purge cycle, because restrictive diets commonly precipitate binges (11). Guidelines for an appropriate, yet safe (i.e., not conducive to weight gain) caloric intake will help the athlete to realize that she is *supposed* to eat (unlike in her self-imposed, crash-diet regimen).

Initially, eating may seem safest if it's mechanical with few decisions to be made. The American Dietetic Association's exchange lists can be helpful; also try menus based on unit portions, such as one cup of yogurt, a frozen dinner, a single-serving box of cereal, an apple. This structure can reduce anxiety about overeating. Meals should be dealt with one at a time, to reduce anxiety and overwhelming fears of becoming fat. With constant reassurance that food contributes to health, high energy, and top performances, the athlete can practice eating healthfully just as she practices her sport—as an integral part of her training program.

Preventing Eating Disorders

To help prevent problems, a sport nutritionist or registered dietitian should work with athletic females to teach them how to lose weight healthfully or to maintain a realistic weight. When left on their own, athletes tend to crash-diet, then binge, thus falling prey to the vicious cycle of starve/binge routines that set the stage for severe eating disorders.

Tips for Helping Athletes With Eating Disorders

Anorexia and bulimia are self-destructive eating behaviors that may signal underlying depression and can be life-threatening. Here are some tips for approaching the delicate subject:

• Approach the athlete gently but persistently, saying that in watching her you have observed that she seems to have a problem with food. Stress that you're worried about her health. A bulimic will often open up with this approach, but an anorexic may try to deny any problem. She's perfectly fine, she insists. However, she may be concerned about her loss of concentration, light-headedness, or chronic fatigue. These health changes are more likely to be a stepping-stone to accepting help, because the athlete clings to food and exercise for feelings of control and stability.

• Don't discuss weight or eating habits. The anorexic takes great pride in being perfectly thin and may dismiss your concern as jealousy, thinking that you probably yearn to be as successful with weight control. Remember that the starving or bingeing is not the most important issue. Rather it is a smoke screen hiding the fundamental problem—problems with life.

• Focus on the athlete's unhappiness as the reason for seeking help. Point out how anxious, tired, or irritable she has been. Emphasize that she doesn't have to be that way.

• Be supportive and listen sympathetically, but don't expect the athlete to open up and trust you right away. Give it time, but constantly remind her that you are concerned and that you believe in her ability to resolve the problem.

• Give her a written list of resources for professional help. Although the athlete may deny that there's a problem now, she may admit despair at another moment.

Post a list of local resources (with a tear-off phone number at the bottom) in the locker rooms, bathrooms, and dining halls.

If local resources are inadequate, contact one of these national organizations.

Anorexia Nervosa and Associated Disorders (ANAD)
Box 271
Highland Park, IL 60035
Phone 708-831-3438

ANAD runs a national system of free support groups and referral lists of psychotherapists.

National Anorexic Aid Society (NAAS)
1925 East Dublin-Granville Road
Columbus, OH 43229
Phone 614-436-1112

NAAS provides referral services in the United States, Canada, and Great Britain. It also offers a newsletter and additional information on eating disorders.

Anorexia and Bulimia Treatment and Education Center (ABTEC)
621 South New Ballas Road
Suite 7019B
St. Louis, MO 63141
Phone 314-569-6898

ABTEC offers a national referral service, self-help groups, and information on eating disorders. Send a self-addressed, stamped envelope, three stamps, and $1 for details.

• Don't deal with the problem alone. If you feel that you're making no headway and the athlete is becoming more self-destructive, seek help from one of her family members, a medical professional, or a health service. Make an appointment with a mental health counselor and bring the athlete there yourself. Tell the athlete that you choose to involve other people because you care about her. If you are overreacting and there really is no problem, this health professional will be able to ease your mind.

• Talk to someone about your own emotions if you feel the need. Remember that you are not responsible and can only *try* to help. Your power comes from using community resources and health professionals, such as a guidance counselor, a nutritionist, a member of the clergy, or an eating disorders clinic.

Summary

1. Eating disorders such as anorexia and bulimia affect as many as a third of athletic females.

2. Family alcoholism, history of sexual abuse, multiple injuries, menstrual irregularity, abnormal eating habits, and distorted self-image regarding weight are all possible indicators of eating disorders.
3. A medical-team approach to treatment of eating disorders includes coaches, physicians, trainers, sport nutritionists, and counselors who work together to provide helpful information, guidance, and support in sport nutrition programs.
4. Because eating problems and disorders affect approximately one-third of female athletes, sports medicine professionals should learn about the warning signals so that they can identify these devastating conditions, confront the struggling athletes, and hopefully transform disordered eating patterns into healthful sport diets. Optimal sport nutrition is fundamental—not only for the female athlete's performance today, but also for her health and well-being tomorrow.
5. Dietary goals include establishing a normal attitude toward food, body image, and eating.

References

1. Eating disorders in young athletes: a round table. Phys. Sportsmed. 13(11):89-106; 1985.
2. American College of Physicians. Eating disorders: anorexia and bulimia. Ann. Intern. Med. 105:790 794; 1986.
3. APA. Diagnostic and statistical manual of mental disorders III-R, 3rd ed. rev. Washington, DC: American Psychiatric Association; 1987.
4. Benson, J.; Allemann, Y.; Theintz, G.; Howard, H. Eating problems and calorie intake levels in Swiss adolescent athletes. Int. J. Sports Med. 11(4):249-252; 1990.
5. Borgen, J.; Corbin, C. Eating disorders among female athletes. Phys. Sportsmed. 15(2):89-95; 1987.
6. Burckes-Miller, M.; Black, D. Male and female college athletes: prevalence of anorexia and bulimia nervosa. Athletic Training 23:137-140; 1988.
7. Clark, N. letter Phys. Sportsmed. 15(8):24; 1987.
8. Clark, N.; Nelson, M.; Evans, W. Nutrition education for elite female runners. Phys. Sportsmed. 16(2):124-135; 1988.
9. Frusztajer, N.; Dhuper, S.; Warren, M.; Brooks-Gunn, J.; Fox, R. Nutrition and the incidence of stress fractures in ballet dancers. Am. J. Clin. Nutr. 51:779-783; 1990.
10. Mellin, L. Responding to disordered eating in children and adolescents. Nutr. News 51(Summer):5-7; 1988.
11. Polivy, J.; Herman, C.P. Dieting and binging: a causal analysis. Am. Psychol. 40:193-201; 1985.
12. Rosen, L.W.; McKeag, D.B., Hough, D.O.; Curley, V. Pathogenic weight-control behavior in female athletes. Phys. Sportsmed. 14:79-86; 1986.
13. Woititz, J. Adult children of alcoholics. Pompano Beach, FL: Health Communications; 1983.

CHAPTER 11

•

Gender Differences in Circulorespiratory and Metabolic Variables Related to Endurance Performance

Ben R. Londeree

A highly trained endurance athlete is able to maintain high exercise intensity without accumulating significant lactic acid. Important contributors to success in endurance activities include a high maximal oxygen uptake ($\dot{V}O_2$max), a high lactate threshold (LT); variously called aerobic threshold, anaerobic threshold, ventilatory threshold, onset of plasma lactate, onset of blood lactate accumulation, and maximal steady state), and economical performance (41). For events that last over an hour, delay of glycogen depletion is important (39).

Circulorespiratory and Metabolic Factors Affecting Endurance Performance

Female performances in events involving circulorespiratory endurance are significantly poorer than male performances. It follows that gender differences in physiological and metabolic variables important to success in these events may contribute to the performance deficits.

Maximal Oxygen Consumption

Maximal oxygen consumption involves delivery of a high volume of oxygen to the active tissues that, in turn, process it during very intense activity. Because a steady supply of oxygen is required to sustain exercise and oxygen consumption is related to exercise intensity, it follows that a high rate of oxygen delivery is imperative for sustained, high intensity exercise. A high rate of oxygen delivery depends on several key steps: high rate of ventilation ($V_E$max), high rate of diffusion across the alveolar-capillary membranes, high cardiac output (Qmax), high oxygen carrying capacity of blood (total hemoglobin-Hb), optimal distribution of blood to the active tissues, high rate of diffusion of the oxygen from capillaries to the mitochondria of active tissues, and a high rate of muscle mitochondrial activity.

In healthy, normal individuals ventilation probably is not a limiting factor. In elite female runners VEmax has been reported to be 66% of maximal ventilatory volume (MVV; 45). However, three elite male runners were reported to have $V_E$max values exceeding 90% of MVV, although these individuals had below normal MVV (46).

There is some controversy regarding the extent that pulmonary diffusing capacity limits $\dot{V}O_2$max. The widening alveolar- to arterial-oxygen difference [(A-a)O_2] as exercise intensity increases supports the hypothesis that pulmonary diffusing capacity can limit $\dot{V}O_2$max in endurance athletes (63). Factors that contribute to the increasing (A-a)O_2 include inhomogeneities in ventilation-perfusion ratios, limited pulmonary diffusion per se, and admixture of venous shunt blood. Dempsey (22) suggested that pulmonary diffusing capacity may limit VO_2max in some situations, particularly with reduced ambient oxygen tension. Magel and Andersen (43) felt that training does not change the diffusion capacity per se, rather the increased lung volume found in endurance athletes provides a larger surface area for exchange.

Maximal cardiac output is a function of maximal heart rate (HRmax) and maximal stroke volume (SVmax). Because the coefficient of variation for HRmax is relatively low in young adults (6%) and HRmax is lower in endurance-trained individuals (42), it is not an important contributor to an enhanced Qmax. On the other hand, SVmax of endurance athletes is nearly two times that of sedentary individuals and tends to increase with endurance training (59); therefore, it is the major determinant of variability in Qmax. Stroke volume is a function of heart volume, myocardial contractility, and venous return which, in turn, is influenced by blood volume. Endurance training will increase heart volume (16), myocardial contractility (58), and blood volume (49).

The oxygen-carrying capacity of blood is a function of hemoglobin concentration ([Hb]) and blood volume. Modification of blood volume or Hb concentration via blood withdrawal and subsequent reinfusion has demonstrated that $\dot{V}O_2$max is related to the total Hb in the circulatory system (38). Endurance training has had a variable effect on hemoglobin concentration but has increased blood volume and total hemoglobin (40).

Optimal distribution of blood to active tissues has not been studied much. Blood flow to a muscle influences oxygen uptake and work by that muscle (7). However, blood flow to a working muscle has been shown to change little (and perhaps even to decrease) with endurance training (31). But, increases in active muscle mass have produced incremental increases in $\dot{V}O_2$max, probably because an increase in active muscle would increase total blood flow and hence be a potential cause of higher $\dot{V}O_2$max. Nevertheless, differences in blood distribution per se probably do not contribute significantly to differences in $\dot{V}O_2$max under normal circumstances.

Barring disease effects (e.g., diabetes), the rate of diffusion of oxygen from blood into muscle probably is not a rate-limiting step. Normally such diffusion is thought to be a function of an oxygen gradient resulting from rapid oxygen use in the muscles. However, $(a-v)O_2$ has been shown to increase as a result of endurance training (59); whether this change is due to changes in diffusion or to increased oxidative capacity of active tissues has not been determined.

The rate of oxygen use at the tissue level depends on two factors (1) active muscle mass and (2) oxidative capacity of the active muscle. To the extent that recruited muscles can process oxygen, the larger the active muscle mass, the greater the oxygen consumption (60). For a given activity that presumably would use a constant muscle mass, the oxidative capacity of that muscle mass determines the limit to oxygen consumption (35). On the other hand, among individuals of different sizes the active muscle mass for a particular activity is probably related to body size (BW) or actually to lean body weight (LBW). Therefore, oxygen consumption for weight-bearing activities generally is expressed in $mL \cdot kg\ BW^{-1} \cdot min^{-1}$ or sometimes $mL \cdot kg\ LBW^{-1} \cdot min^{-1}$.

Because the oxygen cost of weight-bearing activity is related to BW (44), $\dot{V}O_2$max usually is expressed per kilogram of BW. It follows that nonessential body fat increases BW (the denominator) and hence reduces the weight-adjusted $\dot{V}O_2$max.

In summary, factors that contribute significantly to $\dot{V}O_2$max probably include (1) a high, maximal cardiac output via a high stroke volume (stroke volume is a function of heart size, contractility, and venous return; the latter depends on the nature of the activity and blood volume); (2) the oxygen-carrying capacity of the blood, which is dependent on hemoglobin concentration and blood volume; and (3) the oxidative capacity of the recruited muscles, which is a function of the muscle mass and oxidative capacity of the same. When weight-adjusted $\dot{V}O_2$max is used, excess body fat decreases $\dot{V}O_2$max.

Lactate Threshold

Lactate threshold has been defined variously as that oxygen consumption or exercise intensity above which lactate begins to accumulate or elicits a blood lactate of 2.0 mmol or 4.0 mmol. These definitions infer that lactate production exceeds clearance. Because elevated lactate concentrations are associated with fatigue, the ability to perform high intensity exercise without lactate accumulation would be very important to endurance performance.

Several mechanisms have been proposed for lactate threshold: (1) local pockets of hypoxia, (2) excessive stimulation of glycogenolysis and glycolysis (via local metabolic factors or epinephrine), (3) recruitment of fast-twitch glycolytic

(FG) muscle fibers, (4) reduced blood flow to sites of lactate removal, and (5) substrate use (65). There has been considerable controversy regarding which mechanism controls lactate threshold.

The traditional view holds that lactic acid accumulation occurs due to hypoxia (66). However, the degree of hypoxia required to elevate lactic acid production does not occur at the tissue level during submaximal exercise (65).

Epinephrine increases exponentially with exercise intensity and stimulates glycogenolysis that leads to excess lactate production in muscle fibers with low oxidative capabilities (65). Endurance training reduces the epinephrine concentration at a given exercise intensity (67), thereby decreasing the stimulus for excess lactate production and increasing the lactate threshold intensity (absolute and percent of $\dot{V}O_2$max).

Slow-twitch oxidative (SO) and fast-twitch oxidative-glycolytic (FOG) muscle fibers (in contrast to FG muscle fibers) have a well-developed mitochondrial system (with its oxidative enzymes) and tend to have a greater proportion of heart-type lactate dehydrogenase (LDH-H) and a higher activity of the malate shuttle system. LDH-H favors the conversion of lactate to pyruvate that subsequently is metabolized oxidatively. The malate shuttle system oxidizes cytosolic nicotine adenine dinucleotide (NAD) by shuttling reducing equivalents into mitochondria; this decreases the need for converting pyruvate to lactate. Endurance training increases the oxidative activities of SO, FOG, and some FG (convert to FOG) muscle fibers (1, 29), thereby decreasing recruitment of FG muscle fibers and excess lactate production. In fact, training changes in these variables have tended to be relatively greater than the change in $\dot{V}O_2$max (21).

Both lactic acid production and clearance increase during mild and moderate exercise, but clearance declines at higher intensities (23). The reduced lactate clearance was hypothesized to result from decreased blood flow to regions of lactate use. Data collected recently in our lab suggested that initial increases in lactate concentration emanated from FG muscle fibers and reduced blood flow to all regions may have led to rapid accumulation of lactate at higher exercise intensities.

Because lactate production is dependent upon glucose or glycogen metabolism, it follows that anything that modifies carbohydrate metabolism could affect the lactate threshold. Endurance training increases fat use (9) and LT (21), though a cause-and-effect relationship has not been established. Ingestion of a fatty meal will increase the LT (34). Also, lowering muscle glycogen will increase LT (33). Although these dietary modifications can alter LT, they can be controlled.

In summary, lactate threshold probably is due to excess lactate production by FG muscle fibers resulting from epinephrine stimulation of glycogenolysis or recruitment. Rapid accumulation of lactate may be due to reduced blood flow to sites of lactate removal. The increased LT resulting from endurance training may be related to increased fat use and hence reduced carbohydrate use.

Running Economy

Running economy is defined as a relatively low oxygen consumption for a particular exercise intensity. If two runners have the same maximal, steady state oxygen consumption, the runner who is more efficient will be able to run faster.

The oxygen cost of running at steady state speeds is quite variable even when expressed relative to weight. This variability exists even among elite distance runners who had $\dot{V}O_2$ ranges of from 48.7 to 57.8 mL · kg⁻¹ · min⁻¹ at 268 m · min⁻¹ and of 60.6 to 74.4 mL · kg⁻¹ · min⁻¹ at 322 m · min⁻¹ (55). However, intraindividual variation can average 3% to 5% of the mean individual $\dot{V}O_2$ with an extreme variation of 9% (48). When running experience, footwear, time of day, and training activity were controlled, intraindividual variability decreased to 1.6% (a range of 0.4%-3.4%; 48).

Economical running performance has several factors. First and foremost, because the oxygen cost of weight-bearing activity is directly related to weight (44), excess weight in the form of fat increases the oxygen cost of performing at a given intensity. Stated another way, if a runner decreases fat weight, she will be able to run faster using the same amount of oxygen. Endurance athletes have very low percent body fat values.

Second, learning to eliminate wasteful motion can reduce oxygen consumption. When endurance athletes decreased their oxygen consumption for a given exercise intensity with prolonged training (62), part of this improved efficiency probably was related to a less wasteful running style.

Finally, slow-twitch muscle fibers have been shown to have a slower cross-bridge turnover, which means less splitting of adenosine triphosphate (ATP) and hence less oxidation to replace ATP (6, 28). Endurance athletes have been reported to have higher than normal to very high percentages (85%-98%) of SO muscle fibers (27). Some athletes may gravitate to endurance events because they have a high percentage of SO fibers; however, long-term training as done by elite long distance athletes may have increased the number of slow-twitch muscle fibers (38). In addition, the nonlinear relationship between $\dot{V}O_2$ and speed of running when a wide range of speeds is chosen (19) suggests that the recruitment of fast-twitch muscle fibers at higher speeds may reduce efficiency.

Substrate Use

Another factor that may affect performance in events lasting over 1 hour is glycogen depletion. Endurance training increases utilization of fat, thereby decreasing glycogen use and delaying glycogen depletion (32). A possible mechanism for this effect is reduced epinephrine accumulation. Lower epinephrine levels reduce glycogenolysis and lactate production. Lower lactate levels would reduce lactate inhibition of fat mobilization.

Circulorespiratory and Metabolic Factors Related to Gender Differences in Endurance Performance

The previous discussion suggests which variables might explain differences in circulorespiratory endurance among individuals or groups of individuals. Of particular interest is the explanation of *gender* differences in circulorespiratory endurance. Current world-record performances by gender are shown in Table 11.1. If we assume that the improvements in women's records are approaching an asymptote, we may compare elite male and female performers; these individuals are expected to train optimally and near to their genetic limits. Physiological, metabolic, and performance data on a substantial number of elite, male middle-distance (sub-4:00 mile) and long-distance runners (sub-2:15:00 marathon) have appeared in the literature during the past 20 years. Comparable data on elite females has been published in the past 7 years. These data may reveal physiological and metabolic explanations for gender performance differences (see Tables 11.2 and 11.3). Where data on certain variables is limited or lacking on elite runners, data from other sources may be useful.

Maximal Oxygen Consumption

The mean value of $\dot{V}O_2$max for elite, female distance runners averaged 70% of that for men. When adjusted for body weight, the value rose to 85%, and when adjusted for lean body weight, it increased to 94%. Because the energy cost of running generally is considered to be a function of body weight (43), it is logical to use the 85% figure. Conversely, this 15% deficit exceeded performance differences; therefore, adjusting $\dot{V}O_2$max on a 1 mL-to-1 kg ratio is not quite appropriate. Actually, a ratio of $1 \text{ ml} \cdot \text{kg}^{-.7} \cdot \text{min}^{-1}$ might be a more appropriate way to express $\dot{V}O_2$max (8). However, this ratio produced minor changes in the percent deficits when compared to $1 \text{ ml} \cdot \text{kg}^{-1} \cdot \text{min}^{-1}$.

Oxygen transport is dependent on cardiac output via heart rate and SV and on the oxygen-carrying capacity of blood through Hb concentration and blood volume. Recent studies of elite endurance runners reported HRmax and [Hb] but not Q, SV, or blood volume. The gender differences in HRmax were small, variable, and consistent with the conclusion that there is no gender difference in HRmax (42). In 1964, Astrand et al. (4) reported that Qmax was 23% lower (18.5 vs. 24.1 $\text{L} \cdot \text{min}^{-1}$) and SVmax was 25% lower (100 vs. 134 mL) in trained

Table 11.1   Current World Records for Running Events

Event	Females	Males	Female/male %
800 m	1:53.28	1:41.73	111.4
1,500 m	3:52.47	3:29.46	111.0
Mile	4:15.61	3:46.32	112.9
3,000 m	8:22.62	7:29.45	111.8
5,000 m	14:37.33	12:58.39	112.7
10,000 m	30:13.74	27:08.23	111.4
Marathon (26 mi 385 ft)	2:21:06	2:06:50	111.2

Note. Data compiled from *Track and Field News* (1991; 44[1], p. 40; 44[2], p. 32).

Table 11.2 Means for Anthropometric and Physiological Variables at Rest

Variable	Elite M-D males	Elite L-D males	Mixed elite males	Elite M-D females	Elite L-D females	Mixed elite females
Height (cm)	177.3	180.0	179.0	165	167	160.8/166
Weight (kg)	65.0	60.6	63.1	50.3	53.2	47.0/51.9
Age (yrs)	24.9	28.8		23.0	22.8	27.2/22.9
% body fat	6.0	7.5	4.6			14.3
LBW (kg)	61.1	56.0	60.2			40.3
% ST	61.3	82.0	82.9	60	80	68.8
SDH	20.4	18.7	21.6			13.3
RBC (mil · cm^{-3})			5.01/5.1	4.45	4.45	4.45
Hct (%)			43.8/44.9	39.9	40.6	40.9/40.3
Hb (g · dL^{-1})			15.5	13.6	13.6	14.0/13.6
S-Ferritin (ng · mL^{-1})			42.3	28.6	35.5	34.0/32.4
S-Iron (μ · dL^{-1})			85.9			102.0
% saturation of transferrin			25.3			29.0
LVEDD (cm)			5.10			4.8
LVESD (cm)			3.42			3.1
PLVWT (cm)			0.98			0.9
IST (cm)			1.13			1.0

(continued)

Table 11.2 *(continued)*

Variable	Elite M-D males	Elite L-D males	Mixed elite males	Elite M-D females	Elite L-D females	Mixed elite females
EF (%)			67			77
SV (mL)			96.4			91
FVC (L)	5.78	5.40	5.88			3.96
RV (L)	1.53	1.78	1.64			1.25
TLC (L)	7.31	7.18	7.27			5.23
RV/TLC (%)	20.9	24.6	23.0			24.0
FVC1.0 (% FVC)	78.4	80.4	82.0			85.8

Note. LBW = lean body weight, % ST = percent slow twitch muscle fibers, SDH = sucinnate dehydrogenase activity, RBC = red blood cell count, Hct = hematocrit, LVEDD = left ventricular end diastolic diameter, LVESD = left ventricular end systolic diameter, PLVPWT = posterior left ventricle wall thickness, IST = interseptal thickness, EF % = ejection fraction, SV = stroke volume, FVC = forced vital capacity, RV = residual volume, TLC = total lung capacity, FVC1.0 = timed vital capacity.

Data compiled from *Track and Field News* (1991; 44[1], p. 40; 44[2], p. 32).

Table 11.3   Means for Physiological Variables During Exercise

Variable	Elite M-D males	Elite L-D males	Mixed elite males	Elite M-D females	Elite L-D females	Mixed elite females
$\dot{V}O_2$max (L · min^{-1})	5.06	4.50	5.00	3.37	3.71	3.15/3.55
$\dot{V}O_2$max (mL · kg^{-1} · min^{-1})	78.1	74.4	79.3	68.0/67.0	66.4/68.8	67.1/67.9
$\dot{V}O_2$max (mL · kg LBW^{-1} · min^{-1})	82.8	80.3	83.1			78.2
HRmax (bpm)	197.0	193.5	189.0	195	184/188	189/191
$V_E$max (L · min^{-1})	166.4	161.7	166.0	111.5	126.2	106.2/119.3
HLactate max (mmol)	12.8	10.3	11.9	10.3	8.2	8.9
Ventilatory threshold (% VO_2max)			88.2			
Ventilatory threshold (HR)			178			
HLactate threshold (% VO_2max)				> 71	> 73	> 72
HLactate threshold (HR)				> 172	> 157	> 163
VO at 268 m (mL · kg^{-1} · min^{-1})	54.8	49.9		51.5	50.3	50.9
HR at 268 m (bpm)	166.3	158.5		161	155	158

Note. Data compiled from *Track and Field News* (1991: 44[1], p. 40; 44[2], p. 32).

females; HRmax was 4% lower in the females. When adjusted for body weight, the differences were reduced to 8% for Qmax and 11% for SVmax. These gender percent differences were less than those reported for $\dot{V}O_2$max for the elite runners but might have been due to an adjustment to offset the lower oxygen-carrying capacity of blood in females.

Hemoglobin concentration for the elite female runners was 12% lower than the elite male runners. Corresponding blood volume data were not available; however, the 1964 Astrand et al. cohort showed a 22% lower absolute plasma volume (8% when adjusted for body weight) for the females. In addition, PO_2 for mixed venous blood for these females was equal to that in the males so that $(a-v)O_2$ difference was 8% lower in females. Cureton et al. (17), using active, healthy subjects, equated male Hb levels with females by withdrawing blood from the males and reduced the gender difference in $\dot{V}O_2$max from 4.8 to 1.6 mL · kg^{-1} · min^{-1} (67%). However, the time to exhaustion on a cycle ergometer test was reduced only 12% following blood withdrawal. These differences (67% vs. 12%) support the conclusion that $\dot{V}O_2$max does not fully explain endurance performance.

The oxidative capacity of the total musculature is a function of active muscle mass and the enzyme activity per unit mass. If we assume that the active muscle mass:LBW ratio is similar for males and females, then LBW differences can represent the relative active muscle mass differences. The LBW value for the elite female runners was about 67% (or 33% less) of that for males.

Oxidative capacity per unit of muscle is a function of fiber type proportions and oxidative enzyme concentrations. The proportion of slow-twitch fibers for the elite males and females were quite similar. However, the concentration of succinate dehydrogenase (an aerobic enzyme of the Kreb's cycle) was about 33% lower in the females.

Lactate Threshold

Very little published data exist for the LT (or aerobic-anaerobic threshold, etc.) for elite runners. A group of males, including both elite middle- and long-distance runners, had an average ventilatory threshold of 88.2% of $\dot{V}O_2$max, a very high value. The Aerobics Center male runners had a mean lactate concentration of 3.3 mmol (nearly twice the threshold level) at 85% $\dot{V}O_2$max (55). No comparable data are available for elite females. However, at an average of 72% $\dot{V}O_2$max (71% and 73% for middle and long distance, respectively), elite female runners had lactate concentrations averaging 1.2 mmol. Generally, lactate concentration at LT averages about 1.70 to 1.80 mmol, so these women runners were clearly below their thresholds. Therefore, we cannot make direct comparisons of LTs for elite male and female runners. Fay et al. (26) reported that well-trained, but certainly not elite, females had a lactate concentration of 2.0 mmol at an average of 78% $\dot{V}O_2$max and a lactate concentration of 4.0 mmol at an average of 87% $\dot{V}O_2$max. Elite female runners could be expected to have higher lactate thresholds than the Fay et al. runners, so it is reasonable to expect that the former would have LTs near the values reported in the elite male runners.

LT relative to $\dot{V}O_2$max is related to the percentage of slow-twitch muscle fibers (36). This percentage was similar for the elite males and females, so this supports the conclusion that their LTs were similar.

On the other hand, the elite male runners had higher succinate dehydrogenase activities than the elite female runners. Aunola et al. (5) reported that LT was related closely to citrate synthase and malate dehydrogenase activities (mitochondrial markers) and moderately to succinate dehydrogenase activity. Other reports show that trained females have lower SDH activities than trained males (13, 15) but there may not be a gender difference in sedentary subjects (13). In addition, Ivy (36) showed that LT was related closely to the ability of muscle tissue to oxidize pyruvate. These results suggest that the elite male runners might have had higher LTs.

In conclusion, the indirect analyses suggest that the LT relative to $\dot{V}O_2$max of the elite female runners was equal to or slightly less than that of their male comparison groups. However, because $\dot{V}O_2$max was higher in the males, the absolute LT values for males were higher also.

Running Economy

Submaximal $\dot{V}O_2$ data are available both for elite females (230, 248, 268, and 293 m · min^{-1}) and elite males (268 and 322 m · min^{-1}). Unfortunately, the two studies on elite females reported $\dot{V}O_2$ values that differed about 2 to 3 mL · min^{-1}. At the common male-female speed of 268 m · min^{-1}, only the study that reported the lower $\dot{V}O_2$ values presented data. These values averaged 50.9 mL · kg^{-1} · min^{-1} which was between the male long-distance (49.9 mL · kg^{-1} · min^{-1}) and middle-distance (54.8 mL · kg^{-1} · min^{-1}) values. When divided into middle- and long-distance runners, these females did not display the magnitude of the difference exhibited by the males. Subelite females and good males in these studies had $\dot{V}O_2$ values similar to or greater than elite middle-distance males. Thus, when controlled for type and level of conditioning, there is little difference in running economy between genders.

Substrate Use

Submaximal RER data are not available for elite male runners, so gender substrate use comparisons are not possible. However, Costill et al. (15) reported that for males and females matched for $\dot{V}O_2$max and training background, fat use was similar when working at 70% $\dot{V}O_2$max.

Summary

1. A number of variables important to endurance performance may explain gender endurance performance differences. These variables include $\dot{V}O_2$max, Qmax, total Hb, LBW, percent body fat, oxidative capacity of muscles, LT, percentage of SO muscle fibers, running economy, and ability to use fat as a source of energy.

2. Gender differences in endurance performance can be attributed to lower weight-adjusted $\dot{V}O_2$max values in females. Contributing to this deficit are higher percent body fat, lower Qmax due to lower SV and blood volume, lower total Hb due to lower [Hb] and blood volume, and lower concentration of mitochondrial enzymes. Because the $\dot{V}O_2$max is lower the absolute LT is lower.

3. There are important gaps in the physiological data on elite distance runners, for example, ventilatory and lactate thresholds. Even less information is available on other types of elite endurance athletes. Obtaining these data would be very worthwhile.

References

1. Andersen, P.; Henriksson, J. Training induced changes in the subgroups of human type II skeletal muscle fibers. Acta Physiol. Scand. 99:123-125; 1977.
2. Anon. All-time world and U.S. list. Track and Field News 44(1):40; 1991.
3. Anon. All-time world and U.S. list. Track and Field News 44(2):32; 1991.
4. Astrand, P.O.; Cuddy, T.E.; Saltin, B.; Stenberg, J. Cardiac output during submaximal and maximal work. J. Appl. Physiol. 19:268-274; 1964.
5. Aunola, S.; Marniemi, J.; Alanen, E.; Mantyla, M.; Saraste, M.; Ruskoi, H. Muscle metabolic profile and oxygen transport capacity as determinants of aerobic and anaerobic thresholds. Eur. J. Appl. Physiol. 57:726-734; 1988.
6. Aura, O.; Komi, P.V. Effects of muscle fiber distribution on the mechanical efficiency of human locomotion. Int. J. Sports Med. 8(Suppl.):30-37; 1987.
7. Barclay, J.K.; Stainsby, W.N. The role of blood flow in limiting maximal metabolic rate in muscle. Med. Sci. Sports Exerc. 7:116-119; 1975.
8. Bergh, U.; Sjodin, B.; Forsberg, A.; Svedenhag, J. The relationship between body and oxygen uptake during running in humans. Med. Sci. Sports Exerc. 23:205-211; 1991.
9. Callow, M.; Morton, A.; Guppy, M. Marathon fatigue: the role of plasma fatty acids, muscle glycogen, and blood glucose Eur. J. Appl. Physiol. 55:654-661; 1986.
10. Carter, J.E.L.; Kasch, F.W.; Boyer, J.L.; Phillips, W.H.; Ross, W.D.; Sucec. A. Structural and functional assessments on a champion runner—Peter Snell. Res. Quart. 38:355-365; 1967.
11. Conley, D.L.; Krahenbuhl, G.S.; Burkett, L.N.; Millar, A.L. Following Steve Scott: physiological changes accompanying training. Physician Sportsmed. 12(1):103-106; 1984.
12. Costill, D.L. Rodgers: the right stuff. Runner 2(3):46; 1980.
13. Costill, D.L.; Daniels, J.; Evans, W.; Fink, W.; Krahenbuhl, G.; Saltin, B. Skeletal muscle enzymes and fiber composition in male and female track athletes. J. Appl. Physiol. 40:149-154; 1976.
14. Costill, D.L., Fink, W.J.; Flynn, M.; Kirwan, J. Muscle fiber composition and enzyme activities in elite female distance runners. Int. J. Sports Med. 8(Suppl.):103-106; 1987.
15. Costill, D.L.; Fink, W.J.; Getchell, L.H.; Ivy, J.L.; Witzmann, F.A. Lipid metabolism in skeletal muscle of endurance trained males and females. J. Appl. Physiol. 47:787-791; 1979.
16. Cox, M.L.; Bennett, J.B., III; Dudley, G.A. Exercise training-induced alterations of cardiac morphology. J. Appl. Physiol. 61:926-931; 1986.

17. Cureton, K.; Bishop, P.; Hutchinson, P.; Newland, H.; Vickery, S.; Zwiren, L. Sex difference in maximal oxygen uptake. Eur. J. Appl. Physiol. 54:656-660; 1986.
18. Daniels, J.T. Running with Jim Ryan: a 5-year study. Physician Sportsmed. 2(9):62-67; 1974.
19. Daniels, J.; Krahenbuhl, G.; Foster, C.; Gilbert, J.; Daniels, S. Aerobic responses of female distance runners to submaximal and maximal exercise. Ann. N.Y. Acad. Sci. 301:726-733; 1977.
20. Daniels, J.; Scardina, N.; Hayes, J.; Foley, P. Elite and subelite female middle- and long-distance runners. In: Landers, D.M., ed. Sport and elite performers. Champaign, IL: Human Kinetics; 1986:57-72.
21. Davis, J.; Frank, M.H.; Whipp, B.J.; Wasserman, K. Anaerobic threshold alterations caused by endurance training in middle-aged men. J. Appl. Physiol. 46:1039-1046; 1979.
22. Dempsey, J.A. Exercise-induced imperfections in pulmonary gas exchange. Can. J. Sport. Sci. 12(Suppl. 1):665-705; 1987.
23. Donovan, C.M.; Brooks, G.A. Endurance training affects lactate clearance, not lactate production. Am. J. Physiol. 244:E83-E92; 1983.
24. Durstine, J.L.; Pate, R.R.; Sparling, P.B.; Wilson, G.E.; Senn, G.E.; Bartoli, W.P. Lipid, lipoprotein, and iron status of elite women distance runners. Int. J. Sports Med. 8(Suppl.):119-123; 1987.
25. Ebashi, H.; Goto, Y.; Nishijima, Y.; Imaizumi, T. Maximal aerobic power and maximal isokinetic strength of male Japanese elite marathon runners. Bulletin of the Physical Fitness Research Institute 71:10-24; 1989.
26. Fay, L.; Londeree, B.R.; LaFontaine, T.P.; Volek, M.R. Physiological parameters related to distance running performance in female athletes. Med. Sci. Sports Exerc. 21:319-324; 1989.
27. Fink, W.J.; Costill, D.L.; Pollock, M.L. Submaximal and maximal working capacity of elite distance runners. Part II. Muscle fiber composition and enzyme activities. Ann. N.Y. Acad. Sci. 301:323-327; 1977.
28. Goldspink, G. Energy turnover during contraction of different types of muscles. In: Asmussen, E.; Jorgensen, K., eds. Biomechanics VI-A. Baltimore: University Park Press; 1978: 27-39.
29. Gollnick, P.D.; Armstrong, R.B.; Saltin, B.; Saubert, C.W., IV; Sembrowich, W.L.; Shepherd, R.E. Effect of training on enzyme activity and fiber composition of human skeletal muscle. J. Appl. Physiol. 34:107-111; 1973.
30. Graves, J.E.; Pollock, M.L.; Sparling, P.B. Body composition of elite female distance runners. Int. J. Sports Med. 8(Suppl.):96-102; 1987.
31. Grimby, G.; Hagendal, E.; Saltin, B. Local xenon-133 clearance from quadriceps muscle during exercise in man. J. Appl. Physiol. 22:305-310; 1967.
32. Holloszy, J.O.; Coyle, E.F. Adaptations of skeletal muscle to endurance exercise and their metabolic consequences. J. Appl. Physiol. 56:831-838; 1984.
33. Hughes, E.F.; Turner, S.C.; Brooks, G.A. Effects of glycogen depletion and pedalling speed on anaerobic threshold. J. Appl. Physiol. 52:1598-1607; 1982.
34. Ivy, J.L.; Costill, D.L.; Van Handel, P.J.; Essig, D.A.; Lower, R.W. Alteration in the lactate threshold with changes in substrate availability. Int. J. Sports Med. 2:139-142; 1981.
35. Ivy, J.L.; Costill, D.L.; Maxwell, B.D. Skeletal muscle determinants of maximum aerobic power in man. Eur. J. Appl. Physiol. 44:1-8; 1980.

36. Ivy, J.L.; Withers, R.T.; Van Handel, P.J.; Elger, D.H.; Costill, D.L. Muscle respiratory capacity and fiber type as determinants of lactate threshold. J. Appl. Physiol. 48:523-527; 1980.

37. Jansson, E.; Sjodin, B.; Tesch, P. Changes in muscle fiber distribution in man after physical training. A sign of fiber types transformation. Acta Physiol. Scand. 104:235-237; 1977.

38. Kanstrap, I.; Eklbom, B. Blood volume and hemoglobin concentration as determinants of maximal aerobic power. Med. Sci. Sports Exerc. 16:256-262; 1984.

39. Karlsson, J.; Saltin, B. Diet, muscle glycogen, and endurance performance. J. Appl. Physiol. 31:203-206; 1971.

40. Kjellberg, S.; Rudhe, U.; Sjostrand, T. Increase in the amount of hemoglobin and blood volume in connection with physical training. Acta Physiol. Scand. 19:146-151; 1949.

41. Londeree, B.R. The use of laboratory test results with long distance runners. Sports Med. 3:201-213; 1986.

42. Londeree, B.R.; Moeschberger, M.L. Effect of age and other factors on maximal heart rate. Res. Quart. Exer. Sport 53:297-304; 1982.

43. Magel, J.; Andersen, K. Pulmonary diffusing capacity and cardiac output in young trained Norwegian swimmers and untrained subjects. Med. Sci. Sports Exerc. 1:131-139; 1969.

44. Margaria, R.; Cerretelli, P.; Aghemo, P.; Sassi, J. Energy cost of running. J. Appl. Physiol. 18:367-370; 1963.

45. Martin, D.E.; May, D.F. Pulmonary function characteristics in elite women distance runners. Int. J. Sports Med. 8(Suppl.):84-90; 1987.

46. Martin, D.E.; May, D.F.; Pilbeam, S.P. Ventilation limitations to performance among elite male distance runners. In: Landers, D.M., ed. Sport and elite performers. Champaign, IL: Human Kinetics; 1984:121-131.

47. Martin, R.P.; Haskell, W.L.; Wood, P.D. Blood chemistry and lipid profiles of elite distance runners. Ann N.Y. Acad. Sci. 301:346-360; 1977.

48. Morgan, D.W.; Martin, P.E.; Krahenbuhl, G.S. Factors affecting running economy. Sports Med. 7:310-330; 1989.

49. Oscai, L.; Williams, B.; Hertig, B. Effect of exercise on blood volume. J. Appl. Physiol. 24:622-624; 1968.

50. Pate, R.R., Sparling, P.B.; Wilson, G.E.; Cureton, K.J.; Miller, B.J. Cardiorespiratory and metabolic responses to submaximal and maximal exercise in elite women distance runners. Int. J. Sports Med. 8(Suppl.):91-95; 1987.

51. Pollak, S.J.; McMillan, S.T.; Mumpower, E.; Wharff, R.; Knopf, W.; Felner, J.M.; Yoganathan, A.P. Echocardiographic analysis of elite women distance runners. Int. J. Sports Med. 8(Suppl.):81-82; 1987.

52. Pollock, M.L. Characteristics of elite class distance runners. Overview. Ann. N.Y. Acad. Sci. 301:278-282; 1977.

53. Pollock, M.L. Submaximal and maximal working capacity of elite distance runners. Part I: Cardiorespiratory aspects. Ann. N.Y. Acad. Sci. 301:310-322; 1977.

54. Pollock, M.L.; Gettman, L.R.; Jackson, A.; Ayres, J.; Ward, A.; Linnerud, A.C. Body composition of elite class distance runners. Ann. N.Y. Acad. Sci. 301:361-370; 1977.

55. Pollock, M.L.; Jackson, A.S.; Pate, R.R. Discriminant analysis of physiological differences between good and elite distance runners. Res. Quart. Exer. Sport 54:521-532; 1980.

56. Raven, P.B. Pulmonary function of elite distance runners. Ann. N.Y. Acad. Sci. 301:371-381; 1977.

57. Ready, A.E. Physiological characteristics of male and female middle distance runners. Can. J. Appl. Spt. Sci. 9:70-77; 1984.

58. Ritzer, T.F.; Bove, A.A.; Carey, A.A. Left ventricular performance characteristics in trained and sedentary dogs. J. Appl. Physiol. 48:130-138; 1980.

59. Saltin, B.; Blomquist, B.; Mitchell, J.H.; Johnson, R.L., Jr.; Wildenthal, K.; Chapman, C.B. Response to submaximal and maximal exercise after bed rest and training. Circulation 38(Suppl. 7):vii-1, vii-78; 1968.

60. Shephard, R.J.; Bouhlel, E.; Vanderwalle, H.; Monod, H. Muscle mass as a factor limiting physical work. J. Appl. Physiol. 64:1472-1479; 1988.

61. Sparling, P.B.; Wilson, G.E.; Pate, R.R. Project overview and description of performance, training, and physical characteristics in elite women distance runners. Int. J. Sports Med. 8(Suppl.):73-76; 1987.

62. Svendenhag, J.; Sjodin, B. Physiological characteristics of elite male runners in- and off-season. Can. J. Appl. Sport Sci. 10:127-133; 1985.

63. Thews, G. Theoretical analysis of the pulmonary gas exchange at rest and during exercise. Int. J. Sports Med. 5:113-119; 1984.

64. Underwood, R.H.; Schwade, J.L. Noninvasive analysis of cardiac function of elite distance runners—echocardiography, vectorcardiography, and cardiac intervals. Ann. N.Y. Acad. Sci. 301:297-309; 1987.

65. Walsh, M.L.; Bannister, E. Possible mechanisms of the anaerobic threshold: a review. Sports Med. 5:269-302; 1988.

66. Wasserman, K.; Beaver, W.; Whipp, B. Mechanisms and pattern of blood lactate increase during exercise in man. Med. Sci. Sports Exerc. 18:344-352; 1986.

67. Winder, W.W.; Hagberg, J.M.; Hickson, R.C.; Ehsani, A.A.; McLane, J.A. Time course of sympathoadrenal adaptation to endurance exercise training in man. J. Appl. Physiol. 45:370-374; 1978.

CHAPTER 12

•

Nutritional Problems and Training Intensity, Activity Level, and Athletic Performance

Nancy Clark

In order to train hard, maintain a high level of activity, and achieve optimal competitive performance, athletic females should eat a daily carbohydrate-rich and nutrient-dense diet that provides the needed energy, vitamins, minerals, and protein. This wholesome training diet should target about 6 to 10 g carbohydrate/kg body weight (3), 0.8 to 1.5 g protein/kg (7), and the remainder of calories from fat.

Under weight-maintenance conditions, this is equivalent to a diet that is about 60% to 70% carbohydrate (CHO), 10% to 15% protein (PRO), and 25% to 30% FAT. When calories are restricted (a common occurrence among female athletes), women should restrict calories from fat to spare the carbohydrates they need for glycogen storage and the protein they need for muscular growth and development.

Adequate vitamins and minerals are essential for the body to perform optimally. Theoretically, women who eat more than 1,200 to 1,500 calories from a variety of wholesome foods can obtain most nutrients necessary for top athletic performance (with the possible exception of iron). Surveys of the general population of American women suggest, however, that teenage girls and adult women tend to have diets low in calcium (60-72% RDA) and iron (37-71% RDA), among other nutrients (11). These two nutrients tend to be correlated positively with calorie consumption.

Energy Intake of Athletic Females

The current energy requirement for the reference 128 lb, 18- to 25-year-old woman who maintains light to moderate activity is 2,300 calories a day (18 Cal/ lb; 10). In comparison, national surveys of food consumption suggest that adult women actually eat about 1,700 calories a day (4). Although one might expect the athletic female, when compared to her sedentary counterpart, to enjoy a higher intake of calories (and consequently vitamins and minerals), studies suggest otherwise if we can assume food intake data is accurate.

Untrained women who started a marathon training program and built up their running over the course of 18 months to about 50 miles a week consumed about 60 more calories a day during training but lost only about 2 pounds of fat. They averaged about 2,000 calories a day (35 Cal/kg; 16 Cal/lb). Their male counterparts, in comparison, ate about 500 more calories a day (2,700 total Cal/ day; 38 Cal/kg; 17 Cal/lb) and lost about 5 pounds of fat (8). Recreational women runners who ran about 3 hours a week reported eating about 1,600 calories. This was only 4% higher than their sedentary counterparts' intake of 1,540 calories (9).

Note that these caloric intakes are less than the recommended 2,300 calories for the reference (nonathletic) woman (10). Athletic females in weight balance reportedly eat fewer calories than might be expected; those who strive to lose weight commonly eat even less. These restrictive diets often jeopardize the nutritional quality of their sports diets, because nutrient intake tends to correlate positively with total calories consumed.

Dietary Analysis of Athletic Females

A brief review of the literature regarding the nutrition of female athletes indicates that females on the U.S. Nordic ski team (14 women ages 15-31; average age 20 yr) consumed 2,400 to 4,000 Calories a day. These calories were approximately 42% to 50% CHO, 13% to 14% PRO, 34% to 41% FAT, and 0.5% to 4.5% alcohol (ALC). Eighty percent to 100% of the women ate a diet with greater than 30% of the calories from fat and fewer than 55% from carbohydrates. This ratio not only is inappropriate for optimal glycogen storage, but it also misses the target heart-healthy 30% FAT diet recommended by the American Heart Association. Their intakes of thiamine, riboflavin, niacin, and vitamin C met the RDA, but 45% to 70% of the skiers ate less than the 18 mg RDA of iron, and 20% to 40% of the skiers ate less than the 800 mg RDA of calcium (6).

Highly trained female marathoners, who were volunteers from the 1984 Olympic marathon trials (19-43 years old; average age 29 yr) and ran about 70 miles a week, reported eating about 2,400 calories a day. These calories were about 55% CHO, 13% PRO, and 32% FAT. Again, they missed the target sports diet/ American Heart Association recommendations of more than 60% CHO and less than 30% FAT. Although the mean calcium intake was 1,200 mg, 23% of the women ate less than the calcium RDA. Forty-three percent ate less than the RDA

Table 12.1   Calorie Expenditures of Female Athletes

Subject	Cal/kg	Cal/lb	Total calories
Recreational runners	27.5	12.5	1,600
Nordic skiers	42-71	19-32	2,400-4,000
Gymnasts	44	20	1,700
Elite runners	46	21	2,400
Reference woman 18-25 yr old	39	18	2,300
25-50 yr old	37	17	2,200

Note. Data compiled from Bernadot, Schwarz, and Heller (1989); Deuster, Kyle, Moser, Vigersky, Sirgh, and Schoomaker (1986); Ellsworth, Hewitt, and Haskell (1985); Pate, Sargent, Baldwin, and Burges (1990); and Pellet (1990).

of iron, and 35% had a serum ferritin less than 12 ng/mL, indicative of absent iron stores. Seventy-seven percent ate less than the RDA of zinc, and 29% had low serum zinc levels (5).

Among a group of women (average age 30 yr) who ran recreationally about 3 hours a week for both fitness and competitive enjoyment, the reported intake was about 1,600 calories: 49% CHO, 15% PRO, and 32% FAT. Mean intakes of both calcium and iron were below the RDAs (630 mg calcium; 11 mg iron), as were those of magnesium, vitamin D, vitamin B-6, and zinc (9).

Among elite young gymnasts (ages 11-14), reported intake was 1,700 calories a day: 52% CHO, 15% PRO, and 32% FAT. Ninety-five percent ate less than the RDA of iron, and 50% ate less than the RDA of calcium. The average intakes of B-vitamins, C, and A met or exceeded the RDAs, but there was a wide variation in intakes (2; see Table 12.1).

This brief overview documents the repeated pattern of lower calorie intakes than might be anticipated and inadequate intakes of carbohydrates, iron, and calcium. Many dieting athletic females, as well as those with eating disorders, consume even fewer calories than reported in these studies; consequently, they consume fewer of the nutrients that could optimize their training diet and enhance their competitive excellence.

Summary

1. Unlike male athletes who consume large quantities of calories with increased athletic performance, female athletes report maintaining a high athletic output on fewer calories than might be expected. If there, this energy efficiency seems to protect women from (undesirable) weight loss. They suffer reduced caloric intake and consequently reduced intake of

vitamins, minerals, protein, carbohydrates—all nutrients that are important for optimal performance.

2. Iron deficiency can contribute to (a) anemia, and in the case of swimmers and women participating in outdoor winter sports (b) poor thermoregulation during cold exposure (1).

3. Calcium deficiency can compromise bone health, possibly contributing to current problems with stress fractures and future problems with osteoporosis.

4. Zinc deficiency can contribute to poor healing of the microtrauma that occurs with rigorous training or to increased susceptibility to colds, flu, and other ailments related to decreased immune function.

5. Carbohydrate deficiency can contribute to glycogen depletion and muscular fatigue.

6. Protein and calorie deficiency can contribute to amenorrhea and its commonly accompanying stress fractures.

7. Without question, nutrition education programs are essential for teaching athletic females how to make the wisest food choices that will invest in both current health and performance, as well as future longevity.

References

1. Beard, J.; Borel, M.; Derr, J. Impaired thermoregulation and thyroid function in iron-deficiency anemia. Am. J. Clin. Nutr. 52:813-819; 1990.

2. Bernadot, D.; Schwarz, M.; Heller, D.W. Nutrient intake in young, highly competitive gymnasts J. Amer. Diet. Assoc. 89:401-403; 1989.

3. Costill, D. Carbohydrates for exercise: dietary demands for optimal performance. Int. J. Sports Med. 9:1-18; 1988.

4. CSFII. November. Nationwide food consumption survey continuing survey of food intake by individuals. Women 19-50 years and their children 1-5 years, 1 day. US Dept. Agriculture. NFCS CSFII Report No. 85, 1985.

5. Deuster, P.; Kyle, S.; Moser, P.; Vigersky, R.; Singh, A.; Schoomaker, E. Nutritional survey of highly trained women runners. Am. J. Clin. Nutr. 45:954-962; 1986.

6. Ellsworth, N., Hewitt, B.; Haskell, W. Nutrient intake of elite male and female nordic skiers. Phys. Sportsmed. 13(2):78-92; 1985.

7. Friedman, J.; Lemon, P. Effect of chronic endurance exercise on retention of dietary protein. Int. J. Sports Med. 10(2):118-123; 1989.

8. Janssen, G.; Graef, C.; Saris, W. Food intake and body composition in novice athletes during a training period to run a marathon. Int. J. Sports Med. 10(Suppl. 1): S17-S21; 1989.

9. Pate, R.; Sargent, R.; Baldwin, C.; Burges, M. Dietary intake of women runners. Int. J. Sports Med. 11(6):461-466; 1990.

10. Pellet, P. Food energy requirements in humans. Am. J. Clin. Nutr. 51:711-722; 1990.

11. Pennington, J.; Young, B. Total Diet Study nutritional elements, 1982-1989. J. Amer. Diet. Assoc. 91:179-183; 1991.

CHAPTER 13

•

Strength Training and the Athletic Female

Terry R. Malone
Barbara Sanders

Strength training has become synonymous with male athletic participation in intercollegiate and interscholastic events. Its extension to the competitive female has been much slower but is now considered the norm, particularly in interscholastic and intercollegiate settings. There are major physiologic differences between females and males, primarily because of the varying levels of androgen. However, with proper strength training, major gains can be seen; thus, it seems tenable to conclude that strength training for females will provide benefits similar to those seen in males. This will be accomplished with lesser physical enlargement or hypertrophy and may be related instead to increased neurologic drive, recruitment, and synchronization (27, 36).

Assessing Changes in Muscle Strength

Strength, in and of itself, is difficult to define, particularly as our knowledge of physiologic processes has increased to allow multiple techniques to evaluate particular activities. We therefore recommend that any definition of strength be based upon the particular method used to assess muscular output and that clinicians refer to force, torque, power, or work if such strength assessments are to have relative meaning.

Strength assessment is an attempt to determine objectively the mechanical energy generated by muscular tissues through a chemical energy conversion. We must accept that we are assessing this output in an indirect fashion, relying rather on indirect measurements that are dramatically affected by the skeletal system. These indirect measures mean that we assess not only changes in muscle tension but also those changes related to the specific activity, such as rotation, compression, leverage, and angulation (47). One response to these limitations has been the use of controlled isometric measurements (34). These measurements, taken at the same point in the range of motion, may offer the best assessment of tension produced within the musculoskeletal system (34). However, this is not an assessment of *performance* and may, in fact, give a very poor estimation of the ability to be involved in a specific activity, because dynamic assessment includes movement over articular surfaces, the integrity of such surfaces to withstand compressive loads, the ability to sustain neural drive or appropriately recruit (type of fiber and number of fibers), and the ability to coordinate other patterns of muscular activity required to allow the specific goal of contraction. These problems have led many clinicians to do dynamic assessment, in the belief that it more closely reflects performance.

Dynamic muscular output is more difficult to assess, because of many confounding variables that must be defined. *Force* is a linear measure and is thus sensitive to changes in the length of the lever arm (i.e., 20 lb placed 12 in. from the axis of rotation is much different than 20 lb placed 18 in. from the axis of rotation). *Torque* is a rotational assessment, which provides a better assessment more reflective of actual output but does require appropriate alignment to the axis of rotation. Torque is measured in foot-pounds or Newton-meters. Often, clinicians wrongly assume the objectivity of these measurements. It is imperative not to forget the tremendous influence of effusion, pain, altered recruitment, and inhibition from both physiologic and psychologic factors (11).

We must also define the type of muscular contraction or activation. The ability of muscle to contract allows one to raise the limb (concentric contraction), maintain the position of the limb (isometric contraction), or controllably lower the limb (eccentric contraction or activation). Indeed, *eccentric contraction* may be an inappropriate term, because the muscle is actually undergoing a lengthening process, thus the use of the term *muscle activation*. Both concentric and eccentric data are now available, and we must be careful to assess both of these functions, because some patients will exhibit alterations in one or the other but not necessarily in both (17). It is imperative that we become more exact in our assessments if we are to match them to athletic performance problems. Thus, the type of exercise used to elicit the action should be directly related to that required for action (e.g., isometric activation is best to assess tension capability but not necessarily high velocity activity).

Only recently have we been able to assess eccentric as well as concentric values objectively. Although there are machines now that are able to do this, it is interesting to note the differences in effort required to perform eccentric activities when measured using a dynamometer versus isotonically lowering a weight. It is very likely that the neurophysiologic drive required of dynamometric assessment may be somewhat different than that seen in an actual sport environment requiring the absorption of energy through a closed kinetic chain (e.g., placing a foot on the floor). Different mechanisms for assessing muscular activity have different strengths and weaknesses.

Manual Muscle Testing

Manual muscle testing (MMT) is frequently used to assess an individual's ability to contract muscles against resistance, utilizing gravity or gravity-eliminated positions and manually applying loads to determine the voluntary response. Application of force must be consistent and of a contract-against-resistance or hold-against-resistance pattern (30).

MMT has numerous drawbacks, the two primary difficulties being a lack of reproducibility on persons approaching or surpassing normal levels of strength and the tremendous difficulty in developing correlation or reliability among testers (30). Other problems include test position, stabilization, individual effort, leverage differences, and alterations in length and tension related to specific ranges of motion. Two other major factors are the time allowed for the person to generate tension and the individual's ability to reproduce this tension during sporting activity. MMT is useful in screening but is of limited value in objectifying muscular output.

Handheld Dynamometry

To overcome some of MMT's problems, use of handheld devices that objectify the pressure applied during MMT (e.g., the handheld dynamometer) is acceptable in clinical settings (5). Most of these units operate like pressure or strain gauges and are limited by the clinician's ability to overcome the musculature in question while not allowing uncontrolled movements.

Cable Tensiometry

Another isometric approach is cable tensiometry. This measures isometric output by the development of tension within a cable that is perpendicular to the attachment to the body site (9). Clarke popularized this device, but it has not been used in most clinical settings in part, perhaps, because of clinicians' lack of confidence regarding isometric assessment.

Isotonic Assessment

Isotonic exercise involves the controlled movement of a weight through a range of motion. The difficulties with this assessment approach include limited access to the muscle system (i.e., indirect assessment rather than tension within the muscle itself), inhibition of the neural drive that allows or controls access to the muscular system, damage to articular cartilage, and different types of muscular function (concentric, eccentric, endurance, power, etc.). To minimize these problems, the clinician must take into account lever arm length, speed of movement, and the interplay between neural and muscular performance.

Most isotonic concentric assessments evaluate the ability to lift a skeletal mass through a specific movement pattern. Certain biomechanical "stick points" limit the assessment to the weakest portion of the range of motion. Also, speed and acceleration are not controlled, thus maximal effort is not adequately assessed (12). (Movement with a weight typically occurs at about 60°/second.) Another difficulty is that fatigue becomes a factor before reaching a maximal assessment. Also, concentric effort may not be indicative of eccentric effort. Accurate isotonic assessment continues to be problematic, but it is still frequently used (37).

Isokinetic Assessment

Isokinetic exercise can best be likened to a dynamometer that controls the maximum speed at which a limb is allowed to move during a particular pattern of exercise. The individual attempts to accelerate against the lever arm while the machine, or clinician, prevents movement beyond a preset, maximum velocity. With the development of computer technology during the 1960s, objective assessment using dynamometers became possible (41). Numerous isokinetic devices are available now that allow reliable concentric and eccentric assessment (10, 23, 40). This is not necessarily maximal assessment, because the results depend on the level of effort expended by the individual being assessed. Also, the data collected from these devices must be reviewed in a machine-specific format, because different manufacturers correct for gravity or generate their values in different ways. Clinicians must also be aware that the inverse relationship of concentric force to velocity is much larger than that seen when eccentric measurement is used. Table 13.1 presents a basic outline of muscle activation, output, metabolic demand, and torque generation.

Assessment of strength is a multifaceted problem, complicated by the necessity of indirect assessment. The values derived must be used not in isolation but in conjunction with other clinical assessments. Manual muscle testing may be the most appropriate screening technique, but it lacks the objectivity required for research or individual evaluation, particularly when larger muscle groups or athletic individuals are being assessed. Isometric techniques yield values that may be very consistent and reliable but that may not reflect functional capacity. Concentric isokinetic assessment may be very appropriate to determine dynamic capabilities, but concentric values may not always agree with eccentric values.

Through continued research and clinical experience, the dynamics of muscular contraction and performance are becoming more clearly understood. Computer-controlled or -enhanced equipment provides us much information, and the future is bright for continued improvements in the clinical assessment of strength. Parameters still to be evaluated include anaerobic as well as aerobic limitations. Our present efforts show us only a small piece of the overall picture.

Applications of Strength Training by Athletic Females

In recent years, there has been a dramatic increase in women's sports, both in number of participants and in sports played. The traditional female sports are

Table 13.1 Muscular Activation Sequence Related to Different Factors

Exercise	Action	Output per unit	Metabolic demand	Torque generation
Isometric	Tension only, no skeletal motion	Moderate	Intensity related	No speed factor
Concentric	Movement of skeletal mass through a range of motion	Low	High	Increases as speed decreases
Eccentric	Controlled lowering of skeletal mass through a range of motion	High	Low	Stays about the same at various speeds

field hockey, basketball, softball, gymnastics, and tennis. Other sports that have been increasingly popular are soccer, volleyball, baseball, and even football. In addition, fitness and recreational sports have seen a major rise in interest; more females are running, cycling, and participating in aerobic activity programs.

Though many girls and women participated in sports activities in the past, far too few trained or conditioned properly. Fortunately, this is changing rapidly. Athletic opportunities continue to increase as do training opportunities. Societal attitudes have also changed, and it is now much more socially acceptable for females to participate in training and conditioning activities.

With this 20th-century phenomenon of increased female participation in sports and fitness activities comes the problem of determining the optimal stress level for conditioning and training of females. Unfortunately, research and experience in these areas is lacking primarily because the history of participation by females is so much more recent than that of males. Still, the benefits of exercise for the child, the adolescent, and the adult are well documented, and a well-rounded fitness program, whether for general fitness or for sports fitness, should include three components—flexibility activities, cardiovascular training, *and* strength training.

Strength training is the use of progressive resistance exercise to increase one's ability to exert or resist force. A wide range of training modalities are available to provide resistance training.

Weight training is a specific type of resistance exercise that uses free weights.

Resistance training is exercise that increases strength against some kind of resistance.

Weight lifting is a competitive sport and is the same as Olympic lifting. This sport incorporates two activities, the clean and jerk lift and the snatch lift, and the competitor attempts to lift a maximal amount of weight one time in each lift.

Powerlifting is another competitive sport and uses three lifts: the squat lift, the dead lift, and the bench press. The object in this sport is also a maximal weight lifted one time.

Body building is also a competitive sport that uses several resistance training methods to develop muscle size, symmetry, and definition, though not necessarily strength.

Women traditionally have not participated in strength training for several reasons. For years, it was considered unfeminine and was socially unacceptable. There were few training facilities available, and finally, women were intimidated by many myths and fears about strength training, such as fear of becoming muscle bound.

Strength training can enhance performance and prevent injuries, and it has positive effects on athletic performance and motor skills of male and female athletes and sports activity participants. As strength develops gradually over a period of time, adaptations occur in the musculoskeletal system, a result of the overload principle (22).

The athletic female goes through three stages of development: childhood (prepubertal), adolescence (pubertal), adulthood (postpubertal). Her athletic abilities differ in each stage as demonstrated by the successful national and international competitions of prepubescent females in gymnastics and figure skating, and of adult females in track and field and marathon running.

Anaerobic Training

Strength training is an anaerobic activity, and changes in anaerobic capacity can be expected with resistance training. In boys 11 to 15 years old, Eriksson found that such conditioning increases the concentration of muscle ATP, creatinine phosphate (CP), and glycogen and increases the activity of phosphofructokinase (though only to one-third of adult values) and the rate of glycogen utilization (13). Lammert et al. studied the endurance of the elbow flexors in children 9 to 17 years old; interestingly, girls exhibited a dip in their trainability at the time of peak height growth rate or within the next 6 months (20). Reybrouck concluded that boys 6 to 18 years old have a higher value for anaerobic threshold than do girls at all ages (32). In addition, children are less capable than adults of performing anaerobic exercise. The ability of girls to perform intense anaerobic tasks that last 10 to 60 seconds is significantly less than that of adults. The peak muscle power of 8- to 10-year-old girls was only about 60% that of the 20-year-old woman (4), in contrast to maximal aerobic power (per kg body weight), which is higher in adolescent girls. Bar-Or concludes that repeated activities that last a few seconds and are interspersed with short periods of rest are best suited to children.

Strength Training

During childhood, the strength of prepubescent females is similar to males and is growth dependent. However, it does not increase linearly with growth in body size or height. The main increase in strength occurs in conjunction with the "growth spurt," that is, just before, during, or a few months after the peak height growth rate (4). In one study, peak strength gain preceded peak weight gain in half of the girls and vice versa in one fourth of the girls. Therefore, strength development is a less meaningful indicator of maturity in girls (24). Boys reach their peak strength gains about 1 year after their growth spurt. In contrast to boys, there is little strength difference between early- and late-maturing girls. By age 16 to 17, any strength differences have disappeared (24).

Espenschade studied motor performance of boys and girls 5 to 17 years old in sprint running, jump-and-reach, standing long jump, softball throw, and the Brace test of motor ability. In the 5- to 11- to 13-year-olds, the sexes were identical in performance except in the softball throw (14). Wilmore found that in the softball throw, using the nondominant arm, boys and girls ages 5 to 10 to 12 performed the same (48).

Vrijens compared strength development in 16 prepubescent and 12 postpubescent males (43). The subjects trained for 8 weeks with one set of 8 to 12 repetitions at 75% of 1 RM. Significant increases occurred only in trunk strength and arm circumference in the prepubescent boys. The postpubescent boys increased in strength significantly in all areas. Since this research in 1978, many studies have refuted Vrijen's findings. Most research points out the methodological errors in Vrijen's study, such as the failure to use a control group, the assessment of static strength while training dynamically, and the use of only one set of repetitions. Nevertheless, this study is quoted extensively and still used as the rationale for *not* developing prepubescent strength-training programs.

In several studies that contradict Vrijen's findings, Sailors and Berg evaluated 11 junior high boys' (mean age 12.6 years; SD .69) and 9 college males' responses to an 8-week weight-training program using free weights (35). Control groups were used. Both treatment groups experienced significant increases in the squat lift, bench press, and arm curl. The boys' training group also showed significant decreases in their sum of skinfolds (i.e., percent body fat). They concluded that the strength and muscle endurance gains made by Greulich group 2 and 3 pubescents were comparable to gains made in adult males.

In 1985, Servedio et al. presented a paper at the ACSM annual conference studying the effects of weight training on prepubescent boys (38). The boys' mean age was 11.9 years (SD 0.5) and maturity was Tanner Stage 1.4 (SD 0.6). The boys trained 3 times a week for 8 weeks using Olympic lifts, whereas a control group did no weight training. There were no injuries during the eight-week session. Shoulder flexion strength, left ventricular end diastolic dimension and volume, and therefore, calculated stroke volume and cardiac output, were all greater in the weight-lifting group than in the control group. Systolic blood pressure was unchanged, but diastolic blood pressure decreased in the weight-lifting group. There was no change in resting heart rate, percent body fat, or flexibility in either group. The authors concluded that prepubescents can achieve benefits similar to adults through weight training. One particularly interesting aspect of this study is the use of free weights and Olympic-style lifts. Weight *lifting* has generally been regarded as unsafe for prepubescents, whereas weight *training* has not.

Pfiffer and Francis studied the effects of resistance training across age groups, from 8 to 21 years of age (29). Subjects were classified as prepubescent, postpubescent, and pubescent, based on Tanner stages, and then randomly assigned to experimental and control groups. Subjects trained 3 times a week for 9 weeks using free weights, machines, and their body weights. The results showed that males of all three maturity levels can gain strength through resistance training, and the effects seem to be similar across all groups. The study disagreed with Watt's study, which found that the greatest rate of change of strength and muscle endurance occurred between the skeletal ages of 13 and 15 (44). In some tests in Pfieffer's study, the prepubescent group made significantly greater gains than the other two groups.

Sewell and Micheli looked at both boys and girls (Tanner Stages 1 and 2), who trained three times a week for 9 weeks (39). Subjects used machines for three sets of 10 repetitions. Results showed greater strength improvements for the experimental group than for the control group in shoulder flexion and extension, and knee extension; only shoulder flexion was significantly greater. Testing was performed isometrically, supporting the conclusion that true strength gains, rather than neuromuscular learning, were achieved.

In addition to evidence that strength gains can be made before the onset of puberty, there is evidence that resistance training in prepubertal children has other benefits. Weltman et al. studied 19 6- to 11-year-old boys during a 14-week, thrice weekly strength-training program and compared them to a control group (N = 10; 46). The strength-training group used Hydra-Fitness equipment, sit-ups, and cycling and not only increased in strength, but significantly increased vertical jump, flexibility, and maximal oxygen consumption as well. Musculoskeletal scintigraphy showed no evidence of damage to epiphyses, bone, or muscle. In addition, the total serum cholesterol level decreased significantly in the strength-training group as did the total cholesterol:HDL-C ratio.

Nielsen et al. looked at the effects of isometric strength training on a performance activity and reported that girls who trained with isometric knee extension exercise also improved in the vertical jump (28). Weltman reported that prepubertal boys who strength-trained improved in the vertical jump by 10.4% compared to a control group, which decreased performance by 3% (45).

The average female reaches puberty 2 years earlier than the male; therefore, at age 11, the female is taller and heavier and, from age 12 to 15, more mature and stronger. The female at 16 years has about two thirds the strength of most males her age. There is, of course, a wide range of differences that are accounted for not only by maturity but also by habit and activity.

Following the growth spurt, the female has a higher proportion of fat, whereas the male increases in muscle mass and size. This increase in body fat is a disadvantage to the female in activities requiring that body mass be lifted; it is similar to carrying extra pounds of dead weight.

Exercise during prepubescence may delay menarche, which poses no medical hazards but may necessitate medical evaluation if delayed past age 16, or if after age 14 the female has not experienced breast development or pubic and axillary hair growth.

In the teenage female, menstrual cycle irregularity and the lack of normal ovulation is not unusual; however, both seem more prevalent among exercising teenagers. Menstrual cycles appear to have no significant effect on female sports participation or performance; in fact, some studies have shown that vigorous athletic participation has decreased the incidence of menstrual complaints. But alterations in the menstrual cycle are not infrequent and may prove worrisome. These menstrual abnormalities—irregular menstruation or secondary amenorrhea—seem to result from a combination of psychologic and physiologic stresses in these young women (2, 8).

The adult female has less muscle mass and more body fat per total body weight than her male counterpart. Generally, she has a smaller heart and rib cage, lower vital capacity, and higher respiratory rate. The adult male is generally heavier, taller, and stronger than the female and, in general, has a 10% superiority in athletic competition.

Wilmore et al. found that strength gains (i.e., percent of improvement) due to weight training are similar between men and women (49). Women may actually have a larger relative gain, because their initial strength levels are lower. Brown and Wilmore studied nationally ranked female field athletes and found that they could bench-press several hundred pounds (6). Wilmore also stated that females may never attain the same absolute level of strength as males, but they can expect close to a 30% improvement with training. When adjusted for variance in body size, women were weaker in the upper extremities than men and actually slightly stronger in the lower extremities.

Laubach found that women's mean total body strength was 63.5% of men's (21). In upper extremity activities involving pushing and pulling, and lifting and lowering weights, women had 55.8% of male strength. Lower extremity strength was 71.9% of men's in knee and hip extension and flexion.

Hoffman et al. supported Wilmore's 1974 study (16). In an isokinetic study, women could bench press 50% and 24% of the male, when results were adjusted for height and lean body mass, respectively. Women had an adjusted 4% greater strength in the leg press. The researchers speculate that this is due to the traditional gender-assigned activities of daily living. Women are involved in few activities requiring upper extremity strength but have expectations similar to those of men for lower extremity exercise.

Falkel et al. found in isokinetic testing that arm and leg strength of females were equal to males relative to lean body mass (15). However, when the researchers matched the subjects on aerobic fitness, they found that the female participants were very fit and the men only slightly above the average fitness level.

In the majority of research, the average female's absolute arm and leg strength is less than the average male's. However, if expressed relative to lean body mass, their leg strength is equal, but the female's arm strength is less.

A decline in muscle strength generally has been associated with aging; however, research has not yet explained what occurs—is it physiological or activity-related? With fitness programs primarily targeted toward aerobic fitness, many older females are increasing participation in those activities. Today, we realize that fitness programs must be balanced to include muscular strength and endurance, and flexibility, as well as aerobic work. Exercise and physical fitness are important to the postmenopausal woman if she is to offset those structural and functional losses that accompany aging. Not only will fitness programs benefit an individual's health, it will also greatly benefit society by reducing medical costs (3).

Safety

There is little more than anecdotal evidence regarding concerns for injury in strength-training prepubescents. More injuries occur in the activities of daily living and organized and unorganized sporting activities than in resistance training (45). The injuries that have occurred in weight-related accidents have been in unsupervised settings (emergency room visits indicate that many injuries occur when younger siblings try to imitate what they have observed their older siblings doing on home weight equipment) or when maximal weight or Olympic-type movements are used. Rooks and Micheli feel that young athletes should restrict themselves to weight training and avoid weight lifting until after puberty (33) and make specific recommendations on developing weight-training programs based on age, ranging from 9 to 17 years old.

In contrast, Totten feels that Olympic-style weight lifting should be incorporated into the program for the prepubescent athlete. He contends that this age group learns more readily than their older counterparts and that the correct mechanics can be taught and reinforced more easily (42). Totten also espouses the importance in developing explosive power relative to sports skills, as well as the additional cardiovascular benefits of Olympic weight lifting. He recommends that very light weights be used (perhaps only a broomstick) and that weight lifting be incorporated only after achieving a solid weight-training base. He also emphasizes the importance of proper supervision.

Weltman provides these guidelines for children's participation in a strength-training program:

1. A careful preparticipation evaluation should be performed.
2. The program must be closely supervised by knowledgeable, trained individuals.
3. Proper form should be emphasized.
4. Lifting maximal weight, as well as performing ballistic movements, should be avoided until skeletal maturity is attained (45).

Injuries

Studies have found that injuries sustained by females in sports are very similar to those sustained by males and are considered sport-specific, not gender-specific. Women may have slightly more knee and ankle injuries, though studies of specific rate of injury to females are rare. One type of injury more frequently observed in females than males is the overuse syndrome. Such injuries result from collective microtraumas from repeated impact and occur primarily in runners. These injuries are generally attributed to errors in training, such as too much too fast; anatomic malalignments; imbalance between musculotendinous units in strength or flexibility; improper equipment (e.g., poorly fitting shoes); or training on inappropriate surfaces (25). Young females seem particularly susceptible to these syndromes because of a lack of adequate, long-term preparation for sports, which might be remedied by earlier and more thorough development of a training base (26).

Two additional concepts that should be included in any discussion of strength training are plyometrics and closed-chain activities.

Plyometrics

Plyometrics is best described as an intensive training regimen designed to enhance explosive activities performed at high intensity and rapid speed. Plyometrics can be functionally defined as the application of hops, jumps, leaps, or rhythmic movements to gain explosive power. Komi popularized use of the stretch-shortening cycle, which is the basis of these techniques (18, 19).

The sequence of the stretch-shortening cycle can best be described as being composed of three distinct activities: the eccentric phase, the amoritization phase, and the concentric phase. The eccentric phase (yielding, or "cocking") involves the rapid application of force to the muscle fibers, leading to an eccentric muscle activation. This can best be described as a stretching or storing action being forced upon the muscle-tendon unit. The amoritization phase is the time between the storage or application of stretch before the muscle is activated into movement or shortened, leading the opposite movement. The concentric phase is the resultant explosive effort, that is, the jump or bounding movement.

The principles of this cycle include application of a resistive overload (the force, frequently the body weight, that causes muscle stretching). The second principle is the exaggeration of the range of motion through which this force is allowed to act, thus increasing the stretch-reflex impulse to the muscle-tendon unit. The final principle is execution of the movement as intensely and as rapidly as possible after the force has been applied, thus enhancing the cycle.

It is important to note that these principles require intense, high quality movement for optimal results. Because beginning such training frequently leads to delayed-onset muscle soreness, these activities are typically implemented in the off-season.

One of the more frequently used plyometric techniques is depth jumping, which involves hopping from a height of 16 inches or more. Use of plyometrics must be limited by the level of preparedness and conditioning of the individual athlete and is best applied during the final stages of preparation for competitive events and is not for general adult fitness training. Rather, these are activities for the intensely trained athlete who executes ballistic, high intensity movements that require power and explosive performance. In fact, only a small portion of a preseason conditioning program should involve plyometrics, because they must be performed in a limited volume and at a high intensity for appropriate integration. Additional information on plyometrics can be found in Cavagna et al. (7) and Radcliffe and Farentinos (31).

Closed Kinetic Chain Activities

Closed kinetic chain activities are activities that involve the integration of muscle joints acting in sequential order with combined weight bearing and shear forces that are mediated by eccentric muscle action. This concept has become more popular in the literature and in professional seminars, though research on the effects of closed-chain principles is minimal. Empirical evidence in clinical trials shows apparent succcess in rehabilitation and functional training in athletes and warrants additional research into the clinical applications. Eccentric exercise, or closed kinetic chain activities, can be incorporated into any strength-training program whether the equipment being used is free weights, isokinetics, or weight machines (1).

Recommendations for Strength-Training Programs

Strength-training programs should include warm-ups, cool-downs, and flexibility exercises, both general and sport-specific. The equipment, whether free weights or weight machines, should be well maintained, appropriate in design, and allow individualization. Incorporating proper technique under supervision, workouts should require 1 hour or less to complete.

One caveat in weight training for the average or recreational young athlete is that this should not be her primary means of exercise. There is abundant evidence that children and adolescents need to be involved in an exercise program. However, evidence does not support weight training as the best form of exercise to increase one's overall fitness level. Adolescents are better advised to participate in controlled aerobic activities.

Another question that must be asked is, do we want children to start early with an organized weight-training program and risk burnout, which frequently happens in organized sports? Children need to play and enjoy exercise, so activities should be geared in that direction. If the goal is lifetime fitness, we must find the balance between beginning good habits early in life with enjoyment and possibly developing resentment of the demands imposed by organized activities. Family and group physical activities may incorporate resistance training as a component of an overall fitness program.

In summary, our recommendations are these:

1. Resistance training in prepubescent through adult females is safe and can provide many positive physical benefits.
2. Resistance training can be incorporated as part of a voluntary, organized sporting activity (i.e., part of training for soccer, track, volleyball, etc.).
3. Olympic lifts should be prohibited until skeletal maturity.
4. Power lifting should be performed only for practice of proper form and without weights until skeletal maturity.
5. Any resistance training *must* be closely supervised by a knowledgeable professional.
6. *No* maximal lifts should be performed until skeletal maturity. Sets of 12 to 15 repetitions should be performed with adequate rest between sets.
7. A preparticipation physical is essential.
8. Strength-training programs should include the three phases of training—base phase, strength phase, and conversion phase. The base phase is a 2- to 3-week period for development of a general foundation. The strength phase develops a high level of strength. The conversion phase emphasizes strength maintenance and power or endurance development (36). These phases should be cycled to coordinate with sport-specific competition.
9. All strength-training programs should be based on the overload principle with sport-specific exercises that include components of duration, frequency (at least 3 times a week), and intensity (6-9 repetitions in 3 sets).

Summary

1. In general, upper and lower extremity strength in the female is less than in the male. However, when adjusted for lean body mass, the female's lower extremity strength equals that of the male, whereas her upper extremity strength is similar to the male's.
2. Females in any age group should participate in well-rounded fitness programs that include flexibility, cardiovascular, and strength-training components.
3. The athletic female can develop the same percentage strength improvement as the male while undergoing strength training. Specificity of training is important.
4. The acquisition of strength is a slow, progressive process. Women can become quite strong without the development of markedly enlarged musculature.
5. Strength training can enhance performance and prevent injury and can be safely incorporated into overall fitness and sports programs.
6. Proper supervision and a conservative approach to strength training (i.e., no uncontrolled Olympic lifting, power lifting performed only without weights, and no maximal lifts until skeletal maturity) are necessary.
7. The effects of strength training on the athletic female must be further studied.

References

1. Albert, M. Eccentric muscle training in sports and orthopaedics. New York: Churchill Livingstone; 1991.
2. Anderson, J.L. Women's sports and fitness programs at the U.S. Military Academy. Phys. Sportsmed. 7:72; 1979.
3. Bachmann, G.A.; Frill, J. Exercises in the postmenopausal woman. Geriatrics 42:75-85; 1987.
4. Bar-Or, O. The prepubescent female. In: Shangold, M.; Mirkin, G., eds. Women and exercise: Physiology and sports medicine. Philadelphia: F.A. Davis Co; 1988.
5. Bohannon, R. Test-retest reliability of handheld dynamometry during a single session of strength assessment. Phys. Ther. 66:206; 1986.
6. Brown, C.H.; Wilmore, J.H. The effect of maximal resistance training on the strength and body composition of women athletes. Med. Sci. Sport 6:174-177; 1974.
7. Cavagna, G.A.; Disman, B.; Margaria, R. Positive work done by previously stretched muscle. J. Appl. Phyisol. 24:21-32; 1968.
8. Corbitt, R.W.; et al. Female athletes. J. Phys. Ed. Rec. 46:45; 1975.
9. Clarke, H.H. Cable tension strength tests: a manual. Springfield, MA: Stuart E. Murphy; 1953.
10. Davies, G. A compendium of isokinetics in clinical usage, 2nd ed. LaCrosse, WI: S & S Publishers; 1985.
11. DeAndrade, J.; Grant, C. Joint distention and reflex inhibition in the knee. J. Bone Joint Surg. 47:313; 1965.

12. DeLorme, T.L.; Watkins, A.L. Techniques of progressive resistance exercise. Arch. Phys. Med. Rehab. 29:263; 1948.

13. Eriksson, B.O. Physical training, oxygen supply, and muscle metabolism in 11- to 15-year-old boys. Acta Physiol. Scand. Suppl. 384:1-48; 1972.

14. Espenschade, A. Motor development. In: Johnson, W.R., ed. Science and medicine of exercise in sport. New York: Harper & Row; 1960.

15. Falkel, J.E.; Sawka, M.N.; Levine, L.; Pandolf, K.B. Upper to lower body muscular strength and endurance ratios for women and men. Ergonomics 28(12):1661-1670; 1985.

16. Hoffman, T.; Stauffer, R.W.; Jackson, A.S. Sex difference in strength. Am. J. Sports Med. 7:265-267; 1979.

17. Jones, N.L.; McCartney, N.; McComas, A.J., editors. Human muscle power. Champaign, IL: Human Kinetics; 1986.

18. Komi, P.V. The stretch-shortening cycle and human power output. In: Jones, N.L.; McCartney, N.; McComas, A.J., eds. Human muscle power. Champaign, IL: Human Kinetics; 1986.

19. Komi, P.V.; Bosco, C. Utilization of stored elastic energy in leg extension muscles by men and women. Med. Sci. Sports 10:261-265; 1978.

20. Lammert, O.; Froberg, K.; Murer, K.; Andersen, P.E. The effect of training in relation to chronological age and developmental stages in children 9 to 17 years of age (abstract). Acta Physiol. Scand. 105:61A; 1980.

21. Laubach, L.L. Comparative muscular strength of men and women: a review of the literature. Av. Space Environ. Med. 47:534-542; 1977.

22. Leard, J.S. Flexibility and conditioning in the young athlete. In: Michell, L.J., ed. Pediatric and adolescent sports medicine. Boston: Little, Brown & Company; 1984.

23. Lesmes, G.R.; Costill, D.L.; Coyle, E.F.; Fink, W.J. Muscle strength and power changes during maximal isokinetic training. Med. Sci. Sports 10:266; 1978

24. Malina, R.M. Growth, performance, activity, and training during adolescence. In: Shangold, M.; Mirkin, G., eds. Women and exercise: physiology and sports medicine. Philadelphia: F.A. Davis Co.; 1988.

25. Micheli, L.J., et al. Etiologic assessment of overuse stress fractures in athletes. Nova Scotia Med. Bull. 59:43; 1980.

26. Micheli, L.J.; LaChabrier, L. The young female athlete. In: Micheli. L.J., ed. Pediatric and adolescent sports medicine. Boston: Little, Brown & Co.; 1984.

27. Moritani, T.; DeVries, H.A. Neural factors versus hypertrophy in the time course of muscle strength gains. Am. J. Phys. Med. 58(3):115-130; 1979.

28. Nielsen, B.; Nielsen, K.; Behrendt, H.M.; Asmussen, A. Training of functional muscular strength in girls 7-19 years old. In: Berg, K.; Erikson, B.K., eds. Children and exercise, Vol. 9. Baltimore: University Park Press; 1980.

29. Pfeiffer, R.D.; Francis, R.S. Effects of strength training on muscle development in prepubescent, pubescent, and postpubescent males. Phys. Sportsmed. 14(9):134-143; 1986.

30. Poland, J.; Hobart, D.; Payton, O. The musculoskeletal system: Body system series. Garden City, NY: Medical Examination Publishing Co., Inc.; 1981.

31. Radcliffe, J.; Farentinos, R. Plyometrics: explosive power training. Champaign, IL: Human Kinetics; 1985.

32. Reybrouck, T.M. The use of anaerobic threshold in pediatric exercise testing. In: Bar-Or, O., ed. Advances in pediatric sport sciences, Vol. 3. Champaign, IL: Human Kinetics; 1989.

33. Rooks, D.S.; Micheli, L.J. Musculoskeletal assessment and training: the young athlete. Clin. Sports Med. 7(3):641-677; 1988.
34. Rothstein, J.M., ed. Measurement in physical therapy. New York: Churchill Livingstone; 1985.
35. Sailors, M.; Berg, K. Comparison of responses to weight training in pubescent boys and men. J. Sports Med. 27:30-37; 1987.
36. Sanders, M.T. Weight training and conditioning. In: Sanders, B., ed. Sports physical therapy. Englewood Cliffs, NJ: Appleton & Lange; 1990.
37. Sanders, M.; Sanders, B. Mobility: active-resistive training. In: Gould, J., ed. Orthopaedic and sports physical therapy. St. Louis: C.V. Mosby; 1985.
38. Servedio, F.J.; Bartels, R.L.; Hamlin, R.L.; et al. The effects of weight training, using Olympic-style lifts, on various physiological variables in prepubescent boys. Abstract. Med. Sci. Sports Exerc. 17:288; 1985.
39. Sewell, L.; Micheli, L.J. Strength training for children. J. Pediatr. Orthop. 6:143-146; 1986.
40. Sherman, W.M.; Pearson, D.R.; Plyley, M.J.; et al. Isokinetic rehabilitation after surgery. Am. J. Sports Med. 10:155; 1982.
41. Thistle, H.G.; Hislop, H.; Moffroid, M.; Lowman, E.W. Isokinetic contraction: a new concept of resistive exercise. Arch. Phys. Med. Rehab. 48:279; 1967.
42. Totten, L. Practical considerations in strengthening the prepubescent athlete. NSCA 8(2):38-40; 1986.
43. Vrijens, J. Muscle strength development in the pre- and postpubescent age. In: Borms, J.; Hebbelinck, M., eds. Medicine and sport. Vol. 11: Pediatric work physiology. New York: S. Karger AG; 1978.
44. Watt, N.S. Maturity, structural strength, and motor convergence growth analysis of boys 7 through 17 years of age. Eugene, OR: Univ. of Oregon; 1963. Unpublished dissertation.
45. Weltman, A. Weight training in prepubertal children: physiologic benefit and potential damage. In: Shangold, M.; Mirkin, G., eds. Women and exercise: physiology and sports medicine. Philadelphia: F.A. Davis Co.; 1989.
46. Weltman, A.; Janney, C.; Rians, C.B.; Strand, K.; Katch, F.I. The effects of hydraulic resistance strength training on serum lipid levels in prepubertal boys. AJDC 141:777-780; 1987.
47. Williams, M.; Lissner, H.R. Biomechanics of human movement. Philadelphia: W.B. Saunders; 1966.
48. Wilmore, J.H. Body composition, strength, and development. J.H. Phys. Ed. Rec. 46:38; 1975.
49. Wilmore, J.H.; Parr, R.B.; Girandola, R.N.; Ward, P.; Vodak, P.A.; Barstow, T.J.; Pipes, T.V.; Romero, G.T.; Leslie, P. Physiological alterations consequent to circuit weight training. Med. Sci. Sports Exerc. 1:79; 1978.

•

CHAPTER 14

Conditioning the Aging Female

Gregory A. Peters

Unlike at any previous time in American society, elderly people constitute the fastest growing segment of our population. In 1880, less than 3% of the total population, or fewer than 2 million people, were over age 65. By 1980, the elderly population had reached approximately 25 million, representing over 11.3% of the population (18). By the year 2035, the U.S. Bureau of Census (1982) estimates that 20% of the total population will be elderly (4).

This growth of the aging population has increased interest in the use of exercise as a means of maintaining independence and functional capacity of older individuals. The aging female can improve her functional capacity through a systematic program of low-intensity exercise.

Defining the Aging Female

In attempting to define old age, gerontologists have three different categories: the *young-old*—those who have retained a sufficient level of fitness to continue a normal living pattern; the *middle-old*—those who are independent for activities of daily living but require assistance with certain activities; and the *old-old*—those who are disabled and require nursing care (2). These groups correspond presently to chronological ages of 60 to 75 years, 75 to 85 years, and greater than 85 years. Apparent physiologic age and actual chronologic age vary greatly, and it is the duration of the young-old phase (currently at 60-75 years of age) that may be extended by maintaining a higher fitness level as one ages. For the purposes of this discussion, a woman beyond 60 years of age is defined as an aging female (3).

The Aging Process in Women and Men

There appears to be little evidence of a difference in the aging process between women and men (1).

In both women and men as the body ages, bone mass decreases, tissues become more inflexible, muscles atrophy, and aerobic fitness levels decline. These aging changes lead to weaker bone, slower reactions, and less strength and endurance.

In both women and men there is weakening of muscle, shortening of stature, and osteoporosis. In general, body weight usually declines with a general decrease of lean body mass, due to concomitant lessening of bone mass and muscular atrophy.

Relative body fat increases, usually both in women and men, with percent body fat in elderly women at 38% (5). Changes in muscle mass and tendon strength are evident in appearance. Generally the body contours of the elderly have a less firm and muscular appearance than those in middle age (45-55 years; 6). Abdominal girth commonly increases 25% to 35% in women.

Definition of Aging

Much of what has been considered aging in the past is considered functional disuse today. With aging, muscle undergoes decrease in size and strength. This appears related to loss of muscle fibers and reduction in size of existing fibers. There appears to be very little loss of metabolic potential of muscles with aging. Exercise training can increase the size and strength of contitioned muscle through hypertrophy of both Type I and II fibers (20).

Respiratory dynamics change due to changes in elastic tissue (14). The VO_2max, resting cardiac output, and stroke volume decrease (8). Response to submaximal exercise in the elderly woman indicates that more frequent and more prolonged rest periods are necessary with advancing age to complete work tasks (13).

The physical conditioning of the aging female is often limited by fear of overexertion, muscular weakness, poor motivation, and shortness of breath (Shephard & Sidney, 1978). Maximal cardiac output decreases with each decade (16). The maximal aerobic power of the sedentary 60- to 70-year-old woman is 19 to 30 mL/kg/min (20). The loss of aerobic power is significantly greater in sedentary than in active women and men (10). Because of the reduction in concentration of lactic acid, pulmonary diffusing capacity, and alveolar ventilation, the quality of work that can be performed in a given period is greatly reduced (21).

Research on Exercise and Aging Females

There appears to be a change in the activity patterns of and attitudes toward exercise in the aging female of today's fitness-oriented society. Early retirement, changed cultural expectations, and increased opportunity for exercise each play a role. Activities such as walking, jogging, rowing, golfing, tennis, cycling, swimming, and alpine skiing and the proliferation of fitness clubs have increased the young-old athletic female's opportunities for exercise. Yet as recently as the early 1970s, Shephard and Sidney had found that exercise at this age was believed to be hazardous (24).

Conditioning the aging female is fraught with differences of opinion. Factors such as initial fitness level, bone demineralization, conditioning methods employed, and types of training all lead to different opinions. The work of Sidney and Shephard (1976; 24, 25, 1977; 23) and Adams and deVries (26) both indicate that the aging female is quite capable both of participating in a physical training program and benefiting from it, though little change occurs in blood pressure or heart rate (3).

Adams and deVries (1973; 26) reported improvement caused by walking, swimming, and jogging in women 52 to 79 in O_2 (19%), oxygen uptake (21%), and working capacity (37%; 26). The aging female has the same ability as the younger individual to benefit from physical conditioning (15).

As a result of running, walking, and endurance training, there is an apparent increase in lean body mass, cardiovascular improvement, and skinfold reduction (15, 17). Most studies also show that osteoporosis is delayed by exercise. Increased stress with exercise increases the mineralization of bone in the aging female, a result of increased weight-bearing. Muscular contraction also increases the stress applied to bone. Increased blood flow to bone due to cardiovascular stimulation further depresses demineralization. Finally, bone growth increases due to increased physical activity.

There are very few reports on conditioning of aging females (sportswomen more than 60 years of age; 19). Most conclusions on females are drawn from male data, and their response to exercise is the same as that of younger women and older men.

In 1981, Vaccaro, Dummer, and Clarke (27) compared female geriatric swimmers to sedentary females. As expected, the swimmers had lower percent body fat (23.5% vs. 44.6%) and were comparable to younger ages 19 to 24 (8). This helps illustrate the importance of exercise at an early age with a maintenance program.

Exercise is desirable for everyone including the aging female. In a healthy, young-old female the best approach would be to develop a reasonable program that is easy to adhere to.

Suggested Athletic Activities

It is never too late to begin exercise, especially for the aging female, and there are beneficial exercises for everyone, even the bedridden. But a thorough medical examination, which includes testing of cardiorespiratory function, is advisable for all aging females who wish to add regular exercise to their daily routines. This will assure their ability to participate safely and will ease the monitoring of their progress. Aging females at high risk of cardiovascular disease and those classified as having fair-poor fitness (when measured by ergometry) require more detailed evaluation before they embark on *any* exercise program.

Healthy athletic or nonathletic females over 60 years of age should begin with walking. Not doing too much, too fast, too soon is important. Proper warm-up, footwear, posture, walking mechanics, and terrain are important. Shoes are the single most important piece of equipment.

A progressive walking program begins with walking one block, then increasing that distance by one block every 3 days. After 1 week, the walker should carefully evaluate her progress, the suitability of her footwear, and any aches and pains. There is no data to support the concern that past athletic participation will make the onset of arthritis more likely. The walker can increase her endurance by walking faster, farther, or both, or by increasing her arm swing to make the walking session more strenuous.

The aging woman has several choices of exercise, including walking, swimming, bicycling, and playing golf or tennis. Recently, local fitness clubs have developed aerobic movement classes for seniors. Older women can also find classes for women of similar age at YMCAs and YWCAs, preventive medical clinics, and senior clubs. Exercise supervision is important at any age, but competitive situations should be avoided.

Women in their 80s (i.e., old-old females) and older should perform imagery workouts and flexibility exercises (22). (Imagery is an internal psychological process that evokes the physical characteristics of objects or events (e.g., an exercise workout) that are absent from one's daily activities; 12.) These exercises can be done while sitting on a chair or in a wheelchair. By doing such exercises, one can maintain a complete range of motion in the joints even though one's actual mobility is limited.

Benefits of Exercise for Aging Females

Regular exercise is desirable at any age, but especially for the aging female. Exercise helps maintain proper body weight, decreases body fat, prevents osteoporosis, increases or maintains muscle strength, and maintains joint flexibility. Performance of regular exercise also diminishes the loss of cardiovascular reserve. For example, Ruth Rothfarb, an 80-year-old marathon competitor, began running at age 72 and now runs 10 miles a day.

Any conditioning program of regular exercise has tremendous psychological benefits in the aging female—an elevation in mood, relief of tension, even an increase in one's self-esteem. Aging females who exercise often improve their self-images (9). They become addicted both to exercise and to its overt and subtle benefits. Highly active older women are more satisfied with the way they look than are less active women, which suggests that physical activity may have positive influences on body image, perceived health, and probably on physical health as well (7).

Health care professionals who work with aging athletic females will do well to recognize that masters athletes are, in some significant ways, qualitatively different from nonathletic females. Athletic aging females are more highly motivated, more goal-oriented, and more persistent than nonathletes. Only about 8% of adult Americans meet the government standard of 15 to 25 minutes of exercise 3 to 4 days a week to achieve good health (20), but aging, formerly athletic females are much more likely to follow through on a regular exercise program in pursuit of that goal.

It is never too late—in the aging female's life, or anyone's life—to begin an exercise program (1). At any age, the improvement in the quality of life is well worth the effort.

There is no reason for the aging female to suffer unnecessary injuries, overuse syndromes, or other aches and pains (2). Beginning a regular exercise program after years of less activity is never easy, but it is rewarding. As when running or jogging, flexibility and stretching exercises should be included daily to prevent muscle soreness and injury.

Recommendations for Future Research

No significant research has been done over the past decade on the aging female athlete. Nor has the effect of exercise on the pre-, peri-, and postmenopausal athletic and master athletic female been addressed. How does menopause affect the body image, competitive performance, or psychological profile of the aging, master athletic female? Few studies assess even the fitness levels of the older female. Most studies have been done on males and the conclusions applied to female athletes.

Summary

1. There is little difference in the aging process between women and men. Among other physiological changes, muscles decrease in size and strength with aging. Exercise can increase the size and strength of muscles and decrease other effects of aging.
2. Although in the past, exercise was considered to be contraindicated for aging females, research now shows that it provides both physical and psychological benefits.
3. Activities such as walking, swimming, bicycling, tennis, and golf can be included in exercise programs for aging females. Women over 80 should perform exercises to increase their flexibility to its maximum potential.
4. Before starting an exercise program, a thorough medical examination is recommended for all aging females.

References

1. Jake, P.; Demaio, M; Garrett, W.E. Exercise and athletic conditioning. Orthopedic knowledge update 3. Home study syllabus. Parkridge, IL: American Academy of Orthopedic Surgeons 52; 1990.

2. Kolanowski, A.M.; Gunter, L.M. Do retired career women exercise? Geriatr. Nurs. Nov./Dec.:351-352, 1988.

3. Lichtenstein, M.J.; Shields, S.L.; Shiavi, R.G.; Burger, C. Exercise and balance in aged women: a pilot controlled clinical trial. Arch. Phys. Med. Rehabil. 70:138-143; 1989.

4. Menard, D.; Standish, W.D. The aging athlete. Am. J. Sports Med. 17:187; 1989.

5. Metivier, G.; Gravell, F.; Mews, L.; Ouellette, R. Physical work capacity of older women and men living in rural communities of eastern Ontario, Canada. Gerontol. 35:1-6; 1989.

6. Michelsen, S.; Hurlen, M.; Stugaard, M.; Otterstad, J.E. Influence of age on physical performance, heart rate, and systolic blood pressure response during exercise in apparently healthy women. Scand. J. Clin. Lab. Invest. 49:97-102; 1989.

7. Michelsen, S.; Otterstad, J.E. Blood pressure response during maximal exercise in apparently healthy men and women. J. Intern. Med. 227:157-163; 1990.

8. Miller, W.C.; Lindeman, A.K.; Wallace, J.; Niederpruem, M. Diet composition, energy intake, and exercise in relation to body fat in men and women. Am. J. Clin. Nutr. 52:426-430; 1990.

9. Molloy, D.W.; Richardson, L.; Crilly, R.G. The effects of a 3-month exercise programme on neuropsychological function in elderly institutionalized women: a randomized controlled trial. Age and Aging 17:303-310; 1988.

10. Notelovitz, M.; Fields, C.; Caramelli, K.; Dougherty, M.; Schwartz, A.L. Cardiorespiratory fitness evaluation in climacteric women: comparison of two methods. Am. J. Obstet. Gynecol. 1009-1013; 1986.

11. Patrick, J.; Bassey, J.; Morrant, J.; Macdonald, I. Effects of a week's beta-adrenoceptor blockade with atenolol and metoprolol CR/ZOK on the response to exercise in healthy women aged 50 to 70 years. J. Clin. Pharmacol. 30:S108-S116; 1990.

12. Riccio, C.M.; Nelson, D.L.; Bush, M.A. Adding purpose to the repetitive exercise of elderly women through imagery. Am. J. Occup. Ther. 44(8):714-719; 1990.

13. Sawada, S.G.; Ryan, T.; Fineberg, N.S.; Armstrong, W.F.; Judson, W.E.; McHenry, P.L.; Feigenbaum, H. Exercise echocardiographic detection of coronary artery disease in women. J. Am. Coll. of Cardiol. 14(6):1440-1447; 1989.

14. Sedgwick, A.W.; Davidson, A.H.; Taplin, R.E.; Thomas, D.W. Effects of physical activity on risk factors for coronary heart disease in previously sedentary women: 5-year longitudinal study. Austral. New Zea. J. Med. 18:600-604; 1988.

15. Shangold, M.M. Exercise in the menopausal woman. Obstet. Gynecol. 75(4):53S-83S; 1990.

16. Shephard, R.J. Physical training for the elderly. Clin. Sports Med. 5:515-533; 1986.

17. Sinaki, M.; Grubbs, N.C. Back strengthening exercises: quantitative evaluation of their efficacy for women aged 40 to 65 years. Arch. Phys. Med. Rehabil. 70:16-20; 1989.

18. Warner, K.E. Health and economic implications of a tobacco-free society. JAMA 258:2080-2086, 1987.

19. Wells, C.L. Women, sport, and performance. Champaign, IL: Human Kinetics; 1991:217-305.

20. Wilmore, J.H. The aging of bone and muscle. Clin. Sports Med. 2:231-244, 1991.

21. Xusheng, S.; Yugi, X.; Shuqin, X. Observation on the frequency of sister chromatic exchanges in the peripheral blood lymphocytes of healthy old women with taichiquan exercise. Int. J. Sports Med. 11:166-167, 1990.

22. Yoder, R.M.; Nelson, D.L.; Smith, D.A. Added-purpose versus rote exercise in female nursing home residents. Am. J. Occup. Ther. 43(9):581-586; 1989.
23. Shephard, R.J. Physical activity and aging. Chicago, IL: Year Book Medical Publishers: 1978.
24. Shephard, R.J. Endurance fitness. Toronto: University of Toronto Press: 1977.
25. Shephard, R.J.; Sidney, S. Exercise and aging. In R.S. Huttin's (Ed.) Exercise and sport series review. 6:1-57; 1978.
26. Adam, C.M.; de Vries, H.A. Physical effects of an exercise program on an exercise training regimen upon women. J. Gerontol. 28:52-70; 1973.
27. Vaccaro, D.; Dummer, G.S.; Clarke, D.H. Physiological characteristics of female master swimmers. The Physician and Sports Medicine. 9(2):75-78; 1981.

CHAPTER 15

•

Off-Season Conditioning

John W. Uribe
Merl J. Miller

If an athletic female is to reach optimal performance during the competitive season, she must follow a year-round conditioning program. The level of competitive athletics has steadily risen demanding that athletes come closer to reaching their genetic potential, to reach for higher levels of physical conditioning, to become faster, stronger, and more powerful. Each sport has its own conditioning requirements and musculoskeletal demands; yet conditioning programs for all sports have the common goal of improved athletic performance potential during the competitive season. By using scientific training principles in the off-season conditioning program, the athletic female may return from the off-season with her muscular fitness, cardiovascular fitness, flexibility, and body composition maintained or even improved.

To help the athletic female reach peak performance during the competitive season, coaches and athletes have implemented cycles of specific training. Known as cycling, or periodization, this training system is designed to prepare an athlete for maximum performance during the competitive season. Traditionally, training programs have been divided into phases of preseason, competitive season (in-season), and postcompetitive season (off-season; 21). Further divisions implemented for those athletes who are preparing for the Olympics include a macro (multiyearly), meso (yearly), and micro (weekly) cycle (31, 34). Each season has specific goals and objectives. The off-season is defined as the period between the postcompetitive season and the preseason. Goals for the off-season conditioning program include prevention of deconditioning, increasing strength, power, and endurance, increasing or maintaining aerobic fitness, increasing or maintaining flexibility, maintaining or altering body composition, and improving performance in areas of weakness (22).

Preventing Deconditioning

The end of the competitive season moves the athlete into a period of time away from competition. If the athlete becomes inactive, deconditioning begins. It is important for the athlete to remain physically fit and yet not experience the deleterious effects of overtraining. Varying the volume and intensity of training will reduce the amount of work being done and yet retain the desired level of sport-specific conditioning. But periods of physical inactivity will lead to losses in strength, power, muscular endurance, flexibility, and aerobic fitness and changes in body composition (8, 15, 33). To prevent this deconditioning and maintain these components of physical fitness, a variety of exercises may be used in the conditioning program.

Resistance Training

Strength differences between females and males have been studied and, generally, males are stronger than females (7, 19, 37). When differences in lean body mass and body size are considered, relative strength differences are considerably less (18). The functional quality of muscle is the same in females and males in regard to contractile properties and the ability to develop muscular strength. Females and males have similar fiber type and distribution. Hypertrophy may be less in females than males perhaps due to testosterone; however, females can become very strong with resistance training. The female response to conditioning is similar to males; therefore, their training programs should be very similar. It is well known that the strength characteristics of muscle are affected by the type and amount of work performed over a period of time (1, 12, 28).

It is beneficial for most athletes to include resistance training in their conditioning programs. Proper conditioning of the musculoskeletal system enhances performance and decreases injury potential. Gains in strength or muscular hypertrophy produced by resistance training result in "improved motor performance and, therefore, improved sports performance" (16, p. 4). Incremental increases in the work load placed on muscle will cause physiological changes within the musculoskeletal system (24), such as muscular hypertrophy, increases in the size of myofibrils, increased strength of ligaments and tendons, hyperplasia (an increase in the number of muscle fibers), as well as enzymatic changes developed through anaerobic exercise. These changes depend on the type and amount of work performed consistently. When maximum strength, endurance, or power is the ultimate goal, the athlete must follow a specifically designed program (11).

The resistance training program that will best develop strength remains a controversial issue. However, the accepted range is six to eight repetitions of maximum load (RM, repetitions maximum) performed three times a week (1, 3, 5, 6). This will progressively adapt a muscle to a given work load. For adaptation to occur, a muscle must be overloaded, that is, stressed beyond the demand of its normal work load. *Load* is the amount of weight used in an exercise. *Intensity* is the rate at which work is performed. The response and gains in strength are specific to the muscle group being exercised, the type and speed of the contraction, and the intensity. As the muscle adapts to overload, new demands must be introduced to promote further progress. However, it is important to watch for overtraining (31). Overtraining occurs when the body is worked beyond its limits of recovery. The length of time between sets and training sessions (i.e., rest) is another variable. Different exercises may be used to vary the conditioning stimulus to a particular muscle group (32).

Strength Training

Development of a resistance training program begins with an assessment of a sport's performance requirements, including analysis of exercise movements, the specific muscles utilized, joint angles, and types of muscular contraction. Once this is accomplished, program variables may be selected: exercise load, resistance or intensity, order of exercise, rest periods, and number of sets (18).

The exercises chosen should target those muscle groups used in the specific sport. The angles, velocities, and types of contraction should resemble those of the sport skill. In addition, to promote total body fitness, major muscle groups in the body should be involved, including upper and lower extremities and the torso. Core exercises that require contraction of several major muscle groups during one movement also should be included, such as the deadlift, squat, power clean, and power snatch (16, 26). Sport-specific body part exercises will vary with the demands of the sport.

The amount of load and variations of resistance and intensity provide the stimulus for strength gains. Two methods are frequently used to determine the load to be used in repetitive exercise. The first takes a percentage (70%-85%) of a single maximal lift (1 RM); this weight is then lifted for several sets, each set consisting of six to eight repetitions. The second method uses a load that can be lifted only for six to eight repetitions maximum (RM); this weight is then lifted for several sets with six to eight RM. The 1-RM and RM methods yield approximately equal load values, but the RM method is preferred by many, because of the ease by which the load is determined. In both methods, the load is increased incrementally as the athlete becomes stronger. Training results are related to the number of sets performed (1). Typically, three to six sets are used to achieve optimal gains in strength. Multiple-set programs improve the rate of strength gains more rapidly than single-set systems.

Rest periods are important to strength-training-program design. Lactic acid accumulates in exercised muscle, and rest allows for it to be removed. Thus, varying the amount of rest between sets may allow the athlete to tolerate higher levels of lactic acid. The traditional, three-times-a-week workout, with a recovery day every other day, appears to allow adequate recovery (16).

Aerobic Fitness

Aerobic conditioning is a critical component of any athlete's off-season conditioning program (8). The measure of aerobic fitness is expressed in terms of the athlete's ability to uptake oxygen. This is limited by the delivery and utilization of oxygen. Depending on the demands of the sport, aerobic fitness requires 8 to 12 weeks to develop.

Low aerobic capacity causes fatigue and poor performance. Fatigue reduces strength, speed, and reaction and movement time. These losses may increase the athletic female's risk of injury. In contrast, the athlete who has a high degree of aerobic fitness has the ability to work at greater intensities for longer periods and is able to recover from the fatigue of exercise faster. Although cardiovascular demands differ from sport to sport, the aerobic power of an athlete will be a major determinant of athletic performance (35).

The measure of aerobic fitness is defined as the oxygen consumption relative to body weight. It is expressed by maximum oxygen uptake difference ($\dot{V}O_2max$) with $\dot{V}O_2max$ = heart rate (HR) $\times$ stroke volume (SV) $\times$ arteriovenous oxygen difference ($(a-v)O_2$). $\dot{V}O_2max$ represents the maximum capabilities of the oxygen transport system and aerobic ATP resynthesis. Two components of $\dot{V}O_2max$, HR and SV, determine cardiac output (Q). HR $\times$ SV = Q. Thus, if cardiac output is improved by aerobic conditioning, $\dot{V}O_2max$ also improves. The other factor limiting utilization of oxygen is the ability of the muscles to extract and utilize oxygen from the blood delivered. Proper off-season conditioning will stimulate physiologic changes in the muscles, which will improve their ability to extract and use oxygen for ATP resynthesis. Aerobic training also increases the size and number of mitochondria (M).

Training Principles

Any exercise prescription should use sound, scientific principles to maintain aerobic fitness in the off-season. Females do not differ from males in terms of response to aerobic training; both will respond by increasing $\dot{V}O_2max$. But differences in $\dot{V}O_2max$ may be genetic or physiologic (18).

The principles that guide the design of an aerobic conditioning program include specificity, overload, progression, and individuality. Gains are specific to the metabolic system utilized, muscles involved, and sport-specific requirements. The aerobic system must be stressed beyond what is normally encountered, and as aerobic capacity improves, either the intensity or volume (or both) should be increased to continue to produce the overload response effect. Each athlete responds to the demands placed on her in similar but unique ways.

Athletic activity may be classified as aerobic or anaerobic, or be a combination, depending on the sport. The aerobic demands placed on a slalom skier differ from those placed on a basketball player; however, both require a high level of aerobic fitness. The exercise prescription for an off-season program should allow for these differences, and so help an individual become more physically fit for her specific sport.

Aerobic Conditioning

The type of activity performed should promote rhythmical contractions of large muscle groups, as in running, cycling, or swimming (2). The intensity at which the activity is performed should be monitored. To maintain conditioning, exercise intensity should stress the cardiovascular system to at least 70% of the athlete's maximum heart rate (20).

Exercise may be continuous or interval, depending on the sport. Continuous training and interval training are equally effective in improving cardiovascular fitness. Continuous training, such as long-distance running at a slow pace, is effective when performed at a constant intensity maintained for 20 to 60 minutes. Interval training should be performed at 75% to 85% maximum speed with a work-to-rest ratio of 1:1. Interval training can be adapted to better stimulate sport-specific needs and incorporate anaerobic endurance. Other considerations include duration of exercise (at least 30 to 60 minutes) and frequency (three times a week for maintenance; 18).

Optimal Body Composition

Another goal of the off-season is to maintain or alter body composition. Optimal body composition can be maintained during the off-season through physical training and attention to nutrition. Body weight is often the only measure by which athletes determine if they are maintaining an appropriate body composition. However, total body weight measured on a standard scale does not distinguish between lean tissue and fat.

It is important in most sports to maximize the lean body mass (LBM) to body fat ratio. Increasing functional muscle mass while decreasing fat is advantageous, because fat has no force production capacity, whereas increased muscle mass improves performance in strength and power sports.

Alteration of body composition requires following sound nutritional guidelines and incorporating proper training principles. With proper design, the off-season conditioning program *can* maintain or alter body composition (7, 9, 25, 27, 36). For example, isotonic strength training performed three times a week for 8 weeks using three sets of six RM increases muscle hypertrophy and lean body mass and reduces body fat. Another method of changing body composition is aerobic exercise performed at low to moderate intensities, which reduces body fat if caloric intake remains the same.

Body Composition Assessment

The first step in designing a program requires assessment of the athlete's body composition. Two commonly used methods are hydrostatic weighing and skinfold measurements. Both methods require the assistance of a trained professional to make an accurate assessment. When the percent body fat is known, the ideal body weight can be calculated, as can the amount of weight loss required to reach that goal. The most effective method of reducing body fat is a combination of moderate increase of physical activity and moderate reduction of caloric intake. A deficit of 500 to 1,000 Kcal a day will ensure slow fat loss of 1 to 2 pounds a week. One pound of fat is equal to 3,500 Kcal. Individual caloric intake can be easily calculated by recording the amounts and types of food and drink consumed in a 24-hour period. Caloric expenditure is calculated by multiplying the athlete's basal metabolic rate (BMR) by the active caloric expenditure, giving the total Kcal expenditure (18). A well-balanced, high-carbohydrate, low-fat diet is necessary to provide adequate nutrition and decrease the use of protein (i.e., muscle) as an energy source (4, 30).

To maximize the fat loss and minimize the loss of LBM, vary the intensity, duration, and frequency of exercise. Exercise of low intensity and long duration is more effective than high intensity and short duration. Duration of 45 to 60 minutes, up to five times a week are best (18). Continual monitoring of the body composition throughout the off-season is necessary to ensure maintenance of body composition once the goal is met.

Female athletes may engage in pathogenic weight-control behavior or use fad diets in an attempt to control body weight (29, 30). These individuals should be identified and referred to appropriately trained professionals for counseling.

Optimal Flexibility

Flexibility is defined as the ability of a joint to move through a range of motion (ROM). Two types of flexibility have been described—static and dynamic. Static flexibility is the total joint range of motion. Dynamic flexibility is the resistance soft tissue structures provide to joint movement during motion. Progressive overload allows soft tissue structures to adapt and increase joint ROM. These modifiable structures will increase flexibility over a period of 6 to 12 weeks (18).

The value of flexibility is well known; however, excessive flexibility has not been shown to improve athletic performance (10, 17). Flexibility demands of each sport are unique; particular sport skills require specialized joint flexibility. The potential for injury increases whenever inflexible muscles and joints are stretched beyond their capacity (17).

Developing Flexibility

Sport requirements for flexibility differ. An analysis of the demands and needs for individual areas of flexibility should be assessed. The female athlete needs both general body flexibility and specific flexibility to perform specific sport skills to decrease the potential for injury. Flexibility exercises for upper and lower extremities and torso should be included.

Several methods of developing flexibility exist. Slow static (passive), partner (passive-assisted), ballistic (active), and proprioceptive neuromuscular facilitation (PNF), as well as other modes of stretching, have been studied, and each produces some improvement in flexibility (13, 23).

Slow, static stretching performed daily is best suited for the off-season program, because of the ease with which it is accomplished. The intensity should overload the muscle to a point of producing stretch without causing injury. The stretch may be repeated several times in one exercise session and be held for up to 30 seconds.

Program Design

Planning an off-season conditioning program for a specific sport requires significant attention to the sport activities performed. The individual responsible for designing a program should do the following.

1. Assess the physical demands of the sport activity.
2. Plan the conditioning exercises to accomplish the physiological adaptations necessary.
3. Know the musculoskeletal actions through kinesiological and biomechanical analysis.
4. Identify those muscles responsible for prime movement, synergistic action, and stabilization.
5. Determine the speed and type of muscular contraction.
6. Understand which energy system is utilized during the sport. With this information, an off-season program can be prepared specifically for a particular sport.

Summary

1. When the competitive season ends, the athlete must continue activity in order to maintain or improve physical conditioning.
2. The goal of the off-season conditioning program is to bring the athlete into the preseason with improvement or maintenance of muscular strength, power, or endurance, aerobic fitness, increase or maintenance of flexibility, individual alterations or maintenance of body composition, and improvement in areas of individual weakness.
3. Although individual capacities and sport requirements vary, a program may be adjusted to meet the needs of each athlete.
4. Using the principles of specific adaptations to imposed demands, specificity, progression, and overload, a program may be developed that will return the athlete physically prepared for the demands of competition (16).

References

1. Atha, J. Strengthening muscle. Exerc. Sport Sci. Rev. 9:1-73; 1981.
2. American College of Sports Medicine. Guidelines for graded exercise testing and exercise prescription. 2nd ed. Philadelphia: Lea & Febiger; 1980.
3. Anderson, T.; Kerarney, J.T. Effects of three resistance training programs on muscular strength and absolute and relative endurance. Res. Q. Exerc. Sport. 53:1; 1982.
4. Behnke, A.R.; Wilmore, J.H. Evaluation and regulation of body build and composition. Englewood Cliffs, NJ: Prentice Hall; 1974:116-123.
5. Berger, R. Comparative effects of three weight training programs. Res. Q. 34:396; 1963.
6. Berger, R. Optimum repetitions for the development of strength. Res. Q. 33:334; 1962.
7. Brown, C.; Wilmore, J.H. The effects of maximal resistance training on the strength and body composition of women athletes. Med. Sci. Sports 6(3):174-177; 1974.
8. Brynteson, P.; Sinning, W.E. The effects of training frequencies on the retention of cardiovascular fitness. Med. Sci. Sports 5:29-33; 1973.
9. Clarke, D.H. Adaptations in strength and muscular endurance resulting from exericse. In: Wilmore, J.H., ed. Exercise and sports science review. Vol. 1. New York: Academic Press; 1973.
10. Corbin, C.B. Symposium on profiling: flexibility. Clinics in Sports Med. 3(1):101-117; 1984.
11. Costill, D.L.; Coyle, E.F.; Fink, W.F.; et al. Adaptations in skeletal muscle following strength training. J. Appl. Physiol. 46:96-97; 1979.
12. DeLorme, T.; Watkins, A. Techniques of progressive resistance exercise. Arch. Phys. Med. Rehabil. 29:263-271; 1948.
13. deVries, H.A. Evaluation of static stretching procedures for improvement of flexibility. Res. Q. 33:222-229; 1962.
14. deVries, H.A. Physiology of exercise. Dubuque, IA: William C. Brown; 1980.
15. Drinkwater, B.L.; Horvath, S.M. Detraining effects in young women. Med. Sci. Sports 4:91-95; 1972.
16. Fleck, S.J.; Kraemer, W.J. Designing resistance training programs. Champaign, IL: Human Kinetics; 1987.
17. Garrett, W.E., Jr. Muscle strain injuries: clinical and basic aspects. Med. Sci. Sports Exerc. 22(4):436-443; 1990.
18. Heyward, V.H. Designs fo fitness. New Yok: Macmillan Publishing Co.; 1984.
19. Heyward, V., McCreary, L. Analysis of the static strength and relative endurance of women athletes. Res. Q. 48:703; 1977.
20. Hickson, R.C.; Foster, C.; Pollock, M.L.; et al. Reduced training intensities and loss of aerobic power and cardiac growth. J. Appl. Physiol. 58:492-499; 1985.
21. Hilyer, J. A year-round strength development and conditioning program for men's basketball. NSCA Journal 11(6):16-19; 1989.
22. Hitchcock, W. Individualized strength and conditioning program for women's basketball. NSCA Journal 10(5):28-29; 1988.
23. Holt, L.E.; Travis, T.M.; Okita, T. Comparative study of three stretching techniques. Perceptual & Motor Skills 31:611-616; 1970.
24. Houtz, S.J.; Parish, A.M.; Hellebrandt, F.A. The influence of heavy resistance exercise on strength. Physiother. Rev. 26:299; 1946.

25. Mayhew, J.; Gross, P. Body composition changes in young women with high-resistance weight training. Res. Q. Exerc. Sport 45:433-440; 1974.

26. O'Shea, J.P. Scientific principles and methods of strength training. Reading, MA: Addison-Wesley Publishing Co.; 1976.

27. Oyster, N. Effects of a heavy resistance weight training program on college women athletes. J. Sports Med. 19:79-83; 1979.

28. Penman, K. Ultrastructure changes in human striated muscle using three methods of training. Res. Q. 40:764; 1969.

29. Rosen, L.W.; McKeag, D.B.; Hough, D.O.; Curley, V. Pathogenic weight-control behavior in female athletes. Physician Sports Med. 14(1):79-86; 1986.

30. Smith, N.J. Weight control in the athlete. Clinics in Sports Med. 3(3):693-704; 1984.

31. Stone, M.H. Muscle conditioning and muscle injuries. Med. Sci. Sports Exerc. 22(4):457-462; 1990.

32. Stone, M.; O'Bryant, H. Weight training: A scientific approach. Minneapolis, MN: Burgess; 1987.

33. Thorstensson, A. Observations on strength training and detraining. Acta Physiol. Scand. 100:491-493; 1977.

34. Van Handel, P.J.; Puhl, J. Sports physiology: testing the athlete. 2(1):19-30; 1983.

35. Wilmore, J.H. Training for sport and activity. Boston: Allyn & Bacon, Inc.; 1982.

36. Wilmore, J.H. Alterations in strength, body composition, and anthropometric measurements consequent to a 10-week weight-training program. Med. Sci. Sports 6:133; 1974.

37. Wilmore, J.H. Morphologic and physiologic differences between men and women relevant to exercise. Int. J. Sports Med. 5(Suppl.):193-194; 1984.

CHAPTER 16

•

Sport-Specific Training

Barbara Hoogenboom

Sport-specific training is an important topic for the athletic female. It relates directly to many topics that have appeared in preceding chapters and to some that will follow. Sport-specific training is the preparation (training) for those activities required by a particular sport (1, 18, 26). Common sense indicates that such training as a form of off- or preseason conditioning should prevent injury and deconditioning, enhance specific muscle strength and length, and facilitate appropriate aerobic or anaerobic conditioning. However, there are no prospective longitudinal studies or research to examine these concepts. Yet, the number of women in sport and fitness participation continues to rise, and many athletic females wish to improve their preparticipation condition and to prevent common, sport-specific overuse injuries. Can women of all ages and abilities optimally prepare for their chosen sports? Sport-specific training may help them accomplish this.

Injury Prevention as a Rationale for Sport-Specific Training

Experience shows that large numbers of athletic women sustain injuries in their chosen sports—from aerobics to water polo—both in individual activities and in those that involve team participation. Medical professionals who treat all levels of athletes see many injuries (3, 8, 9, 14, 15, 16), including numerous common sport-specific injuries that must be treated and rehabilitated (e.g., rotator-cuff overuse in the throwing athlete or the racquet-sport participant). Thus, target populations for sport-specific training include elite or professional athletes, collegiate athletes, recreational athletes, and fitness participants. Though injury rates in organized athletics are carefully documented by the National Athletic Trainers Association (NATA) and the National Collegiate Athletic Association (NCAA; 3, 8), little data exist on recreational athletes and their injury rates. Yet women who participate in sport for fitness and recreation may play several different sports in a given year and need to condition for each specific activity. For them, sport-specific training and its role in injury prevention is an extremely important concept.

Studies show that injury rates can be tied to improper conditioning; hence, it follows that by improving an athlete's preparticipation condition level, her injury rate may be reduced (17, 24). Obviously, some accidents will happen regardless of the condition of the athlete, for example, when equipment failure is involved— equipment used either in the performance of a given sport (e.g., tennis racquet, ski equipment) or as essential elements that compose the "conditions" of a given sport (e.g., the bases used or field conditions in softball, and court surfaces used in tennis; 2, 11, 12, 14, 15, 17). However, many soft-tissue, overuse injuries, training errors, or strain injuries may be prevented with proper training.

Defining Sport-Specific Training

Sport-specific training is training that consists of stretching, strengthening, and aerobic or anaerobic conditioning, which is designed and targeted to optimally prepare an athlete for her chosen sport.

Analyzing Sport Motions

To determine the appropriate components of a sport-specific training program, one must first define the needs or critical demands of a given sport (7, 22, 23, 25, 26). The movements that comprise the essence of the sport must be analyzed to determine which muscles are being utilized (primary movers, secondary movers, or joint stabilizers) and in what type of movement and contraction (concentric vs. eccentric; closed- or open-chain movement; speed of contraction). The length over which a muscle must distend (e.g., one-joint or two-joint muscle) is critical in sport movement analysis. For example, the quadriceps function as two-joint muscles in all running activities; failure to stretch them over both the knee and the hip may predispose a runner to quadriceps strain.

Analyzing Aerobic and Anaerobic Demands

Next, to decide the aerobic or anaerobic demands of the sport, one must determine the intensity and duration of a competition or bout of exercise (21). This will indicate how important aerobic conditioning is in the sport-specific training program (20). The more aerobic demands a sport has, the more preparticipation time an athlete will need to achieve the appropriate level of physiological conditioning.

Developing a Sport-Specific Training Program

When the biomechanics of sport actions and the aerobic and anaerobic demands have been determined, the three important components of the sport-specific training program can be assembled: flexibility and stretching exercises, endurance and aerobic conditioning, and specific muscle group strengthening. These components of the training program and general suggestions have been discussed by several authors (10, 15, 19, 26).

Stretching

Stretching should be performed in a slow, consistent manner using static stretches that are held for 15 to 30 seconds. Avoid ballistic (bouncing) stretches (4, 6, 13), because the muscle spindle and the golgi tendon organ act in a counterproductive manner when stretched ballistically. Stretching should be appropriate to the biomechanical demands of the specific support motions needed; for example, stretch in sport-functional patterns (as though pitching a ball or swinging a bat), and stretch two-joint muscles appropriately.

Aerobic and Anaerobic Conditioning

There are many ways to achieve aerobic conditioning, and cross-training or using various types of exercise machines or devices are good options. Many activities can be used to achieve the desired level of cardiovascular fitness: walking, running, biking, swimming, upper body ergometry, stairclimbing, or using a rowing machine, or a machine that mimics cross-country-skiing motion.

When training for a specific sport, use an activity that will develop endurance in the muscle groups most utilized in that sport (e.g., use upper body ergometry when training for tennis or throwing sports). Anaerobic training should also utilize muscles or sport-specific patterns most needed for burst or sprint-type activities. For example, use baseline length sprints to condition the softball player.

Muscular Training

Achieving strength in the desired muscle groups can be as simple as using weighted household items (partially filled milk jugs), or as complex as using free weights, or elastic resistance (surgical tubing or theraband), Nautilus or other isotonic machinery, hydrotherapeutic exercise, inertial training, or isokinetics. But note that athletic females should use strength equipment that is fitted to their needs, especially in size and resistance. Most female athletes should use light resistance and more sets or repetitions for strengthening, instead of the heavy resistance and low number of repetitions used by power lifters (13, 18). Number of sets and repetitions should be prescribed and tailored to the individual and her sport-specific needs.

Reproducing Sport Pattern

Be creative when using sport pattern simulation. Sport pattern simulation with resistance can be used for strength training unique to a specific sport. For example, use surgical tubing, one end tied to a tennis racquet and the other to a post, when going through the stroking motions of the forehand, backhand, overhead smash, or serve.

Suggestions for Further Study

Clinical experience suggests that sport-specific training, cross-training, and off-season conditioning enhance performance and prevent injury. Sport-specific strength training is important for the athletic female and should be included in programs for recreational, as well as for competitive, athletes. Research is needed in *all* areas of women's sport, including comparative studies of athletic females who undergo off-season conditioning and sport-specific training and those who do not. Longitudinal studies will determine if those who train sport specifically do indeed display improved performance and decreased injury rates. Many challenges lie ahead in collecting data and discerning fact in this increasingly popular area.

Summary

1. Sport-specific training is a concept that has been little written on since the 1970s. Further studies are needed on the effects of sport-specific training on the athletic female, both as it relates to injury prevention and performance enhancement.
2. Sport-specific training is closely related to preparticipation conditioning/preparation for any sport; it can be applied to many types of female athletes (professional, collegiate, high school, and recreational).
3. Sport-specific training consists of stretching, strengthening, and anaerobic and aerobic conditioning designed to optimally prepare an athlete for her chosen sport.
4. To assemble a sport-specific training program, one must first define the critical demands of a sport, including the biomechanics of characteristic motions and the anaerobic and aerobic demands.
5. Muscular training can be done many ways. Be creative when training in sport-specific patterns, and use a variety of resistances.
6. There are many options for aerobic conditioning, both for primarily upper extremity and primarily lower extremity sports.

References

1. American College of Sports Medicine. Guidelines for graded exercise testing and exercise prescription. 2nd ed. Philadelphia: Lea & Febinger; 1980.

2. Bouter, L.M.; Knipschild, P.G.; Volvics, A. Binding function in relation to injury risk in downhill skiing. Am. J. Sports Med. 17(2):226-233; 1989.
3. Clark, K.; Buckley, W. Womens' injuries in collegiate sports. Am. J. Sports Med. 8:187-191; 1980.
4. Corbin, C.B. Symposium on profiling: flexibility. Clinics in Sportsmed. 3(1):101-117; 1984.
5. Deutsch, E.; Deutsch, S.L.; Douglas, P.S. Exercise training for competitive tennis. Clin. Sports Med. 7(2):417-427; 1988.
6. deVries, H.A. Evaluation of static stretching procedures for improvement of flexibility. Res. Q. 33:222-229; 1962.
7. Elliott, B.C. Biomechanics of the serve in tennis: a biomedical perspective. Sports Med. 6(5):285-294; 1988.
8. Garrick, J.; Requa, R. Girls' sports injuries in high school athletics. JAMA 239:2245-2248; 1978.
9. Gecha, S.R.; Torg, E. Knee injuries in tennis. Clin. Sports Med. 7(2):435-452; 1988.
10. Hageman, C.E.; Lehman, R.C. Stretching, strengthening, and conditioning for the competitive tennis player. Clin. Sports Med. 7(2):211-228, 1988.
11. Janda, D.H.; Hankin, F.M.; Ten Hoor, F. Softball injuries: cost, cause, and prevention. Am. Fam. Phys. 33(6):143-144; 1986.
12. Janda, D.H.; Wojtys, E.M.; Hankin, F.M. Softball sliding injuries: a prospective study comparing standard and modified bases. JAMA, 259(12):1848-1850; 1988.
13. Leard, J.S. Flexibility and conditioning in the young athlete. In: Micheli, L.F., ed. Pediatric and adolescent sports medicine. Boston: Brown & Co.; 1984.
14. Lehman, R.C. Surface and equipment variables in tennis injuries. Clin. Sports Med. 7(2):229-232; 1988.
15. Locke, S. Alpine skiing—injuries and prevention. Aust. Fam. Phys. 16(6):793-795; 1987.
16. Maylock, F.H. Epidemiology of tennis, squash, and racquetball injuries. Clin. Sports Med. 7(2):233-243; 1988.
17. Nadeau, M.T.; Brown, T.; Boatman, J.; Houston, W.T. The prevention of softball injuries. the experience at Yokota. Military Medicine 155(1):3-5; 1990.
18. Nielsen, B.; Nielsen, K.; Behrendt, H.M.; Asmussen, A. Training of functional muscular strength in girls 7-19 years old. In: Berg, K.; Erikson, B.K., eds. Children and exercise, Vol. 9. Baltimore: University Park Press; 1980.
19. Nirschl, R.P. Prevention and treatment of elbow and shoulder injuries in the tennis player. Clin. Sports Med. 7(2):277-287; 1988.
20. Ready, A.E.; Humber, H.R. Physiologic response of nordic ski racers to three modes of sport specific exercise. Can. J. Sports Sci. 15(3):213-217; 1990.
21. Ryu, R.K.; McCormick, J.; Jobe, F.W.; Moynes, D.R.; Antonelli, D.J. An electromyographic analysis of shoulder function in tennis players. Am. J. Sports Med. 16(5):481-485; 1988.
22. Smith, G.A. Biomechanics of cross-country skiing. Sports Med. 9(5):273-285; 1990.
23. Steadman, J.R.; Swanson, K.R.; Atkins, J.W.; Hagerman, G.R. Training for alpine skiing. Clin. Orthop. 216:34-38; 1987.
24. Thomas, P. Avoiding skiing injuries. Practitioner 233(1461):90, 92, 94; 1989.
25. Williams, M.; Lissner, H.R. Biomechanics of human movement. Philadelphia: W.B. Saunders; 1966.
26. Wilmore, J.H. Training for sport and activity. Boston: Allyn & Bacon, Inc.; 1982.

CHAPTER 17

•

Muscle Imbalances in the Athletic Female

Shirley A. Sahrmann

A variety of studies have reported the characteristics of normal gait (2) and normal shoulder motion (3), the range of motion of specific joints, and even strength values. But as any investigator or even observer of human movement knows, there is great variation in these characteristics. In fact, identifying individuals whose gait or even whose joint range of motion, particularly rotation, meets the established standard is relatively rare. Thus the major difficulty for the clinician is to distinguish deviations that are individual from those that are signs of dysfunction and potential pathology. When variations of movement are signs of dysfunction, I believe the underlying factor is muscle imbalance.

Defining Muscle Imbalances

Muscle imbalances, though referred to by others (4, 5), have not been defined. Most often the implication is that an imbalance is a weakness of a muscle that alters its relationship with its antagonists. Of course, antagonists have differences in strength, and different individuals have varying degrees of strength in any given muscle. Thus distinguishing a weak muscle is difficult unless it is compared to its contralateral counterpart. Kendall (4) identifies imbalances by manual muscle testing for weakness, and her methods are used primarily by physical therapists. Others, taking advantage of the quantitative values provided by isokinetic testing, call alterations in agonist-antagonist muscle strength ratios, such as that between the quadriceps and hamstrings, imbalances (6, 9).

The definition I propose for muscle imbalances is the condition arising when forces, both passive and active, exerted by a muscle or muscles contribute to faulty joint alignment, deviations from the ideal path of the axes of joint rotation, or disruption of the ideal recruitment patterns of muscles designated as prime movers and those believed to be accessory contributors. Obvious distortions of joint alignment by excessive pull of specific muscles as was commonly found in the patient with polio are readily understood. This type of muscle imbalance can be classified as passive, because it is apparent without movement. The important and relatively easily recognizable component of a passive imbalance is the associated alteration in muscle length, which is readily recognized by trained examiners of posture and alignment. Consideration of the muscular arrangement about any joint indicates that a balance between agonist-antagonists, between synergists with antagonistic secondary actions, and between supporting tissues is the factor that controls segmental alignment. For example, the anterior-posterior tilt of the pelvis is a function of the length of the abdominals and hip extensors versus the hip flexors and paraspinal muscles. Any deviation from an individual's ideal alignment is an indication of changes in muscle length. The Kendalls (4) have formulated standards and specific tests of muscle length that can be used to supplement or verify the information obtained from examination of postural alignment.

The Relationship Between Stretching and Muscle Imbalances

Stretching, which is strongly advocated for athletes, can be considered a preventive and corrective means of reducing the tendency to develop muscle imbalances. Unfortunately, neither the precise objectives for stretching nor the endpoints of muscle length are well understood. Information on stretching often implies the more, the better, though the exact angle of the joint, which represents a muscle's length and at which the stretching should stop, is not presented (1). Furthermore multijoint muscles can develop compensatory actions at any or all of the many joints that they cross. For example, shortness of the tensor fascia lata can cause excessive hip medial rotation instead of a lack of hip extension or adduction. Furthermore shortness of the band can produce excessive lateral rotation of the tibia instead of affecting hip motions. There are no guidelines about slight substitutional motions or joints that may be sites of compensatory motion. For example, when stretching the hamstrings, if an individual is allowed to medially rotate the hip during knee extension while sitting, shortness of the medial hamstrings will go undetected as will the excessive length of the lateral hamstrings. Thus, a common finding when examining athletic stretching programs is that they have stretched the wrong segments or have stretched a specific muscle excessively. The hamstring and calf muscles are the focus of many stretching programs, though the most widely recommended methods for stretching these muscles allow the subject to substitute lumbar or thoracic flexion for hip flexion in the case of the hamstrings. Excessive subtalar motion is a common substitution for the talocrural range when stretching the calf muscles. Inappropriate stretching creates problems of faulty flexibility of secondary joint segments (a concept I call relative flexibility, 8), which causes additional exaggeration rather than elimination of muscle imbalances.

In addition to the problems that can arise from faulty stretching, many programs focus entirely on the short muscle and make no attempt to correct the problem of the antagonist that has become too long. Studies using animals have shown changes in the length-tension properties of muscles that undergo anatomical changes in length after 4 to 6 weeks of immobilization in either a maximally lengthened or shortened position (11). The insights arising from these studies have caused me to question the value of strength developed without regard to ideal muscle length.

Strong muscles that develop their peak tension at faulty lengths that permit or require faulty joint alignment contribute to problems rather than prevent them. To that end, corrective exercises must focus on muscles that are too long. Stretching short muscles will not correct the problems of muscles that have become excessively lengthened. Therefore, specific exercises that require activity of the lengthened muscles while in a shortened position are necessary. The key to this type of program is very precise instruction and performance. In an era in which emphasis is placed on strengthening muscles according to their group actions by the use of machines, a program of precision exercises that emphasize the use of very specific muscles is relatively rare.

Consider the hip abductors. Most often, their length is not adequately assessed. Consequently, many individuals are led to believe that they have a bony leg-length discrepancy rather than a postural fault of hip adduction on one side and hip abduction on the other, arising from muscle length problems. A program designed to strengthen muscles that are faulty in length will only reinforce the existing imbalance.

If exercises to strengthen the hip abductors are performed with the hip in flexion and, worse yet, medial rotation, the tensor fascia lata and the gluteus minimis and anterior gluteus medius muscles will contribute the most strongly to the motion. The hip abductor lateral rotators (such as the posterior gluteus medius) will be overplayed and not contribute as strongly to the motion, eventually developing faults in length. An individual can substitute for the desired hip abduction motion by hip abduction of the contralateral hip abductors, or even use the ipsilateral abdominals to perform lateral pelvic tilt. The necessary specificity requires palpation of the gluteus medius and careful observation of the motion to ensure action of the correct prime mover, not the sartorius or abductor-medial rotator muscles. Just as fine tuning is required for any machine with rotating segments, no matter how powerful its ultimate output, so the human body needs fine tuning for balanced, precise motion.

Identifying Muscle Imbalance

Usually alterations in muscle length are preceded by slight faults in movement, or active muscle imbalances. During the past 10 years, I have attempted to classify the slight faults in motion that can be observed in athletes with musculo-skeletal pain and to develop appropriately named syndromes. By appropriately named, I mean a name that directs a physical therapist's treatment to the offending fault. These pain syndromes are usually diagnosed as forms of tendinitis, though often there are no specific points of tenderness to palpation or any pain with resistance to contraction of the affected muscle. But even if a tendinitis is present, the question is, why did it occur? Why should the tendon of one muscle in one limb become inflamed when the sport requires comparable participation from both limbs? Surely the injured limb is performing differently. Intervention programs based on precise, corrective exercises combined with instruction in correct movement patterns during functional activities (such as sit-to-stand, going up or down stairs, walking and running) seem to be effective.

A central theme to the concepts underlying the classification of these faulty movement-based syndromes is that small faults in alignment and the associated slight changes in muscle length contribute to imbalances of movement that create microtrauma within and about joints, which eventually produces macrotrauma. A reasonable analogy is that just as the wheels on an automobile need balancing and alignment so that the tires do not undergo excessive wear, so joint movements need to be fine-tuned to remain precise. Because joint movement is based on the force-couple action of muscles, slight changes in muscle length and potential corresponding changes in the length-tension properties would alter the path of the instant axis of joint rotation (PIAR). The instantaneous axis of rotation is the center about which a rigid body rotates at a given instant of time. This axis of rotation may change at each instant of time because of joint surfaces, configurations, and other external constraints (7, 10). The characteristics of a syndrome including an alteration in the PIAR from the kinesiological standard and the muscle imbalances believed to be responsible will be described.

The Anterior-Medial Hip Impingement Syndrome

The anterior-medial hip impingement syndrome is an example of a musculoskeletal pain syndrome that occurs frequently in athletic females. This syndrome occurs primarily in runners, hikers, dancers, and in individuals who participate in aerobic exercise and karate. It can also occur in men but is less common.

Symptom Characteristics

The syndrome is characterized by pain in the groin that is particularly evident with hip and knee flexion. The pain can progress from localized pain in the anterior thigh in the region of the inguinal ligament to a deep, aching pain in the posterior aspect of the hip joint. Points or areas of tenderness are not common. Except in the severe case in which the pain has progressed to a constant ache, the pain in the inguinal ligament region is usually transient and occurs primarily during motion.

Posture Analysis

The standing postural alignment of individuals with this syndrome is usually swaybacked. In the terminology used by Kendall (4), swaybacked posture consists of a thoracic kyphosis, loss of the normal lumbar curve, with the upper back swayed back and the pelvis swayed forward. The pelvis is tilted posteriorly and the hip joint is extended. In this type of posture, the abdominals, particularly the external oblique muscles, are excessively long as is the iliopsoas muscle. Importantly, even though the iliopsoas is long, other hip flexors such as the tensor fascia lata (TFL) and the rectus femoris, are short. The combination of the posterior pelvic tilt and the swayed back thorax moves the line of gravity markedly posterior to the hip joint axis. The result is disuse atrophy of the posterior hip girdle muscles, which is evident in diminished definition of the buttocks. Occasionally asymmetry of iliac crest height is also present.

Muscle Length and Strength Assessment

In order to demonstrate the faults in hip-flexor muscle length, a modification of the two-joint hip-flexor test first described by Kendall (4) is used. The subject is supine at the edge of a table, one knee held toward the chest in order to flatten the lumbar spine. If hip flexor length is normal, the thigh should contact the top of the table while the hip joint is in neutral position with respect to abduction or adduction. If any or all hip flexors are short, the thigh will not extend completely and thus will not contact the table. A modification to Kendall's test allows subjects to abduct their hips while attempting to reach full hip extension. If there is a gain in hip extension range associated with hip abduction, it indicates shortness of the TFL. Passively extending the knee in this position is a means of assessing the length of the rectus femoris: if the hip extends further, the rectus femoris is short. Any residual lack of complete hip extension indicates shortness of the iliopsoas. In this syndrome, most commonly, the iliopsoas is long, whereas the TFL is short.

Hip-abductor length is assessed in the side-lying position by the Ober test. Most often the hip abductor-medial rotators are short.

Hamstring length is assessed by the straight-leg raise (SLR) while the patient is supine. According to Kendall (4), the hip should be able to flex to a minimum of 80° when the pelvis is posteriorly tilted enough to flatten the lumbar spine. The length of the biceps femoris versus that of the semimembranosus and the semitendinosus muscles is an important point. If the hip joint is medially rotated and the hip flexion range is greater than when the hip is laterally rotated, it indicates that the biceps femoris muscle is long, whereas the semimembranosus and semitendinosus are short, a common finding in this syndrome. These results further support the pattern of shortness of the hip medial rotators and excessive length of the lateral rotators.

Hip rotation to examine the length of the muscles affecting this motion is assessed with the subject in the prone position with the knee flexed. The typical finding is limited lateral rotation and excessive medial rotation. As expected, anteverted hips are a contributing factor.

The most important manual muscle tests are those of the iliopsoas, the posterior gluteus medius, and the gluteus maximus. These tests indicate muscle performance at its short length rather than tests of the muscle's ability to generate its peak tension. Typically, these muscles test weak.

Movement Tests

When the subject stands on one leg—the affected extremity—hip medial rotation may be exaggerated. In the supine position, hip flexion to more than 90° elicits pain in the region of the inguinal ligament. If hip flexion is performed completely passively and the hip is rotated slightly laterally, the range of hip flexion without pain is greater. The most definitive test is the movement of the greater trochanter during SLR. Ideally, the trochanter would remain in a constant position during the straight-leg raise, because the axis of joint motion passes through the spherical head of the femur. In patients with this syndrome, the path of the trochanter is anterior and medial, which also occurs with excessive medial rotation. If the examiner performs passive SLR while maintaining a constant axis of rotation, the differences between the passive and the active motions makes the faulty movement easily discernable.

Analysis of this fault combined with the information obtained from the specific muscle length and strength tests suggests that the lateral rotators are too long and do not provide the necessary counterbalancing control. Also, the iliopsoas (with its insertion on the lesser trochanter) should prevent medial rotation if it is the prime mover during hip flexion. I propose that the TFL and rectus femoris muscles have become the prime movers and the iliopsoas an accessory contributor, thus the change in muscle dominance. Because these muscles attach relatively far from the axes of rotation, precise control of the motion is compromised.

In severe cases, corresponding faults can be observed during hip extension when performed in the prone position. When the patient is asked to perform hip extension, often the contraction of the hamstrings is obvious by the visual change in the muscle belly. In contrast, the gluteal muscle will not show any change in muscle definition. Palpation further supports the observation of a lack of activity in the gluteal muscles. The hamstrings have become the dominant muscle in hip extension.

The action of the greater trochanter further supports a fault in the PIAR resulting from a change in muscle balance. During hip extension, instead of the greater trochanter rotating laterally and moving slightly posteriorly, it rotates medially and moves anteriorly. The passive, and even active, restriction of the TFL and rectus femoris muscles contributes to this faulty movement of the PIAR. The hamstrings, which originate on the ischial tuberosity and insert primarily on the tibia and fibula, are far from the axis of rotation and thus can contribute to the movement fault. In contrast, the gluteal muscles with their attachments on the greater trochanter would provide optimal control if their participation was ideal.

Hand-Knee Rocking.   In this position, the patient typically assumes a position of less than 90° of hip flexion. When rocking backward to sit on her heels, an asymmetry in the amount of hip flexion occurs; the affected hip does not flex as much as the contralateral hip. Interestingly, when performing hip flexion by rocking backward in this position, the patient will most often be able to achieve complete hip flexion without pain. Usually, after 8 to 10 repetitions of rocking backward to sit on her heels, the hip flexion will become symmetrical if the patient is guided appropriately. Any preexisting asymmetry in the level of the iliac crest will also be resolved by this exercise.

Walking.   These patients most often demonstrate the same faults in gait that were observed during the movement tests. During stance phase, there is excessive hip medial rotation. The lack of change in muscle definition and in firmness, detected by palpation, indicates a lack of gluteal participation. These changes in muscle dominance patterns can also contribute to hamstring strains. The work load placed on this muscle is enormously increased if the gluteus maximus is not fully contributing to the extension moment at the hip. Often, the action of the biceps femoris muscle is a major source of hip lateral rotation, further adding to the demands on this muscle. In such cases, there may be rotational problems at the knee because the force of the hamstrings on the tibia is not counterbalanced by the development of equal force on the femur by the proximally inserting hip lateral rotators.

The best explanation of these findings is that in the individual with this syndrome, the head of the femor is not undergoing the posterior glide that is part of the normal pattern of hip flexion. The pain arises from pinching of anterior joint capsule structures because of the faulty movement of the femoral head. The change in pattern of participation of the muscles that control the motion has contributed to this problem.

Treatment Recommendations

The corrective exercise program is guided by the faults of the syndrome. The objective is to eliminate the anterior-medial motion of the femur during flexion and to restore the proper pattern of muscle participation. The exercises are essentially the same as the tests, only adjusted to produce precise performance. The contraindicated exercise would be hip-flexor stretching, because that would contribute further to the anterior-medial displacement of the femoral head.

The specific exercises would be these:

1. Hip and knee flexion while supine by sliding the foot along the floor and monitoring the path of the greater trochanter.
2. Passive hip and knee flexion with slight lateral rotation in the ranges of 90° to 120°, always stopping with pain.
3. Active hip abduction with lateral rotation while sidelying and being sure that the posterior gluteus medius muscle is being used. This exercise

should be started with the hip and knee slightly flexed and resting on a pillow, if the muscle is extremely weak or long.

4. After regaining adequate control of the hip abductor-lateral rotators, iliotibial band stretch by allowing the hip to adduct so the foot contacts the floor but without either pelvic tilt or hip medial rotation.

5. Hip lateral rotation while prone with the knee flexed.

6. Hip extension with the knee flexed and the gluteus maximus working maximally. A pillow should be placed under the abdomen so that the hip is slightly flexed and substitute motion by lumbar extension is avoided. The hip extension range should be limited to 10°.

7. Hand-knee rocking in the backward direction.

8. Sitting and using the hands to passively flex the hip to the maximum amount of hip flexion without pain and then releasing the hands so that the hip flexion is maintained by contraction of the iliopsoas. After the patient can perform this isometric exercise, she can progress to giving resistance to isometric maintenance of the hip flexion.

9. Sitting and performing knee extension while the hip is in lateral rotation (to stretch the medial hamstrings, if they are short).

10. Standing on one leg and controlling the hip medial rotation by tightening the buttocks muscles.

11. Practicing walking with active effort to use the gluteals during stance phase.

Recommendations

Muscle imbalances probably arise from alterations in recruitment patterns of synergistic muscles that change muscle dominance during a particular motion. Specific sports and activities favor the use of certain muscles or cause excessive lengthening of others, thus creating the potential for problems. Distance running especially uses the thigh muscles more than the hip girdle muscles; doing resistive quadriceps and hamstring exercises while sitting on machines only adds to the imbalances that the sport induces. Dancers perform excessive amount of hip flexion in ranges that utilize the flexors originating farther from the axis of joint rotation than is ideal. Participants in karate do many kicks that emphasize hip medial rotation and thus induce the syndrome I have described. Detailed observation of joint motions and attention to specific muscle use patterns are necessary to prevent and correct muscle imbalances and the eventual dysfunction and pathological changes in joints and muscles that they can produce. The simplistic notion that strong is good no matter how achieved does more harm than good. I hope these ideas have been presented clearly enough to stimulate interest in appreciating the complexity of exercise. Like any complex piece of machinery, the human movement system needs fine tuning of its rotating segments to maintain optimal efficiency and longevity.

Efforts should be made to encourage studies of the muscle and mechanical imbalances that contribute to the development of musculoskeletal and overuse

pain syndromes. Recognition of signs of developing syndromes and early attention to their correction could reduce the incidence and severity of joint and
skeletal injuries. As the medical profession continues to emphasize the importance
of physical activity to optimal health, developing effective means to prevent
injury associated with that activity is critical.

Summary

1. Muscle imbalances and how they can contribute to the development of
   musculoskeletal pain syndromes is a poorly understood topic, though there
   are many examples of how alterations in muscle length and patterns of
   recruitment can result in inappropriate stresses being imposed on joints
   and muscles.
2. A specific syndrome, the anteriomedial hip impingement syndrome, which
   results from such imbalances, illustrates that identification and remediation
   is relatively specific and simple.
3. Many of the so-called overuse syndromes are muscle and mechanical
   imbalance problems in which synergists are underused. Rather than symptomatic treatment of the injured tissues, such syndromes are best remedied
   by correcting the etiological imbalances.
4. Correction requires individual examination and instruction in well-
   designed, fault-specific exercises.

References

1. Anderson, R.A. Stretching. Bolinas, CA: Shelter Publications; 1980.
2. Inman, V.T.; Ralston, H.J.; Todd, F. Human walking. Baltimore: Williams & Wilkins;
   1981.
3. Inman, V.T.; Saunders, M.; Abbott, L.C. Observations on the function of the shoulder
   joint. J. Bone Joint Surg. 26:1-30; 1944.
4. Kendall, F.P.; McCreary, E.K. Muscles: testing and function. Baltimore: Williams &
   Wilkins; 1983.
5. Kendall, H.O.; Kendall, F.P.; Boynton, D.A. Posture and pain. Baltimore: Williams &
   Wilkins; 1952.
6. Knight, K.L. Strength imbalance and knee injury. Physician Sportsmed. 8:140; 1980.
7. Panjabi, M.M. Centres and angles of rotation of body joints: a study of errors and
   optimization. J. Biomech. 12:912-920; 1979.
8. Sahrmann, S.A. Movement system balance theory for musculoskeletal pain syndromes.
   Submitted to Phys. Ther. 1992.
9. Sandersson, D.J.; Musgrove, T.P.; Ward, D.A. Muscle balance between hamstrings
   and quadriceps during isokinetic exercise. Arch. Phys. Med. Rehab. 61:68-72; 1980.
10. Soudan, K.; Van Auderkercke, R.; Martens, M. Methods, difficulties, and inaccuracies
    in the study of human joint kinematics and pathokinematics by the instant axis concept.
    Example: The knee joint. J. Biomech. 12:27-33; 1979.
11. Williams, P.E.; Goldspin, G. Changes in sarcomere length and physiological properties
    in immobilized muscle. J. Anat. 127:459-468; 1978.

•

CHAPTER 18

Incidence and Pattern of Injury in Female Cadets at West Point Military Academy

John T. McBride
William C. Meade, III
Jack B. Ryan

Ever since the admission of women into the military academies in 1976, there has been keen interest in the injury pattern and injury rates in the female cadet population. Our specific interest was the relative injury rate with regard to stress fractures. This was first elucidated by Protzman (3) in 1977, when he noted a significant increase in stress fractures in the women versus the men performing the same or similar activities. This was followed in 1979 by Cox (1) in his report of female cadets at the naval academy. Since that time, there has been a relative paucity of information pertaining to the cadets. In a follow-up study by Cox and Lenz (2), it was clearly evident that through training women could compete at a higher level than at first anticipated. This was most readily apparent in reviewing the minimum requirements for successfully completing certain activities over the 5 years before their most recent article (2). Standards had, in fact, become more demanding, and the women rose to the challenge. Most of the data was based on the performance of the women in specific, military relevant activities. The question has been raised as to the incidence of injury rates with regard to the female cadets now that they have, in fact, become more competitive and better physically conditioned since entering the academy. This chapter is a retrospective review of a randomized sample of the class of 1992 over the past 2-1/2 years and represents a comprehensive review of medical records as well as a computer search of our health care data base. Injury patterns, as well as the healing rates are discussed in this chapter.

This retrospective review of the United States Military Academy class of 1992 includes injuries from the time of enrolling in West Point in July 1988 through January 1991. The class of 1991 was not chosen because the medical records were not readily available due to the commissioning and graduation process at the academy. The classes of '93 and '94 have been enrolled only 6 months and 18 months, respectively, not long enough to give the information that we were trying to obtain.

Survey Population

Medical records of 74 female and male cadets were selected randomly from those of the class of '92. The class of '92, at this time, consists of 996 cadets, of which 884 are males and 112 are females. (The females are 11% of the class, which reflects the total female officer population in the United States Army.) Their medical records were reviewed for musculoskeletal injuries. Total days excused from full athletic participation as well as types of injuries were evaluated. Relative injury frequency rates were determined based on the number of cadets in the class as of January 1991. The injury patterns are divided into subcategories (Table 18.1). The frequency of injuries is low for the majority of the injuries identified; however, certain injuries had an incidence of greater than 5 and these will be the subject of most of our discussion. For some injuries, the number of duty days lost due to injury were more than two standard deviations greater than the normal and these will be discussed separately.

Duty days lost is a numerical way to quantitate cadet disability, or the number of days stated on the official cadet excusal slip for an injury. Any West Point cadet unable to participate fully in all activities (military formation and training, physical education classes, and varsity, club, or intramural athletics) must obtain a cadet excusel form that lists the diagnosis and duration of limited activity. Each excusel is entered into a computerized injury record using a predetermined injury vocabulary agreed upon by all physicians, physician assistants, and therapists. Orthopedic sick call is held Monday through Friday at 6:30 a.m. in the cadet health center and 5:00 p.m. in the intramural and varsity training rooms. Injured outpatient cadets must attend physical therapy in lieu of extracurricular activities. Return to full activities requires a change or termination of the profile by the orthopedic physician or physical therapist. This injury surveillance system is described to show that, although not impossible, it is difficult for an injured cadet to avoid diagnosis and treatment (5).

Training Activities

Before enrolling in the academy, the applicants, or ''new cadets'' as they are called, are given a list of activities and an exercise training program. It is recommended that they start this well in advance to their arrival at the academy. The

Table 18.1 Type of Injury and Length of Disability

Injury	Male			Female			
	N	Days/injury	Range	N	Days/injury	Range	NOTR
Upper							
Rotator cuff injury	5	7.6	4-12	6	12.3	8-17	
Dislocated shoulder	(1)	(220)					
Sublux shoulder	5 (6)	43.8 (103.2)	10-400	2 (3)	66.5 (127.1)	13-250	400d = 1 male
A/C separation	5	29.6					250d = 1 fem
Triceps strain	1	25		1	1		
Elbow contusion	2	15	13-17	3	7.7	3-14	
Wrist sprain	8	22.4	2-48	1	21		
Wrist tendinitis				1	325		
Gamekeeper's thumb	5	29	14-68				
Hand contusion	3	5	2-10	4	12.3	6-18	
MCP/PIP injury	4	11.8	4-30	5	20.2	9-30	
Lower							
Trochanteric bursitis	1	2		3	27	14-45	
Groin strain	4	12	4-21	9	11.9	4-45	
Quad contusion	4	8	5-14	4	16.3	6-30	
ITB tendinitis	2	14.5	10-19	4	23.5	6-45	
MCL, UCL knee strain,							
Grade I	6 (7)	11.7 (229)	1-90	2	13	12-14	90d = 1 male
Grade II/III	4	23	14-50				

(continued)

Table 18.1 (*continued*)

Injury	Male			Female			NOTR
	N	Days/injury	Range	N	Days/injury	Range	
ACL tear	4	217.3	115-300	1	194		115 recent
PCL tear	1	137					
PFP	5	17.8	5-30	18 (19)	19 (25.1)	6-135	135 female
Shin splints	3	16.7	14-19	10	14.5	8-23	
Low leg muscle strain	1	4		4	13.3	5-26	
Ankle sprain, Grade I	4	8	2-11	18	8.6	1-20	
Grade II	9	20.8	12-35	12	17.9	10-30	
Grade III	2	25	20-30	0			
?	2	16	13-19	2	19.5	14-25	
Foot sprain				2 (3)	5.5 (28.7)	3-75	75 female
Plantar fasciitis	1	34		3 (5)	11 (67)	7-152	2f.152/150
Metatarsalgia				6	19	4-40	
Contusion	2	16.5	7-26	6	8	1-18	
Blister	9	7	4-15	14 (15)	8.6 (9.7)	4-26	26d/female
IGT	2 (3)	7 (12.3)	7-23	2	4.5	4-5	23d/male
Prepatellar bursitis	3	31	11-27				
Meniscal repair	(1)	(190)					
Foot contusion	2	16	12-20	4	10.3	7-14	
Achilles tendinitis	1	3		1	16		
Back/spine							
Cervical strain	4 (5)	26.5 (112.2)	15-455	3	7.3	3-10	455 C7 rad
Low back strain	7	25.7	2-69	12	15	3-45	

						295 atyp.
Stress Fractures						
Pelvis	2		2	72.5	60-85	
Femur			1	60 (177.5)	60-295	
Tibia			5	84.4	80-95	
Calcaneal			1	56		
Metatarsal			2	53.5	34-73	
Fracture						
Nose	7		1	7		
Spine		7	2	287.5	180-395	
Clavicle	77		1			
Olecranon	133		1			
Radius	55		1			
Scaphoid	375		1			
MC	34	30-38	2			
Femur			1	90		
Ankle	53		1	195		
Toe			1	20		
Sesamoid	120		1	30		
Miscellaneous						
Muscle strain	34		6	8	1-18	
Contusion	16.5	7-26	2	28.5	10-47	
Plantar warts			2	34	7-61	
Laceration	50	5-10				
Tendinitis	7.5		7	16.3	8-28	

Note. Numbers in parentheses include unique injuries. (See Table 18.3 for further information.)

first 6 weeks at the Academy is called cadet basic training, or "beast barracks." This is when the majority of overuse or stress injuries occur. The cadets have all been premeasured for boots, shoes, athletic shoes, glasses, and uniforms. During the next few weeks, these items are "broken in." A typical day for a cadet starts at approximately 0500 (5 a.m.). During basic training, they begin an exercise program that includes physical training in the morning and unit runs in formation after calisthenics. During their last week in basic training, they make a 12-mile forced road march out to a field camp environment. When they road-march back into the West Point academy area, they are considered plebes.

Athletic and military activities are performed throughout the school year. All cadets participate in the Army's physical fitness test and also in the indoor obstacle course test. Both of these test upper body strength, lower body strength, and aerobic endurance. The indoor obstacle course test specifically requires the use of the arms overhead in climbing up on to a shelf and also on a horizontal ladder, which can put the rotator cuff tendons at risk of overuse injuries. Both the men and the women participate equally in these events. This may explain why the relative rate of rotator cuff injuries is essentially the same. Male cadets, however, are required to participate in boxing and wrestling, which may account for the increased rate in subluxing and dislocated shoulders among the men. Men are also involved in intramural contact sports, such as football and lacrosse, which may predispose them to acromio-clavicular (A-C) separations as well as shoulder dislocations.

Injuries in Female and Male Cadets

Seventy-four men sustained 138 injuries with an average duty time lost of 42 days an injury. Seventy-four women sustained 197 injuries and averaged 41 lost duty days an injury. The men lost 5,391 injury days, or 73 days per male cadet. The women lost 5,870 injury days, or 80 days per female cadet.

The cadets averaged 20 days lost per injury for upper extremity injuries. The incidence for men was 39 versus 22 for women. There were five gamekeeper's thumbs and five acromioclavicular separations for men, injuries that were not seen in the females (Tables 18.2 and 18.3).

Overall, there were far more lower extremity injuries in females than in males. The average days lost per injury were 29.5 for the men and 23 for the women. The men sustained more anterior cruciate ligament tears (4 for the men, 1 in the women). The women had a threefold incidence of patellofemoral pain, 18 versus 5 for the men. The time to return to full activity was essentially the same, 18 days in the men and 19 days in the women with respect to anterior knee pain. For shin splints, the women had a threefold increased injury rate (Table 18.2). The healing time was similar, 16 days for men versus 14 days for women. For Grade I ankle sprains, the women had a fourfold increase in injuries as opposed to the men and an approximate 50% increase in Grade II ankle sprains. Again, for both of these injuries, the number of days out of full activities because of

Table 18.2 Injury With Frequency > 5

Injury	Male			Female		
	N	Days/injury	Range	N	Days/injury	Range
Upper						
Rotator cuff injury/tendinitis	5	7.6	4-12	6	12.3	8-17
A/C separation	5	29.6	2-52	0		
Wrist sprains	8	22.4	2-48	1	21	
Gamekeeper's thumb	5	29	14-68			
MCP/PIP injuries	4	11.8	4-30	5	20.2	9-30
Lower						
Groin strain	4	12	4-21	9	11.9	4-45
ITB tendinitis	2	14.5	10-19	4	23.5	6-45
Quad contusion	4	8	5-14	4	16.3	6-30
Knee strain[1]	6	11.7	1-27	2	13	12-14
ACL tear	4	217.3	115-300	1	194	

(continued)

Table 18.2 (continued)

Injury	Male			Female		
	N	Days/injury	Range	N	Days/injury	Range
PFP[2]	5	17.8	5-30	18	19	6-46
Shin splints	3	16.7	14-19	10	14.5	8-23
Ankle sprains, Grade I	4	8	2-11	18	8.6	1-20
Grade II	9	20.8	12-35	12	17.9	10-30
Metatarsalgia				6	19	4-40
Blisters[3]	9	7	4-15	14	8.5	4-26
Back						
LBS	7	25.7	2-69	12	15	3-45
Stress fractures[4]	0			11	65.1	34-295

[1] = 90-day Grade I MCL omitted, male

[2] = 135-day PFP omitted, female

[3] = 26 blister omitted, male

[4] = 295-day hip stress fracture omitted, female

Table 18.3 Summary of Injury Types and Length of Recovery

Injury	Male			Female		
	N	Days/injury	Range	N	Days/injury	Range
Upper extremity	39	21		22	20.1	
Lower extremity	72	29.5		125	23	
Spine	11	26.1		15	11.2	
Stress fractures	0			11	65.3	
Fractures	10	106.1	7-375	7	104.9	7-395
Miscellaneous	6	27		17	21.7	

Omitted	Male	Female	
D/L shoulder	220 days	Football player	
Sublux shoulder	400 days	Surgery, both cadets	250 days
Wrist tendinitis		Arthroscopy	325 days
Atypical femoral neck SF		Surgery—hip pinning	295 days
Cervical radiculopathy	455 days	Schwannoma	
Ingrown toenail	23 days		
Blistered feet	26 days		

(continued)

Table 18.3 (continued)

Omitted	Male		Female		Lacrosse player
Foot sprain			75 days		
Plantar fasciitis			152 days		
Plantar fasciitis			150 days		
PFP			135 days		
Grade I MCL	90 days				
Meniscal repair	190 days				
	6 male		8 female		
Overall	138 injuries	42 days/injury	197 injuries	41 days/injury	
Omitted	6	229.7	8	176	
By cadet	74/5391–73 days		74/5920–80 days		

the injury was essentially the same (Table 18.2). There were also 11 stress fractures, all in women.

Hand and Wrist Injuries

Hand and wrist injuries were much more frequent in the male cadets. The reason for this is much debated and further study as the etiology of these injuries is warranted. The method of injury may be the way in which men tackle and throw each other in sports such as rugby, lacrosse, and football, the prime culprits.

Knee Injuries

Knee injuries are common among West Point cadets. Fortunately, most of these are not serious, major ligamentous knee injuries. On this matched sample, there were four times as many male anterior cruciate ligament (ACL) tears as female ACL tears. This may be due to the contact-type sports in which the male cadets participate. Dr. Cox (2) reported that the noncontact, ACL injury rate among women basketball players is twice that of the male varsity basketball players at the naval academy, though this was not borne out by our study where the ACL injury rate was higher in the males than in females. Of the other knee injuries seen, patellofemoral pain, or anterior knee pain syndrome, occurred in both men and women at West Point. The incidence was higher in the women cadets, however, the healing rates were essentially the same (Table 18.2).

Stress-Related Injuries

The most striking finding in this review was that of the stress-related injuries, in particular, the incidence of stress fractures. In our random sample of the charts of 74 men, there were no stress fractures documented. This is strictly a sampling bias, for even though there are stress fractures in men at West Point, there were none among the men in this retrospective review. There were, however, 11 stress fractures in the random sampling of 74 female charts. All of these stress fractures were of the lower extremity and required an average of 65 days to heal. Protzman noted a 10-to-1 incidence of stress fractures with respect of females to males (4), and this agrees with our findings. He also noted that at the end of basic training, 25% of the women were on a limited duty profile as opposed to only 5% of the men (3). Over the ensuing 2 years, we noted that the average duty time lost per cadet, whether male or female, is about equal in contrast to the findings of Protzman.

The higher incidence of stress injuries and overuse injuries in females is a cause for speculation. Though only 10% of the Corps are women, there are 10 varsity athletic teams for women and 14 for men. But many more women than men participate in two varsity sports, which may be one reason for the higher incidence of stress-related injuries (Table 18.4).

Low back strain was more prevalent in the female population, though women resolved their low back strain significantly faster than the men. The men had an

Table 18.4   Required and Elective Athletic Activities

Activity	Men	Women	Coed
DPE Classes (Required)[1]			
Boxing	x		
Swimming			x
Gymnastics			x
Wrestling	x		
Self-defense		x	
Combatives			x
Intramurals (Required)			
Basketball			x
Football	x		
Team handball			x
Racquetball			x
Wrestling/boxing	x		
Area hockey			x
Wallyball			x
Swimming			x
Flickerball			x
Cross-country			x
Softball	x		
Lacrosse	x		
Corps Squad (Varsity)			
Baseball	x		
Basketball	x	x	
Cross-country	x	x	
Football	x		
150-lb Football	x		
Gymnastics	x	x	
Hockey	x		
Lacrosse	x		

(continued)

Table 18.4 *(continued)*

Activity	Men	Women	Coed
Corps Squad (Varsity)			
Soccer	x	x	
Softball		x	
Swimming	x	x	
Tennis	x	x	
Track	x	x	
Wrestling	x		
Volleyball		x	
Powerlifting	x	x	
Club Sports	x		
Crew		x	
Cycling	x	x	
Fencing	x	x	
Judo	x	x	
Karate	x	x	
Lacrosse		x	
Marathon	x	x	
Rugby	x		
Skiing	x		
Nordic		x	
Alpine	x	x	
Volleyball	x		
Team handball	x	x	

[1]Required of all cadets first 2 years. More optional sports are taught in which cadets may participate during the last 2 years.

average duty loss of almost 1 month per low back strain injury compared to 2 weeks in the women (Table 18.3).

Unique Injuries

Certain injuries have been omitted from the calculations. The first is a male cadet who sustained a dislocated shoulder. He has had approximately 200 lost duty days. He is a corps squad football player, who is able to play with a brace for his shoulder. He has elected not to have surgery for his shoulder dislocation and occasionally experiences subluxation episodes for which he is symptomatic.

Another such individual is a male cadet with a subluxing shoulder who has had a Bankart repair and has missed approximately 400 days of full duty before and after surgery.

A female in the class also is in a similar situation; she has missed over 250 days. This is one of our corps squad female basketball players who injured her shoulder during close quarters combat and had difficulty with basketball her plebe year. She elected to wait until after the basketball season to have her shoulder surgery. She was on profile to prohibit overhead activities, performing the overhead ladder on the indoor obstacle course test, and taking the APFT. At the end of her plebe year, she underwent a shoulder reconstruction and since that time has been able to return to duty and fully participate in activities.

One cadet had a wrist tendinitis that required arthroscopy and synovectomy. She had been on profile for 325 days, which is atypical.

A cross-country runner who was training for the Marine Corps marathon last summer presented atypical hip pain associated with activity. Her X rays were negative, but lacking significant relief with rest and activity restrictions, she eventually was evaluated with a bone scan and an MRI. A stress fracture was diagnosed and subsequently a hip pinning was performed, resulting in resolution of her hip pain.

A male cadet sustained a neck injury that did not resolve with a conservative treatment. He was found on MRI to have a C-7 schwannoma and has had this surgically removed. He has significant weakness 1/5 of his triceps from a C-7 radiculopathy and has remained on profile for 455 days.

Other atypical cases include a cadet with an ingrown toenail, which required a profile for 23 days; a male cadet with blisters on the feet, which became secondarily infected with cellulitis, requiring hospitalization and antibiotics as well as a subsequent 26-day restriction of activities; a female cadet who had a severe foot sprain that required over 75 days to resolve; two female cadets who developed plantar fasciitis and who required over 5 months to return to full activity; and one female cadet with patellofemoral pain requiring a 135-day profile. Again, these are very atypical.

One cadet with a torn meniscus and subsequent meniscal repair, required 190 days to return to full activity. This is according to protocol for meniscus repair at the United States Military Academy, wherein cadets are restricted after they have a meniscal repair for approximately 6 months.

Summary

1. Female West Point cadets demonstrated higher incidence of patellofemoral pain, shin splints, ankle sprains, and stress fractures. They had almost twice as many lower extremity injuries as male cadets.

2. Overall, female and male cadets are excused from full activities for an equal amount of time over their 4 years at West Point. This contradicts previous reports (3, 4).
3. For similar overuse injuries, other than low back strains, the time it took for male and female cadets to return to fully duty was essentially the same.
4. The male cadets showed a higher incidence of ACL tears and dislocated shoulders, probably due to the activities they participate in that the female cadets do not (e.g., boxing, wrestling, football, lacrosse).
5. The male cadets required a week more to resolve lower extremity injuries and twice as much time to resolve back injuries than did female cadets.

Note

The opinions and assertions contained in this chapter are the personal views of the authors and are not to be construed as official or as reflecting the views of the Department of Defense, Department of the Army, or the United States Military Academy.

Acknowledgment

We would like to thank Ms. Jane Reddington for all her help in preparing this manuscript.

References

1. Cox, J.S.; Lenz, H.W. Women in sports: the Naval Academy experience. Am. J. Sports Med. 7:355; 1979.
2. Cox, J.S.; Lenz, H.W. Women midshipmen in sports. Am. J. Sports Med. 12:241; 1984.
3. Protzman, R.R. Women in sports. Am. J. Sports Med. 7:145; 1979.
4. Protzman, R.R.; Griffis, C.G. Stress fractures in men and women undergoing military training. J. Bone Joint Surg. 59A:825; 1977.
5. Ryan, J.B.; Wheeler, J.H.; Hopkinson, W.J.; Arciero, R.A.; Kolakowski, K.K. Quadriceps contusions: West Point update. Am. J. Sports Med. 19:299; 1991.

CHAPTER 19

•

Upper Extremity Injuries

Letha Y. Griffin

The literature on women's upper extremity injuries occurring during participation in sport is far less extensive than that written on lower extremity injuries (1, 9, 13, 36). One reason may be that more women are involved in sports that maximize on lower extremity skills (track, cross-country, dance, aerobics, soccer, skiing, and basketball) than are involved in sports that maximize on upper extremity skills (swimming, gymnastics, and archery).

Furthermore, injuries to the upper extremity appear to be less common than injuries to the lower extremity, even in sports that employ both. For example, in women's volleyball, surveys have recorded more lower extremity injuries than upper extremity injuries (9).

Frequency of Upper Extremity Injuries

When upper extremity injuries do occur, just as with lower extremity injuries, their nature and frequency do not differ markedly from those sustained by males (4, 39). Kosek (20) reported on the incidence of injuries in women's field hockey, basketball, and track and field at the University of Washington over a 2-year period (1970-1972). Just as in men's sports, the most common injuries were sprains, strains, tendinitis, contusions, and patella overuse injuries. Unfortunately, she did not distinguish between upper and lower extremity injuries.

Haycock and Gillette (13) in 1976 reported the results of an injury survey of 19 major women's sports in 361 schools during the 1973-1974 school year. There were far fewer hand and finger injuries than knee and ankle injuries (13 vs. 151;

Table 19.1   Most Common Injuries to Female Athletes

Injury	No. of positive responses	Total responses, %
Sprained ankles	96	100
Knee	59	61
Contusions	53	55
Lower back	25	26
Muscle pulls and strains	23	24
Shin splints	20	21
Fractures	15	16
Hand and finger	13	14
Lacerations	10	10
Dislocations	10	10
Blisters	8	8
Soft tissue	7	7
Concussions	7	8
Wrist	6	6
Eye	3	3

Note. From "Susceptibility of Female Athletes to Injury" by C. Haycock and J. Gillette, 1976, *Journal of the American Medical Association, 236*(2), pp. 163-165. Copyright 1976 by the American Medical Association. Reprinted by permission.

see Table 19.1). The incidence of fractures, dislocations, contusions, and other soft tissue injuries was not classified by anatomic area.

In Moretz and Grana's (24) report on 60 female and 51 male basketball players who played in the 1975-1976 and 1976-1977 seasons, there were 32 girls and 7 boys injured, with upper extremity injuries being far less frequent than lower extremity injuries in both sexes (Table 19.2).

Eisenberg and Allen (9) surveyed 114 female athletes participating in eight varsity collegiate sports during the 1975-1976 season. They found that whereas ankle and knee injuries comprised 55.2% of injuries, shoulder, elbow, and wrist injuries were only 11.4% (Table 19.3). They agreed with La Cava's (21) earlier report that upper extremity injuries were generally sprains, strains, and dislocations resulting from an "intrinsic dynamic action, which has been poorly executed" (p. 9).

A slightly higher incidence of upper extremity injuries (19.3%) was reported by Garrick and Requa (10) in their survey of 192 injuries that occurred in four Seattle high school girls' sport programs in the 1973-1974 season, with a total

Table 19.2   Anatomic Locations of Injuries

Injured area	Boys	Girls
Upper extremity	3	4
Back	0	2
Facial lacerations	0	4
Hip	0	2
Thigh	0	6
Knee	1	5
Leg	0	4
Ankle	3	13
Foot	1	3
Total	8	43

Note. From ''High School Basketball Injuries'' by A. Moretz and W. Grana, 1978, *The Physician and Sportsmedicine,* **6**(10). Copyright 1978 by McGraw-Hill. Reprinted with permission of McGraw-Hill, Inc.

of 870 participant-seasons (Table 19.4). This number, although a higher percentage of all injuries than that reported by Eisenberg and Allen (19.3% vs. 11.4%), was still far less than the incidence of lower extremity injuries in these same athletes (65.7%).

In 1980, Whiteside (39) reported on injuries occurring in games and practices in the paired female and male sports of basketball, gymnastics, and softball (baseball for men) in the 1975-1976 and 1976-1977 seasons. She defined a *reportable injury* to be one that caused the athlete to stop playing on that day, whereas a *significant injury* prevented the athlete from returning to sport for 7 days. The rate of significant forearm and hand injuries was similar for female and male gymnasts (1.1 for women; 1.2 for men). The rate of significant upper extremity (shoulder, arm, forearm, and hand) injuries in women gymnasts was 1.7, compared to 3.2 for significant lower extremity (hip, leg, knee, ankle, and foot) injuries (Table 19.5).

In softball (baseball, for men), like gymnastics, the rate of significant upper extremity injuries in women and men was similar (1.0 compared to 0.6). Whereas the rate of significant upper extremity injuries in men was similar to their rate of significant lower extremity injuries (0.6 compared to 0.4), the rate of significant upper extremity injuries in women was substantially less than the rate of significant lower extremity injuries (1.0 compared to 5.2). The author did not speculate on why these differences existed.

Table 19.3   Sites of Injury in Each Sport (Frequency and Percentage of Total Injuries)

Injured area	Volleyball	Basketball	Track	Swim-ming	Gymnastics	Softball	Tennis	Golf	All sports
Toes			1(.9%)		3(2.6%)				4(3.5%)
Ankle and feet	5(4.4%)	4(3.5%)	10(8.8%)	1(.9%)	5(4.4%)	3(2.6%)	3(2.6%)		31(27.1%)
Knee and leg	2(1.7%)	3(2.6%)	15(13.1%)	2(1.7%)	5(4.4%)	5(4.4%)			32(28.1%)
Thighs			3(2.6%)	1(.9%)	5(4.4%)			1(.9%)	10(8.8%)
Fingers	1(.9%)	3(2.6%)				3(2.6%)		1(.9%)	8(7.0%)
Hands and wrist					1(.9%)		1(.9%)	1(.9%)	3(2.6%)
Elbows and shoulders		1(.9%)		2(1.7%)	5(4.4%)	2(1.7%)	3(2.6%)		10(8.8%)
Heads and faces		4(3.5%)				3(2.6%)		1(.9%)	8(7.0%)
Necks					1(.9%)	1(.9%)			2(1.7%)
Chest and backs		1(.9%)	1(.9%)	1(.9%)	2(1.7%)		1(.9%)		6(5.3%)
Totals	8(7%)	16(14%)	30(26.3%)	7(6.1%)	27(23.7%)	17(14.9%)	5(4.4%)	4(3.5%)	114(100%)

Note. From "Injuries in a Women's Varsity Athletic Program" by I. Eisenberg and W. Allen, 1978, *The Physician and Sportsmedicine*, **6**(3). Copyright 1978 by McGraw-Hill. Reprinted with permission of McGraw-Hill, Inc.

Table 19.4   Injury Location

Injured area	No. of injuries	% of total
Head	7	3.6
Spine/trunk	22	11.5
Upper extremity		
Shoulder	7	3.6
Wrist/hand	17	8.9
Other	13	6.8
Lower extremity		
Thigh	24	12.5
Knee	27	14.1
Ankle	32	16.7
Other	43	22.4
Total	192	100.1

Note. From "Girls' Sports Injuries in High School Athletics" by J. Garrick and R. Requa, 1978, *Journal of the American Medical Association,* **239**, pp. 2245-2248. Copyright 1978 by the American Medical Association. Reprinted by permission.

In basketball, the rate of signfiicant upper extremity injuries in women and men was similar (0.3 compared to 0.4). Both experienced substantially more significant lower extremity injuries (4.8 and 3.0) than significant upper extremity injuries.

A later study by Shivley, Grana, and Ellis (36) of injuries reported by 79 Oklahoma high schools in 1978-1979 analyzed 165 injuries in 6,478 boys and 132 injuries in 4,807 girls with similar injury rates of 25.4 and 27.4 injuries per 1,000 participants, respectively. Of these, 115 were lower extremity injuries (50 major) and 21 upper extremity injuries (12 major) in men, compared to 101 lower extremity injuries (66 major) and 14 upper extremity injuries (7 major) in women. Again, for female and male athletes at the high-school level, upper extremity injuries were far less common than lower extremity injuries.

DeHaven and Lintner's (7) study of injuries in recreational, high school, and collegiate athletes (average age 21.6 years) seen over a 7-year period (1976-1983) and representing 4,551 sequential cases at the University of Rochester Sports Medicine Clinic substantiated this low ratio of upper extremity to lower extremity injuries (17.5% upper extremity to 61.2% lower extremity injuries in males, and 9.3% upper extremity injuries to 76.9% lower extremity injuries in females, Table 19.6).

Change in the Frequency of Occurrence of Upper Extremity Injuries Over the Last Several Decades

Some had theorized that as women became more aggressive in their sports participation throughout the 1970s and 1980s, we would see an increase in the

Table 19.5   Men's and Women's Reportable and Significant Injuries According to Body Part*

Sport	Head/neck/ spine		Face/ scalp		Shoulder/ arm		Forearm/ hand		Torso		Hip/ leg		Knee		Ankle/ foot	
	No.	R	No.	R	No.	R	No.	R	No.	R	No.	R	No.	R	No.	R
Women																
Basketball																
Reportable	12	0.6	32	1.8	3	0.2	31	1.4	15	0.7	66	3.2	57	2.9	166	8.7
Significant	3	0.1	10	0.6	0	0.0	6	0.3	2	0.1	12	0.6	34	1.7	49	2.5
Gymnastics																
Reportable	1	0.1	0	0.0	8	1.0	26	4.2	12	1.1	8	0.9	18	0.9	30	2.7
Significant	0	0.0	0	0.0	3	0.6	9	1.1	4	0.3	12	0.1	12	1.1	20	2.0
Softball																
Reportable	8	0.3	1	0.0	15	0.6	21	0.8	1	0.0	7	0.3	11	0.4	12	0.4
Significant	1	0.1	0	0.0	7	0.3	8	0.7	0	0.0	1	0.0	5	1.0	4	4.2
Men																
Basketball																
Reportable	13	0.4	61	1.8	13	0.4	40	0.9	35	0.8	91	2.7	86	2.3	217	6.1
Significant	1	0.1	21	0.6	6	0.2	10	0.2	8	0.2	17	0.5	38	1.0	52	1.5
Gymnastics																
Reportable	8	0.6	1	0.1	17	1.3	26	2.1	13	1.0	3	0.2	9	0.8	18	1.6
Significant	3	0.2	1	0.1	9	0.6	15	1.2	5	0.4	1	0.1	7	0.6	8	0.6
Baseball																
Reportable	12	0.2	33	0.9	24	0.5	29	0.6	14	0.3	54	1.3	9	0.2	21	0.4
Significant	2	0.0	2	0.0	15	0.4	10	0.2	3	0.1	6	0.1	4	0.1	10	0.2

Note. From "Men's and Women's Injuries in Comparable Sports" by P. Whiteside, 1980, *The Physician and Sportsmedicine,* **8**(3). Copyright 1980 by McGraw-Hill. Reprinted with permission of McGraw-Hill, Inc. *Some areas of the body are not shown due to the low number of injuries sustained.

Table 19.6   Commonly Injured Areas by Gender

Diagnosis	No. male	% male injuries	No. female	% female injuries
Knee	1157	42.1	401	59.2
Ankle	326	11.9	89	13.1
Shoulder/upper arm	224	8.1	15	2.2
Hand/finger	151	5.5	20	3.0
Hip/thigh	126	4.6	11	1.6
Elbow/forearm	107	3.9	28	4.1
Foot/toe	72	2.6	20	3.0

Note. From "Athletic Injuries: Comparison by Age, Sport, and Gender" by K. DeHaven and D. Lintner, 1986, *American Journal of Sports Medicine,* 14(3), p. 219. Copyright 1986 by the *American Journal of Sports Medicine.* Reprinted by permission.

number of serious injuries occurring in both upper and lower extremities. However, the study by Hunter and Torgan (14) comparing injuries that occurred in the 1980-1981 season to those sustained in the 1975-1976 season showed no increase in major injuries in women.

Garrick and Requa (10) felt that the injury rate did not increase because although women became more aggressive in their sports participation, they also became better conditioned, thus minimizing injuries.

Effects of Conditioning
on Upper Extremity Strength in Women

The relationship of inadequate conditioning to poor upper body strength in women in the 1970s is perhaps best illustrated by the military's experience. When Public Law #94-106 passed in 1975, requiring the admission of women into the military academies beginning in the summer of 1976, there was great concern on the part of educators at those academies over whether the existing programs that challenged male cadets to achieve peak physical performance would fairly challenge entering women cadets.

To investigate the physical performance capabilities of women, Project 60 was organized in the summer of 1975 (38). Sixty-three women ages 16 to 18 participated in this 10-week study. Although they were considered well-conditioned athletes, none of these women could do a single pull-up. Although the flexed arm hang subsequently was substituted for pull-ups in the service academies' physical fitness exercise programs, many of those who were reviewing the performance exercise protocols believed that women cadets should still be encouraged to develop greater upper body strength. These physical educators were not convinced that the poor upper body strength of these preentrance study groups reflected an inherent physiologic inferiority. They felt that the women's poor performance represented instead a lack of adequate conditioning.

Time proved these experts correct, for although in that first class of 119 women entering West Point, 86% could not do one pull-up, within 6 months, 65% of the class could do at least one pull-up. Even more impressively, in the second entering class, 59% of the women could not do one pull-up, and of the 1978 entering class, only 30% of the women could not do pull-ups (2).

Occurrence of Upper Extremity Injuries in Specific Sports

Sports in which upper extremity injuries are seen frequently include gymnastics (11), swimming (17), tennis (12), racquetball (34), field hockey (33), and roller skating (28). Finger injuries are also common in flag football; Collins (5) reported that 39% of 114 injuries seen at Mississippi State in a season of flag football were to the fingers.

Although one may think of gymnastics as dangerous, actually the injury rate is low for club, high school, and recreational gymnastics. Higher injury rates are seen primarily in very skilled gymnasts who perform routines that have high degrees of difficulty.

Unlike men's gymnastics, which stresses upper body strength in three of the four apparatuses (high bar, ring, pommel horse), women's gymnastics capitalizes on balance, coordination, and agility, with the vault and the uneven bars being the two primarily upper-extremity apparatuses (22). Garrick and Requa (11) reported that upper extremity injuries in high school, club, and collegiate gymnasts account for 31%, whereas lower extremity injuries are responsible for 52% of the total injuries occurring.

Acute shoulder injuries are rare, but overuse injuries of the shoulder are common—15% reported by Snook (37) in his 5-year study of 70 women gymnasts and by Garrick and Requa (15) in their 2-year study of gymnastic injuries in high schools, clubs, and colleges in the Seattle, Washington, area. The incidence of elbow injuries in gymnasts is small, less than 7% in Snook's (37), Garrick and Requa's (11), and Priest and Weise's (29) series. The most common elbow injury is fracture of the medial epicondyle, followed by dislocation of the elbow.

Priest and Weise (29) analyzed 32 elbow injuries occurring in 30 female gymnasts. Of the 32, 30 injuries were acute traumatic injuries, but 2 were actually the beginning development of Panner's disease. Stress reactions have been reported not only in the elbow, but also in the distal radial physis (35).

Roller skating is associated with a very high incidence of upper extremity injuries, far higher than the incidence of lower extremity injuries. The most common upper extremity injury is fracture of the distal radius sustained when the skater loses her balance and falls on the outstretched hand. In their study of

62 patients seen over an 8-month period, Perlik et al. (28) reported a much higher incidence of upper extremity acute injuries in women (58.7%) than in men (20.7%) but gave no explanation for this disparity.

Forearm abrasions are seen in volleyball (13). Blisters of the hand commonly occur not only in gymnastics but also in racquet sports.

Upper extremity overuse injuries are also common in swimming and diving (31). Immature divers, both male and female, may develop olecranon apophysitis from repetitive maximal triceps contractions needed to stabilize the elbow at the time of water entry (15).

In 1974, Kennedy and Hawkins (18) stated that swimmer's shoulder, or supraspinatus and biceps tendinitis secondary to impingement, was by far the most common complaint among the 2,486 swimmers surveyed. Freestyle and butterfly were the strokes most frequently blamed in the complaints, although occasionally swimmers related their complaints to the backstroke. The authors felt that veteran competitive swimmers who train all year long needed to be careful not to push heavy yardage on a year-round basis.

Surveying the 1978 World Championship Swimming Team, Dominguez (8) found that 57% of them complained of shoulder pain. He, like Kennedy and Hawkins, blamed the high mileage executed by swimmers during their long training season, some of whom were training at 20,000 meters a day almost 300 days a year.

Richardson, Jobe, and Collins (31) surveyed 137 of our country's best swimmers and found that 58 had shoulder complaints. They stated that complaints were more common in male than female swimmers (46% vs. 40%) and were related, they thought, more to sprinting than to distance swimming. They agreed with earlier reports that the cause of the pain was impingement of the rotator cuff under the coracoacromial arch.

Common Upper Extremity Injuries

Evaluation and treatment of upper extremity injuries is similar for athletic females and males. Discussion of a few of the more common injuries follows.

Shoulder Dysfunction Syndrome

Women engaged in sports that require the arm to be either forcefully or repetitively placed in an overhead, pronated position may develop overuse injuries of the rotator cuff due to either shoulder subluxation or impingement or a combination of both. Although at one time, overuse shoulder pain in such athletes was thought to be primarily due to impingement, Jobe (16) reports that shoulder dysfunction resulting in rotator cuff pathology is distinctly different in young and old athletes.

Jobe attributes shoulder dysfunction syndrome in young athletes (less than age 35) to anterior instability secondary to asynchronous firing in the rotator cuff and scapular rotation muscles, combined with the breakdown and stretching of the static ligamentous stabilizers (inferior glenohumeral ligament, medial glenohumeral ligament, posterior capsule, and anterior and posterior labrum) due to the repetitive eforts required to develop effective, overhead sport technique. In athletes over age 35, the pathology generally is due to a degenerative process characterized by spurs that develop underneath the acromion, resulting in a decreased subacromial space producing an impingement-type phenomenon and "ringing out" of cuff tissue, with loss of adequate blood supply causing dysfunction and ultimate tearing of the cuff.

Jobe feels that instability and impingement represent a continuum of pathology, all resulting in the development of shoulder dysfunction secondary to rotator cuff strain or tear. He has established a four-group classification of shoulder pain:

1. Patients with pure, isolated impingement (typically, older age athletes)
2. Patients with impingement findings and concurrent instability due to chronic labral and capsular microtrauma (seen frequently in overhand athletes)
3. Patients with impingement findings and associated instability due to hyperelasticity in a lax joint
4. Patients with isolated instability due to blunt trauma without impingement

Thus, an accurate history and physical examination of the athlete with shoulder pain are needed to effectively diagnose and classify the pathology. One should ask questions regarding the athlete's onset of pain, localization of pain, point in time during the throwing act when pain occurs, associated numbness, tingling, or weakness, and report of night pain or pain with rest versus pain following or during activity. It is also important to know the athlete's training schedule and any additional sports or activities she pursues.

In the physical examination, one should inspect for atrophy, physical asymmetry, and bony abnormalities. The area of tenderness should be palpated and the range of motion assessed, as well as neurologic testing performed to rule out cervical radiculopathy, entrapment syndromes, or brachial plexus or thoracic outlet pathology.

An impingement maneuver performed with the athlete's arm flexed to 90° and internally rotated to bring the supraspinatus tendon under the acromial process (26) will produce pain in those athletes who exhibit the painful shoulder syndrome of Groups 1 to 3. However, to distinguish between impingement as a primary phenomenon or as a later factor produced by repetitive subluxation, the laxity of the shoulder should be assessed. The athlete remains supine, with the arm off the table, abducted to 90°, and externally rotated. The examiner grasps the humeral head gently with one hand while supporting the patient's elbow with the other hand. Gently, the humeral head is lifted anteriorly, returned to the position of rest, and then slid posteriorly to note anterior and posterior subluxation with resultant relocation (40). (This test is very similar to that used for hip subluxation or dislocation in infants.) Anterior subluxation is more common than posterior subluxation (32). Normal posterior translation may be significant, but it is not usually accompanied by the apprehension displayed by the patient with a subluxable shoulder when stability tests are performed.

Inferior instability, which is usually associated with multidirectional instability, can be demonstrated by the examiner placing downward traction on the relaxed extremity and noting inferior displacement of the humeral head from the acromion, the so-called sulcus sign (25).

Diagnostic tests that help differentiate athletes in these four groups include routine X rays, arthrograms with CAT scans, and MRIs. Subacromial spurs present in Group 1 athletes can be detected on 30°-tilt view of the shoulder, as described by Rockwood (32). Arthrograms are useful for evaluating rotator cuff pathology, and CAT scans following the administration of contrast material are used to evaluate the glenoid labrum. Lesions of the cuff and labrum may also be seen on MRI or by direct anthroscopic visualization.

Lesions of the anterior inferior labrum can be seen in athletes with shoulder subluxation or frank dislocation (Groups 3 and 4 athletes) and are caused by the humeral head "rolling" forward and traumatizing the glenoid in this area. The "slap" lesion, or irregularity or detachment of the anterior superior labrum, is most likely produced by the pull of the biceps on the labrum at its superior glenoid attachment at the time of arm deceleration, especially in the presence of a muscular imbalance (e.g., weakness of the rotator cuff).

Treatment for all four groups of athletes involves strengthening of the rotator cuff, the scapular rotators, and the large positioning muscles of the shoulder (deltoid, pectoralis major, and latissimus dorsi). All exercises should be done within the scapular plane with less than 90° of abduction. Most athletes in the four groups (approximately 95% in Jobe's recent studies) will improve on an exercise program. Those athletes who fail to improve with conservative care after 9 to 12 months probably warrant surgical evaluation.

Arthroscopic subacromial decompression may be helpful in Group 1 and 2 athletes with repair of rotator cuff lesions either arthroscopically or open, where applicable (Group 2 and 3 athletes). Arthroscopic debridement of superior labral lesions may decrease the symptoms of clicking and pain in Group 2 and 3 athletes, but one should be careful not to debride lax or torn inferior labrums, which may convert a subluxing shoulder into one that frankly dislocates (40). Arthroscopic repair of these inferior glenoid labrums may prevent recurrent frank dislocations, but at present, the technique is not as reliably effective as open capsulorrhaphy.

Pericapsulitis of the Shoulder

Pericapsulitis of the shoulder (i.e., adhesive capsulitis, or frozen shoulder) may occur in the older athlete. The pathology of this syndrome is not well understood. In fact, Cailliet (3) in his 1979 book on shoulder pain said the so-called frozen shoulder "a term widely used and poorly understood." The syndrome is characterized by pain perceived initially at the deltoid insertion, but generally becoming global in nature as range of motion decreases. Night pain is not uncommon. The limited range of motion is thought to be secondary to scarring of the capsular or pericapsular structures, with obliteration of the inferior capsular recess. The syndrome seems to affect women more often than men (27). On physical examination, range of motion is markedly decreased. Muscle atrophy may be present, secondary to disuse. Neurologic exam, however, is normal. Routine radiographs may demonstrate mild osteopenia from disuse. A shoulder arthrogram may reveal obliteration of the inferior capsular recess with a decrease in the total volume of the shoulder noted when the contrast material is initially instilled.

There is no consensus regarding treatment. Some experts prescribe rest, believing this is a benign process that will resolve in time. Others believe that physical therapy to maintain or increase motion will decrease the duration of symptoms. Injections of Xylocaine and corticosteroid into the joint to dilate the capsule, soften scar, and decrease the inflammation have also been prescribed. Manipulative therapy, popular in the 60s and early 70s, is no longer commonly employed.

Neurologic Entrapment Syndromes Around the Shoulder

Neurologic lesions of the upper extremity, cervical disc radiculopathy, thoracic outlet compression, and other nerve entrapment syndromes can cause diffuse shoulder pain in the athlete (40). Symptoms are generally present with activities (particularly the abducted, externally rotated position in thoracic outlet syndrome; 32) and often with forceful downward traction in cervical disc radiculopathy. Thoracic outlet syndrome can be caused by an aneurysm of the subclavian artery, a cervical rib, or hypertrophy of the scalene anticus, which causes compression (30). A thorough neurologic exam of the athlete with shoulder pain will rule out these causes of shoulder discomfort.

Signs and symptoms of thoracic outlet syndrome are neurologic or vascular, or both (30), and include upper extremity pain, hypoesthesias, paresthesias, and weakness. Cervical disc radiculopathy generally presents as a radiating pain starting in the neck, with tightness often noted in the trapezius muscle. Numbness and tingling in the distribution of the affected root may also be present, as well as frank weakness. Neurologic compromise may be gradual, although at times the presentation may be acute.

Frequently the Adson maneuver is positive. For this test, the athlete turns her head to the symptomatic side with the neck extended. The affected shoulder is abducted, causing obliteration of the radial pulse in the athlete with this syndrome (19).

Treatment of neurologic problems depends on the specific diagnosis made. Conservative management generally is recommended, with surgical intervention used only if conservative therapy fails.

Fractures of the Humerus

Stress fractures of the neck of the humerus can occur especially in swimmers and athletes who throw. The athlete typically complains of a painful shoulder, with pain increasing markedly during activity and improving with rest. The pain may be difficult to localize, and the athlete may simply hold her upper arm when asked to describe the site of pain. Treatment consists of rest of the upper extremity, followed by a strengthening program for muscles about the shoulder, and then a slow return to sport.

Fractures of the greater tuberosity of the humerus can occur from a direct blow to the tuberosity itself, such as that sustained in a fall when skiing. Again, rest with early range-of-motion and strengthening exercises is the prescribed treatment.

Valgus Overload Syndrome

The underarm pitching style of softball may be the reason there are fewer reported incidences of osteochondritis dissecans of the capitellum and medial epicondylar apophysitis in young athletic females and of the valgus extension overload that produces posteromedial osteophytes in the older athletic female when compared to athletic males.

Epicondylitis of the Elbow

Medial and lateral epicondylitis are as common in women as in men, particularly in the sports of tennis, golf, and racquetball. Patients with these diagnoses typically present with symptoms of pain over several weeks (and even several months) that at first occur only after playing and then occur during play and that may be severe enough to limit their participation. Not only is the athlete symptomatic with sport participation, but she may also complain of pain when doing common activities of daily living, such as opening jars, shaking hands, or lifting bags of groceries out of the car. Generally, the pain is perceived at the epicondyle, but it may radiate down either the flexor or extensor muscle mass.

On physical examination, there is no effusion in the joint. The area of tenderness is limited to the area of the epicondyle where the tendons of the wrist extensors (lateral epicondyle) or wrist flexors (medial epicondyle) arise. There is full range of motion of the elbow, and the extremity is neurovascularly intact.

X rays of the elbow are typically normal but are taken to exclude other potential causes of epicondylar elbow pain, such as osteochondritis dissecans in the young athlete, bony spurs in the older athlete, stress reaction of bone, or the presence of an osseous tumor.

Treatment consists of warming up before activity, increasing muscle flexibility, and applying ice after activity to decrease inflammation. Tennis-elbow bands, which alter the pull of the muscle mass at the epicondyle, may be helpful. Exercises for the involved muscles, as well as all muscles of the upper extremity, may increase circulation, and hence, promote healing, as well as help to alter the muscle pull at its origin.

The exact pathology of these so-called overuse injuries, which occur because the body is unable to heal the damage caused by repetitive, submaximal stresses, is not fully known. Some have theorized that, for a yet unknown reason, the acute inflammatory reaction is not followed by the fibroplastic repair stage.

Massage, various physical therapy modalities, such as ultrasound and electrical stimulation, and strengthening exercises may help to increase circulation and promote healing.

Antiinflammatories, either oral agents or corticosteroids injected into the site of maximum tenderness, may help ease symptoms. Surgery to release this muscle mass from the epicondyle is rarely needed.

Capsular Impingement of the Wrist

Repetitive, forced dorsiflexion of the wrist in a weight-loading situation, as seen in a gymnast, can cause posterior capsular impingement (23). The gymnast generally complains of pain on the dorsal aspect of the wrist, which on physical examination, may be tender to palpation. There also may be some thickening and swelling of the dorsal wrist. Treatment is rest, modalities to decrease the swelling and inflammation, and protection of the wrist from the hyperextended position.

Fractures and dislocations of the carpus, metacarpals, and phalanges are not common but do occur in a variety of sports (6). Phalangeal fractures are perhaps the most frequently seen fractures of the wrist and hand. Treatment depends on the fracture site and the degree of displacement.

Summary

1. Upper extremity injuries in female athletes are less common than lower extremity injuries, even in sports using both extremities.
2. The nature and frequency of upper extremity injuries that occur in women's sports are similar to those seen in men's sports.
3. Upper body conditioning is integral to the overall conditioning program for athletic females, enhancing strength and flexibility and reducing the risk of injury.
4. Though high rates of acute, traumatic, upper extremity injuries have been reported in some women's sports (such as gymnastics and roller skating), overuse injuries of the upper extremity are generally more common.

References

1. Albohm, M. How injuries occur in girls' sports. Physician Sportsmed. 4(2):46-49; 1976.
2. Anderson, J. Women's sports and fitness programs at the U.S. Military Academy. Physician Sportsmed. 7(4):72-78; 1979.
3. Cailliet, R. Shoulder pain. Philadelphia: F.A. Davis; 1979.
4. Clarke, K.; Buckley, W. Women's injuries in collegiate sports. Am. J. Sports Med. 8(3):187-191; 1980.
5. Collins, R. Injury patterns in women's intramural flag football. Am. J. Sports Med. 15(3):238-242; 1987.

6. Culver, J. Sports-related fractures of the hand and wrist. Clinics in Sports Med. 9(1):85-109; 1990.
7. DeHaven, K.; Lintner, D. Athletic injuries: comparison by age, sport, and gender. Am. J. Sports Med. 14(3):218-224; 1986.
8. Domingues, R. Shoulder pain in swimmers. Physician Sportsmed. 8(7):37-47; 1980.
9. Eisenberg, I.; Allen, W. Injuries in a woman's varsity athletic program. Physician Sportsmed. 6(3):112-120; 1978.
10. Garrick, J.; Requa, R. Girls' sport injuries in high school athletics. JAMA 239:2245-2248; 1978.
11. Garrick, J.; Requa, R. Epidemiology of women's gymnastics injuries. Am. J. Sports Med. 8(4):261-264; 1980.
12. Gregg, J.; Torg, E. Upper extremity injuries in adolescent tennis players. Clinics in Sports Med. 7(2):371-385; 1988.
13. Haycock, C.; Gillette, J. Susceptibility of women athletes to injury: myths versus reality. JAMA 236(2):163-165; 1976.
14. Hunter, L.; Torgan, C. Personal communication, 1982.
15. Ireland, M.; Andrews, J. Shoulder and elbow injuries in the young athlete. Clinics in Sports Med. 7(3): 473-512; 1988.
16. Jobe, F.; Bradley, J.; Pink, M. Impingement syndrome in overhand athletes: Part I. Surgical Rounds for Orthopaedics. 1990 Aug.:19-24; Part II. Surgical Rounds for Orthopaedics. 1990 Sept.:39-41.
17. Johnson, J.; Sim, F.; Scott, S. Musculoskeletal injuries in competitive swimmers. Mayo Clinic proceedings 62:289-304; 1987.
18. Kennedy, J.; Hawkins, R. Swimmer's shoulder. Physician Sportsmed. 2(4):34-38; 1974.
19. Knortz, K.; Reinhart, R. Women's athletics: the athletic trainer's viewpoint. Clinics in Sports Med. 3(4).851-868; 1984.
20. Kosek, S. Nature and incidence of traumatic injury to women in sports. Proceedings, National Sports Safety Congress, Cincinnati, 1973, 50-52.
21. LaCava, G. A clinical and statistical investigation of traumatic lesions due to sport. Clinics in Sports Med. 2:8-15; 1962.
22. McAuley, E.; Hudash, G.; Shields, K.; Albright, J.; Garrick, J.; Requa, R.; Wallach, R. Injuries in women's gymnastics: the state of the art. Am. J. Sports Med. 15(6):558-565; 1987.
23. Mellion, M.; Walsh, W.; Shelton, G., eds. The team physician handbook. Philadelphia: Hanley & Belfus; 1990.
24. Moretz, A.; Grana, W. High school basketball injuries. Physician and Sportsmed. 6(10):92-96; 1978.
25. Neer, C.; Foster, C. Inferior capsular shift for involuntary inferior and multidirectional instability of the shoulder. J. Bone and Joint Surg. 62A:897-908; 1980.
26. Neer, C.; Welsh, R. The shoulder in sports. Orthop. Clin. N. Am. 8:583-591; 1977.
27. Parker, R.; Froimson, A.; Winsberg, D.; Arsham, N. Frozen shoulder. Part I: Chronology, pathogenesis, clinical picture, and treatment. Orthopedics:869-873; 1989.
28. Perlik, P.; Kalvoda, D.; Wellman, A.; Galvin, E.; Stojic, B. Roller skating injuries. Physician and Sportsmed. 10(4):76-80; 1982.
29. Priest, J.; Weise, D. Elbow injury in women's gymnstics. Am. J. Sports Med. 9(5):288-295; 1981.
30. Rayan, G. Lower trunk brachial plexus compression neuropathy due to cervical rib in young athletes. Am. J. Sports Med. 16(1):77-79; 1988.

31. Richardson, A.; Jobe, F.; Collins, H. The shoulder in competitive swimming. Am. J. Sports Med. 8(3):159-163; 1980.
32. Rockwood, C.; Matsen, F., eds. The shoulder. Philadelphia: W.B. Saunders; 1990.
33. Rose, C. Injuries in women's field hockey: a 4-year study. Physician Sportsmed. 9(13):97-100; 1981.
34. Rose, C.; Morse, J. Racquetball injuries. Physician Sportsmed. 7(1):73-78; 1979.
35. Roy, S.; Caine, D.; Singer, K. Stress changes of the distal radial epiphysis in young gymnasts. Am. J. Sports Med. 13(5):301-307; 1985.
36. Shively, R.; Grana, W.; Ellis, D. High school sports injuries. Physician Sportsmed. 9(8):46-50; 1981.
37. Snook, G. Injuries in women's gymnastics: a 5-year study. Am. J. Sports Med. 7(4):242-244; 1979.
38. Tomasi, L.; Peterson, J.; Pettit, G.; Vogel, J.; Kowal, D. Women's response to Army training. Physician Sportsmed. 5(6):32-37; 1977.
39. Whiteside, P. Men's and women's injuries in comparable sports. Physician Sportsmed. 8(3):130-140; 1980.
40. Zarins, B.; Andrews, J.; Carson, W., eds. Injuries to the throwing arm. Philadelphia: W.B. Saunders; 1985.

CHAPTER 20

•

Dance, Gymnastics, and Skating Injuries in Athletic Females

Carol C. Teitz

Gymnastics, dance, and skating have much in common. All require a combination of athletic ability, creativity, and artistic expression. Strength, coordination, rhythm, balance, timing, and flexibility are critical. The average age at which children begin participating in these activities is 8 years. Peak performance often occurs between the ages of 15 and 19 years in gymnastics and skating, whereas in dance, peak performance is seen most commonly in dancers in their late teens and early twenties.

There are various subtypes of dance (ballet, modern, tap, aerobics), events in gymnastics (balance beam, floor exercise, uneven parallel bars), and events in skating (individual, pairs, and dance). Each of these subgroups has specific requirements and types of movements. To a certain extent different injuries are a function of the specific activity in which the athlete is involved.

Incidence of Injuries

Comparing injury incidence in these activities is difficult due to differences in reporting and in defining injury. The incidence of injury in gymnastics varies as a function of the level of expertise (27). Weiker found a 12% injury rate in a group of club gymnasts, slightly higher in female than male gymnasts (55). Garrick and Requa reported that women's gymnastics ranked only behind football, wrestling, and softball as a producer of injuries at the interscholastic level (11).

The NCAA injury surveillance over the last few years has consistently noted a high rate of injuries both in women's and men's gymnastics, though female gymnasts sustain more injuries that require surgery (32).

Rovere et al. studied 218 dancers (162 females and 56 males) in the North Carolina School of the Arts for 1 year and found that 185 students sustained 352 injuries that merited the attention of a physician (38). Solomon and Micheli surveyed 164 modern dancers (127 women and 37 men) who reported 229 injuries over a 5-year period (48). Garrick et al. followed 351 students (87% female) and 60 instructors (80% female) of aerobic dance from six different facilities for 16 weeks. There were 327 medical complaints, only 84 of which resulted in any disability and only 2.1% of which required medical care (10). In Quirk's study of 664 ballet dancers, 472 of whom were females, he found an injury rate of 2.87 per female dancer and 3.96 per male dancer over a 15-year period (37).

In a study of elite pairs skaters and ice dancers followed for one competitive season (9 months), Smith and Ludington found 33 serious injuries (i.e., missing 7 or more days of training) in 24 skaters and 16 less serious injuries in 13 skaters (46). Smith and Micheli reported an incidence of 0.12 serious injuries/year/skater in a group of 19 highly competitive skaters, 15 of whom were female. Fourteen of these skaters (11 females) reported 16 acute and 36 overuse injuries. Only eight of these were considered serious (i.e., off the ice > 3 days; 45). Brock and Striowski reported on injuries in 60 Canadian nationally ranked figure skaters over a 1-year period. Of the 33 females, 17 reported a significant injury (i.e., an injury that kept the skater off ice or that impaired performance; 2).

None of these studies has included the vast number of children and adults dancing or participating in skating or gymnastics recreationally in a nonorganized fashion, so actual incidence of injury in these activities is unknown.

Types of Injury

Dancers sustain predominantly overuse injuries (36, 38, 54), whereas gymnasts suffer slightly more traumatic injuries than overuse injuries (see Table 20.1; 11, 32, 34, 47, 55). Skaters appear to have more traumatic than overuse injuries, but the incidence varies depending on the study and the population examined (Table 20.2).

Quirk analyzed 2,113 consecutive ballet injuries over a 15-year period. Muscle and tendon injuries together accounted for 465 of the injuries, of which 34% were muscle strains and 10.7% tendinitis. Stress fractures comprised 1.1% (36).

In the 1989-1990 NCAA injury surveillance, the most common type of injury in women's gymnastics was a sprain (31% of total gymnastic injuries), followed by strain (28%), and ligament rupture (8%; 32). The types of injuries seen in skaters are shown in Table 20.2. Of the 49 injuries in Smith and Ludington's study of elite skaters, 27 were acute (55%) and 22 (45%) were due to overuse. The acute injuries included an avulsed peroneal tendon, concussion, patellar fracture, torn knee ligaments (unspecified), a 5th metatarsal fracture, and an

Table 20.1 Injuries in Gymnasts

	Female & Male[a]	Club				Collegiate	
		Female & Male[b]	Male[c]	Female[c]	Female[d]	Female[d]	Female[e]
Number of participants	2,558	873	21	370	72	24	70
Total number of injuries	52	105	16	260	16	17	66
Number of overuse injuries	11	43	9	98	4	11	15
Number of traumatic injuries	51	62	7	162	12	6	51
Rate of overuse injuries/100 athletes	0.4	12	43	26	6	46	21
Rate of traumatic injuries/100 athletes	2	7	33	44	17	25	73

[a]Data compiled from Petrone & Ricciardelli (1987).
[b]Data compiled from Weiker (1985).
[c]Data compiled from Lowry & Le Veau (1982).
[d]Data compiled from Garrick & Requa (1980).
[e]Data compiled from Snook (1979).

Table 20.2   Types of Injuries in Figure Skaters

Injury	Male & Female[a]	Female[b]	Male & Female[c]
Low back pain	4	5	
Bursitis	4	5	
Patellofemoral pain	3	2	2
Shin pain	0	5	
Tendinitis	5	1	10
Concussion	2	1	
Fracture	3	2	1
Strain	6	2	
Laceration	3	1	
Sprain	3	2	
Contusion	6	0	
Miscellaneous	10	7	15
Total injuries	49	33	28
Total skaters	29	11	28

[a]Data compiled from Smith & Ludington (1989).
[b]Data compiled from Smith & Micheli (1982).
[c]Data compiled from Brock & Striowski (1986).

ischial tuberosity avulsion. The overuse injuries included low back pain, patellofemoral pain, shin pain, a 1st metatarsal stress fracture, bursitis, and tendinitis (46). In Smith and Micheli's study, rates were 0.22/year/skater for acute injuries and 0.78/year/skater for overuse injuries, although this differed slightly by sex. Twenty-seven percent of the women's injuries were acute compared to 37% of injuries in the men (45). In Brock and Striowski's study, 50% of the injuries were acute (i.e., fractures and soft tissue injuries) and 43% were overuse injuries (tendinitis and patellofemoral symptoms; 2).

Another type of injury, which might be called an adaptive problem rather than an injury per se, occurs secondary to standing or working in unusual positions for long periods of time. In dancers these include subungual hematomas, avascular necrosis of the head of the metatarsals, hallux valgus and bunions, hammertoes, and hallux rigidus (41, 42, 50). Osteoarthritis is prevalent in professional ballet dancers, predominantly in lower extremity joints (42). Hammertoes are also prevalent in skaters, as is hypertrophy of both the anterior tibial and posterior tibial tendons (4, 5). Another adaptive problem seen in all three groups of athletes is ankle impingement. This occurs anteriorly due to osteophyte formation on the talus, the tibia, or both (24, 33) and posteriorly due to an os trigonum or long posterior process of the talus (18, 19, 37).

Anatomical Injury Sites

The vast majority of injuries in these athletes occurs in the lower extremities, which accounts for from 37% to 71% of gymnastics injuries (Table 20.3; 11, 32, 47, 55), from 58% to 88% of dance injuries (Table 20.4; 10, 36, 38, 54), and from 68% to 79% of skating injuries (Table 20.5; 45, 46).

Knee

Within the lower extremity the rate of knee injuries has ranged from 9% to 27% in gymnasts (11, 32, 47, 56), from 13% to 17% in dancers (10, 36, 38, 54), and from 10% to 20% in skaters (45, 46). During a 78-month period, Andrish found that "chondromalacia patellae" and patellar tendinitis accounted for 36.5% and 3.5%, respectively, of all gymnasts' knee injuries (1); 84% of these injuries were in women. In Quirk's study of professional ballet dancers, each of these diagnoses accounted for approximately 16% of knee injuries, patellar subluxation accounted for 0.3%, and meniscal problems for 16% (36). Patellar tendinitis is also seen in aerobic dancers (10). Donati et al. described a case of bilateral patellar tendon rupture in a 21 year-old female gymnast (6). Among traumatic knee injuries in gymnasts, subluxation and dislocation of the patella accounted for 9.4%, sprains of the anterior cruciate ligament for 6.4%, medial collateral ligament for 9.4%, posterior cruciate ligament for 1.2%, meniscal tears for 14.1%, and contusions for 7.1% of the knee injuries reported in Andrish's study (1). In skaters, patella-related injuries (patellofemoral dysfunction, patellar fractures, contusions, and tendinitis) are the most common type of knee injuries (45, 46).

Shin

Muscular "shin splints" are quite common, seen in 5% to 29% of dancers, particularly aerobic dancers, and in 10% of skaters (10, 36, 45). In aerobic dancers, these injuries are seen more commonly in female than male students but equally in instructors of both sexes. Furthermore, students sustained two-thirds as many shin problems as did instructors. Of the students with shin problems, 43% had previous similar problems, whereas 50% of the instructors had previous similar problems. However, in neither case was the recurrent injury more severe than the primary injury. Garrick was unable to find any consistent association between floor type and shin injuries (10).

Ankle

Ankle injuries account for 9% to 27% of injuries in gymnasts (Table 20.3; 11, 32, 47, 55), for 11% to 23% of injuries in dancers (Table 20.4; 10, 36, 38,

Table 20.3 Percent of Injuries in Gymnasts by Anatomical Location

Site	Club			Collegiate			
	Male[a]	Female[a]	Female[b]	Female[b]	Female[c]	Female[d]	Male[d]
Foot	—	13	*	+	5	14.5	7
Ankle	9.5	21	25	24	27	17	20
Shin/leg	—	9	*	+	6	4	2
Knee	27.5	25	19	18	9	23	9
Hip/thigh	—	3	*	+	8	5	3
Total lower extremity	37	71	69	58	55	63.5	41
Spine/trunk	9	6	—	18	15	11	12
Upper extremity	36	19	25	18	30	17	41
Other	18	4	6	6	3	8.5	6

[a]Data compiled from Weiker (1985a, 1985b).
[b]Data compiled from Garrick & Requa (1980).
[c]Data compiled from Snook (1979).
[d]Data compiled from National Collegiate Athletic Association; 2-year mean.
*Other lower extremity injuries not detailed but total 25%.
+Other lower extremity injuries not detailed but total 16%.

Table 20.4 Percent of Injuries in Dancers by Anatomical Location

Site	Aerobic student[a]	Aerobic instructor[a]	Ballet/ modern student[b]	Theatrical mixed[c]	Ballet professional[d]
Foot	23	24	15	10	20
Ankle	11	23	22	13	22
Shin	29	24	5	14	8
Knee	15	13	15	14	17
Hip/thigh	5	4	14	7	13
Total lower extremity	83	88	71	58	80
Back	12	7	18	18	9
Other	5	5	11	24	11

[a]Data compiled from Garrick, Gillien, & Whiteside (1986).
[b]Data compiled from Rovere et al. (1983).
[c]Data compiled from Washington (1978).
[d]Data compiled from Quirk (1983).

54), and 16% to 37% in skaters (Table 20.5; 45, 46). Most commonly, these injuries were sprains (16, 25), but they also included tendinitis of the Achilles, peroneals, and flexor hallucis longus tendons in the dancers and skaters, malleolar bursitis in the skaters, and anterior and posterior ankle impingement in all groups.

Ankle sprains are common in dancers and gymnasts because of the frequent plantar-flexed position of the foot. Achilles tendinitis is common in all types of dancers also due to a great deal of work with the foot in a plantar-flexed position. Peroneal and posterior tibial tendinitis are more common in student dancers using poor technique. Tendinitis of the flexor hallucis longus is seen commonly in ballet dancers *en pointe* (15, 17, 40), probably because when the dancer is *en pointe*, the flexor hallucis longus is predominantly responsible for pushoff as well as maintenance of position.

Stress fractures are one of the more serious overuse injuries seen in these athletes and tend to occur predominantly in the metatarsals and in the distal fibula (30). Amenorrhea and dietary deficiencies may contribute to the high incidence of stress fractures in dancers and gymnasts but are beyond the scope of this chapter (22, 53).

Table 20.5   Percent of Injuries in Skaters by Anatomical Location

Site	Female[a]	Male[a]	Male & Female[b]
Foot	12	5	12
Ankle	27	37	16
Shin/leg	15	0	4
Knee	10	16	20
Hip/thigh	15	10.5	19
Total lower extremity	79	68.5	71
Spine/trunk	15	10.5	8
Upper extremity	3	10.5	14
Other	3	10.5	7

[a]Data compiled from Smith & Micheli (1982).
[b]Data compiled from Smith & Ludington (1989).

Table 20.6   Skating Injury Rates as a Function of Expertise and Event

Event	Level	Injury rate
Pairs	Senior	1.4 (females)
Pairs	Senior	0.4 (males)
Pairs	Junior	0.5 (females)
Pairs	Junior	0.8 (males)
Dance	Senior	1.2 (females)
Dance	Senior	1.0 (males)
Dance	Junior	0.5 (females)
Dance	Junior	0.0 (males)

Note. Adapted from Smith and Ludington (1989).

Rate: Number of severe injuries per skater per study period. *Severe* is defined as an injury resulting in 7 or more consecutive days of training missed.

Spine

The spine is also a common site of complaint in these athletes; various authors note incidence of back injuries of 6% to 18% in dancers and gymnasts (9, 10, 12, 14, 29, 31, 36, 38) and 8% to 15% in skaters (45, 46; see Tables 20.3, 20.4, 20.5). Spine problems take the form of strains, scoliosis, and spondylolysis. Micheli has also described vertebral body fractures and discogenic back pain in gymnasts (31). Spondylolysis is four to five times more common in dancers and gymnasts (11%-15%) than in the general population (13, 21). This is often attributed to the hyperextension maneuvers required in dance and gymnastics. Concern has been raised about this possibility in skaters but has not been studied specifically. The arabesque in dance and the camel in skating produce great hyperextension of the spine, as do back walkovers and scales in gymnastics (12, 14).

A higher prevalence than normal of scoliosis has been found in dancers and skaters. Smith and Micheli found scoliosis in 33% of their female skaters compared to 15% in the general population (45). A 24% prevalence of scoliosis was found in a group of professional ballet dancers and was thought to be related to menarchcal delay. However, a high prevalence was also found in the *families* of these dancers compared to those of dancers without scoliosis, suggesting that both heredity and delayed maturation may be involved (53).

The frequency of hyperextension and the great demands for shock absorption during jumps may contribute to the high incidence of back pain in these athletes (12, 14).

Upper Extremity

The upper extremity is less commonly injured in dance and skating than in gymnastics (see Tables 20.3, 20.4, 20.5), although shoulder injuries are fairly common in low impact aerobic dance. Garrick found that one-fourth of interscholastic and club female gymnasts' musculoskeletal problems occurred in the upper extremity (11), as did Snook's study (47) which found of female collegiate gymnasts, 20 of 66 injuries were in the upper extremity. Priest and Weise described 30 female gymnasts who suffered 30 acute traumatic events involving their elbows. Some of these events produced more than one anatomic injury such that 41 elbow injuries were reported: 17 dislocations, 16 medial epicondylar fractures, 3 radial head fractures, 2 supracondylar fractures, 1 radial nerve palsy, 1 chip fracture of the proximal ulna, and 1 osteochondral fracture of the olecranon. Fifty-nine percent of these traumatic injuries occurred without a spotter. In other cases, the spotter was often inexperienced or poorly positioned. Nine out of 16 injuries, including all six from the balance beam, were due to falls onto thin mats or the bare floor. Priest and Weise also found two additional nonacute injuries in the form of osteochondritis of the humeral capitellum (35). Singer and Roy reported on five female gymnasts with osteochondritis of the capitellum in seven elbows (44). This type of problem may be related to impact loading and the frequently locked position of the elbows during floor, vault, and beam.

Another upper extremity problem that may be due more to overuse than trauma is dorsal wrist pain attributed to the hyperextension required at the wrist as well as to the fact that the upper extremity becomes weight bearing in gymnastics. Roy et al., in a 3-year period, noted 21 young high performance gymnasts (19 of whom were females) with wrist complaints. Eleven of these gymnasts (10 females) had radiographic changes of the distal radial epiphysis thought to represent stress fractures, and their recoveries took at least 3 months. Ten gymnasts with similar symptoms but no radiographic changes recovered in an average of 4 weeks (39).

In skating, upper extremity injuries range from 3% to 14% of all injuries and include sprains of the wrist and fingers and strains of the shoulder musculature (45, 46).

Dance Form, Gymnastic and Skating Events, and Injury

Various authors have tried to associate specific injuries with particular events in gymnastics and skating or with the school of discipline in dance. In gymnastics, Pettrone and Ricciardelli have been unable to find any association between type of injury and event (34). Such an analysis is also difficult in dance, because many dancers take classes in more than one type of dance. However, the style of holding the torso fairly stiffly, the great external rotation of the hips, as well as the pointe position for the female dancers, all produce certain kinds of problems more common to ballet than to other forms of dance (51). Tap and jazz dancing are less commonly associated with any specific, significant injuries.

Modern dancers contract, release, and fold the torso, flexing and extending, and their movements are more angular. The head and neck are more likely to move out of phase with the lower torso. Rovere et al. found roughly twice as many cervical and upper back strains in modern than in ballet dancers (38). Within the discipline of modern dance, injuries also vary as a function of the particular technique (48, 51).

In aerobic dance, foot and leg injuries are very common and are influenced by the design of the aerobic program. In the study by Garrick at al., 37% of the injuries to males occurred in the foot compared to 21% of the females. The shin and leg were responsible for 20% of the male injuries and 28% of female injuries (10). In other words, although one can make associations, there is no musculoskeletal injury that occurs *exclusively* during a specific gymnastic event or in a specific dance form.

In skating, the individual and pairs events tend to be more acrobatic including jumps, lifts, and throws, whereas in ice dancing, the emphasis is on precise, coordinated movement of the partners, body lean, and speed. In Smith and Ludington's study (46), the rate of injury varied as a function of expertise and event (see Table 20.6, on p. 258). The senior pairs females were the most frequently injured, and almost one-third of their injuries were in the head, trunk, and upper extremities. This is most likely due to the overhead lifts. All four senior dance females sustained serious injuries. The dancers also had more boot-related injuries.

The Relationship Between Technique, Ability, and Injury

Technique (appropriate positioning and muscle use) is a factor in many overuse injuries (48). Lack of efficiency in movement, due either to poor instruction or lack of readiness (i.e., inadequate flexibility, strength, experience), or both, leads to unnecessary overuse of certain muscle groups with subsequent imbalance in the musculoskeletal system, strains of poorly positioned joints, and an increased potential for traumatic injury (49).

Despite the importance of proper technique in the prevention of most injuries, the incidence of serious injuries increases proportionately with skill and experience (1, 27, 47, 55, 56). Snook noted that 27 (40%) of the 66 major injuries reported in a group of 47 female collegiate gymnasts occurred in the 7 most accomplished gymnasts in the group, in fact, 3 of the 7 were All-Americans (47). In Weiker's study, the more severe injuries were sustained by Class I gymnasts who were doing more difficult maneuvers, and the least severe by the preparation-level gymnast. Even when hours of exposure were incorporated into the calculation, the absolute number of injuries was highest in Class I gymnasts (55, 56). Noncompetitors generally have closer supervision and additional spotting and spend less time in the gym than competitive gymnasts. However, in the case of competitors, more coaches per competitor may mean more pressure exerted on the gymnast by the coach or more encouragement to attempt difficult skills, less time spent waiting in line or resting, and therefore, greater fatigue (34, 52).

In skaters, the incidence of injury varies with the study (see Table 20.2). In some studies, it appears that the more experienced skater is more likely to be injured, perhaps because of the increased difficulty of her routine (46). However, others disagree (2). Most authors have not been able to pin down specific muscular imbalances that attribute to injury. Technique can play a role here, too, as evidenced by peroneal tendinitis in a skater who leans too far over on the outside edge of her skate.

Schedule Considerations

Pettrone and Ricciardelli, and Lowry, and coauthors found statistically significant correlations between the number of injuries and the duration of the gymnastics workout (27, 34). Aerobic dance instructors are also more likely to be injured than students (10). Many injuries occur in the weeks immediately preceding performances or competitions, when practicing too many repetitions of the same movements can cause overuse injuries. During this time, the time spent training also increases; hence, fatigue and stress can interact negatively to increase the chances of traumatic as well as overuse injuries.

Athletic Equipment and Injuries

Equipment can also play an etiologic role in injuries. In skating, many injuries are attributed to the boot, and lacerations occasionally occur due to the skate blade. In dance and gymnastics, a sprung-wood floor is important (43). Aerobic shoes have improved markedly in the last 5 years with improvements in shock-absorbing material, control of the heel and forefoot, arch support, and room in the shoe for accommodative and supportive devices. However, ballet and jazz dancers and gymnasts wear soft slippers with no shock absorbancy and no room for orthotics. Modern dancers often dance in bare feet, which contributes to cracking of the skin on the feet, a different problem from the corns and bunions seen in ballet dancers *en pointe*. Also, the high forces on the toes in the *pointe* shoes may lead to hallux rigidus seen commonly in professional ballerinas (50).

Gymnastics requires the use of various apparatuses (beam, uneven bars, etc.) and safety equipment such as mats and harnesses (27). Tricks are often practiced on a trampoline, which has been implicated in severe neck injuries that have caused quadriplegia (52). In two studies, the event associated with the most injuries in women gymnasts was floor exercise, followed by uneven bars (27, 32). When separating acute from overuse injuries, Weiker found that the highest rate of acute injuries occurred on the balance beam (55). Priest and Weise found that twice as many injuries occurred on thin (1- to 2-inch) mats as on thick (4-inch) mats (35).

In skating, ice conditions might bear consideration but do not seem to account for any serious injuries in the studies to date. Boots, on the other hand, are frequently implicated in causing blisters, callosities, bursitis, and even tendinitis (2, 4, 46), though competitive skaters still have problems despite their use of custom-made boots (5). Development of a more flexible boot that will allow more ankle motion to decelerate the limb and to absorb shock during jumps is currently underway. Such boots may also decrease the incidence of shin pain.

Rules of Competition That Promote Injury

Scoring of dismounts has been proposed as an indirect cause of injury in gymnastics (20, 34). Hunter and Torgan noted in 11 high school and college gymnasts with serious knee injuries that 7 were injured as a result of dismounts from the beam or the uneven bars (20); 5 of the 7 used a twist in the maneuver. Pettrone and Ricciardelli found that 16 of 51 acute injuries occurred during dismount: 6 from vault, 7 from beam, and 3 from uneven parallel bars (34). At the high school level, a deduction in score is given if the degree of difficulty of the dismount is not equal to that of the routine (i.e., too easy or too difficult). In international rules, however, the routine must build, and the degree of difficulty of the dismount must be at least equal to if not greater than that of the routine, even though by the end of her routine, the gymnast may be tired and have lost concentration. Obviously, the scoring of dismounts must be reconsidered. The use of mats of various thickness for different events and allowing spotters during competition also may decrease the incidence of injuries.

Preventing Injuries

A thorough discussion on prevention and treatment of these injuries is beyond the scope of this chapter. Nevertheless, certain critical areas should be considered. Because of the anatomic requirements of these activities, a child who is found on preparticipation screening to have limited flexibility, significant lower limb rotational abnormalities, or increased lumbar lordosis should be discouraged from competitive gymnastics and skating or a career in dance (23, 49). Conditioning should include flexibility exercise, upper and lower extremity strengthening, and cardiovascular endurance exercise to decrease the possibility of fatigue leading to injury (28, 51). Amenorrheic athletes appear to be at greater risk for musculoskeletal injury, particularly stress fractures; therefore, the menstrual status of the female dancer, gymnast, or skater needs to be considered also (3, 7, 22, 26).

Safety should also be a primary concern to participants, parents, and coaches (9, 35, 52, 57). Finally, proper training with regard to the frequency, duration, intensity, and specificity of activity and with emphasis on proper technique is also critical (8, 9).

Summary

1. Women's gymnastics ranks behind only football, wrestling, and softball as a producer of injuries among interscholastic athletes.
2. In general, dancers sustain predominantly overuse injuries, whereas gymnasts and skaters are more likely to sustain traumatic injuries.
3. Overwhelmingly, these injuries occur in the lower extremity.
4. Poor technique is a factor in many injuries.
5. In gymnasts, the incidence of serious injuries increases with skill and experience.
6. Changes in athletic equipment and rules of competition may decrease the incidence and severity of injuries in gymnasts and skaters.

References

1. Andrish, J.T. Knee injuries in gymnastics. Clin. Sports Med. 4:111-122; 1985.
2. Trock, R.M.; Striowski, C.C. Injuries in elite figure skaters. Phys. Sportsmed. 14(1):111-115; 1986.
3. Cann, C.E.; Martin, M.C.; Gerrant, H.K.; Jaffe, R.B. Decrease in spinal mineral content in amenorrheic women. JAMA 251:626-629; 1984.
4. Cummings, T. Lace-bite padding. Phys. Sportsmed. 12(2):166; 1984.
5. Davis, M.W.; Litman, T. Figure skater's foot. Minn. Med. 62:647-648; 1979.
6. Donati, R.B.; Cox, S.; Echo, B.S.; Powell, C.E. Bilateral simultaneous patellar tendon rupture in a female gymnast: a case report. Am. J. Sports Med. 14:237-239; 1986.

7. Drinkwater, B.L.; Nilson, K.; Chestnut, C.H. III; Bremmer, W.; Shainholtz, S.; Southworth, M. Bone mineral content of amenorrheic and eumenorrheic athletes. New Engl. J. Med. 311:277-281; 1984.

8. Fukushima, S. Physical conditioning: a review. Int. Gymnast 22:57-59; 1980.

9. Ganim, R.J. Gymnastics safety for the physician. Clin. Sports Med. 4:123-133; 1985.

10. Garrick, J.G.; Gillien, D.M.; Whiteside, P. The epidemiology of aerobic dance injuries. Am. J. Sports Med. 14:67-72; 1986.

11. Garrick, J.G.; Requa, R.K. Epidemiology of women's gymnastics injuries. Am. J. Sports Med. 8:261-264; 1980.

12. Gelabert, R. Dancers' spinal syndromes. J. Orthop. Sports Phys. Therap. 7:180-191; 1986.

13. Goldberg, M.J. Gymnastic injuries. Orthop. Clin. North Am. 11:717-726; 1980.

14. Hall, S.J. Mechanical contribution to lumbar stress injuries in female gymnasts. Med. Sci. Sports Exerc. 18:599-602; 1986.

15. Hamilton, W.G. Tendinitis about the ankle joint in classical ballet dancers. Am. J. Sports Med. 5:84-88; 1977.

16. Hamilton, W.G. Sprained ankles in ballet dancers. Foot Ankle 3:99-102; 1982.

17. Hamilton, W.G. Stenosing tenosynovitis of the flexor hallucis longus tendon and posterior impingement upon the os trigonum in ballet dancers. Foot Ankle 3:74-81; 1982.

18. Hardaker, W.T.; Margello, S.; Goldner, J.L. Foot and ankle injuries in theatrical dancers. Foot Ankle 6:59-69; 1985.

19. Howse, A.J.G. Posterior block of the ankle joint in dancers. Foot Ankle 3:81-84; 1982.

20. Hunter, L.Y.; Torgan, C. Dismounts in gymnastics: should scoring be reevaluated? Am. J. Sports Med. 11:208-210; 1983.

21. Jackson, D.W.; Wiltse, L.L.; Cirincione, R.J. Spondylolysis in the female gymnast. Clin. Orthop. 117:68-73; 1976.

22. Kadel, N.J.; Teitz, C.C.; Kronmal, R.J. Stress fractures in ballet dancers. Am. J. Sports Med. 20:445-449; 1992.

23. Kendall, H.O.; Kendall, F.P. Normal flexibility according to age groups. J. Bone Joint Surg. 30A:690-694; 1948.

24. Kleiger, B. Anterior tibiotalar impingement syndromes in dancers. Foot Ankle 3:69-73; 1982.

25. Liebler, W. Injuries of the foot in dancers. Foot Sci. 23:284-286; 1976.

26. Lindberg, J.S.; Fears, W.B.; Hunt, M.M.; Powell, M.R.; Boll, D.; Wade, C.E. Exercise-induced amenorrhea and bone density. Ann. Intern. Med. 101:647-648; 1984.

27. Lowry, C.B.; LeVeau, B.F. A retrospective study of gymnastic injuries to competitors and noncompetitors in private clubs. Am. J. Sports Med. 10:237-239; 1982.

28. McMaster, W.C.; Liddle, S.; Walsh, J. Conditioning program for competitive figure skating. Am. J. Sports Med. 7:43-47; 1979.

29. Micheli, L.J. Back injuries in dancers. Clin. Sports Med. 2:473-484; 1983.

30. Micheli, L.J.; Sohn, R.F.; Solomon, R. Stress fractures of the second metatarsal involving Lisfranc's joint in ballet dancers. J. Bone Joint Surg. 67A:1372-1375; 1985.

31. Micheli, L.J. Back injuries in gymnastics. Clin. Sports Med. 4:85-93; 1985.

32. National Collegiate Athletic Association Injury Surveillance System. Unpublished data.

33. Parkes, J.C.; Hamilton, W.G.; Patterson, A.H.; Rawles, J.G., Jr. The anterior impingement syndrome of the ankle. J. Trauma 20:895-898; 1980.

34. Pettrone, F.A.; Ricciardelli, E. Gymnastic injuries: the Virginia experience, 1982-1983. Am. J. Sports Med. 15:59-62; 1987.
35. Priest, J.D.; Weise, D.J. Elbow injury in women's gymnastics. Am. J. Sports Med. 9:288-295; 1981.
36. Quirk, R. Ballet injuries: the Australian experience. Clin. Sports Med. 2:507-514; 1983.
37. Quirk, R. Talar compression syndrome in dancers. Foot Ankle 3:65-68; 1982.
38. Rovere, G.D.; Webb, L.X.; Gristina, A.G.; Vogel, J.M. Musculoskeletal injuries in theatrical dance students. Am. J. Sports Med. 11:195-199; 1983.
39. Roy, S.; Caine, D.; Singer, K.M. Stress changes of the distal radial epiphysis in young gymnasts. A report of 21 cases and a review of the literature. Am. J. Sports Med. 13:301-308; 1985.
40. Sammarco, G.J.; Miller, E.H. Partial rupture of the flexor hallucis longus tendon in classical ballet dancers. J. Bone Joint Surg. 61A:149-150; 1979.
41. Sammarco, G.J.; Miller, E.H. Forefoot conditions in dancers: Part I. Foot Ankle 3:85-92; 1982.
42. Schneider, H.J.; King, A.Y.; Bronson, J.L.; Miller, E.H. Stress injuries and developmental change of lower extremities in ballet dancers. Diagnostic Radiol. 113:627-632; 1974.
43. Seals, J.G. A study of dance surfaces. Clin. Sports Med. 2:557-561; 1983.
44. Singer, K.M.; Roy, S.P. Osteochondritis of the humeral capitellum. Am. J. Sports Med. 12:351-360; 1984.
45. Smith, A.D.; Micheli, L.J. Injuries in competitive figure skaters. Phys. Sportsmed. 10(1):36-47; 1982.
46. Smith, A.D.; Ludington, R. Injuries in elite pair skaters and ice dancers. Am. J. Sports Med. 17(4):482-488; 1989.
47. Snook, G.A. Injuries in women's gymnastics. Am. J. Sports Med. 7:242-244; 1979.
48. Solomon, R.L.; Micheli, L.J. Technique as a consideration in modern dance injuries. Phys. Sportsmed. 14:83-92; 1986.
49. Teitz, C.C. Sports medicine concerns in dance and gymnastics. Pediatr. Clin. North Am. 29:1399-1421; 1982.
50. Teitz, C.C.; Harrington, R.M.; Wiley, H. Pressures on the foot in pointe shoes. Foot Ankle 5:216-221; 1985.
51. Teitz, C.C. Gymnastic and dance athletes. In: Mueller, F., ed. Prevention of athletic injuries. Philadelphia: Davis; 135-158; 1991.
52. Torg, J.S. Trampoline-induced quadriplegia. Clin. Sports Med. 6:73-85; 1987.
53. Warren, M.P., Brooks-Gunn, J.; Hamilton, L.H.; Warren, L.F.; Hamilton, W.G. Scoliosis and fractures in young ballet dancers: relation to delayed menarche and secondary amenorrhea. New Engl. J. Med. 314:1348-1353; 1986.
54. Washington, E.L. Musculoskeletal injuries in theatrical dancers: site, frequency, and severity. Am. J. Sports Med. 6:75-98; 1978.
55. Weiker, G.G. Injuries in club gymnastics. Phys. Sportsmed. 13:63-66; 1985.
56. Weiker, G.G. Club gymnastics. Clin. Sports Med. 4:39-44; 1985.
57. Wettstone, E., editor. Gymnastics safety manual, 2nd ed. University Park, PA: Pennsylvania State Univ. Press; 1979.

CHAPTER 21

•

Lower Extremity Injuries

Jerome V. Ciullo

We have learned a lot in 20 years. Concurrent with the development of sports medicine as a modern discipline, the Women's Movement, Title IX, and the introduction of female cadets into the military academies were misguided efforts pitting female against male in an attempt to achieve athletic equality. This resulted in nationally televised "battles of the sexes," locally publicized introductions of female members into the ranks of the male high school football squads, and unusual position statements from the AMA (8).

As the data have carefully been analyzed, myths have become discredited. It has become obvious that given an adequate level of conditioning, training, and coaching, injury patterns vary little from gender to gender and are more sport-specific than sex-specific (Table 21.1 and Figure 21.1; 1, 7, 14, 26, 38).

Table 21.1   Lower Extremity Injuries by Collegiate Sport (NAIRS Data: 1975-1978)

Sport	Male	Female
Baseball	37	—
Softball	—	40
Basketball	69	82
Gymnastics	33	67
Soccer	76	—
Field hockey	—	72
Track and field	72	92

Note. Adapted from Clark and Buckley (1980).

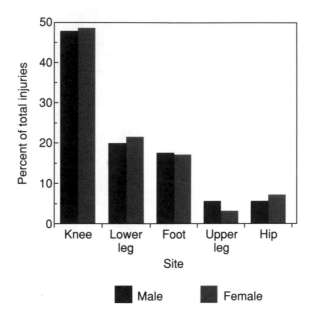

Figure 21.1   Runners' lower-extremity injury sites by gender. *Note.* Adapted from Macintyre, Taunton, Clement, et al. (1991).

Injury Patterns in Female and Male Athletes

If we try to compare male to female sporting injury patterns, we are making a great mistake. For example, males tend to play rugby as a contact sport, whereas females play with much greater finesse. The female in karate tends to use speed and combination techniques common in forms like tae kwon do; the male has a higher tendency to participate in forms like shoto-kan, shito-ryu, and kickboxing, where power and lock-out technique is evident. These athletes are merely practicing what has been taught in this sport for centuries in that if you are small, speed is to your advantage; if you are large, power is your advantage. That females or males cluster toward certain events within a sport can be considered profiling, or natural selection due to advantage of certain physiologic parameters. The gender-specific injury patterns that tend to emerge clinically are caused by overuse or abuse on a specific phenotype and are directly related to factors of socialization, training, and conditioning (16, 18, 20, 38). These phenotypic patterns become important in dealing with treatment once injury has occurred.

The athletic female generally has a higher tendency toward a wide pelvis, femoral neck anteversion with a varus hip, valgus at the knee, compensatory external tibial tubercle rotation, and pronation of the hindfoot (34). This leads to an increased Q-angle (Figure 21.2) and overall turning in of the lower extremity. Coupled with genu recurvatum and a tendency toward looser joints, the turning

Q angle

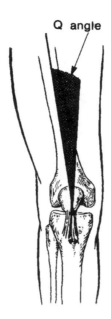

Figure 21.2   Q-angle formed by intersection of line down femoral shaft (essentially in line of pull of the quadriceps) and second line between the center of the patella to the tibial tubercle (the tail of the Q).

in of the lower extremities gives the impression of ''squinting'' patellae and a widened or ''splay'' foot, which has been labeled as a ''miserable alignment syndrome'' (22) based on clinical appearance rather than biomechanical analysis (Figure 21.3).

The wider female pelvis necessitates a more valgus orientation to the knee in order to reestablish a mechanical axis through the hip, knee, and ankle. In conjunction with this, there is femoral neck anteversion and relative internal rotation of the lower extremities. There is no proof that squinting of the patellae, or miserable alignment syndrome necessarily interferes with athletic performance. Muscles and tendons have developed in relation to their origins and insertions to bone and rotational osteotomies, proximal or distal extensor mechanism realignments, or other surgical maneuvers may radically change such musculotendinous relationships. Although the AP X-ray may *look* improved after surgery, athletic performance may be seriously compromised.

The athletic female characteristically has a lower center of gravity at 56.1% of her height compared to the 56.7% of her male counterpart. This is due primarily to differences in extremity length; the legs of men make 56% of their height, compared to 51.2% in women (24). This allows the female to have the advantage of a lower center of gravity on the balance beam in gymnastics (20), whereas the male has the advantage (when combined with increased muscle mass) in power activities such as kicking a football or locking out a karate kick.

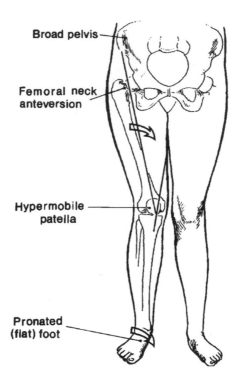

Broad pelvis

Femoral neck
anteversion

Hypermobile
patella

Pronated
(flat) foot

Figure 21.3   Miserable alignment syndrome: femoral neck anteversion, hip varus, knee valgus, and external placement of tibial tubercle with pronation of the heel is a phenotypic difference in the athletic female that has been misinterpreted as malalignment.

The larger male frame is associated with higher muscle mass and greater articular surface (24), which is necessary to support the larger frame as well as possibly allowing a higher capacity for impact loading (Figure 21.4). This increased muscularity is reflected in the ratio of muscle to body weight in the male and is associated with a higher metabolic rate (Table 21.2). The heart, being a muscle, is also larger in the male and is associated with higher stroke volume and $\dot{V}O_2$max. Muscle density is hormonally regulated, and there is high variability in both males and females. Even though the female is generally more flexible and less muscular and has a lower $\dot{V}O_2$max, this does not mean that she cannot benefit from conditioning, flexibility, and weight training to prevent sports injuries as does the male athlete. Large increases in strength have been documented in the athletic female without concurrent increase in clinical bulk (38).

Differences in physique correlate with differences in the way athletic activity is performed (37). It is incorrect to extrapolate from the data that her lower lean body mass and shorter extremity length would lead to overuse of the upper and lower extremities in the female swimmer attempting to cover the same distance

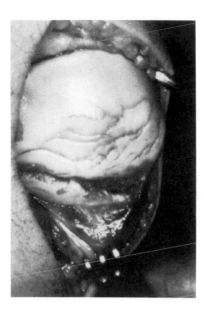

Figure 21.4   Increased patellofemoral compression due to blunt trauma in the female athlete cannot be underplayed as in this 14-year-old soccer goalie with continued knee pain in spite of 3 weeks immobilization. Chondral fracture occurred with blunt contusion; X ray was delayed 6 weeks. It must not be assumed that injuries in athletic females are less significant than those in athletic males.

as her male counterpart. Her increased body fat makes her more buoyant, such that each stroke or kick requires less effort and, thus, is more efficient. Therefore, if we were to compare male to female injury patterns for a specific sport, we would essentially be comparing apples to oranges. The NCAA has recently decreased the size of the ball in women's basketball; perhaps a proportional decrease in size of the court, height of the net, and length of the quarter might be considered as well.

Psychosocial factors are hard to quantitate and do radically alter perception of pain and body composition of the athletic female (20). Eating disorders and exercise can decrease adiposity leading to menstrual irregularities and even jeopardizing calcium hemostatis (33, 35). There is evidence that each year of training before menarche can delay menarche by 5 months (12). Decreasing body fat below 10%, in pursuit of a critical lean/fat ratio or increased mileage, or decreasing weight (i.e., fat) too quickly have been thought to cause menstrual irregularity (11, 13). Reflex sympathetic dystrophy is much more common in the athletic female than in the athletic male. There is nothing more challenging than the female swimmer presenting with knee pain that does not correlate with a typical clinical pattern. Her parents want the problem corrected, so that she can push a little harder to get a college swimming scholarship (which they feel entitled to

Table 21.2   Gender Differences That May Account for Variance in Athletic Performance or Injury Patterns

Problem	Female	Male
Flexibility/elasticity	Higher	Lower
Pelvic width	Wider	Narrower
Bone mass	Less	More
Articular surface	Less	More
Hip varus	More	Less
Knee valgus	More	Less
Ankle pronation	More	Less
Q-angle	12-16°	8-10°
Leg length (% height)	51.2%	56%
Center of gravity (% height)	56.1%	56.7%
Average college student body fat	25%	15%
Average college track athlete body fat	10-12%	5-7%
Percentage muscle to body weight	23%	40%
Basal metabolic rate	Decreased	Increased
Heart size and stroke volume	Less	More
$\dot{V}O_2$max	Less	More

Note. Adapted from Klafs and Lyon (1978).

for the years of carting her around from meet to meet); she would rather be going to the mall with her friends or dating, instead of participating in twice-daily training sessions. There is no brace or physical therapy program capable of correcting the stress on her knee.

Because of phenotypic factors combined with the sports they participate in, athletic females do present with common clinical problems of the lower extremities. For purposes of analysis, let us divide the lower extremity in three segments: the *proximal* (or upper) *segment*, including the hip and proximal two-thirds of the thigh; the *middle segment*, including the knee, distal one-third of the thigh, and proximal one-third of the leg; and the *distal segment*, including the distal two-thirds of the lower leg, the ankle, and the foot.

Proximal Segment Injuries

Around the hip, iliotibial band friction syndrome is extremely common in the athletic female. Pain or snapping across the greater trochanter is much more prevalent than associated lateral knee pain. What has been termed *snapping hip* often is associated with a visible tissue shift across the greater trochanter as the hip is flexed, adducted, or internally rotated. This is frequently experienced without pain and can be voluntarily produced. After adequate X ray, reassurance that this probably will not lead to disabling arthritis of the hip as the athlete ages is usually all she needs. If however, such snapping is painful or interferes with athletic performance, iliotibial band stretching, iontophoresis over the greater trochanter, Indomethacin, strengthening, and occasionally weight loss are necessary to help alleviate the problem. Most often conservative management is best. If this remains a disabling problem, surgery can be contemplated, but it is very rarely needed.

I do not recommend elliptocyzing or feathering tissue over the greater trochanter. I have not done either of these procedures but have seen patients in follow-up who have had such procedures done. Elliptocyzing tissue over the trochanter may lead to protrusion of the trochanter through the defect and even greater snapping than occurred preoperatively. Feathering of tissue leads to the same result. I prefer surgical exploration to find the area of snapping, which is usually the posterior border of the iliotibial band or the anterior border of the gluteus maximus. Direct visualization allows surgical release of the iliotibial tract over the greater trochanter with reattachment in a step cut fashion (Figure 21.5). Rotation of the leg before release and reattachment should reproduce the snapping, though snapping should be gone following lengthening. The patient is on crutches for 2 weeks postoperatively and is usually capable of returning to full activity in 4 to 6 weeks.

If the snapping cannot be directly visualized clinically, then other causes must be investigated, particularly if groin pain is associated. When this occurs, the snapping can be due to capsular damage or labral detachment, and a vacuum sign (32) or hip laxity may be evident by push-pull films (Figure 21.6). Internal derangement would be treated exactly as it would be in a male, that is, by arthroscopic debridement of the labrum, or open debridement combined with capsular reattachment. With pain over the lesser trochanter, snapping of the iliopsoas tendon may be suspected and documented by iliopsoas bursography. If this is the case, iliopsoas Z-lengthening or debulking of the lesser trochanter could be considered; however, stretching and steroid injection has been sufficient to manage this problem in the fencers and ballet dancers I have treated. Anterior hip pain without snapping may be due to anterior capsulitis related to muscle imbalance.

In the young female, apophysitis may be a problem, particularly in the iliac origin of the iliotibial band. This leads to pain without snapping. The only treatment needed is reassurance, because the pain diminishes as the apophysis closes. Apophyseal problems are generally just as apparent in the female as they are in the male; however, they may occur at an earlier age as with Sever's disease. For example, Osgood-Schlatter, common in the 14- to 16-year-old male runner may occur in the female runner in the same sports at ages 11 to 13. Triplane and Type III Salter fractures of the ankle occur slightly earlier in the female than in the male, as do slipped capital femoral epiphyses of the hip.

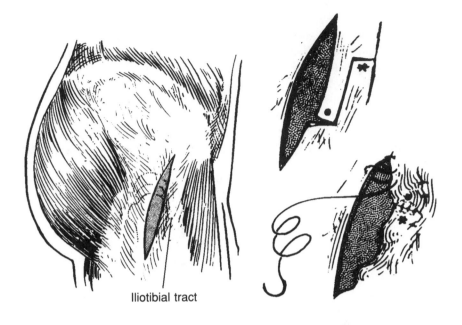

Iliotibial tract

Figure 21.5   Step-cut lengthening of iliotibial band over the greater trochanter can eliminate snapping hip symptoms.

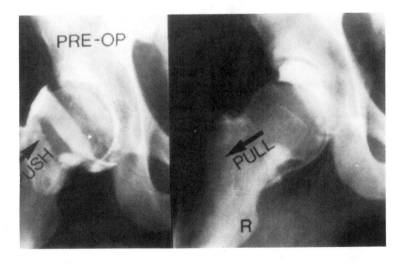

Figure 21.6   Push-pull films documenting hip laxity as the cause of a ''snapping hip.''

There is some variance occurring in athletic females that the sports physician should be aware of. The large, unconditioned, overweight junior high male who is asked to go out for football to play "the left side of the line" is in fact prone to sustaining a slipped capital femoral epiphysis. An overweight, unathletic female of the same age group can sustain the same injury. However, the preadolescent athletic female often has delayed menarche related to decreased body fat, which in turn leads to delayed fusion of the physeal plates, which are more exposed to injury due to athletic performance (12). Therefore, the preadolescent, thin, female gymnast or ballet dancer may be as prone or even more prone to slipped capital femoral epiphysis than her male, overweight, unathletic counterpart (30, 39).

Another classic injury more particular to the female athlete is that of greater trochanteric bursitis. This is assumed to be due to the more varus angulation of the hip, femoral neck anteversion, and a tight iliotibial band that compresses tissue in this area. Greater trochanteric bursitis usually responds to iliotibial band stretching, antiinflammatory medication, such as Naproxyn or Indomethacin, antiballistic strenghtening activity, and general conditioning. Occasionally, a steroid injection may diminish symptoms, although iontophoresis without injection technique can be as effective if done in a therapeutic setting. I have only had two patients who presented with need to drain an inflamed greater trochanteric bursa; both were female athletes. The first was a young long-distance runner who developed spontaneous swelling and responded to aspiration of the bursa of 50 cc of clear, yellowish fluid and then 35 cc of similar fluid a week later. It has not reoccurred since. The second athlete was a female rugby player who had sustained a blunt contusion to the area and had 185 cc, 130 cc, and 60 cc of serosanguinous fluid drained from the greater trochanteric bursa 2 weeks apart, with no reaccumulation since; no steroid injection was used (Figure 21.7). Most clinical cases resolve under conservative treatment.

Middle Segment Injuries

Clinical pain around the knee is the most common orthopedic complaint of the athletic female: It is also one of the most challenging to treat. As in most sport injuries, these are commonly problems of *use*: mis*use*, dis*use*, ab*use*, or over*use*. The individual who is flexible and well conditioned before participating in athletic endeavors is less likely to get hurt.

Females often take up athletics, particularly on a recreational level, later in life. The importance of their preparticipation conditioning to avoid injury must be stressed. Muscle balance is essential at the knee to avoid the onset of knee pain.

Retropatellar pain is the most common athletic complaint and is aggravated by running on hills, squatting, knee flexion and extension exercise, and even walking. The patella does not make contact with the femoral trochlea until 20° to 30° of flexion. With the knee in an extended position and the patient relaxed, the patella can be tilted, and the inferior facet surfaces palpated. There may be tenderness on the medial or lateral side. The patella compression test commonly

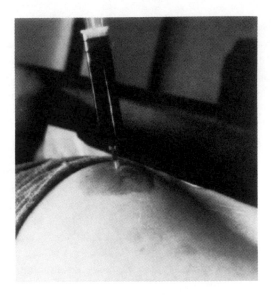

Figure 21.7   Aspiration of inflamed greater trochanteric bursa is occasionally helpful, as in this female rugby player.

causes pain with or without crepitation. With crepitation, there is often hypertrophic synovial or fibrotic adipose tissue caught between the patella and femur above the articular surface superiorly, or between the nonarticular patella and the femoral trochlea distally. Producing a fluid wave and feeling crepitation in the patellofemoral groove that begins at 30° to 60° of flexion and persists is more indicative of chondromalacia, or fibrillation (Table 21.3) of the infrapatellar surface, ranging from minor blistering to fissuring, fibrillation, or areas of complete cartilage loss (28). Articular cartilage loss on the trochlear side with chondral flaps around the periphery may be a posttraumatic change, associated with obesity, or an early sign of diabetes and occasionally can be seen in female body builders who use anabolic steroids (although this may be associated with excessive use of an extension machine in quadriceps strengthening). In the athletic females the articular cartilage is very rarely affected on both sides of the patellofemoral joint.

Articular cartilage works like a sponge. It normally has no blood supply or nerve supply. The proper amount of pressure helps release waste products, and release of pressure allows absorption of nutrients from the synovial fluid (22). With the improper amount of pressure, either too much or too little, cartilage breaks down, first blistering, then fissuring, then shredding, and eventually breaking off. Loose fragments of cartilage within the joint irritate the joint lining, which releases chondrolytic enzymes to help in the absorptive process but, unfortunately, speeds up the breakdown of the articular cartilage as well. Macrotrauma such as articular compression or forceful patellar subluxation with associated osteochondral fracture can augment the process. A grade 2 effusion in the knee decreases

Table 21.3   Chondromalacia or Retropatellar Articular Cartilage Damage

Level of damage	Injury
Grade 1	Blistering
Grade 2	Fissuring
Grade 3	Fragmentation greater than 1.5 cm
Grade 4	Erosion to subchondral bone

Note. Adapted from McCarroll, O'Donoghue and Grana (1983).

strength as measured by Cybex from 10% to 40% (40). This encourages muscle atrophy, which increases patellofemoral friction and accelerates the breakdown process. If the fat pad becomes involved with inflammation and hypertrophy, this can further tilt the patella, impinge in the patellofemoral joint, and lead to inflammation at the patellar tendon origin. The quadriceps, which help balance the patella in the trochlear groove (Figure 21.8), is not uniform musculature. The vastus medialis obliquus (VMO) has more speed fibers, and the vastus lateralis has more endurance fibers. The VMO is the first to atrophy and the last to return. With VMO atrophy combined with the internal rotation to the lower leg associated with femoral anteversion, increased stress occurs across the medial capsule leading to tension on the medial synovial plica. A triad of abnormal patellofemoral tracking, fat pad hypertrophy with associated inflammation of the patellar tendon, and medial plical tenderness can set up (Figure 21.9); traumatic compression of the medial plica as an initiating incident can start this process in reverse.

Treatment in this situation is *not* routine arthroscopy or lateral release, because the majority of female athletes presenting with retropatellar pain can be treated conservatively. Conservative management consists of the use of NSAIDs to decrease inflammation and synovial reaction and to stabilize breakdown of articular cartilage. Naproxyn can be used in the young athletes whose parents are concerned about Reye's syndrome. Exercise is the therapeutic modality of choice. Quadriceps setting exercises that progress to short arc exercises and avoid use of extension machines, Cybex, or Biodex are the cornerstone of management. Ballistic activity such as running and high-impact aerobics must be avoided until the pain is diminished. Instead, development of muscular strength and cardiovascular endurance should be encouraged by bicycling, swimming, and weight training (beginning with quad setting, progressing toward short arc exercises with weights, isometrics, and then, finally, to isokinetic and functional, or closed-kinetic-chain, exercises). When patellar tendinitis is a component of injury, then iontophoresis to the anterior fat pad and origin of the patellar tendon three times a week for up to 2 weeks may decrease inflammation and pain and allow exercises to progress. With medial capsular pain, a lateral felt wedge taped to the knee, the use of a Neoprene sleeve with a lateral wedge, or the use of TENS

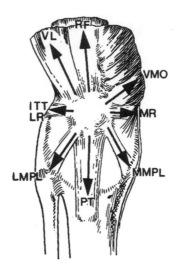

Figure 21.8   Soft tissue stabilization of the patellofemoral mechanism is accomplished by combined musculotendinous insertions and ligament capsular retinacular tethers: VL-vastus lateralis; RF-rectus femoris; VMO-vastus medialis obliquus; MR-medial retinaculum; MMPL-medial meniscal patellar ligament; PT-patellar tendon; LMPL-lateral meniscal patellar ligament; LR-lateral retinaculum; ITT-iliotibial tract.

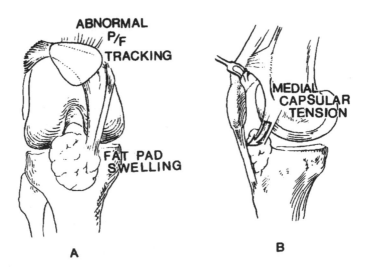

Figure 21.9   Triad injury combining patellofemoral friction and subsequent cartilage debris with fat pad hypertrophy (and related patellar tendinitis) along with medial capsular traction, or plica syndrome (largely due to VMO atrophy).

to decrease medial pain, which allows muscle strengthening to proceed, can be useful. I like using a muscle stimulator to hypertrophy the vastus medialis; in addition to muscle stimulation, it has a crossover TENS effect of pain relief, though this is not universally accepted and warrants further investigation (20). The use of an orthotic to decrease tension on the medial side of the knee, specifically with tenderness of the plica, is extremely useful.

Conservative measures usually work. If not, and especially if swelling persists within the knee, arthroscopy may be indicated. Even a limited lateral release may be indicated if X-ray evidence of maltracking and evidence of maltracking due to lateral retinacular fibrosis is documented arthroscopically. It must be stressed to the athlete than an injured extremity is never normal and that it is exercise, not surgery, that is the ultimate therapeutic technique. Surgery is often necessary to alter the cycle of injury that occurs, such as irrigating and debriding chondral fragments that cause effusion and potentiate muscle atrophy. Arthroscopic debridement allows the athlete to get back to a rehabilitative exercise regime but is not a cure-all in itself. A lateral release is rarely indicated unless at the time of arthroscopy there is maltracking past 30° of flexion that cannot be compensated for by a slight manual pressure on the lateral side of the joint. If necessary, the minimal amount of lateral retinacular release, starting proximally and working distally, should be done and stopped when tracking is corrected. The danger of a lateral release when digital pressure can correct patellar tracking is that relief of pain may in fact be due to denervation of the lateral structures (41) and not to correcting mechanics of the extensor mechanism (17, 36). In itself, relief of pain is fine; however, if such relief allows postoperative recovery of the vastus medialis, overpull of the patella medially can and does occur (see Figure 21.10, pp. 280-282). Further research into the cause of pain and appropriate therapeutic modalities is indicated.

Treatment of retropatellar pain when there is no effusion and no crepitation beyond 30° of flexion requires an even more conservative approach. In the young athlete, knee pain may occur during growth spurts when musculotendinous functional length may not keep pace with bone growth (29). At an older age, elimination of the use of wrist weights, which is totally unphysiologically valid, can in itself relieve knee pain encountered in fitness walking. Weighting the upper extremities in preference to the lower extremities can unbalance the crossed-extensor reciprocal innervation mechanisms that are used in energy amplication and linkage systems, thus leading to pain (6). This is more commonly found than chondral damage and also responds well to a conservative program; if not successful in 12 weeks, the use of orthotics, Neoprene bracing, muscle stimulation of the VMO, and antiinflammatories should continue for even a longer period of time rather than proceeding to arthroscopy, especially in a recreationally athletic female. Exposure of subchondral neuroendplates leading to peripatellar pain has been hypothesized (41), which brings up the possibility of capsular injection of neurologic sclerosing agents such as guanethidine to diminish pain and allow muscle strengthening to proceed. I have seen this used successfully in a few cases of reflex sympathetic dystrophy in adult females.

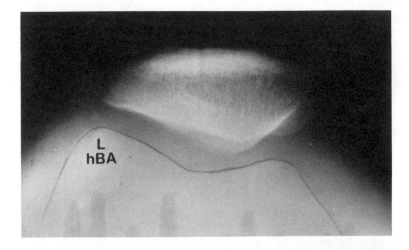

(continued)

Figure 21.10 Patients occasionally complain of and are able to clinically demonstrate medial patellar displacement with flexion and quad contraction following lateral release. This patient has had a lateral release on the left symptomatic side, but not the right. Patellar rotation increases (A) compared to the normal knee (B). Lateral tilt and subluxations increase with a 15-lb medial force (C vs. D). With 15-lb lateral force, the clinical medial subluxation is reproduced on the left, mimicking lack of retinacular stabilization combined with VMO overpull (E vs. F). *Note.* Photos courtesy Dr. Robert Teitge, Detroit MI. (36).

Because chondral breakdown is not usually retropatellar pain in the athletic female, what had previously been labeled *chondromalacia* has been relabeled *patellofemoral stress syndrome.* This implies increased patellofemoral friction leading to subchondral irritation and increased intraosseous pressure, and further implies that core decompression or osteotomy of the patella may successfully

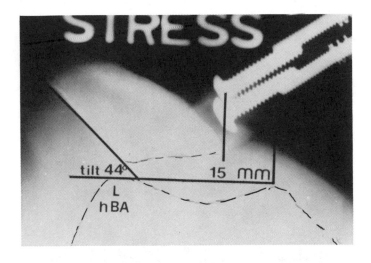

C

D

(continued)

Figure 21.10   *(continued)*

alleviate pain. Again, eccentric and concentric muscle balance, flexibility, and proper training techniques are the mainstays of rehabilitation; surgical maneuvers are, for all practical purposes, *salvage techniques* that are done to disrupt the pathologic breakdown cycles associated with pain.

Parapatellar pain may be associated with lateral tilt of the patella on the 45° Merchant X-ray view. This is generally found in the recreational athlete who is beginning a higher level of athletic activity. This is most commonly associated with weakness of the vastus medialis and responds to home exercises or physical therapy; a lateral release is not necessarily needed. If VMO atrophy persists, lateral tilt may allow increased lateral patellofemoral compression, and the medial

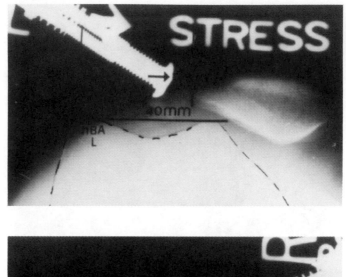

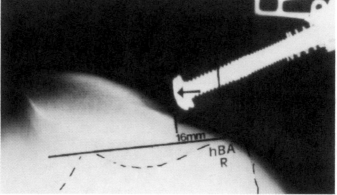

Figure 21.10   *(continued)*

cartilage may calcify to fill in "dead space" in an effort to distribute stress more evenly (see Figure 21.11, pp. 283-284). A limited lateral release at this point may possibly denervate the capsule and eliminate pain, thus allowing exercise to be more effective in redistributing force and reestablishing vastus medialis pull, but once the cartilage calcifies and large osteophytes have developed, the kneecap is locked in place and weight loss, antiinflammatory medication, and strengthening are less effective. This is a disaster when the recreational athlete is too young to be considered a candidate for total knee arthroplasty, though lateral osteophyte resection and VMO strengthening, perhaps even with a myostimulator, may be of some use.

Lateral knee pain is the second most common problem seen in the athletic female and is commonly associated with synovial interposition, fat pad interposition, or iliotibial band friction against the lateral condyle. All of these are seen

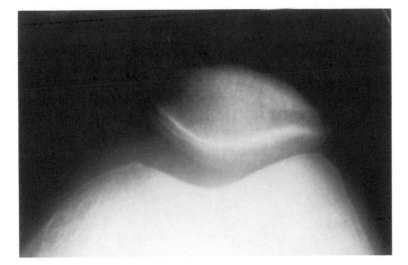

A

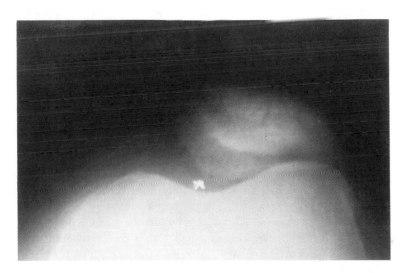

B

(continued)

Figure 21.11   Lateral tilt of patella is generally due to vastus medialis atrophy and is commonly seen in the recreationally athletic female. Treatment of initial patellar tilt (A) consists of VMO strengthening, weight loss, and antiinflammatory medications, as in this 14-year-old athlete. (B) With progressive medial enchondral ossification calcification to distribute stress, limited lateral release, weight loss, and resection of the lateral patellar osteophyte may have some success as in this 25-year-old recreational athlete. (C) If she decides to begin athletic activity after significant cartilage remodeling has occurred, lateral osteophyte resection, weight loss and antiinflammatories would be the appropriate salvage technique, rather than total knee arthroplasty, in this 38-year-old female.

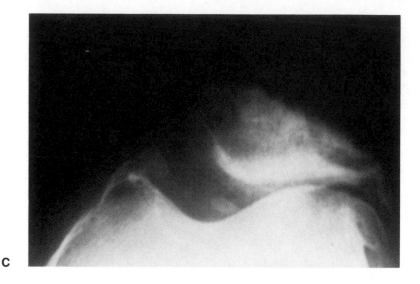

C

Figure 21.11   *(continued)*

frequently in the female cross-country runner, the recreational jogger, and the aerobic enthusiast. Lateral meniscal sprain is considered in differential diagnosis.

With lateral entrapment of tissue, a Neoprene brace with a lateral wedge can make symptoms worse. Antiinflammatory medication (Naproxyn or aspirin), icing, iliotibial band stretching, and increasing flexibility and strengthening of hamstrings and quadriceps are most often effective treatments. If not, an arthroscopic synovectomy and minimal debridement of fat pad can be done, taking care to avoid creation of an iatrogenic peripheral lateral meniscal tear. Feathering of the iliotibial insertion into Gerdy's tubercle may be necessary to eliminate pain in this area. Early motion and flexibility are mandatory to help prevent recurrence of scar tissue following operative intervention.

The most common cause of lateral knee pain is the training error of running on an uneven surface. It may be associated with a recent shoe change but is more commonly associated with running on the same angle, that is, compressing the same side of the knee while running into a curve (Figure 21.12). This is common in recreational athletes and is easily corrected by reversing the course on the return trip. Essentially, the jogger retraces her steps and avoids either running with traffic or against traffic for the entire training session (6).

Medial knee pain, whether called *chronic medial collateral ligament sprain* or *medial plica syndrome*, is a real challenge. The cause is vastus medialist atrophy, primarily in the unconditioned athlete and secondarily following injury, occasionally even in a conditioned athlete. Use of crutches until pain is gone will ease tenderness along the medial collateral ligament, although water exercises and nonballistic exercises, such as bicycle riding and quad setting, can usually be tolerated. Again the use of a myostim in therapy 4 times a day for 15 minutes

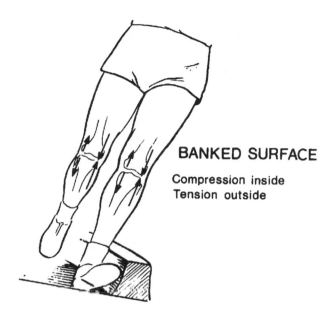

BANKED SURFACE

Compression inside
Tension outside

Figure 21.12   Running on an angle, as on the apron of a roads, can cause compression on one side of the knee and distraction on the opposite side, leading to peripatellar pain. Reversing direction halfway through the run and retracing her steps, usually eliminates the athlete's pain.

can help hypertrophy the VMO and decrease stress along the medial structures. The use of an orthotic within the shoe on a temporary basis to derotate the knee is often effective in management.

The same treatment modalities are useful in management of a tender medial plica. The worse thing that can be done here is to resect a medial plica arthroscopically in an externally rotated valgus knee with vastus medialis atrophy. The medial pain can be exacerbated by surgery, accelerating further vastus medialis atrophy and leading to a prolonged recovery phase. Iontophoresis over the tender medial plica or even the use of a TENS unit in therapy is indicated at first to help strengthen the vastus medialis. If pain persists after rehabilitation of the vastus medialis and use of a medial shoe orthotic to unload the medial joint, arthroscopic plica resection will be much more successful. Nevertheless, if there is no medial condylar articular edge notch or fraying associated with the plica making contact in flexion, then there is no need to resect the plica.

Lateral patella dislocation occurs in the athletic female as it does in the athletic male. Osteochondral fractures of the patella and femur associated with patellar subluxation, at least in my practice, have been more common in females than males (Figure 21.13). Rupture of the medial retinacular fibers may lead to elongation or what has been called a high attachment in the recovery phase leading to some extensor mechanism dysfunction that is accentuated in the female by the

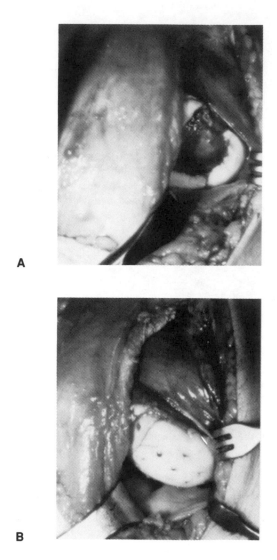

Figure 21.13   Lateral patellar dislocation occurred and karate instructor pushed the patella back with a palm-strike, leading to chondral avulsion of lateral femoral condyle (A). This was repaired (B).

increased Q-angle. If repair is indicated, then advancement of the vastus medialis in the female may be more necessary (Figure 21.14). Further research concerning patellar rotation is needed.

Posterior knee pain, specifically associated with recurvatum, is extremely difficult to manage. When found with tight hamstrings, often the case in gymnasts, there is often a history of back injury. Hamstring tightness, acting as a protective

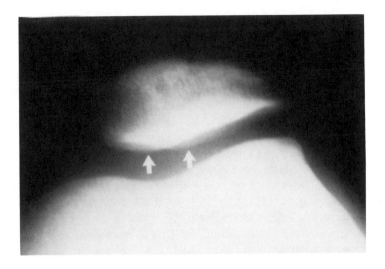

Figure 21.14 When the medial ridge does not line up well within the trochlea on the 45° Merchant film, lateral subluxation with vastus medialis stretch associated with vastus medialis tearing may be suspected and may imply advancement of vastus medialis and perhaps minimal lateral release to balance the extensor mechanism. Further research is needed on patellar rotation.

mechanism to splint the back, leads to secondary pull distally. Stretching of the hamstrings with quadriceps strengthening is usually effective in management. A popliteal cyst must be ruled out; if one is found, the cause of the inflammation within the joint that led to secondary cyst formation must be sought and treated.

In the past, it was falsely assumed that the athletic female was more prone to injury because of the valgus orientation to her knee and its increased flexibility. This is not the case. In contact and ballistic sports, like volleyball, the incidence of ligament disruption, particularly of the anterior cruciate, is essentially the same as that of male participants in the sport (14). There is some evidence, though, that knee and ankle sprain may be more common in female athletes (7, 21, 24). Hinged knee braces to prevent hyperextension are not well tolerated, particularly in gymnastics, and use of a Neoprene sleeve or figure-8 taping or elastic bandaging can help increase proprioception and diminish pain when eccentric and concentric muscles have been rehabilitated to work together to balance the knee.

Ligament injuries of the knee in the athletic female are treated the same way they are in the male, except for injuries to the medial collateral and the anterior cruciate ligaments. The rehabilitation protocol for medial collateral injury may need to be modified by use of a medial orthotic in the shoe and prolonged antiinflammatory medication and vastus medialis strengthening, if tenderness persists along the medial collateral and posterior oblique ligaments beyond the normal healing time.

The concept of a cruciate dependent knee is important in treating the athletic female. Secondary restraints, particularly the posterior capsule, can compensate in a knee with a positive Lachman but negative pivot shift. When there are not sufficient secondary restraints, then the knee is called cruciate dependent, and the patient is more likely a candidate for anterior cruciate ligament reconstruction. Because of the increased incidence of recurvatum in females, their knees may be more cruciate dependent, therefore, the higher incidence of anterior cruciate surgery for injured athletic females in sports, like volleyball and basketball, where "isolated" anterior cruciate ligament injuries occur (21). Aggressive postoperative therapy is mandatory because synovial inflammation, stiffness, and patellofemoral fibrosis are more common in injured recreationally athletic females than in their male counterparts (19). Also, in spite of achieving isometry at the time of surgery, there is a higher tendency in the athlete with recurvatum for the graft to stretch postoperatively within the first 2 years. Postsurgical loss of hyperextension unbalances lower extremities. Even blocking hypertension in a derotation brace can lead to ankle pain in the same extremity or back pain on the contralateral side.

Unusual injuries also occur about the knee. If there is no joint line tenderness or posterior or retropatellar pain, but point tenderness is experienced within the middle segment above or below the knee, a stress fracture may be suspected. I have had as a patient one female runner who presented with swelling of both knees and shoulders, associated with dyspareunia in her premenstrual period. She was diagnosed as having endometriosis internae or adenomyosis. All symptoms were relieved by a uterine conization, and, although her obstetrician has suggested hysterectomy, she prefers to be considered for arthroscopic synovectomy of her joints so that she can resume running sooner.

Distal Segment Injuries

It has been assumed that increased flexibility and ligamentous laxity in women leads to an increased incidence of ankle sprains (19). Nevertheless, the same training techniques that the male utilizes in preparing for sports played on uneven ground, or for pivoting or landing on one foot, should be incorporated by and their importance emphasized for the female. Four-quadrant ankle strengthening exercises with the use of Theraband or elastic tubing, calf strengthening, and achilles stretching are all mandatory in prevention of ankle injury. The use of lace-front ankle bracing or elastic wrapping should be emphasized. There are foot problems that are perhaps more prevalent in females than males, most likely due to the predominance of female participation in the sports that produce such injury or the splay foot associated with heel pronation.

Coming down short from a dismount in gymnastics or from a jump in volleyball or basketball can dorsiflex the ankle and jam the anterior tibia against the talus. Soft tissue may be impinged in the process, and inflammation can lead to synovial hypertrophy in the anterior/lateral joint (the so-called ankle plica syndrome, or soft tissue impingement; 15) or development of an anterior tibial spur (25). Spur formation along the anterior tibial articular edge can erode further into the talus, releasing chondral debris and increasing inflammation in a cyclic manner (Figure 21.15). Antiinflammatory medication, four-quadrant stretching (with strengthening of the invertors, evertors, planatar flexors, and dorsiflexors), and perhaps iontophoresis along the anterior edge of the tibia can provide symptomatic relief. The use of a soft wrap about the anterior ankle can help minimize aggravation of the injury. Point tenderness in the lateral anterior synovial margin, if it does not respond to conservative therapy, may respond in a last resort to arthroscopic resection.

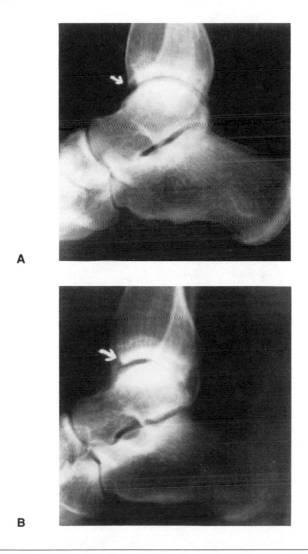

A

B

(continued)

Figure 21.15 Ankle anterior hypertrophic spur: (A) preoperative (B) postoperative (C) conservative management and wrapping in the rehabilitative phase.

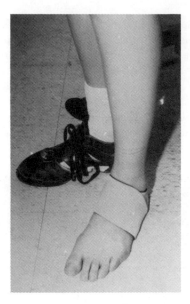

C

Figure 21.15   *(continued)*

Impact loading on the Achilles tendon in activities like basketball and volleyball can lead to symptoms of posterior heel pain when a calcaneal prominence exists. This is commonly confused with retrocalcaneal bursitis and can respond to Achilles stretching, calf strengthening, and the use if Indomethacin—75 mg sustained release every morning for 4 to 6 weeks. If symptoms persist in spite of a prolonged course of attempted conservative management, then resection of the calcaneal ''hatchet'' or prominence can be done (10, 23). Use of a cast is required for 2 to 4 weeks, but a quick return to athletic activity can be anticipated (Figure 21.16).

Posterior ankle pain is common in toe-pointing activity, such as ballet and gymnastics. Synovial interposition, a symptomatic os trigonum, or impingement of the bony posterior talar prominence can lead to pain or may even be associated with formation of loose bodies (Figures 21.16 and 21.17). Loose bodies must be surgically removed, and, if conservative measures of wrapping, antiinflammatories, and strengthening and stretching are not effective, then resection of bone or soft tissue posteriorly may be necessary, even when loose bodies are not present. Posterior/medial ankle pain can be associated with tendinitis of the posterior tibial, flexor hallucis, or flexor digitorum tendons and is commonly seen in ballet and volleyball. When the flexor hallucis does not respond to stretching and antiinflammatories, surgical decompression of the tendon sheath may be necessary (32). If there is tenderness along the course of the posterior tibialis, and pain and swelling do not diminish with the use of a rigid medial orthotic, then use of a cast is mandatory to prevent rupture of the posterior tibial tendon. If this

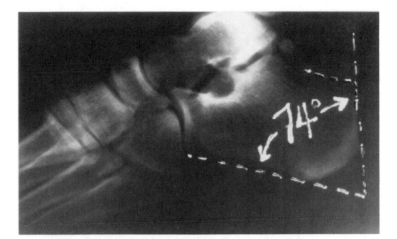

A

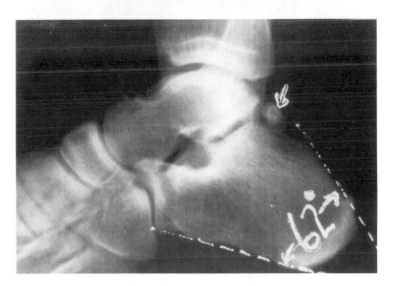

B

Figure 21.16   Calcaneal prominence leading to retrocalcaneal symptoms in college volleyball player: (A) preoperative status; and (B) postoperative result. Unable to complete preoperatively, she returned 4 weeks postoperatively to full varsity training regimen. (*Note.* Posterior talar process was painful when the patient was younger, toe-pointing in ballet, but no longer symptomatic during dorsiflexion impact in volleyball.)

tendon does rupture, surgical reconstruction may be necessary; however, this most likely will result in the inability of the athlete to return to competitive activity.

Peroneal tendinitis in the lateral ankle may in fact be a compressive phenomenon, because medial orthotics in the shoe frequently relieve symptoms when

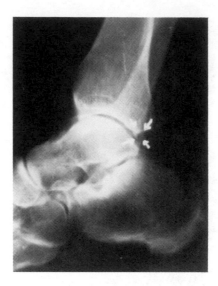

Figure 21.17   Loose body in posterior ankle joint of a 32-year-old ballet instructor.

used in conjunction with weight loss and antiinflammatory medications like Naproxyn, Ibuprofen, or aspirin. Peroneal subluxation after ankle sprain can be treated the same way, though failure of conservative management may necessitate fibular slide or lateral ligamentous reconstruction (2).

Heel pain is a real problem in the athletic female especially if she has recently taken up fast walking or jogging for fitness and is relatively out of condition. The four causes are plantar fasciitis, stress fracture of the calcaneous, saponification of the fat pad, and Sever's disease. Plantar fasciitis is treated just as it is in the male—with Indomethacin, heel pads, stretching, and perhaps cortisone injection; surgery is almost never indicated. Compression of the calcaneous medially and laterally that causes significant discomfort indicates the presence of a stress fracture that may not show up on an X ray immediately. Strengthening, stretching, nonballistic activity, and generalized conditioning are indicated while the stress fracture heals. If there is no pain in the calcaneous with compression medially to laterally, but there is tenderness underneath in the heel pad, saponification of the fatty tissue may have occurred, which is a bruising process of the adipose tissue in the heel, an overuse phenomenon that generally takes longer to heal than a stress fracture and must be treated symptomatically with antiinflammatory medications and the use of crutches or a cane in the opposite hand for ambulation purposes until the patient is asymptomatic.

Sever's disease, or posterior calcaneal apophysitis, presents at average age 8 in males and 7 in females (Figure 21.18). It seems to be more symptomatic in the athletic female, particularly in figure skaters, whose expensive, custom skates often have tight heel counters installed in the boot. Skaters seem to respond to

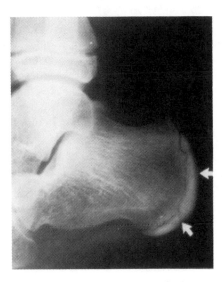

Figure 21.18 Sever's disease, or traumatic apophysitis of the heel, occurs at a slightly younger age in the female than the male and is more symptomatic in sports such as figure skating where a tight heel counter is a factor.

icing, stretching of the heel counter in their boot, if possible, and reassurance of both the young athlete and her parents that this is a temporary phase that she will soon grow out of.

The splay foot associated with femoral anteversion, internal rotation of the lower extremity, and increased pronation at the heel increases the prevalence of symptomatic bunions, Morton's neuroma formation, and sesamoiditis in the athletic female and is directly correlated to shoe wear. Because athletic shoes have become scientifically better designed (i.e., essentially, less narrow), these problems are becoming less evident. Nevertheless, high-heeled shoes worn by females in our society are the direct cause of these compressive phenomena and of the higher incidence of treatment in females (27). It is important in treating a bunion in a young athletic female that plantar flexion of the first metatarsal be compensated for when slight shortening procedures, like Mitchell bunionectomies, are done, otherwise stress fractures of the second and third metatarsals or metatarsalgia may occur postoperatively (20). Compressive neuroma formation or symptomatic sesamoiditis that does not respond to antiinflammatory medication or cortisone injection may require surgical excision.

Stress fractures most often occur in the distal segment of the leg, and, in the past, were more common in female military recruits and high school athletic females than they are today (31). In the 1970s, girl cross-country runners were asked to run indoors to "protect them" from inclement weather. But the cement floors of the school hallways were unforgiving and led to a higher incidence of injury, that is, lower extremity stress fractures, than would have occurred had they been running outdoors. Just as in the male, bone density in the female develops with demand. In the early phases however, absorption may outpace bone deposition during bone remodeling or leave trabecular architecture less capable of managing impact energies causing microfractures to propagate. Plain X rays do not pick up stress fractures well at first; but after a few weeks, the fractures may be more evident during the absorptive phase; a few weeks later, sclerosis may be seen in the healing phase. Point tenderness over a bone, which is made worse with activity and lessens with inactivity, should be treated as a stress fracture until proven otherwise. Decreased ballistic activity is imperative, but this does not mean inactivity. Water-training exercises, low-impact aerobics, step training, bicycling, and strength training along with flexibility improvement and diet counseling can be done while the fracture is healing. Again, ballistic activity must be avoided to prevent propagation of a fracture. Just as in the male, tibial stress fractures, particularly distal fractures, are the predominant overuse phenomenon in athletic females, though there appears to be a wider variety of lower extremity stress fractures in the athletic female, primarily due to the activities in which they participate. For example, both gymnastics and ballet participants have a high incidence of femoral neck fracture; but only the ballet dancers have a high incidence of proximal tibia and fibular stress fractures (Figure 21.19). It is important to realize that stress fractures can displace; the intracapsular femoral neck fractures seen in gymnastics and the proximal tibial fractures seen in runners must be protected (Figure 21.20; 3, 4, 5, 6).

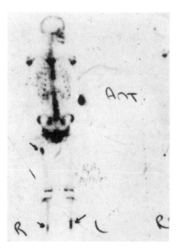

Figure 21.19   Stress fractures in one area tend to mask pain in other areas in that more than one stress fracture commonly occurs in the athletic female. The tibial fracture was clinically evident; however, the femoral fracture was not detected until specifically examined for.

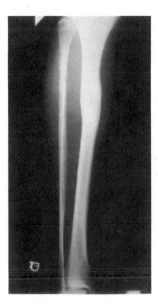

Figure 21.20 When a 14-year-old track athlete with stress fracture pain decided to compete against medical advice, the proximal tibial stress fracture propagated, and displaced tibial and fibular fractures occurred as she jumped off her starting blocks. When she returned to running, stress reaction and microfractures continued to occur in the fibula without displacement.

Overview of Lower Extremity Injuries in the Athletic Female

The benefits of exercise are not gender-specific. Preconceived ideas that female athletes are more prone to sport-related injury due to hypermobility of joints, malalignment of lower extremities, and so on are not true. The fact that females get involved in sport and fitness activity later in life, or to a lesser extent than do males is a social phenomenon, not a physiologic one. This results in skewed statistics. Especially on a recreational level, it is important to realize that premature participation in athletics (i.e., without getting in shape first) is undesirable and injury provoking.

In the last 20 years, as more females have entered the arena of athletic performance, their initially increased lower extremity stress reactions have diminished as they have gotten better conditioning, better training, and better coaching (9). Equal access to conditioning, training, and coaching that encourage fitness and enjoyment of athletic endeavors while decreasing risk of injury was the real purpose of Title IX, not the contest of female against male.

Obviously females are phenotypically different than males in many regards, and the athletic injuries that occur in lower extremities due to these phenotypic variations are directly related to the type of athletic activities that women participate in. Injuries are generally sport-specific, not sex-specific. As conditioning methods improve, stress-related injuries decrease in both sexes.

Summary

1. Females are not injury prone. Sociological factors combined with male/female physiologic differences can explain variants of injury patterns.
2. Females and males may participate in the same sport but execute its movements differently due to phenotypical differences.
3. Lower extremity injuries, like most injuries, appear to be sport-specific, not sex-specific.
4. Benefits of exercise are not gender-specific. Proper training can decrease incidence of injury to the benefit of both sexes.

References

1. Albohm, M.E. How injuries occur in girls' sports. Phys. Sports Med. 4(2):46-49; 1976.
2. Arrowsmith, S.R.; Fleming, L.L.; Allman, F.L. Traumatic dislocations of the peroneal tendons. Am. J. Sports Med. 11:142-146; 1983.
3. Bargren, J.H., Tilson, D.H.; Bridgeford, O.E. Prevention of displaced fatigue fractures of the femur. J. Bone Joint Surg. 53A:1115-1117; 1971.
4. Blickenstaff, L.D.; Morris, J.M. Fatigue fracture of the femoral neck. J. Bone Joint Surg. 48A:1031-1047; 1966.
5. Burrows, H.J. Fatigue in infraction of the middle of the tibia in ballet dancers. J. Bone Joint Surg. 38B:83-94; 1956.
6. Ciullo, J.; Jackson, D. Track and field. In: Schneider, R.C.; Kennedy, J.C., eds. Sport injuries: mechanisms, treatment, and prevention. Baltimore: Williams & Wilkins; 1985:212-246.
7. Clarke, K.; Buckley, W. Women's injuries in collegiate sports. Am. J. Sports Med. 8:187-191; 1980.
8. Corbitt, R.W.; Cooper, D.L.; Erickson, D.J.; Kriss, F.C.; Thornton, M.L.; Craig, T.T. Female athletics. JAMA 228:1266-1267; 1974.
9. Cox, J.S.; Heinz, W.L. Women midshipmen in sports. Am. J. Sports Med. 12:241-243; 1984.
10. Dickinson, P.H.; Coutts, M.B.; Woodward, E.P.; Handler, D. Tendo achillis bursitis: a report of 21 cases, J. Bone Joint Surg. 48A:77-81; 1966.
11. Feicht, C.B.; Johnson, T.S.; Martin, B.J.; Sparks, K.E.; Wagner, W.W. Secondary amenorrhea in athletes. Lancet 2:1145; 1978.
12. Frisch, R.E.; Gotz-Welbergen, A.V.; McArthur, J.W.; Albright, T.; Witschi, J.; Bullen, B.; Birnholz, J.; Reed, R.B.; Hermann, H. Delayed menarche and amenorrhea of college athletes in relation to age of onset of training. JAMA 246:1559-1563; 1981 Oct. 2.
13. Frisch, R.E.; McArthur, J.W. Menstrual cycles: fatness as a determinant of minimum weight for height necessary for their maintenance or onset. Science 185:949-951; 1974.

14. Garrick, J.G.; Requa, R.K. Girls' sport injuries in high school athletics. JAMA 239:2245-2248; 1978 May 26.
15. Guhl, J.F. Soft tissue pathology. In: Guhl, J.F., ed. Ankle arthroscopy. Thorofare, NJ: Slack, Inc.; 1988.
16. Haycock, C.E.; Gillette, J.V. Susceptibility of women athletes to injury: myths vs. reality. JAMA 236:163-165; 1976.
17. Huberti, H.H.; Hayss, W.C. Contact pressures in chondromalacia patella and the effects of capsular reconstruction procedures. J. Orthop. Res. 6:499-508; 1988.
18. Hunter, L.Y.; Andrews, J.R.; Clancy, W.G.; Funk, F.J. Common orthopaedic problems of female athletes and instructional course lectures. AAOS 31:126-151; 1982.
19. Hunter, L.Y. Women's athletics: the orthopaedic surgeon's viewpoint. Clin. Sports Med. 3:809-827; 1984.
20. Hunter, L. Aspects of injuries to the lower extremity unique to the female athlete. In: Nicholas, J.A.; Hershman, E.B. eds. The lower extremity and spine in sports medicine. St. Louis: Mosby; 1986:90-111.
21. Ireland, M.L.; Wall, C. Epidemiology and comparison of knee injuries in elite male and female United States basketball athletes. Med. Sci. Sports Exerc. 22:S82; 1990.
22. James, S.L. Chondromalacia of the patella in the adolescent. In: Kennedy, J.C., ed. The injured adolescent knee. Baltimore: Williams & Wilkins; 1979: ch. 8.
23. Keck, S.W.; Kelly, P.J. Bursitis of the posterior part of the heel. J. Bone Joint Surg. 47A:267-273; 1975.
24. Klafs, C.E.; Lyon, M.J. The female athlete. St. Louis: Mosby Co., 1978.
25. Kleiger, D. Anterior tibiotalar impingement syndrome in dancers. Foot Ankle 3:69-75; 1982.
26. Macintyre, J.G.; Taunton, J.E.; Clement, D.B.; et al: Running injuries: a clinical study of 4,173 cases. Clin. J. Sports Med. 1:81-87; 1991.
27. Mann, R.A.; Coughlin, M.J. Hallux valgus and complications of hallux valgus. In: Mann, R.A., ed. Surgery of the foot. St. Louis: C.V. Mosby Co.; 1986.
28. McCarroll, J.R.; O'Donoghue, D.H.; Grana, W.A. The surgical treatment of chondromalacia of the patella. Clin. Ortho. Rel. Res. 175:130-134; 1983.
29. Micheli, L.J. Overuse injuries in children's sports: the growth factor. Orthop. Clin. N. Am. 14:337-360; 1983.
30. Morden, M.L. Musculoskeletal ailments of young female athletes. Ortho. News 5(6):1; 1983 Nov.-Dec.
31. Protzman, R.R.; Griffis, C.G. Stress fractures in men and women undergoing military training. J. Bone Joint Surg. 59A:825; 1977.
32. Quirk, R. Ballet injuries: the Australian experience. Clin. Sports Med. 2:507-514; 1983.
33. Rigotti, N.A.; Neer, R.M.; Skates, F.; Herzog, D.B.; Nussbaum, S.R. The clinical course of osteoporosis in anorexia nervosa. JAMA 265:1133-1138; 1991.
34. Sady, S.P.; Freedson, P.S. Body composition and structural compositions of female and male athletes. Clin. Sports Med. 3:755-777; 1984.
35. Shangold, M.; Rebar, R.W.; Wentz, A.C.; Schiff, I. Evaluation and management of menstrual dysfunction in athletes. JAMA 263:1665-1669; 1990.
36. Teitge, R. Iatrogenic medial dislocation of the patella. Paper read at the 58th annual meeting of the American Academy of Orthopaedic Surgeons. Anaheim, CA; 1991 March 9, 1991.
37. Williams, K.R.; Kavanagh, P.R.; Ziff, J.L. Mechanical studies of elite female distance runners. Int. J. Sports Med. 8:107-118; 1987.

38. Wilmore, J. Exploding the myth of female inferiority. Phys. Sports Med. 2(5):54-58; 1974.
39. Wolman, R.L.; Harries, M.J.; Fyfe, I. Slipped upper femoral epiphysis in an amenorrheic athlete. BMJ 229:720-721; 1989 Sept. 16.
40. Wood, L.; Ferrell, W.R.; Baxendale, R.H. Pressures in normal and acutely distended knee joints and effects on quadriceps maximal voluntary contractions. Q. J. Exp. Physiol. 73:305-314; 1988.
41. Woytjs, E.M.; Beaman, D.N.; Glover, R.A.; Janda, D. Innervation of the human knee joint by substance-P fibers. Arthroscopy 6:254-263; 1990.

Provocative Issues and Recommendations for Future Research

In addition to presenting the papers that compose the body of this publication, the participants at the AOSSM workshop discussed the topics highlighted by the speakers. A number of provocative issues were raised concerning the athletic female, which led to further discussion. Many of the facts and opinions expressed during these discussions appear in this section.

The need for further research on such issues and in other areas where knowledge about the athletic female is lacking was also discussed, and suggestions for that research follow.

Provocative Issues

During the workshop, participants discussed several provocative issues pertaining to the athletic female. These are the issues and highlights of the ensuing discussions.

Issue #1: Oligomenorrhea before achieving peak bone density influences the ultimate degree of peak bone density.

Current data suggest that females ages 16 to 21 with oligomenorrhea have less bone density than those with regular menstruation. There is insufficient data, however, to support the theory that oligomenorrhea decreases peak bone mineral density in women who have achieved peak bone mass. Normal data for bone mineral density in young people are needed.

A few specific questions were considered:

A participant questioned, ''If a young (age 16 to 21) woman is oligomenorrheic, should she be advised to become an elite athlete?'' Another suggested that the athlete be worked up (endocrinologic work-up) and that the decision should be based on the young woman's bone density.

Another wondered, ''Are there side effects from low-dose use of birth control pills?'' Someone responded that there are side effects, some negative and some positive.

One person asserted that it is a fact that irregular menstrual periods are associated with lower bone density in females between the ages of 19 and 25. Another participant noted that weak data suggest that young women who wish to become physically active are at risk if they

- are oligomenorrheic,
- were late in the onset of menstruation (i.e., menarche),
- never established a regular menstrual pattern,
- have low bone density,
- are likely to make training errors (or if those training them are likely to make training errors), and
- menstruate without ovulation.

A "normal" menstrual cycle is not well defined. There is no evidence to suggest that young females (16-21 years) who have missed a substantial (more than one third of expected) number of menses have less bone density than regularly menstruating classmates.

There was unanimous agreement that amenorrheic and oligomenorrheic states are associated with low bone density in young women. Oligomenorrheic athletic females have less bone density than their oligomenorrheic, sedentary counterparts. Genetic factors, stress, diet, sport-specific factors, and conditioning techniques all can contribute to oligomenorrhea and amenorrhea, which in turn contribute to lower bone density. These factors themselves may be interrelated. One participant noted that an athlete does not need to worry about the other factors if she does not have low bone density. Another added that it is not the number of risk factors a female presents but the intensity of them or each of them.

Another area of discussion was whether bone density scans can be used as diagnostic tools. Some noted that they are not reliable under age 20. Two or three readings are needed over time, and they must be more than one or two standard deviations below the mean to indicate potential concern. One participant felt that a young woman with oligomenorrhea needs a full medical examination. A participant noted that, at her university, all female athletes are medically screened and those with oligomenorrhea are given hormonal therapy.

In considering what amount of lower bone density is replaceable and how long it takes to treat the condition, it was noted that those who are physically active and are oligomenorrheic are more at risk of stress fractures and osteoporosis. They need nutritional counseling, conditioning technique evaluation, and hormone therapy to help restore a more regular menstrual pattern with ovulation. If normalcy cannot be achieved through hormone therapy, the use of birth control pills should be considered. The athlete should also have a full medical and physical examination and seek to establish a regular menstrual cycle. However, the use of birth control pills does not always result in regular menstruation or ovulation. The athlete should also be informed about the potential long-term effects of the use of birth control pills and also about the long-term effects of decreased bone density. Drug intervention is also another treatment choice.

Estrogen seems to have a protective effect on bone mass, although some questioned whether it is appropriate to treat oligomenorrheic athletes with low-estrogen birth control pills even though we do not know whether low estrogen is a secondary factor in or a direct cause of low bone mass. Some wondered whether the level of estrogen in birth control pills is sufficient to ward off the development of low bone mass in later years.

Issue #2: To what extent does strength training for the athletic female enhance performance and decrease injury?

Sport-specific training, off-season training, cross-training, and strength training interact to enhance performance and decrease injury. However, the young athletic female should be discouraged from training exclusively in a single sport. For the young athletic female, a diversity of physical activity is desirable. Intense sport-specific training should not supplant such diversity of physical activity in this age group.

One participant observed that deficits in caloric, carbohydrate, and calcium intakes limit the capacity of the female to achieve maximum performance. Another suggested that these nutritional deficits result from the poor body image of athletic females.

Issue #3: Identification of muscle imbalance and rehabilitation of specific muscle groups are important for optimal body balance for the athletic female.

All but two participants agreed with the issue as stated. Minority opinions were voiced that "it implies more than we know and than we may ever know" and "more research and clinical evaluations need to be done on it"; the statement should be modified so that it is not an absolute.

Research in this area is weak at best. One participant noted that intuitively we say, "This is true. It makes sense, so we teach it." Another participant commented that muscle imbalance does not necessarily result in injury. If an athlete has muscle imbalance but does not stress it, she is not likely to be injured. The statement is an underlying principle of physical therapy.

Discussion also considered whether restoring muscle balance is necessary for optimal performance. One participant stated, "I disagree with the idea of needing to be in 'ideal' body balance. We are all made differently. Maybe all we can say is that there may be an association between muscle imbalance and incidence of injury." Others felt that the emphasis on rehabilitating the muscle groups should be replaced by restoring physiological length, strength, and endurance, noting it is not just balance but also the length of the muscles that is important. At present, we do not have good ways of measuring length.

A participant noted that every joint has an axis around which it moves. The muscles around it should be balanced in terms of length and strength. In motion, there is an order of function. If one muscle does not function, it tends to pass the functional need to the other muscles, and this may cause a problem. Some suggested that this is more related to previous injury and rehabilitation than optimal functioning.

Issue #4: In basketball there is a greater incidence in females than in males of knee injury involving the anterior cruciate ligament.

There was 100% consensus on this issue as stated. One workshop participant noted that this raises questions about whether this is a gender-specific or sport-specific pattern of injury. Research needs to be done to determine whether there may be a similar problem relative to other sports. Another participant suggested that we need to alter the athletic education of young females and stress training for lifelong participation in athletic activities.

In discussing this issue, data from the NCAA surveillance study (1989-1990) were presented (see Table 1).

The following abstract was distributed to the participants.

To determine the incidence and compare the nature of knee injuries in male and females, the 144 basketball athletes selected for participation in the United States Olympic trials completed a detailed questionnaire. In June 1988, 80 males and 64 females completed a detailed knee and history survey and physical exam. Knee injuries occurred in 11 of the 80 males (13%) and in 34 of the 64 females (53%) ($p < .0001$). Forty-five of the athletes (31%) had sustained a knee injury and 20 athletes (18%) underwent surgery. All surgical patients were examined and

Table 1   Incidence of Basketball Injuries in Men and Women

	Men		Women	
Total exposures	147613		135993	
Knee injury	88		130	
rate	.60		.96	
Structures involved				
ACL	7	.047	50	.368
Collateral	35	.24	39	.28
Patella	34	.23	30	.22
Meniscus	27	.18	53	.39

Note. Data from the NCAA Injury Surveillance System (1989-1990). Conclusions drawn from or recommendations based on the data provided by the National Collegiate Athletic Association are those of the author(s) based on analyses/evaluations of the author(s) and do not represent the views of the officers, staff, or membership of the NCAA.

records reviewed. The incidence, severity, and need for surgery was statistically higher in the female athletes. The number of males requiring surgery was 6 (7.5%) compared to 20 (31%) females who underwent 24 surgeries (p < .0007). The anterior cruciate ligament was involved in half of the athletes. Twenty cases were arthroscopies. There were 2 males and 8 females who underwent anterior cruciate ligament reconstructions. There was no statistically significant difference in side of injury, basketball position, time of game or practice, floor, or type of weight or conditioning program. Further prospective studies and investigation of risk factors in hopes of preventing knee injuries are needed. Compared to males, knee injuries are more common and more significant in the elite female basketball athlete.*

Issue #5: Nutritional deficits limit the athletic female's opportunities for maximal performance.

All of the workshop participants agreed, and there was little discussion.

Issue #6. Poor body imaging may lead to or cause poor nutritional habits in the athletic female.

There was consensus that poor nutritional habits are associated with a negative body image, which can be affected by society's portrayal of the "ideal" body. Inappropriate perceived body image can pertain to (a) one's own body or (b) image of what is appropriate. Pressures from society, including the media and press, tend to contribute to this problem.

One participant commented that it is more accurate to refer to "inappropriate" rather than "negative" body image. The athletic female may look at her body and think, "That is not good." So she eats to change her body to what she thinks is an appropriate image. Anorexics are not necessarily influenced by the media—they have a skewed body image. Also worth noting is that in the obese female, body imaging, by conceptualizing what she thinks her body looks like, may be appropriate.

Recommendations for Future Research

During this professional inquiry, the workshop participants enumerated and defined several recommendations for future research and study, goals, and new directions related to the athletic female. The following points are expressions of the participants' thoughts and not the products of a consensual validation process.

---

*From M.L. Ireland and C. Wall, "Epidemiology and Comparison of Knee Injuries in Elite Male and Female United States Basketball Athletes," *Medicine and Science in Sports and Exercise*, 22(2), p. 582, 1990, © The American College of Sports Medicine. Reprinted by permission.

1. Look at other sports and determine if anterior cruciate ligament (ACL) injuries are gender-related.
2. Conduct epidemiological investigation of ACL injuries in high school.
3. Determine the etiologic factors in the ACL injury in the athletic female.
4. Undertake a prospective study of bone density, looking at onset of menarche and injury relationship in pre-Olympic athletes.
5. Study postcollegiate women in an epidemiologic survey of their sport experience and injury rate and pattern.
6. Determine the long-term effect of menstrual disturbances secondary to sport involvement over a prolonged time.
7. Study gender-related participation in informal play and activity.
8. Determine the effect of intensive training in the prepubertal athletic female on growth, development, and attainment of menarche.
9. Conduct a study of the effects of exercise on the fitness level of the aging athletic female.
10. Study the sociopsycholgoical and cultural aspect of organized physical activity and the athletic female.
11. Look at the media and society's influence on the health, fitness, participation, and attitudes of the athletic female.
12. Educate strength and conditioning coaches and make them available to the athletic female.
13. Research nutrition and menses, as well as the effects of eating disorders, compulsive exercises, and dysfunctional family background on menses.
14. Make physical activity as well as competitive sport programs be part of the educational system. It was strongly recommended that this program be carried out in the secondary schools as well as in the lower grades.
15. Stress that strength training is an integral part of conditioning for the athletic female.
16. Determine whether strength training of the growing athletic female should be restricted.
17. Investigate the implications or effects of exercise and physical activity in the postpartum period.
18. Emphasize training techniques and nutrition education as a preventive measure.
19. Give the athletic care physician direction, understanding, and involvement in iron deficiency in the athletic female.
20. Conduct a study to determine a baseline bone density in the athletic female.
21. Conduct further research into the factors that decrease and improve performance.
22. Determine the effect of intensive training in the prepubertal athletic female on growth, development, and attainment of menarche.
23. Determine the role of exercise, diet, and menstrual irregularities in maximizing peak bone mass in the young female.
24. Examine exercise intensity, volume, and duration; caloric expenditures; and hormonal changes, including cortisol and endogenous opioids.

25. Collect normative data on menstrual cycles of the sedentary, active, and developing female using today's endocrine collection potential.
26. Using today's imaging techniques, create standardized tables for bone mass in the female—particularly the developing female under age 20.
27. Research succinic dehydrogenase (SDH): Why is SDH lower in elite female athletes versus elite male athletes? Is SDH lower in nonelite female athletes as well? Does decreased SDH affect lactate threshold? If decreased hemoglobin concentration affects VO_2max, does it also affect lactate threshold?
28. Develop guidelines for the evaluation of community fitness programs.
29. Encourage the development of research guidelines for study of the active female.

It is our sincere hope that readers will examine and reflect on this compilation and that these recommendations and research needs can be addressed for the benefit of the athletic female.

Index

A

Adolescent female athletes. *See* Female athletes

Aerobic and anaerobic conditioning, for specific sports, 205

Aerobic conditioning, 197

Aerobic dance, 2. *See also* Dance

Aerobic demands, analyzing, for specific sports, 204

Aerobic fitness, defined, 196

Aging females. *See also* Athletic females
  conditioning, 185-189
  defining, 185
  exercise for, 186-189
  imagery workouts for, 188
  psychological benefits of regular exercise, 188

Alcohol, 135

Amenorrhea. *See also* Menstrual irregularities
  defined, 42
  and contraception, 104-105. *See also* Oral contraceptives
  dietary habits linked to, 7
  nonreversible loss of bone mineral density linked with, 6, 47-50, 300
  not precluding pregnancy, 5
  prevalence of, 45
  relationship with luteal phase suppression, 44
  risk of osteoporosis associated with, 68
  and stress fractures. *See* Stress fractures
  studies of, 4-5, 45, 46
  treatment for, 6, 46, 54-55

Amphetamines, 131

Anabolic steroids, 109, 125-130

Anaerobic demands, for specific sports, 204

Anaerobic training, 175

Androgyny, 21-22

Ankle injuries, 255, 257, 288-295

Anorexia, 142-143, 144-146

Anovulation, 42-43

Anterior cruciate ligament injuries, 287-288
  increased incidence of among female athletes, 120-121, 302-303

Anterior-medial hip impingement syndrome, 212-216

Apophyseal problems, 274

Appetite suppressants, 131-132

Athletic activity
  for aging females, 185-189
  biological differences affecting, 33
  and body image, 33-36
  considerations for postpartum exercise, 96-99
  decline in participation by females, 4
  during pregnancy, 6, 81-100
  effect of menopause on, 8

effects of, on labor and delivery, 96

enhancing women's sense of competence and control, 27-28

guidelines for post-delivery exercise, 98-99

guidelines for pregnant women, 91-94.

image precluding participation by women, 3

importance of, 2

and older women, 7-8, 185-189

psychological changes resulting from, 27-28

relationship with delayed menarche, 44

and self-perception, 27-28

time as an obstacle to participation in, 2

Title IX prohibiting sex discrimination in, 2-3

women's participation in, 1-2

Athletic amenorrhea. *See* Amenorrhea

Athletic females. *See also* Female athletes
  adolescents, 14, 105, 117-121
  current perspectives of, 8
  definitions of, 1-2
  dietary analysis of, 166-167
  differing in physique from males, 268-272
  historical perspective of concerns, 5-7
  inadequate energy intake of, 166-168
  issues of concern to, 299-303
  lack of support and recognition of, 11
  muscle imbalances in, 209-217
  nutritional needs of, 165, 166
  older women and physical activity, 7-8, 185-189
  and oral contraceptives, 103-110
  preadolescents, 113-117
  problems faced by, 11-12, 13-14
  recommendations for future research, 303-305
  role of Melpomene Institute in awareness of, 4-5
  sports available to, 172, 174
  sport-specific training for, 203-206
  stages of development of, 174-175
  strength training for. *See* Strength training
  substance abuse by, 125-137

Athletic injuries
  ankle injuries, 255, 257, 288-295
  anterior cruciate ligament injuries more frequent among female athletes, 120-121, 287-288, 302-303
  associated with anabolic steroid use, 128-129
  athletic equipment causing, 262
  chondromalacia, 279-280
  chronic medial collateral ligament sprain, 284-285
  in dance, gymnastics, and skating, 251-263
  diet and menstrual status as determinants of risk of, 61-77
  distal segment injuries, 255, 257, 288-295
  documentation of rates of, 203-204

exercise preferred over surgery as therapy for, 279
gender differences in injury patterns, 268-272
gender differences in rates of, for cadets at West Point Military Academy, 224-229, 231-232
gender-specific injury patterns, 268
greater trochanteric bursitis, 275
hand and wrist injuries, 229, 248
hip problems, 272-275
iliotibial band friction syndrome, 272-274
incidence and pattern of, in female cadets at West Point Military Academy, 219-233.
    See also Female cadets
knee injuries, 121, 229, 255, 275-288
lower extremity injuries. *See* Lower extremity injuries
male and female injury patterns compared, 14
medial plica syndrome, 284-285
menstrual irregularities contributing to, 14
middle segment injuries, 121, 229, 275-288
nutritional disorders contributing to, 14
overuse injuries, 179, 252, 254
patellofemoral stress syndrome, 279-280
preventing, 7, 203-204, 263
prevention of, as a rationale for sport-specific training, 203-204
proximal segment injuries, 272-275
psychosocial factors in, 271-272
relationship with technique and ability, 261
risk of fractures increased by use of non-alcoholic carbonated beverages, 132
risk of slipped capital femoral epiphysis, 274-275
risks of, for adolescent female athletes, 120-121
risks of, for preadolescent athletes, 115-117
rules of competition promoting, 262
shin injuries, 255
snapping hip, 272-274
spine injuries, 259
sport-specific, not gender-specific, 179, 267
stress fractures. *See* Stress fractures
stress-related injuries, 229, 231
studies of determinants of risk of, 61-77
susceptibility of women to, 6-7
tight hamstrings causing, 286
upper extremity injuries. *See* Upper extremity injuries
women treated differently from men, 6
Athletic performance
adequate nutrition for, 165, 303
adversely affected by beta blockers, 136
effect of iron deficiency on, 119
enhanced by caffeine, 175
factors affecting, 301
gender bias in evaluating, 30
and menstrual cycle, 109-110
and oral contraceptive use, 109-110

B

Back injuries, in dancers, gymnasts, and skaters, 259
Back problems, during pregnancy, 84-85
Basketball, anterior cruciate ligament injuries more frequent among female players, 120-121, 287-288, 302-303
Bem Sex Role Inventory, 21-23
Beta blockers, 136
Biopsychosocial models, need for, 33
Body building, defined, 174
Body composition, 114, 117-118, 197-198
Body fat
    increased in females after growth spurt, 177
    relationship with delayed menarche, 275
    relationship with menstrual irregularities, 46, 271
Body image, 33-36
    compulsive use of anabolic steroids to maintain, 129-130
    and healthy eating and nutrition, 35, 303
    positive effect of exercise on, 188
Bone fractures. *See* Stress fractures
Bone loss. *See* Osteoporosis
Bone mineral density. *See also* Osteoporosis
    age-dependent changes in, 76-77
    age of achieving peak bone mass, 49, 68, 76-77, 119
    association with menstrual regularity, 66-68
    determinants of peak bone mass, 76, 299-301
    effect of oral contraceptives on, 106-107
    increasing in relationship to stress, 51-52
    influence of exercise on, 51-53, 187
    in long bones, 51
    lower levels associated with menstrual irregularity, 48-50, 64, 67-68, 299-301
    loss linked with amenorrhea, 6, 48-50, 52-53
    loss slowed by exercise, 187
    in lumbar spine, 48-49, 51
    measuring, 51, 76
    nonreversible loss of, 48-49
    protective effect of estrogen, 301
    relationship between spinal bone loss and ovulatory disturbances, 76-77
    relationship with dietary fiber intake, 66, 71
    and time of menarche, 49
    timetable of development of, 49
    variables affecting, 53
Breast cancer, relationship with oral contraceptive use, 108
Breast disease, effect of oral contraceptives on, 108
Breast-feeding, 97-98
Breast-tenderness and enlargement, 107
Bulimia, 143-146

C

Cable tensiometry, 171
Caffeine, 135-136
Calcium deficiency, 119-120

Calcium metabolism, affected by nonalcoholic carbonated beverages, 120, 132
Cancer
    lower incidence of sex-hormone sensitive cancers observed in female athletes, 53
    relationship of breast cancer with oral contraceptive use, 108
Capsular impingement of the wrist, 248
Cardiovascular disturbances
    associated with anabolic steroid use, 128
    caused by drugs, 133, 134
Center of gravity
    differing in males and females, 269
    shifting during pregnancy, 84
Children. See Preadolescent athletes
Cholesterol
    changes in ratios associated with anabolic steroid use, 128
    positive association with menstrual irregularity, 73
    serum levels decreased by strength training, 177
Chondromalacia, 279-280
Chronic medial collateral ligament sprain, 284-285
Circulorespiratory and metabolic factors
    affecting endurance performance, 149-159
    maximal oxygen consumption, 149-151, 154, 158, 270
    related to gender differences in endurance performance, 153-159
Closed kinetic chain activities, 180
Coaching, preventing athletic injury, 7
Cocaine, 132-133
Competition, 11-14
Competitiveness
    gender and cultural influences on, 24-25
Competitive orientation, 22-23
Competitive outcomes, focus on, 28
Conditioning
    ability of aging females to benefit from, 187
    aerobic and anaerobic, 205
    decreasing premenstrual symptoms, 107
    effects of, on upper extremity strength in women, 241-242
    and injury rates, 204
    off-season, 193-199
    reducing injuries, 295
Contraceptives. See Oral contraceptives
Crack, 133-134
Cruciate dependent knee, 287-288. See also Knee injuries

D
Dance
    adaptive problems, 254-255
    injuries in, 252-255, 257, 259-260
    preventing injuries, 262-263
    stress fractures, 294
Dance, gymnastics, and skating injuries, 251-263

Deconditioning, training to prevent, 194-196
Delayed menarche, 44
    of preadolescent athletes, 117-118
    relationship to athletic training, 271
    relationship to decreased body fat, 275
Diet. See Nutrition
Dietary fat, 69-72
Dietary fiber
    and bone mineral density, 66, 71
    effect of on estrogen levels, 65-66, 70, 76
    menstrual irregularities associated with, 65, 70
    metabolic impact of not understood, 71
    reproductive hormone levels modulated by, 69-72
Distal segment injuries, 255-257, 288-295
    ankle strengthening exercises for prevention of, 288
Distance running, for preadolescent athletes, 116
Diving, upper extremity injuries in, 243
Dysmenorrhea, effect of oral contraceptives on, 107

E
Eating disorders. See Pathogenic weight-control behaviors
Eccles's model of achievement, 26-27
Elbow, epicondylitis of, 247-248
Endogenous opioids, 47
Endometrial cancer and hyperplasia, oral contraceptives reducing risk of, 106
Epicondylitis of the elbow, 247-248
Epinephrine, 152
Ergogenic aids, 131-136
Estrogen. See also Reproductive hormones
    levels influenced by diet, 65-66, 69, 70, 76
    metabolism of, 70
    protective effect on bone mineral density, 301
    response of young and postmenopausal women to replacement therapy, 48-49
    as therapy for menstrual irregularities, 55
Exercise. See Athletic activity
Expectations, 25-27

F
Fear of success, 24
Female athletes. See also Athletic females
    adolescent female athletes, 14, 105, 117-121
    differing in physique from male athletes, 268-272
    found to be androgynous or masculine, 21-22
    injury patterns compared to male patterns, 268-272
    lower incidence of sex hormone-sensitive cancers in, 53
    media attention to, 3-4, 12
    problems faced by, 11-12, 13-14
    providing role models for, 4
    studies of reproductive health of, 53-54
Female cadets, incidence of injury in, 219-233

Female sex steroids. *See* Reproductive hormones
Flexibility, 198-199
Follicular phase of menstrual cycle, 42, 43
Fractures of the humerus, 246-247
Frozen shoulder, 245-246

G

Gender, 23-28, 32-33
  belief systems, 28-30, 33
Gender differences
  in anterior cruciate ligament injury in basketball players, 121, 288, 302-303
  assumptions about, 20
  beliefs differing from actuality, 28
  and biological differences, 33
  in body fat, 177
  in center of gravity, 269
  in circulatory and metabolic factors related to endurance performance, 153-159
  in endurance performance, 149-159
  in expectations, 26, 27
  in gymnastics injuries, 251-252
  in hemoglobin concentration, 158
  and inequality in sport, 11-12
  in injury patterns, 268-272
  in injury rates at West Point Military Academy, 224-229, 231-232
  lack of evidence for, 20-21
  in maximum oxygen consumption, 154, 158, 270
  in metabolic rate, 270
  overuse syndrome more common in females, 179
  in performance, related to differences in physique, 268-271
  in pericapsulitis of the shoulder, 246
  phenotypic differences misinterpreted as misalignment, 268-270
  in preadolescent athletes, 114
  in rate of upper extremity injuries, 237, 239
  social context of, 27, 30-31
  world record performances by gender, 153-154
Gender role orientation and research, 21-23
Gender stereotypes, 28-32
Glycogen depletion, 153, 159
Goal orientation, females scoring higher on, 25
Greater trochanteric bursitis, 275
Gymnastics
  adaptive problems, 254-255
  injuries in, 242, 251-255, 259-262, 294
  stress fractures, 294

H

Hand and wrist injuries, 229, 248
Handheld dynamometry, 171
Heel pain, 292-293
Hemoglobin concentration, 150, 158
Hip problems, 272-275
Humerus, fractures of, 246-247
Hyperventilation, during pregnancy, 83

Hypothalamic-pituitary-gonadal axis, role in menstrual irregularities, 46-47
Hypoxia, 152

I

Iliotibial band friction syndrome, 272-274
Injury. *See* Athletic injuries
Iron deficiency, in adolescent female athletes, 118-119
Isokinetic assessment, 172
Isotonic assessment, 171-172

K

Knee injuries, 229, 275-288
  chondromalacia, 279-280
  chronic medial collateral ligament syndrome, 284-285
  in dancers, gymnasts, and skaters, 255
  in high school athletes, 120-121
  lateral patellar dislocation, 285-286
  medial plica syndrome, 284-285
  more frequent among female basketball players, 120-121, 287, 302-303
  patellofemoral stress syndrome, 279-280
  treatment of ligament injuries, 287
Knee pain
  causes of, 275-277, 279
  lateral, 282-284
  medial, 284-285
  parapatellar, 281-282
  posterior, 286-287
  retropatellar, 275-280
  treatment of, 277, 279-281, 284-288
  in young athletes, 279

L

Lactate threshold, 151-152, 158-159
Lateral patella dislocation, 285-286
Lean body weight, relationship to oxygen consumption, 151
Ligaments and cartilage, softening during pregnancy, 85-86
Lipid metabolism. *See also* Cholesterol
  affected by caffeine, 135
  negative effects of oral contraceptives offset by exercise, 108-109
Liver function, affected by anabolic steroids, 127
Lower extremity injuries, 224, 229, 267-296
  ankle injuries, 255, 257, 288-295
  anterior cruciate ligament injuries more frequent among female basketball players, 121, 287-288, 302-303
  chondromalacia, 279-280
  chronic medial collateral ligament syndrome, 284-285
  of dancers, gymnasts, and skaters, 254-258, 260
  distal segment injuries, 288-295
  greater trochanteric bursitis, 275
  iliotibial band friction syndrome, 272-274
  knee injuries, 120-121, 229, 255, 275-288, 302-303
  medial plica syndrome, 284-285
  middle segment injuries, 120-121, 229, 255, 275-288, 302-303

Lower extremity injuries *(continued)*
  patellofemoral stress syndrome, 279-280
  patterns in female and male athletes,
    268-272
  proximal segment injuries, 272-275
  reduced by conditioning, 295
  related to athletic equipment, 261-262
  shin injuries, 255
  slipped capital femoral epiphysis, 274-275
  snapping hip, 272-274
  sport-specific rather than sex-specific, 267
  stress fractures. *See* Stress fractures
Luteal phase suppression, 44

M

Manual muscle testing, 171
Marijuana, 134-135
Maternal fitness programs, 94-96
Maximal oxygen consumption
  and differences in blood distribution,
    150-151
  and endurance performance, 158
  factors contributing to, 151
  gender differences in, 270
  mean value lower for women, 154
  and pulmonary diffusing capacity, 150
  reduced by beta blockers, 136
  used in definition of aerobic fitness, 196
Medial plica syndrome, 284-285
Melpomene Institute
  guidelines for exercise during pregnancy,
    91-94
  recommendations for evaluating maternal
    fitness programs, 94-96
  role in awareness of athletic female, 4-5
  studies of exercise patterns of pregnant
    women, 90-91
  study of exercise and pregnancy, 6
  survey of demands on women's time, 2
Menarche. *See* Delayed menarche
Menopause, effect on athletic activity, 8
Menstrual cycle, 41-44
  and athletic activity, 3, 5-6
  and athletic performance, 110
  effects of specific nutrients on menstrual
    status, 73-76
  function affected by body fat, 46
  issues raised by changes in, 5-6
  manipulating, 106, 110
  mechanisms altering, 46-54
  regulated by oral contraceptives, 104, 105,
    106
Menstrual irregularities
  as a determinant of risk of athletic injury,
    14, 61-77
  amenorrhea. *See* Amenorrhea
  associated with dietary fiber intake, 70
  cholesterol positively associated with, 73
  delayed menarche, 44, 117-118
  and diet, 46
  and dietary fiber intake, 65
  and estrogen metabolism, 70

etiological factors of, 45-46
  evaluating, before using oral contraceptives,
    104-105
  factors contributing to, 300
  lower bone mineral density associated with,
    64, 67-68, 300
  luteal phase suppression, 44
  more prevalent among exercising females,
    177
  and peak bone density, 299-301
  prevalence of, in athletes, 45
  relationship between spinal bone loss and
    ovulatory disturbances, 76-77
  relationship to exercise, 45-46
  role of body fat, 46, 271
  role of endogenous opioids, 47
  role of hypothalamic-pituitary-gonadal axis
    in, 46-47
  and stress fractures, 50-53, 63. *See also*
    Stress fractures
  studies of effects of, 53-54
  survey of incidence and circumstances of,
    4-5
  treatment of, 54-55
Middle segment injuries, 255, 275-288
  anterior cruciate ligament injuries, 120-121,
    287, 302-303
  chondromalacia, 276, 279-280
  chronic medial collateral ligament sprain,
    284
  lateral knee pain caused by, 282, 284
  lateral patella dislocation, 285-286
  ligament injuries, 287-288
  medial knee pain caused by, 284-285
  parapatellar pain caused by, 281-282
  patellofemoral stress syndrome, 279-280
  posterior knee pain caused by, 286
  retropatellar pain caused by, 275-280
Miserable alignment syndrome, 269
Muscle assessment, 169-172. *See also* Strength
    training
Muscle imbalances, 209-217, 245, 301-302
Muscle strength. *See* Strength training
Muscular training, for specific sports, 205

N

Neurologic entrapment syndromes around the
    shoulder, 246
Norepinephrine, effect of cocaine on, 133
Nutrition
  of adolescent female athletes, 118-120
  for breast-feeding women, 97
  dietary changes easing premenstrual symp-
    toms, 107
  effects of specific nutrients on menstrual
    status, 73-76
  emphasis on, important for overweight
    women, 35
  inadequate energy intake of athletic females,
    166-168
  for maintaining athletic performance, 7, 165,
    303

and menstrual irregularities, 46, 64-65
during pregnancy, 86-90
problems arising from lack of essential
nutrients, 167-168
Nutritional disorders. *See* Pathogenic weight-
control behaviors

O

Off-season conditioning, 193-200
Oligomenorrhea, 42, 45. *See also* Amenorrhea;
Menstrual irregularities
Optimal body composition, 197-198
Oral contraceptives, 103-110
Orthopaedics, women in, 16
Osteoporosis. *See also* Bone mineral density
linked with amenorrhea, 6, 68
linked with decreased bone mineral density,
49
oral contraceptives protecting against, 106
relationship with breast-feeding, 97-98
risk of, and menstrual irregularities, 300
role of exercise in delaying or preventing,
49, 187
Ovarian cancer, 107
Overuse injuries, 179, 252, 254
Overweight women, 35
Oxidative capacity of muscle, 151

P

Patellofemoral stress syndrome, 279-280
Pathogenic weight control behaviors
among adolescents, 14
anorexia, 142-143
among athletes, 7, 120, 130, 141-142
bulimia, 143
contributing to injuries, 14
dietary treatment of, 144-145
incidence of, 141-142
national organizations aiding with, 146
predisposing factors for, 144
pressures encouraging, 35
preventing, 145
substances abused for, 130-132
tips for helping athletes with, 145-146
Peak bone density, 49, 68, 76-77, 119
determinants of, 76, 299-301
and menstrual irregularities, 299-301
Pelvic inflammatory disease, occurrence
reduced by oral contraceptives, 107
Pelvic structure, differing in males and
females, 268-269
Pericapsulitis of the shoulder, 245-246
Personal competition, 12-13
Personality, and gender role orientation, 21-23
Personality Attributes Questionnaire, 21-23
Phenylpropanolamine, 131-132
Physical activity. *See* Athletic activity
Physical education, decline in provision for, 4
Plyometrics, 179-180
Powerlifting, defined, 174
Preadolescent athletes, 113-118
gender differences in, 114, 175-177
strength training for, 116-117, 175, 177, 179

Preadolescent female athletes, 113-118. *See
also* Female athletes
Pregnancy
and amenorrhea, 5
avoiding overheating during, 86-87
back problems during, 84-85
changes in cardiovascular and respiratory
systems during, 83-84
changes in eating habits during, 89
current thinking on exercise, 6, 82-83
diet recommendations, 87-90
effects of exercise on labor and delivery, 96
evaluating maternal fitness programs, 94-96
exercise guidelines for, 91-94
heart and lung considerations, 83-84
historical attitudes to exercise during, 91-92
hyperventilation during, 83
importance of diet during, 87-88
ligaments and cartilage softening during,
85-86
metabolic changes maintaining weight
during, 89
muscle and bone effects of, 84-86
posture and back pain, 84-85
post-partum exercise, 96-99
progesterone increasing appetite, 89
studies of exercise during, 83, 84, 90-91
unpleasant side effects of progesterone, 89
upper body strength training during, 85, 86
Premenstrual symptoms, 107
Progesterone, and pregnancy, 89
Propanolol, 136
Proximal segment injuries, 272-275
Psychological skills training, need for, 36
Pulmonary diffusing capacity, 150

Q

Qmax, 150, 154, 158

R

Racial and ethnic stereotypes, 32
Recreational drugs, 132-136
Relaxin, 85-86
Reproductive hormones. *See also* Estrogen
dietary fat and fiber as modulators of levels
of, 69-72
effect of dietary change on, 70-73
levels changing during menstrual cycle, 42
measuring, 43
normative clinical chemistry values of,
68-69
reasons for variances in, 69
Resistance training, 174, 176, 194-195
Retropatellar pain, 275-280
Roller skating, upper extremity injuries in,
242-243
Running
distance running for preadolescent athletes,
116
exercise guidelines for, during pregnancy,
92-93
risk of iron deficiency associated with, 118
Running economy, 152, 153, 159

Ruth Jackson Society, 15

S

Self-perceptions, and athletic activity, 27-28
Sever's disease, 292-293
Sex differences. *See* Gender differences
Sex-typing. *See* Gender stereotypes
Shin injuries, in dancers, gymnasts, and
    skaters, 255
Shoulder injuries, 245-246
Shoulder dysfunction syndrome, 243-245
Shoulder pain, four-group classification of,
    244
Skating, 252-262
Slipped capital femoral epiphysis, risk of,
    274-275
Snapping hip, 272-274
Social context, 31-32
Spine injuries, in dancers, gymnasts, and
    skaters, 259
Sport
    behaviors demanded by, 22
    enthusiasm for contact sports, 12
    gender influences on reactions to, 25
    gender stereotypes in, 29-30
    inequalities in, 11-12
    violence in, 12
Sport achievement, 23-28
Sport and exercise psychology, 32, 35-36
Sport choice, influenced by sex-typing, 28
Sport motions, analyzing, 204
Sport Orientation Questionnaire, 24-25
Sport participation, 22-23
    attitudes of preadolescent athletes to, 114
    decline in, by females, 4
Sport pattern simulation, 206
Sport performance. *See* Athletic performance
Sport sociologists, research by, 31
Sport-specific training
    aerobic and anaerobic demands of, 294
    analyzing sport motions for, 204
    defining, 204
    developing a program for, 205-206
    injury prevention as a rationale for, 203-204
Squinting patellae, 262
Steroids, 109, 125-130
Stimulants, 131-136
Strength development, 175-178
Strength training, 171-174
    anaerobic training, 175
    application of, by athletic females, 172,
        174-180
    assessing changes in muscle strength,
        169-172
    and the athletic female, 169-181
    benefits for prepubertal children, 175,
        177
    closed kinetic chain activities, 180
    determining load, 195
    enhancing performance and decreasing
        injury, 301
    importance of rest periods in, 196

    importance of upper body strength training
        during pregnancy, 85
    injuries sustained during, 179
    plyometrics, 179-180
    for preadolescent athletes, 116-117
    to prevent deconditioning, 195-196
    problems with muscle assessment, 169-171
    recommendations for, 181
    safety considerations, 178-179
    for specific sports, 205
Stress fractures, 132, 292-294
    in dancers, gymnasts, and skaters, 257
    higher incidence in women, 219, 229
    increased in amenorrheic women, 7, 50-53
    more frequent in women with menstrual
        irregularities, 50-53, 63, 300
    of the neck of the humerus, 246-247
Stress-related injuries, 229, 231
Stretching, 205, 210-211
Substance abuse, 125, 130-137
    anabolic steroids, 109, 125-130
    counseling needed for, 136-137
    nonalcoholic carbonated beverages, 119-120,
        132
    pathogenic weight control aids, 130-132
    prevalence of, among athletes, 125
Substrate use, 153, 159
Swimming
    and exercise during pregnancy, 93-94
    upper extremity injuries in, 243

T

Thermoregulation, 86-87, 114-115, 135
Thoracic outlet syndrome, 246
Title IX, 2-3, 13
T-lymphocyte function, decline in associated
    with training at maximal work load, 53
Toxemia, 88
Trochanteric bursitis, risk of, 275

U

Upper body strength training, importance of,
    during pregnancy, 85, 86
Upper extremity injuries, 235-248, 259-260
    in dancers, gymnasts, and skaters, 259-260
    in males and females, 237, 239
Upper extremity strength, 241-242
Uterine fibroids, oral contraceptives preventing
    growth of, 106

V

Vagus overload syndrome, 247
Vegetarian diet, 65-66, 73, 76
Volleyball, upper extremity injuries in, 243

W

Weight control. *See* Body image; Pathogenic
    weight-control behaviors
Weight lifting, 174, 179
Weight training, 174, 176
Win orientation, males scoring higher on, 25
Women. *See* Aging females; Athletic females;
    Female athletes; Gender
Wrist, capsular impingement of, 248